THE HISTORY OF AL-ṬABARĪ

AN ANNOTATED TRANSLATION

VOLUME XXXI

The War between Brothers

THE CALIPHATE OF MUḤAMMAD AL-AMĪN

A.D. 809–813/A.H. 193–198

The History of al-Ṭabarī

Center for Iranian Studies

Columbia University

SUNY

SERIES IN NEAR EASTERN STUDIES

Said Amir Arjomand, Editor

The preparation of this volume was made possible in part by a grant from the National Endowment for the Humanities, an independent federal agency.

Bibliotheca Persica
Edited by Ehsan Yar-Shater

The History of al-Ṭabarī

(Ta'rīkh al-rusul wa'l-mulūk)

VOLUME XXXI

The War between Brothers

translated and annotated
by

Michael Fishbein

University of California, Los Angeles

State University of New York Press

Published by
State University of New York Press, Albany

Printed in the United States of America

For information, address State University of New York Press, State University Plaza, Albany, N.Y., 12246

Library of Congress Cataloging-in-Publication Data

Ṭabarī, 838?–923.
[Ta'rīkh al-rusul wa-al-mulūk. English. Selections]
The war between brothers/translated and annotated by Michael Fishbein.
p. cm.—(The history of al-Ṭabarī = Ta'rikh al-rusul wa'l-mulūk; v. 31) (SUNY series in Near Eastern studies) (Bibliotheca Persica)
Translation of extracts from: Ta'rīkh al-rusul wa-al-mulūk.
Includes bibliographical references and index.
ISBN 0–7914–1085–4. ISBN 0–7914–1086–2 (pbk.)
1. Islamic Empire—History—750–1258.
I. Fishbein, Michael II. Title. III. Series.
IV. Series: Ṭabarī, 838?–923. Ta'rīkh al-rusul wa-al-mulūk. English; v. 31. V. Series: Bibliotheca Persica (Albany, N.Y.)
DS38.2.T313 1985 vol. 31
[DS38.5]
909'.1—dc20 91–38852
10 9 8 7 6 5 4 3 2 1 CIP

Preface

THE HISTORY OF PROPHETS AND KINGS (*Ta'rīkh al-rusul wa'l-mulūk*) by Abū Jaʿfar Muḥammad b. Jarīr al-Ṭabarī (839–923), here rendered as the *History of al-Ṭabarī*, is by common consent the most important universal history produced in the world of Islam. It has been translated here in its entirety for the first time for the benefit of non-Arabists, with historical and philological notes for those interested in the particulars of the text.

Al-Ṭabarī's monumental work explores the history of the ancient nations, with special emphasis on biblical peoples and prophets, the legendary and factual history of ancient Iran, and, in great detail, the rise of Islam, the life of the Prophet Muḥammad, and the history of the Islamic world down to the year 915. The first volume of this translation will contain a biography of al-Ṭabarī and a discussion of the method, scope, and value of his work. It will also provide information on some of the technical considerations that have guided the work of the translators.

The *History* has been divided here into 39 volumes, each of which covers about two hundred pages of the original Arabic text in the Leiden edition. An attempt has been made to draw the dividing lines between the individual volumes in such a way that each is to some degree independent and can be read as such. The page numbers of the Leiden edition appear in the margins of the translated volumes.

Al-Tabarī very often quotes his sources verbatim and traces the chain of transmission (*isnād*) to an original source. The chains of transmitters are, for the sake of brevity, rendered by only a dash (—) between the individual links in the chain. Thus, "According to Ibn Ḥumayd—Salamah—Ibn Isḥāq" means that al-Ṭabarī received the report from Ibn Ḥumayd, who said that he was told by Salamah, who said that he was told by Ibn Isḥāq, and so on. The numerous subtle and important differences in the original Arabic wording have been disregarded.

The table of contents at the beginning of each volume gives a brief survey of the topics dealt with in that particular volume. It also includes the headings and subheadings as they appear in al-Ṭabarī's text, as well as those occasionally introduced by the translator.

Well-known place names, such as, for instance, Mecca, Baghdad, Jerusalem, Damascus, and the Yemen, are given in their English spellings. Less common place names, which are the vast majority, are transliterated. Biblical figures appear in the accepted English spelling. Iranian names are usually transcribed according to their Arabic forms, and the presumed Iranian forms are often discussed in the footnotes.

Technical terms have been translated wherever possible, but some, such as dirham and imām, have been retained in Arabic forms. Others that cannot be translated with sufficient precision have been retained and italicized, as well as footnoted.

The annotation aims chiefly at clarifying difficult passages, identifying individuals and place names, and discussing textual difficulties. Much leeway has been left to the translators to include in the footnotes whatever they consider necessary and helpful.

The bibliographies list all the sources mentioned in the annotation.

The index in each volume contains all the names of persons and places referred to in the text, as well as those mentioned in the notes as far as they refer to the medieval period. It does not include the names of modern scholars. A general index, it is hoped, will appear after all the volumes have been published.

For further details concerning the series and acknowledgments, see Preface to Volume I.

Ehsan Yar-Shater

Contents

The Events of the Year 195 (810–811) / 46

The Events of the Year 196 (811–812) / 92

The Events of the Year 197 (812–813) / 134

Abbreviations

EI[1]: *Encyclopaedia of Islam*, 1st edition. Leiden, 1913–42
EI[2]: *Encyclopaedia of Islam*, 2nd edition. Leiden, 1960–
GAS: F. Sezgin, *Geschichte des arabischen Schrifttums*
IJMES: *International Journal of Middle East Studies*
JRAS: *Journal of the Royal Asiatic Society*
RCAL: *Rendiconti della Reale Accademia dei Lincei*
REA: E. Combe, J. Sauvaget, and G. Wiet, *Répertoire chronologique d'épigraphie arabe*
RSO: *Rivista degli Studi Orientali*

Translator's Foreword

This section of the *History* of al-Ṭabarī covers the four and one-half year reign of Muḥammad al-Amīn, who succeeded to the caliphate upon the death of his father, Hārūn al-Rashīd, on 3 Jumādā II 193 (March 24, 809), and who was killed on 28 Muḥarram 198 (September 25, 813).

A single event, the conflict and eventual civil war between al-Amīn and his half brother al-Ma'mūn, the governor of Khurāsān province, absorbs the attention of al-Ṭabarī for these years. Before his death al-Rashīd had formalized arrangements for the succession in a series of documents signed at Mecca and deposited for safekeeping in the Kaʿbah in the last month of A.H. 186 (December 802) and reaffirmed, with certain additions, some two years later.[1] Under these arrangements, al-Amīn was to succeed to the caliphate; his brother, al-Ma'mūn, was to receive the governorship of the eastern province of Khurāsān, with virtual autonomy from Baghdad. Al-Amīn was not to interfere in any way with the administration of his brother's province. He could neither remove his brother from office nor interfere in any way with his revenues or military support. Furthermore, al-Ma'mūn was named as al-Amīn's successor; al-Amīn was explicitly forbidden to alter the succession. The succession after al-Ma'mūn was fixed in al-Qāsim, a third son of al-Rashīd, although al-Ma'mūn was given the right on his succession to

1. For details of the documents, see Ṭabarī, III, 651–67.

replace al-Qāsim with someone else, if he wished. If either brother violated these conditions, he was to forfeit his rights. These arrangements constituted an unprecedented restriction on a ruling caliph's authority, and although the brothers freely agreed to them, it was obvious that they could be made to work only with the good will of both sides.

It quickly became apparent that such good will did not exist. Trust between the two elder brothers broke down even before the death of al-Rashīd. According to a notice for A.H. 192 (807–8), one year before the death of al-Rashīd, al-Ma'mūn already suspected that his brother would try to eliminate him on accession to the caliphate.[2] He therefore asked to be allowed to accompany al-Rashīd on an expedition to Khurāsān so as not to be in Baghdad and under his brother's control if the already ailing al-Rashīd should die. Al-Rashīd vacillated but eventually granted the request; the chronicle does not make explicit the extent to which he was aware of the mistrust between the two heirs. While on the expedition, al-Rashīd took a step that exacerbated the tension by assigning to al-Ma'mūn the entire army that constituted the expeditionary force. By implying that al-Ma'mūn would have at his permanent disposal a large part of the regular army from Baghdad, in addition to the forces he could raise in his governorate of Khurāsān, al-Rashīd disturbed the military balance that would exist on the accession of al-Amīn. We can deduce that al-Amīn never accepted that this extraordinary arrangement was implied by the terms of succession to which he had agreed. In a letter drafted seven or eight months before al-Rashīd's death and sent to a younger brother, Ṣāliḥ, who had also accompanied the expedition to Khurāsān, with instructions that it be delivered only on the death of al-Rashīd, al-Amīn gave orders that the regular Iraqi troops should return to Baghdad immediately on al-Amīn's succession, under the command of al-Faḍl b. al-Rabīʿ, al-Amīn's most trusted adviser. The secrecy about the letter may imply fear on al-Amīn's part that al-Rashīd might contravene its content if it became known to him before his death.

2. See Ṭabarī, III, 730–31.

Thus, on the death of al-Rashīd the situation already contained the germs of conflict. Al-Rashīd's instructions notwithstanding, the majority of army commanders on the Khurāsān expedition decided to obey the new caliph's orders to return to Baghdad. Al-Ma'mūn was enraged. His first impulse was to use force to prevent the desertion of troops he regarded as under his command, but his chief adviser, al-Faḍl b. Sahl, warned him that his remaining forces were inferior to the task. At the same time, al-Faḍl instructed al-Ma'mūn to work to strengthen his power base in Khurāsān, with a view toward eventually replacing al-Amīn as caliph.

After the account of the episode of the return of the army to Baghdad, al-Ṭabarī's chronicle presents an exchange of letters between the two brothers. Al-Amīn pressed his brother to make a number of concessions that al-Ma'mūn regarded as contrary to the terms of the succession agreement. As there are several accounts of these letters and embassies, the sequence of demands is not always clear. Apparently al-Amīn at first merely requested that al-Ma'mūn allow al-Amīn's infant son, Mūsā, to be added to the order of succession after al-Ma'mūn and al-Qāsim. Al-Ma'mūn, whose military situation in Khurāsān already had improved with the surrender of the rebels, rejected the request and at some point stopped sending al-Amīn official reports of events in his province (via the *barīd* or post service, really an official information service linking provincial governors to the central government in Baghdad). Al-Amīn considered this and a number of associated acts as rebellion and had al-Ma'mūn's name removed from the succession. Other moves by al-Amīn included appointing the infant Mūsā nominal governor of Khurāsān, refusing to allow al-Ma'mūn's private fortune and family to leave Iraq, and summoning al-Ma'mūn back to Baghdad.

These maneuvers continued through A.H. 194 (October 809–October 810). By Jumādā II 195 (March 811) military conflict was imminent. Al-Amīn demanded that certain districts over which al-Ma'mūn had been exercising control from Khurāsān but that lay outside the borders of the province, be returned to the control of Baghdad. When al-Ma'mūn refused to comply, al-Amīn gave a former governor of Khurāsān, ʿAlī b. ʿĪsā b.

Māhān, command of 40,000 men and dispatched him with orders to seize the contested district of al-Rayy and then proceed to Khurāsān. He was to arrest al-Ma'mūn and return him to Baghdad in chains.

Al-Amīn's attempts to settle the dispute by force ended in military disasters. ʿAlī b. ʿĪsā was killed in battle against al-Ma'mūn's commander at al-Rayy, Ṭāhir b. al-Ḥusayn. (Al-Ma'mūn formally accepted the title of caliph shortly after the victory.) A second expedition from Baghdad, led by ʿAbd al-Raḥmān b. Jabalah al-Abnāwī, was defeated as well, leaving al-Ma'mūn in possession of all northern Iran. The year A.H. 196 (September 811–September 812) saw al-Amīn making desperate attempts to recruit support from the Arab tribes of Iraq and Syria, but these efforts, the product of necessity rather than of any personal rapport with the Bedouin Arabs, came to no avail. An expedition by a mixed army of 20,000 regular troops and 20,000 Bedouins sent to prevent Ṭāhir from taking Ḥulwān, the gateway to Iraq, ended in fiasco when the regulars and Bedouins turned against each other at the instigation of agents provocateurs infiltrated into the army by Ṭāhir. A subsequent effort to raise support for al-Amīn in Syria also failed. Even in Baghdad, al-Amīn's support seemed to be melting away. A section of the elite Baghdad garrison (the *Abnā'*) backed a pro-Ma'mūn coup by the son of ʿAlī b. ʿĪsā b. Māhān. Al-Amīn was deposed and imprisoned for two days in Rajab 196 (April 812), until loyal troops from the garrison quarter of al-Ḥarbiyyah put down the coup and freed the caliph.

By the end of A.H. 196, al-Amīn's power was evaporating. After Ṭāhir's victories in northern Iran, al-Ma'mūn, who now considered himself the legitimate caliph because his brother had violated the succession agreement, launched a two-pronged attack on Iraq. While Harthamah b. Aʿyan advanced over the main road from Ḥulwān into Iraq to approach Baghdad from the east, Ṭāhir turned south toward al-Ahwāz, whose governor died in battle rather than renounce his allegiance to al-Amīn. Ṭāhir then turned west, took Wāsiṭ and al-Madā'in, crossed the Tigris, and advanced to Ṣarṣar, only a few miles south of Baghdad.

The siege of Baghdad lasted from 12 Dhū al-Ḥijjah 196 (August 25, 812), when Ṭāhir moved his camp to an open space outside the gate of al-Ḥarbiyyah suburb, the main seat of the Baghdad garrison, until the death of al-Amīn on 25 Muḥarram 198 (September 25, 813). The suburbs that had grown up around the walled city suffered extensive damage from the fighting and from bombardment by siege engines. Al-Amīn could still rely on the loyalty of most of the local troops, and he had large resources of money with which to buy the services of soldiers. Some of Ṭāhir's troops were tempted and changed sides. Gangs of vagrants and unemployed paupers were organized into irregular units to fight a kind of urban guerrilla war. But, with Ṭāhir and Harthamah controlling the approaches to the city and with most of al-Amīn's governors in Iraq having prudently switched their loyalties to the winning side, al-Amīn finally was forced to attempt an escape or negotiate for terms. It was decided that surrender was the best option. The question was whether to turn to Ṭāhir, the obvious choice, as he was in closest proximity to the palace, or to Harthamah, who was across the Tigris on the east bank. The bridges having been cut, the logistics of a surrender to Harthamah were more complicated and would be possible only with the consent of Ṭāhir; however, al-Amīn insisted on Harthamah, whom he knew and believed he could trust.

Terms for the surrender were worked out in three-way negotiations among representatives of al-Amīn, Ṭāhir, and Harthamah. Al-Amīn was to turn over the insignia of the caliphate to Ṭāhir, thereby renouncing his claim to the office. He would then be allowed to proceed to a wharf on the Tigris, where Harthamah would be waiting in a boat to ferry him to safety. The plan was never carried out. What actually happened is not easy to reconstruct. The insignia of the caliphate were never surrendered to Ṭāhir—that is virtually certain. One account presents this neglect as a deliberate attempt by al-Amīn to circumvent the agreement and escape to Harthamah without abdicating. According to this account, al-Ḥasan al-Hirsh, the leader of the irregular troops that had fought for al-Amīn, learned of al-Amīn's intention and denounced al-Amīn to Ṭāhir, who then set up an ambush and frustrated the planned escape. But, according to a second and more detailed account, the failure to hand over the insignia seems not to have been planned. According to this account, Harthamah's messenger came to al-Amīn at the prearranged time and announced that the boat was at the wharf. Presumably, this was the moment when al-Amīn should have sent the insignia to Ṭāhir so that the guards at the gates of the city, under Ṭāhir's command, would be commanded to allow the caliph to depart. However, Harthamah's messenger added that suspicious activity had been noticed on the shore of the Tigris and that Harthamah recommended postponing the surrender for a day; he would return on the morrow with sufficient forces to defend al-Amīn in the event of an ambush. At this point al-Amīn panicked. Convinced that Ṭāhir intended to storm the palace that night, he insisted on riding to the wharf without delay and with only the smallest of escorts. The insignia, one can deduce from Ṭāhir's subsequent account (though full of half-truths, it seems accurate enough on this point), were taken along, carried not by the caliph but by the eunuch Kawthar, who rode in the rear of the cavalcade. Not having received word of a formal surrender by al-Amīn, Ṭāhir's forces attempted to board the boat. A scuffle ensued, and al-Amīn, who fell or jumped into the Tigris and swam to shore, was apprehended, taken to a house being used by one of Ṭāhir's commanders, and executed that night, almost certainly on orders from Ṭāhir. (Ṭāhir's account of how overzealous soldiers mortally wounded al-Amīn at the moment of his capture must be seen as a self-serving lie.) The next morning, Ṭāhir exposed al-Amīn's head to public view, and the civil war—at least this phase of it—was over.

The vigor of al-Ṭabarī's history of this period will be apparent to the reader. There is extensive use of accounts by participants in the events—al-Faḍl b. Sahl for events at the court of al-Ma'mūn and a number of courtiers in the entourage of al-Amīn. The account of the last hours of al-Amīn's life by Aḥmad b. Sallām ranks as one of the most dramatic pieces of early Arabic historical writing. Many diplomatic letters exchanged between al-Amīn and al-Ma'mūn are included verbatim, as well as Ṭāhir's long letter to al-Ma'mūn explaining the circumstances of al-Amīn's death—a letter filled with cold self-justification that is all the more shocking following as it does the heartrending eyewitness narrative of the murder of the caliph. There are long selections from the poetry of the period, both the panegyric and elegy that accompanied all politically significant events and the less formal poetry that commemorated the day-to-day events of the war. A noteworthy inclusion is the 135-verse poem by Abū Yaʿqūb al-Khuraymī describing the devastation of Baghdad.

A Note on the Text

The translation follows the text of the Leiden edition, which appeared in installments between 1879 and 1898 under the general editorship of M. J. De Goeje. The French scholar Stanislas Guyard edited the chronicle for the years A.H. 159–218 (III, 459–1163). The text of the section on the caliphate of al-Amīn survived in only one manuscript known at the time, Istanbul Ms. Köprülü 1041 (siglum C in the apparatus of the Leiden edition but designated in this section simply as "codex," as it provided the only source of the text). The manuscript was described as *"imperfectum, passim parvas lacunas habens."* Restoration of the text was often very difficult, as can be seen from the *apparatus criticus* of the edition. For help in establishing the text Guyard was able to refer to parallel passages by later historians, who often quoted verbatim from al-Ṭabarī: Ibn al-Athīr's *Kitāb al-Kāmil fī al-ta'rīkh*; the anonymous *Kitāb al-ʿUyūn wa-al-ḥadā'iq fī akhbār al-ḥaqā'iq* and Miskawayh's *Kitāb Tajārib al-umam wa-taʿāqib al-himam* (both contained in De Goeje's 1869 edition of *Fragmenta Historicorum Arabicorum*); al-Masʿūdī's *Murūj al-dhahab*; and Sibṭ Ibn al-Jawzī's *Mir'āt al-zamān.*

A photographic copy of one additional manuscript containing part of the section translated here became available for the 1960 Cairo edition of Muḥammad Abū al-Faḍl Ibrāhīm—Istanbul Ms. Ahmet III 2929 (siglum *alif*, or A, in the Cairo apparatus). This manuscript allowed Ibrāhīm to fill in some of the small lacunae in the Leiden edition and occasionally preserved a better reading. Unfortunately, the text of the manuscript stops just before the end of A.H. 197 (III, 902, of the Leiden text), so that the remainder of the Cairo text for this section is the same as the Leiden text, apart from minor differences in punctuation and vocalization. Where my translation follows the Cairo text this is indicated in a footnote.

I have noted where parallel accounts of the events of these years may be found, particularly in the works of al-Yaʿqūbī, al-Dīnawarī, al-Iṣbahānī, al-Masʿūdī, and Ibn al-Athīr, as well as some of the secondary literature available on the period.

The accompanying maps have been reproduced from G. Le Strange's books *The Lands of the Eastern Caliphate* (1905) and *Baghdad during the Abbasid Caliphate* (1900). Unfortunately, they include many features that postdate the caliphate of al-Amīn. The reader should therefore use them as an aid to locating the sites of events narrated by al-Ṭabarī, not as a guide to the topography of Baghdad under al-Amīn.

I wish to express my thanks to Professors Seeger A. Bonebakker, Michael G. Morony, and Moshe Perlmann of the University of California, Los Angeles; to Professor Everett K. Rowson of the University of Pennsylvania; Dr. Michael L. Bates, Curator of Islamic Coins at the American Numismatic Society; and to Dr. Paul E. Chevedden of Salem State College, Salem, Massachusetts, for their help. For any errors and shortcomings, I alone take responsibility.

Michael Fishbein

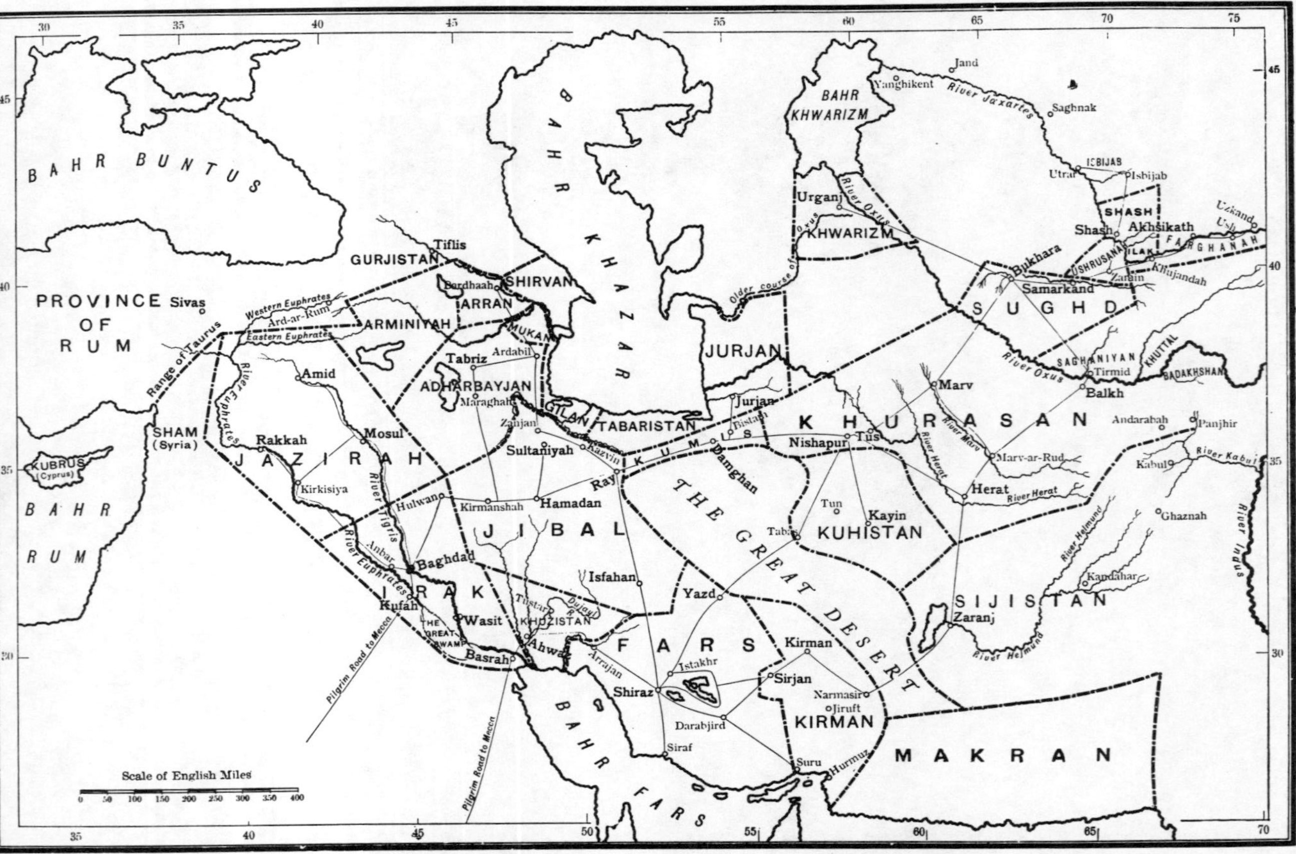

Map 1. The Eastern Lands of the Caliphate. After G. Le Strange, *Lands of the Eastern Caliphate*

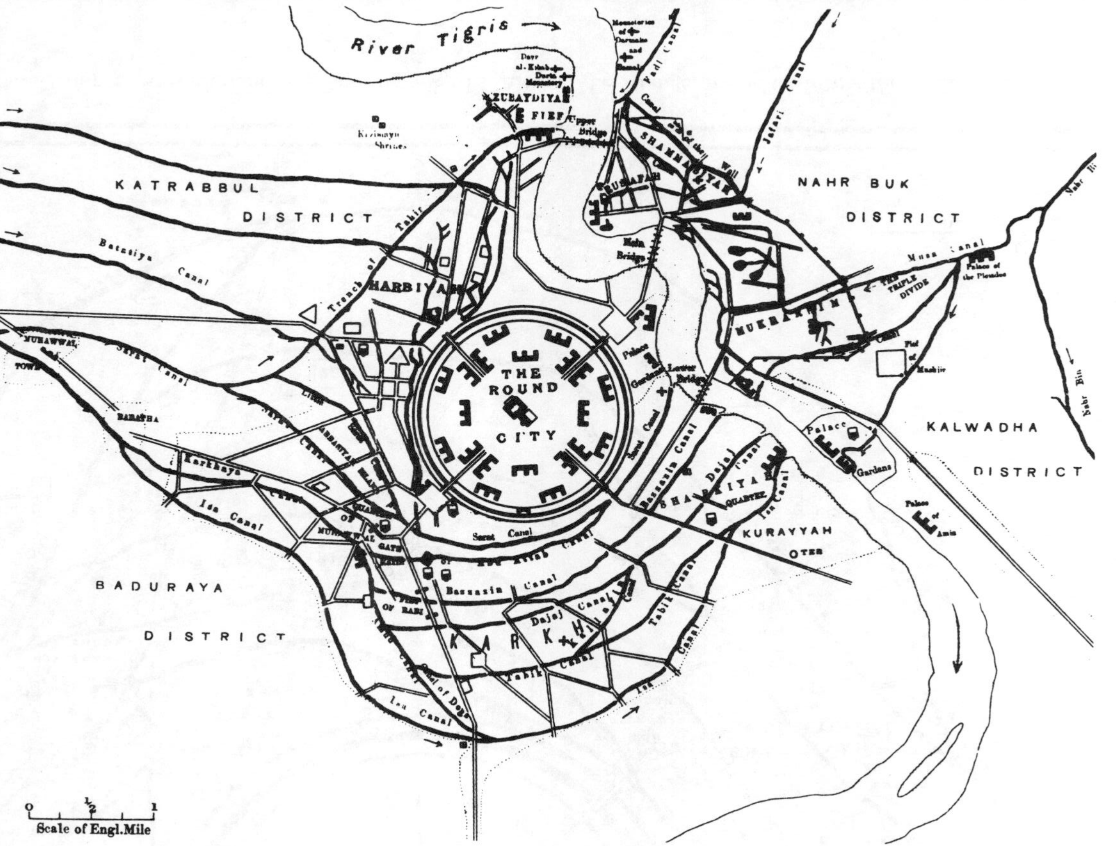

Map 2. Baghdad between A.H. 150 and 300. After G. Le Strange, *Baghdad during the Abbasid Caliphate*

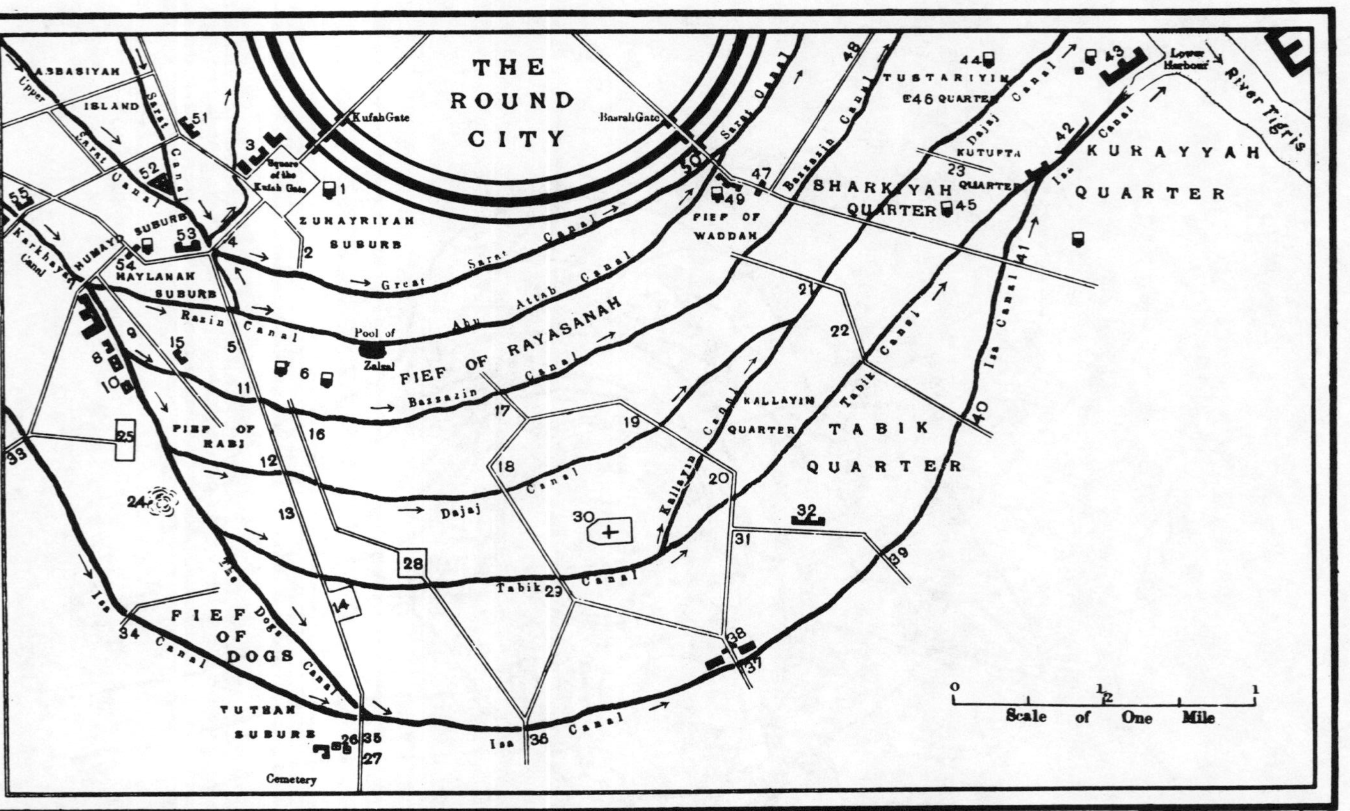

Map 3. Al-Karkh and Neighboring Suburbs. After G. Le Strange, *Baghdad during the Abbasid Caliphate*

1. Mosque of Musayyib with the tall minaret
2. Market of ʿAbd al-Wāḥid
3. Fief of the Gatekeepers, Dīwān of the Ṣadaqah (Office of the Poor Tax), stables, and dromedary house
4. Old Bridge
5. Market of Abū al-Ward
6. Mosque of Ibn Raghbān and Mosque of the Anbārīs
7. Hospital Bridge and Old Hospital (*Bīmāristān*)
8. Darrabāt and Mill of Abū al-Qāsim
9. Quarter of the Wāṣitīs
10. Al-Khafqah (the Clappers)
11. Gate of Karkh
12. Gate of the Coppersmiths
13. Market of Ghālib
14. Square of Suwayd
15. Road of the Painter and House of Kaʿb
16. Market of the Clothing Merchants (*Sūq al-Bazzāzīn*)
17. Butchers' quarter
18. Poultry market
19. Soap boilers' quarter
20. Canal diggers' quarter
21. Reed weavers' quarter
22. Road of the pitch workers
23. Cooks' quarter
24. Mound of the Ass
25. Quadrangle of the Oil Merchant
26. Shrine of Junayd and Sarī al-Saqaṭī, the Ṣūfī convent
27. Tuesday market
28. Quadrangle of Ṣāliḥ
29. Sawwāqīn
30. Fief of the Christians and Monastery of the Virgins
31. Road of Bricks
32. Cotton House
33. Bridge of the Oil Merchants
34. Alkali Bridge
35. Thorn Bridge
36. Pomegranate Bridge
37. Maghīd Bridge and mills
38. Gate of the Mills
39. Garden Bridge
40. Maʿbadī Bridge
41. Banū Zurayq Bridge
42. Myrtle Wharf and Melon House (fruit market)
43. Palace of ʿĪsā, Mosque of Ibn al-Muṭṭalib, and Tomb of Caliph al-Mustaḍī
44. Shrine of ʿAlī (Mashhad al-Minṭaqah)
45. Great mosque of al-Sharqiyyah quarter
46. Shrine of Maʿrūf al-Karkhī and cemetery of the Convent Gate
47. Ḥarrānī archway

47–41. Baṣrah Gate road

47–48. Road to the Lower Bridge, called Barley Street

49. Palace and Mosque of al-Waḍḍāḥ
50. New Bridge and booksellers' market
51. Palace and Market of ʿAbd al-Wahhāb
52. Patrician's Mill
53. Palace in the Fief of ʿĪsā
54. Muḥawwal Gate and Mosque
55. Bridge of the Greeks and House of the *Farrāsh*es

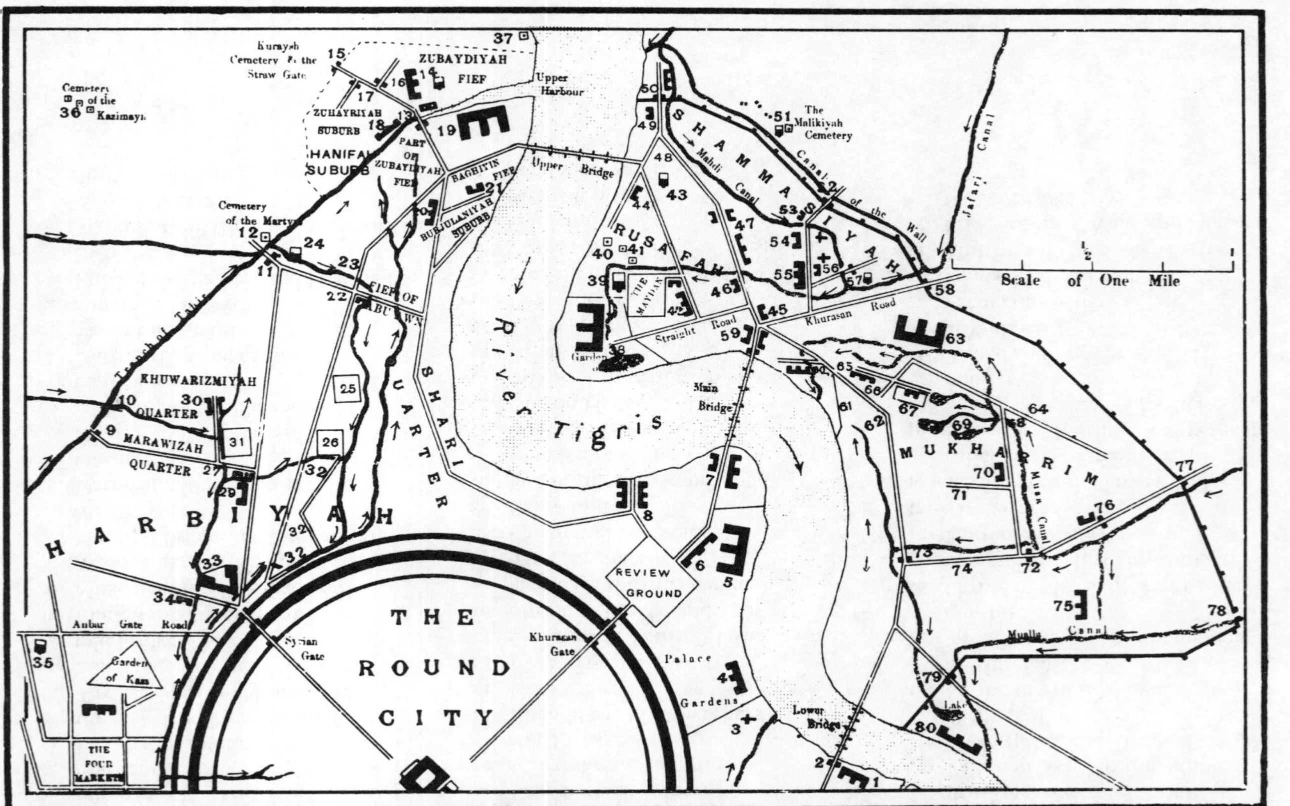

Map 4. Al-Ḥarbiyyah with the Three Quarters of al-Ruṣāfah, al-Shammāsiyyah, and al-Mukharrim. After G. Le Strange, *Baghdad during the Abbasid Caliphate*

1. Palace of Ḥumayd b. ʿAbd al-Ḥamīd
2. Barley Gate (*Bāb al-Shaʿīr*)
3. Old convent at Ṣarāt Point
4. Palace of Zubaydah, called al-Qarār
5. Al-Khuld Palace
6. Royal stables
7. Office of bridge works and hall of the police chief
8. Palaces of Princes Sulaymān and Ṣāliḥ, sons of al-Manṣūr, on Darb Sulaymān
9. Iron Gate and Bridge, leading to Dujayl Road
10. Water conduit (*ʿAbbārat al-Kūkh*)
11. Al-Ḥarb Gate and Bridge, leading to al-Ḥarb Gate Road
12. Tomb of Ibn Ḥanbal
13. Qaṭrabbul Gate and Bridge of Umm Jaʿfar's Mill
14. Palace and mosque of Umm Jaʿfar Zubaydah
15. Straw Gate (*Bāb al-Tibn*)
16. Gate of the Fief
17. Little Gate (*Bāb al-Ṣaghīr*)
18. Palace of ʿUmārah
19. Palace of the Ṭāhirid Ḥarīm
20. Slaves' House (*Dār al-Raqīq*) and Fief of the Pages (*ghulām*s)
21. Palace of Ḥafṣ b. ʿUthmān in Darb Siwār
22. Palace of Ibn Abī ʿAwn
23. Bridge of the Straw Merchants (*Qanṭarat al-Tabbānīn*)
24. Al-Ḥarbiyyah mosque
25. Quadrangle of Abū al-ʿAbbās
26. Quadrangle of Shabīb
27. Abū al-Jawn Bridge
28. Palace of Saʿīd al-Khaṭīb
29. Orphan school
30. Dukkān al-Abnāʾ (Persian shops)
31. Quadrangle of the Persians, with the suburbs of Rushayd, Zuhayr, and ʿUthmān b. Nuhayk
32. Arcades of ʿAkkī, Ghiṭrīf, and Abū Suwayd
33. Prison of the Syrian Gate
34. Road and Palace of Hānī
35. Bukhārī mosque
36. Kāẓimayn shrines: tombs of Zubaydah, Caliph al-Amīn, and the Būyid princes
37. Tomb of ʿAbdallāh son of Ibn Ḥanbal
38. Palace of al-Mahdī in al-Ruṣāfah
39. Al-Ruṣāfah mosque
40. Shrine of Abū Ḥanīfah in Khayzurān cemetery
41. Tombs of the caliphs
42. Palaces of Umm Ḥabīb and al-Faḍl on the road of the Maydān
43. Khuḍayriyyah quarter and mosque; Khuḍayr market
44. Palace of al-Waḍḍāḥ on the Road of the Skiffs
45. Market of Yaḥyā and Bridge Road
46. Palace of Faraj
47. Palaces of Dūr and Jaʿfar al-Barmakī
48. Market of Jaʿfar and Mahdī Canal Road
49. Market of Khālid and Qaṣr al-Ṭīn (Mud Castle)
50. Al-Shammāsīyyah Gate and Palace of Mūnis
51. Three Gates suburb, Place of Vows, and Chapel of the Festival
52. Baradān Gate
53. Baradān Bridge and Palace of Abū Naṣr
54. Palace of Ibn al-Ḥuṭam
55. Barmakid fief and palaces
56. Dār al-Rūm (House of the Greeks) and Nestorian and Jacobite churches of the Christian quarter, with the patriarch's house
57. Market of al-Naṣr, mosque, and Iron Gates
58. Khurāsān Gate of East Baghdad
59. Bāb al-Ṭāq (Archway Gate) and palaces of Khuzaymah, Prince ʿUbaydallāh, and Princess Asmāʾ
60. Street of ʿAmr the Greek
61. Garden of Zāhir at the mouth of the Mūsā canal and Palace of Ibn Muqlah
62. Great Road
63. Palace of al-Muʿtaṣim
64. Long Street
65. Palace of Ibn al-Furāt and Street of the Vine Tendril
66. Thirst Market (*Sūq al-ʿAṭsh*)
67. Palace, quadrangle, and market of al-Ḥarashī
68. Al-Anṣār Bridge
69. Tanks of the Anṣār, Haylānah, and Dāwūd
70. Palace of Ibn al-Khaṣīb in the Road of Saʿd al-Waṣīf
71. Market of al-Ḥajjāj
72. Great Pitched Gate
73. Al-Mukharrim Gate and Bridge of al-ʿAbbās
74. Hay market and booths
75. Palace of Banūjah
76. ʿAmmār Gate and Palace of ʿUmārah
77. Gate of the Horse Market
78. Abraz Gate
79. Gate of the Tuesday Market
80. Firdaws Palace and lake

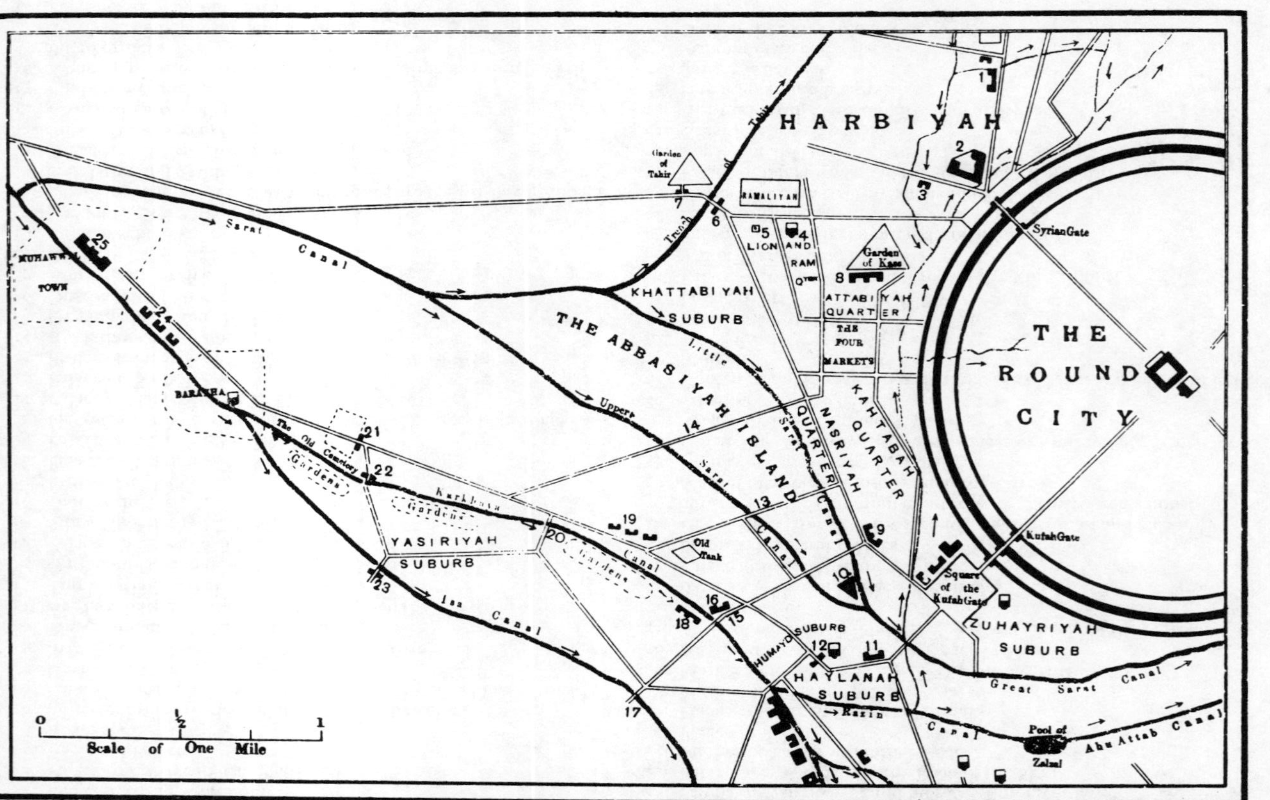

Map 5. Quarters on the Muḥawwal Road. After G. Le Strange, *Baghdad during the Abbasid Caliphate*

1. Palace of Saʿīd al-Khaṭīb and orphan school
2. Prison of the Syrian Gate
3. Road and Palace of Hānī
4. Bukhārī mosque
5. Shrine of Ibrāhīm al-Ḥarbī
6. Al-Anbār Gate and Bridge
7. Garden Gate
8. Dār al-Qazz (Silk House) and Street of Ghāmish
9. Palace and Market of ʿAbd al-Wahhāb
10. Patrician's Mill and Bridge of the Mills
11. Palace in the Fief of ʿĪsā
12. Al-Muḥawwal Gate and Mosque
13. China Bridge
14. Bridge of al-ʿAbbās
15. Bridge of the Greeks
16. House of the *Farrāsh*es
17. Bridge of the Greek Woman
18. Palace of Kaʿyūbah
19. Houses of the Persians
20. Bridge and Street of Rocks
21. Al-Kunāsah Gate and Place of the Sweepings, where beasts of burden were tied
22. Gate of Abū Qabīsah and Jews' Bridge (*Qanṭarat al-Yahūd*)
23. Al-Yāsiriyyah Gate, Bridge, and Quarter
24. Place of the tanners
25. Palace of al-Muʿtaṣim at the town of al-Muḥawwal

The Events of the Year 193 (cont'd)

(October 25, 808–October 14, 809)

The Succession of Muḥammad al-Amīn as Caliph

In this year, allegiance was sworn to Muḥammad al-Amīn b. [764]
Hārūn as caliph at the camp of al-Rashīd.[1] ʿAbdallāh b. Hārūn (al-Maʾmūn) was in Marw at the time.[2] According to what has been mentioned, Ḥammawayh[3] the *mawlā*[4] of al-Mahdī, the

---

1. At the time of his death, the caliph Hārūn al-Rashīd was leading an army raised in Iraq to fight the rebel Rāfiʿ b. Layth in Khurāsān province. He had left Baghdad on 5 Shaʿbān 192 (June 4, 808) and died at Ṭūs (see note 6) on 3 Jumādā II 193 (March 24, 809). His sons ʿAbdallāh al-Maʾmūn and Ṣāliḥ had accompanied him; Muḥammad al-Amīn had remained in Baghdad. Cf. Ṭabarī, III, 730, 738; EI^2 s.vv. al-Amīn (Gabrieli), Hārūn al-Rashīd (Omar), and al-Maʾmūn (Rekaya). Parallel accounts: Yaʿqūbī, II, 524; Dīnawarī, 388; *Fragmenta*, 320; Ibn al-Athīr, VI, 152; Masʿūdī, VI, 415.

2. Marw (Marv, modern Mary in the Turkmen S.S.R.) was the chief city of the second quarter of Khurāsān province. It was often called Marw al-Shāhijān or Great Marw to distinguish it from Marw al-Rūdh or Little Marw. See Le Strange, *Lands*, 397–403; Yāqūt, *Muʿjam*, s.v. Marw al-Shāhijān; EI^2 s.vv. Marv al-Shāhidjān (Yakubovskii) and Khurāsān (Bosworth). During al-Rashīd's final illness, al-Maʾmūn had been sent ahead to Marw with most of the leading commanders of the army to assist Harthamah b. Aʿyan, the governor and commander actually entrusted with the task of subduing Rāfiʿ. Cf. Ṭabarī, III, 733–34.

3. Ḥammawayh, according to Ṭabarī, III, 712, was a eunuch (*khādim*; see note 7 on the term) and had been appointed postmaster of Khurāsān in 191/806–7 by

postmaster[5] at Ṭūs,[6] wrote to Abū Muslim Sallām, his *mawlā* and deputy at Baghdad in charge of the post and information, informing him of the death of al-Rashīd. (Abū Muslim) came before Muḥammad, offered him condolences, and congratulated him about [his succession to] the caliphate. He was the first person to do so. Then Rajā' the eunuch (*khādim*)[7] came to him on Wednesday, the 14th of Jumādā II (April 4, 809),[8] having been sent to him with the news by Ṣāliḥ b. al-Rashīd—some say that this occurred during the night before Thursday, the middle of Jumādā II. The news was made public on Friday; it had been kept secret for the rest of the day and the night [after it was received], while the people spoke confusedly about the matter. When Ṣāliḥ's letter announcing the death of al-Rashīd reached Muḥammad al-Amīn by way of Rajā' the eunuch, (al-Amīn), who was staying in his palace at al-Khuld,[9] moved to the Palace

---

al-Rashīd. See also Abbott, *Two Queens of Baghdad*, 144–45; and Crone, *Slaves on Horses*, 191. For an account of how he obtained an appointment to a seven-year charge of "war and taxes" in Fārs, see *Aghānī*, XV, 79–80.

4. The closest English equivalent of *mawlā* (pl. *mawālī*) is "client." A *mawlā* (often, but not always, a person of non-Arab origin) was bound to his Arab patron by a formal social and legal relationship and obtained protection and something of the patron's social status. See *EI*² s.v. Mawlā (Crone); Bosworth, *'Abbāsid Caliphate in Equilibrium*, 4 n. 4.

5. *Ṣāḥib al-barīd*, "master of post and intelligence": "To make sure that he was well informed about affairs in all corners of the empire and . . . that the representatives of the central government were behaving properly, the caliph appointed his own independent agents who reported directly to him every day, even on such mundane matters as food prices in their respective areas. The official title of such an agent was *ṣāḥib barīd*, postmaster, but more important and to emphasize his direct relationship to the ruler he was also given the honorary status of *mawlā Amīr al-Mu'minīn*"; Shaban, *Islamic History*, II, 9. See also Kennedy, *Early Abbasid Caliphate*, 32; *EI*² s.v. Barīd (Sourdel).

6. Ṭūs (ruins about 25 km north of Mashhad in northeastern Iran) was the second city of the Nishāpūr quarter of Khurāsān province. See Le Strange, *Lands*, 388–91; *EI*¹ s.v. Ṭūs (Minorsky).

7. *Khādim* literally means "servant." Arabic has an explicit term (*khaṣī*) for eunuch, but *khādim* was used as a euphemism. After a proper name as part of the person's title, it is generally not ambiguous. See *EI*² s.v. Khaṣī (Pellat); Bosworth, *'Abbāsid Caliphate in Equilibrium*, 24 n. 100.

8. This represents an average speed of 150 km (94 miles) a day for the 1,900 km (1,188 miles) between Ṭūs and Baghdad. See Kennedy, *Early Abbasid Caliphate*, 33.

9. This palace (its name means "The Palace of Eternity"), overlooking the Tigris amid extensive gardens outside the walls of the Round City, had been

of Abū Jaʿfar[10] in the city. He commanded the people to be present on Friday. They came, and he led them in worship. Having finished his worship, he ascended the pulpit. He praised and extolled God, announced the death of al-Rashīd to the people, and consoled himself and the people. He promised them prosperity, enlarged their hopes, and promised protection[11] to all and sundry. The chief members of his family, his courtiers (*khāṣṣah*),[12] his clients (*mawālī*), and his military commanders (*quwwād*)[13] swore allegiance to him. Then he returned home. He deputed his father's paternal uncle, Sulaymān b. Abī Jaʿfar, to receive the oath of allegiance from those remaining [among the chief people], and the latter did so. He commanded al-Sindī[14] to receive the oath of allegiance from all the [other] people—that is, the military commanders and the rest of the army (*jund*). [765]
He ordered twenty-four months' pay (*rizq*) for the troops who were in the City of Peace,[15] as well as the same months [of pay] for his closest courtiers.

In this year the discord between al-Amīn Muḥammad and his brother al-Ma'mūn began. Each of them determined to oppose the other in what their father, Hārūn, had enjoined them to carry out in the document[16] that we have mentioned that he drew up as an obligation for them and between them.

---

built by al-Manṣūr in 158/774. See Le Strange, *Baghdad*, 101–2; Lassner, *Topography of Baghdad*, 55, 60.

10. The Palace of Abū Jaʿfar al-Manṣūr, also called the Palace of the Golden Gate or the Palace of the Green Dome, was located at the center of the Round City. See Le Strange, *Baghdad*, 31–33.

11. *Amān*: "safety, protection," in military contexts "safe-conduct, quarter." See *EI*² s.v. Amān (Schacht).

12. On the formal distinction between courtiers (*khāṣṣah*) and commoners (*ʿāmmah*) see *EI*² s.v. al-Khāṣṣah wa 'l-ʿĀmmah (Beg).

13. See the discussion of the role and political importance of these army commanders in Kennedy, *Early Abbasid Caliphate*, 82.

14. Al-Sindī b. Shāhak was an important *mawlā* at court. Under al-Rashīd he had been instrumental in the fall of the Barmakids and had been in charge of security in Baghdad. See *EI*² s.v. Ibrahim b. al-Sindī (Pellat); Kennedy, *Early Abbasid Caliphate*, 128; Crone, *Slaves on Horses*, 194–95.

15. *Madīnat al-Salām* was the name given to the original round city of Baghdad laid out by al-Manṣūr in 145/763.

16. This was the so-called Covenant of the Kaʿbah, drawn up in 186/802 to settle the question of the succession. Under its terms al-Amīn, al-Rashīd's younger son by the ʿAbbāsid princess Zubaydah, was given the succession,

Causes of the Discord between al-Amīn and al-Ma'mūn

According to Abū Jaʿfar [al-Ṭabarī]: We have already mentioned that al-Rashīd, when he left for Khurāsān, renewed the oath of allegiance to al-Ma'mūn by the military commanders who were with him. He made the commanders, the remaining troops, and the others who were with him witness that all the soldiers who were with him were to be attached to al-Ma'mūn and that all money, weapons, equipment, and other things that were with him were to be al-Ma'mūn's.[17] When al-Rashīd's son Muḥammad learned that his father's illness had worsened and that he was going to die, he sent someone to bring him a report about him every day. He sent Bakr b. al-Muʿtamir and wrote letters [to be taken] with him, placing them in the hollowed legs of chests that he covered with cowhide and saying: "Do not let the Commander of the Faithful (al-Rashīd) or anyone in his camp find out anything about your business and intention or about what you have with you, even if you are killed, until the Commander of the Faithful dies. When he dies, give each of the men his letter." When Bakr b. al-Muʿtamir reached Ṭūs, Hārūn, having learned of his coming, summoned him and asked him, "What has brought you?" Bakr said, "Muḥammad sent me to find out news about you for him and to bring it to him." Hārūn said, "Do you have a letter with you?" "No," he replied. Hārūn gave orders that what Bakr had with him was to be searched, but they found nothing with him. Hārūn threatened him with blows, but he confessed nothing; so Hārūn ordered him to be
[766] imprisoned and bound. During the night in which he died, Hārūn

---

and al-Ma'mūn, the slightly older son by the slave Marājil, was to have autonomy over the eastern half of the empire during his brother's lifetime, with the right of succession to the caliphate after al-Amīn. See Ṭabarī, III, 654–63; discussion in Gabrieli, "La successione di Hārūn ar-Rašīd," 343–51; Kimber, "Hārūn al-Rashīd's Meccan Settlement"; and Kennedy, *Early Abbasid Caliphate*, 123–27. El-Hibri, in his recent article "Harun al-Rashid and the Mecca Protocol of 802," rejects the text of the protocols as a work of "Ma'munid propaganda."

17. As becomes clear later (p. 13), most of these men had families in Baghdad. Thus their attachment to al-Ma'mūn was an unusual action that al-Rashīd took pains to confirm before leaving for Khurāsān (Ṭabarī, III, 666, 704). Ibn al-Athīr, V, 152, adds that this arrangement "was distressing to al-Amīn."

ordered al-Faḍl b. al-Rabīʿ[18] to go to the place where Bakr b. al-Muʿtamir was being confined and make him confess. He was either to confess or be beheaded. Al-Faḍl went to Bakr and tried to make him confess, but he confessed nothing. Then Hārūn lost consciousness, and the women cried out; so al-Faḍl held back from killing Bakr and went to attend on Hārūn. Hārūn regained consciousness, but he was weak and distracted from thinking about Bakr or anyone else by his sense of [approaching] death. Then he lost consciousness in an attack that they thought was the end. An outcry arose, whereupon Bakr b. al-Muʿtamir sent a note from himself to al-Faḍl b. al-Rabīʿ by way of ʿAbdallāh b. Abī Nuʿaym, asking him that they not be hasty in any affair and informing him that he had with him things that they needed to know about. Bakr was being confined in the house of Ḥusayn the eunuch (*khādim*). When Hārūn died—at the very time at which he died—al-Faḍl b. al-Rabīʿ immediately summoned Bakr and asked him about what he had. Bakr denied having anything—he feared for himself that Hārūn might be alive. But, when Hārūn's death was confirmed to him, and (al-Faḍl) took him into his presence [to see the body], he told him that he had with him letters from the [new] Commander of the Faithful, Muḥammad, but that it was not possible for him to produce them while he was in a state of being bound and confined. Ḥusayn the eunuch refused to release him until al-Faḍl released him; Bakr then gave them the letters that he had. They were in the cowhide-covered legs of the kitchen [chests]. He gave each person his letter. Among the letters there was one from Muḥammad b. Hārūn to Ḥusayn the eunuch in Muḥammad's own hand, commanding Ḥusayn to release Bakr b. al-Muʿtamir and set him free. (Bakr) gave it to him. There was a letter to ʿAbdallāh al-Maʾmūn, and (Bakr) retained al-Maʾmūn's letter with him, so that he might send it to al-Maʾmūn in Marw. They sent for al-Rashīd's son Ṣāliḥ, who had been with his father in Ṭūs, he having been the oldest of Hārūn's children [767]
in attendance on him. He came to them immediately and asked

18. Al-Faḍl b. al-Rabīʿ was Hārūn's vizier. See *EI*² s.v. (Sourdel); Sourdel, *Vizirat ʿabbāside*, I, 183–94; Kennedy, *Early Abbasid Caliphate*, 103; Crone, *Slaves on Horses*, 194.

them about his father, Hārūn. When they told him [of Hārūn's death], he showed intense grief. Then they gave him the letter from his brother Muḥammad that Bakr had brought. Those who had been present at the death of Hārūn were the ones who attended to him, washing him, and preparing him [for burial]. His son Ṣāliḥ prayed [the funeral prayer] over him.

The Letter of Muḥammad al-Amīn to His Brother ʿAbdallāh al-Maʾmūn[19]

If your brother's letter—may God protect him from the loss of you—reaches you on the occurrence of that which can be neither averted nor repelled, it being a thing that departed nations and past ages have bequeathed and transmitted one to another,[20] [console yourself][21] with that whereby God has consoled you. Know that God, whose praise is exalted, has chosen for the Commander of the Faithful the better of two dwelling places and the more abundant of two lots.[22] God has taken possession of him clean and pure. He has rewarded his effort and forgiven his sin, God willing. Take up your affairs like a man of discretion and resolution, one who looks out for his brother, himself, his government, and the generality of Muslims. Take care that grief does not master you; for it annuls the reward [of a deed] and brings a heavy burden [of sin] as its consequence. May God's blessings be upon the Commander of the Faithful in life and in death. Surely we belong to God, and to Him we return![23]

---

19. Cf. the Italian translation by Gabrieli, "Documenti relativi al califfato di al-Amīn in aṭ-Ṭabarī," 200–1.

20. The text is difficult. The translation follows the suggestion in ed. Leiden, *Glossarium*, DXII. Ed. Cairo adds the word *fī* ("in") and can be translated: "according to what has been left behind and transmitted among departed nations and past ages." Gabrieli, ibid., translates, "all' avento di ciò che non si può respingere nè allontare, che ha fatto succedersi e passare dall' uno all' altro i popoli passati e i secoli trascorsi."

21. The bracketed text (Arabic: *fa-ʿazzi nafsaka*) from ed. Cairo, following Ms. Ahmet III, 2929 (A), renders the syntax comprehensible.

22. I.e., heaven.

23. Qurʾān 2:156, traditionally said in time of misfortune.

Have those who are with you—your military commanders, army, courtiers, and commons—swear allegiance to your brother [Muḥammad], then to yourself, and then to al-Qāsim, the son of the [late] Commander of the Faithful, according to the stipulation that the Commander of the Faithful set for you concerning its being annulled or confirmed for the latter.[24] For this you have the mandate of God and His caliph. Make known to those who are with you that my intention is to do them good, satisfy their needs, and be generous to them. As for anyone whom you reject when he swears allegiance or whose obedience you suspect, send me his head with a report of him! Take care that you do not release him, for hellfire is most fitting for him! Write to the financial agents (*'ummāl*) of your frontier regions and the commanders of your armies about the affliction that has befallen you concerning the Commander of the Faithful. Tell them that God, not satisfied with this [768]
world as a reward for him, has taken him to His mercy, His rest, and His Paradise—in a state to be envied and praised, and as a leader into Paradise for all his successors, God willing. Command them to have their armies, courtiers, and commoners swear allegiance in the same way as I have commanded you to have those who are with you swear it. Instruct them to secure their frontiers and to be strong against their enemy. I will acquaint myself with their circumstances and set aright whatever is disordered with them, and will be generous to them. I will not be slow to strengthen my armies and helpers. Let your letters to them be public letters, to be read out to them, because that will set them at ease and enlarge their hopes. Act on the basis of what you[25]

24. That is, al-Qāsim. According to the succession arrangements, al-Ma'mūn could, on succeeding to the caliphate, either confirm al-Qāsim as his own heir or nominate someone else (one of his own children or another brother). See Ṭabarī, III, 658–59.

25. Following the reading of ed. Cairo (*ta'muru*). In the manuscript used by ed. Leiden, the initial letter of the word was left undotted, and the editor restored the word as *na'muru*, "we command." The Cairo reading makes better sense:

command regarding your troops near or far from you, according to what you deem best and perceive; for your brother knows the excellence of your decisions, the soundness of your judgment, and your foresight. He prays that God will keep you and asks God to strengthen his hand through you and gather his affairs into unity through you; and God is gracious to what He will.[26] Written by Bakr b. al-Muʿtamir in my presence and at my dictation in Shawwāl of the year 192 (July–August 808).[27]

The Letter of Muḥammad al-Amīn to His Brother Ṣāliḥ[28]

In the name of God, the Merciful, the Compassionate: If this letter of mine reaches you at the occurrence of what God has foreknown—His Decree that He has executed in regard to His viceroys[29] and His friends, and His established ordinance in regard to the prophets, the apostles, and the angels stationed near Him (so that He has said, "All things perish, except His Face; His is the Judgment, and unto Him you shall be returned"[30])—praise ye God for that to which the Commander of the Faithful has gone: (God's) great reward and the companionship of His prophets, may God's blessings be upon them! To Him we return.[31] We ask Him to render the

---

Al-Amīn begins with praise of al-Ma'mūn's wisdom and concedes him the independence envisaged in the succession settlement.

26. Qur'ān 12:100.

27. Note that the letter is dated in the second month after al-Rashīd's departure from Baghdad, some seven or eight months before his death.

28. Cf. the Italian translation by Gabrieli, "Documenti relativi al califfato di al-Amīn in aṭ-Ṭabarī," 202–4.

29. *Khulafā'*, pl. of *khalīfah*: Cf. Qur'ān 2:30, where God announces to the angels, on the creation of Adam: "I am setting in the earth a viceroy." Cf. also Ṭabarī, I, 974, where the kings of Israel are called *khulafā'*.

30. Qur'ān 28:88. The syntax is loose. Instead of "so that He has said," ed. Cairo reads "so say." The Cairo text yields the following sense: "If this letter of mine reaches you . . . , say: 'All things perish . . . and unto Him you shall be returned; praise ye God. . . .' "

31. See note 23.

caliphate prosperous for the community of His Prophet Muḥammad—may God bless him and give him peace!—for He has been to them a defense and a shelter, and to them He has been gentle and compassionate. Be vigorous in your enterprise. Take care that you do not sit with [769] your hands folded; for your brother has chosen you for what he has sent you to perform and will have an eye out for any places in which you are found wanting.[32] Prove his opinion to be true! We ask God for success. Have the children of the Commander of the Faithful, his family, his *mawālī*, his courtiers, and his commoners who are with you swear allegiance to Muḥammad, Commander of the Faithful, then to ʿAbdallāh, the son of the [late] Commander of the Faithful, and then to al-Qāsim, the son of the [late] Commander of the Faithful, according to the stipulation that the Commander of the Faithful—may God's blessings be upon him!—set concerning its being annulled for al-Qāsim or confirmed. Happiness and prosperity are to be found in upholding his pact and proceeding on his paths. Inform the courtiers and commoners who are with you that I intend to treat them well, to relieve their grievances, to inquire of their conditions, and to pay them their provision allowances (*arzāq*) and stipends (*aʿṭiyāt*). If any troublemaker stirs up mischief or if any unruly person causes a commotion, fall upon him so as to make him "a punishment exemplary for those present and for those to come, and an admonition to such as are God-fearing."[33] Attach to the fortunate man, son of the fortunate man—al-Faḍl b. al-Rabīʿ—the children, servants, and family of the Commander of the Faithful. Command him to travel with them, along with those who are with him, his soldiers, and his horse guards (*rawābiṭ*).[34] Commit the

32. The text may be corrupt; the reading is conjectural.

33. Qur'ān 2:66.

34. That is, to return to Baghdad. The command for a large part of the army assigned to al-Ma'mūn to return to Baghdad was bound to cause friction. See pp. 13–14, below. The exact meaning of *rawābiṭ* (pl. of *rābiṭah*) is unclear. Lane, *Lexicon*, III, 1014, explains the term as synonymous with *murābiṭah*: "a

camp and its policing (*aḥdāth*)[35] to ʿAbdallāh b. Mālik,[36] who is trustworthy in what he undertakes and is favorably received by the regular troops. Attach to him all the police force (*jund al-shuraṭ*)—both horse guards and others—in addition to his soldiers who are with him. Command him to exert himself, be vigilant, and use good judgment in all his affairs night and day; for those who harbor hostility and hypocrisy toward this government (*sulṭān*) will take advantage of an affliction such as this. Confirm Ḥātim b. Harthamah[37] in his post. Command him to guard what the palaces of the Commander of the Faithful contain. He is a man of known and proven obedience, by God's mandate, in accordance with traits of character that were also known to be typical of his father, who was praised in the court of the caliphs. Command the servants to bring their squadrons of horse
[770] guards: by means of them and by means of their soldiers the weak spots of your camp will be closed up, for they are one of your strengths. Entrust your vanguard to Asad b. Yazīd b. Mazyad[38] and your rear to Yaḥyā b. Muʿādh[39] and his soldiers. Command the two of them to report to you each night. Stay on the Great Road. Do not exceed the stages; that will be easier on you. Command Asad b. Yazīd to select someone from his family or one of his commanders to join his vanguard and precede him to prepare the camp sites or part of the road. If some

---

company of horsemen having their horses tied at the frontier in preparation for the enemy." Dozy, *Supplément*, I, 502, notes that the term could be used in the general sense of "mounted guard" or "night watch."

35. For a discussion of the origins of this term, see Dozy, *Supplément*, I, 258.

36. ʿAbdallāh b. Mālik b. al-Haytham al-Khuzāʿī was a leading military figure in al-Maʾmūn's entourage. Cf. Kennedy, *Early Abbasid Caliphate*, 80–81; Crone, *Slaves on Horses*, 181–82. Note that he had already gone ahead with al-Maʾmūn to Marw (p. 14, below).

37. He was the son of Harthamah b. Aʿyan al-Ḍabbī, who had replaced ʿAlī b. ʿĪsā b. Māhān as governor of Khurāsān under al-Rashīd. See Ṭabarī, III, 713–29; *EI*[2] s.v. Ḥātim b. Har<u>th</u>ama (Lewis); Crone, *Slaves on Horses*, 177–78.

38. Asad was the son of Yazīd b. Mazyad al-Shaybānī (d. 185/801), who had been an important military leader with roots in al-Jazīrah (northern Mesopotamia), rather than Khurāsān. See Crone, *Slaves on Horses*, 169–70.

39. Yaḥyā b. Muʿādh b. Muslim was of Khurāsānian origins. See Crone, *Slaves on Horses*, 184.

of those I have named are not present with you in your camp, choose in their stead people whose obedience, loyalty, and respect in the eyes of the populace you trust; God willing, you will not lack such among your commanders and aides. Take care lest you carry out any plan or conclude any affair without the decision of your elder (*shaykh*) and the best minister of your fathers, al-Faḍl b. al-Rabīʿ. Confirm all the servants in charge of the money, weapons, stores, and other things now in their hands. Do not remove any of them from what he is in charge of until you come to me. I have committed to Bakr b. al-Muʿtamir a matter of which he will inform you; act in it according to what you perceive and deem best. If you order pay (*ʿaṭāʾ*) or provision allowance (*rizq*) for the people of your camp, let al-Faḍl b. al-Rabīʿ be the person in charge of paying it to them according to registers that he keeps for himself in the presence of the keepers of the registers. Al-Faḍl b. al-Rabīʿ has always followed such procedures in important affairs. When this letter of mine reaches you, send Ismāʿīl b. Ṣubayḥ[40] and Bakr b. al-Muʿtamir to me on their post horses. There should be for you no staying or delay at the place where you are until you bring me your camp, with the money and stores that are in it, God willing! Your brother asks God to defend you. He prays to God on your behalf that you may be well strengthened [771]
through His mercy. Written by Bakr b. al-Muʿtamir in my presence and at my dictation in Shawwāl of the year 192 (July–August 808).

When Hārūn was buried, Rajāʾ the eunuch left, carrying the seal, the scepter, the mantle,[41] and the announcement of Hārūn's

40. A secretary who served al-Rashīd and al-Amīn; see Sourdel, *Vizirat ʿabbāside*, I, 122, 190.

41. The seal (*khātam*), scepter (*qaḍīb*), and mantle of the Prophet (*burdah*) were insignia of the caliphate. For the story of how the mantle that the Prophet gave to the poet Kaʿb b. Zuhayr was bought by the caliph Muʿāwiyah, see Dozy, *Supplément*, I, 67. Lane, *Lexicon*, I, 184, s.v. *burdah*, gives a description of the garment. See also, Sourdel, "Questions de cérémoniale ʿabbaside," 135; *EI*^{2} s.v. Marāsīm (Sanders).

death. He reached Baghdad the eve of Thursday—some say on Wednesday. The report I have mentioned previously then took place.

Some have said: When the announcement of al-Rashīd's death reached Baghdad, Isḥāq b. ʿĪsā b. ʿAlī [b. ʿAbdallāh b. al-ʿAbbās] ascended the pulpit.[42] Having praised and extolled God, he said, "The man whose loss is greatest and whose survivor is best—we have been afflicted with [his] loss.[43] No one has been afflicted with loss like ours; yet we have been compensated—and who has compensation such as ours?" Then he announced his death to the people and urged the people to obedience.

According to al-Ḥasan the Chamberlain (*al-Ḥājib*)—al-Faḍl b. Sahl:[44] The dignitaries of Khurāsān went to meet al-Rashīd. Al-Ḥusayn b. Muṣʿab[45] was among them. [Continuing, al-Faḍl]

---

42. Al-Yaʿqūbī, II, 525, gives a version of this *khuṭbah* by a senior ʿAbbāsid prince with significant textual variants.

43. The text is difficult. The manuscript used by ed. Leiden (Köprülü 1041) reads, "The man whose loss is greatest and whose survivor is best—we have been afflicted by loss of the *Messenger of God.*" The Leiden editor deleted the words "the Messenger of God." In *Addenda*, DCCLXII, he added this note: "Yaʿqūbī, II, 525, also has 'We have been afflicted with loss of the Messenger of God.' Afterwards, however, Yaʿqūbī has 'and we have been compensated by his successor, his son.'" He added that one perhaps should read, "the Caliph of the Messenger of God." Thus his conjectured reconstruction was, "The man whose loss is greatest and whose survivor is best—we have been afflicted with loss of *the Caliph of* the Messenger of God. No one has been afflicted with loss like ours; yet we have been compensated *by his successor, his son*—and who has compensation such as ours?" Ed. Cairo reads (but gives no textual note): "The man whose loss is greatest and whose survivor is best *is our loss* (*ruzʾunā*). No one has been afflicted. . . . " The original reading of Köprülü 1041 may be correct. As prologue to the announcement of al-Rashīd's death, the speaker may have begun with a reference to how the Muslim community's greatest calamity, the death of Muḥammad, did not mean disaster.

44. On the career of al-Faḍl b. Sahl b. Zadhānfarūkh, the vizier of al-Maʾmūn and perhaps the man most responsible for the war between the two brothers, see EI^2 s.v. (Sourdel). Note that al-Faḍl b. Sahl had been responsible for having al-Maʾmūn accompany al-Rashīd to Khurāsān. Foreseeing that al-Maʾmūn might be in danger of being deprived of his rights if al-Rashīd were to die while both heirs were in Baghdad, he had counseled al-Maʾmūn to accompany his father to the province that had been assigned to him. See Ṭabarī, III, 730–31.

45. Al-Ḥusayn b. Muṣʿab al-Khuzāʿī was the father of Ṭāhir b. al-Ḥusayn, who was to become al-Maʾmūn's main commander in the civil war. On the family and its rise to prominence, see M. Kaabi, "Les Origines ṭāhirides dans la *daʿwa* ʿabbāside."

said: He met me and said to me, "Al-Rashīd is going to die today or tomorrow. The position of Muḥammad b. al-Rashīd is weak. The affair belongs to your master [al-Ma'mūn]. Stretch out your hand." He then stretched out his hand and swore allegiance to al-Ma'mūn as caliph. A few days later, he came to me with al-Khalīl b. Hishām and said, "This is my brother's son. He is someone you can trust. Receive his oath of allegiance."

Al-Ma'mūn had already left Marw for the castle of Khālid b. Ḥammād, a *farsakh*[46] from Marw, intending to go to Samarqand.[47] He had commanded al-ʿAbbās b. al-Musayyab[48] to bring out the troops and go to the camp. Isḥāq the eunuch (*khādim*) passed by the latter, carrying the announcement of al-Rashīd's death. His coming grieved al-ʿAbbās, who then went to al-Ma'mūn and informed him. Al-Ma'mūn returned to Marw, entered the Government House,[49] the house of Abū Muslim, and announced the death of al-Rashīd from the pulpit.[50] He rent his garment and descended. He commanded that money be given to the men and had the oath of allegiance to Muḥammad and then to himself administered. He gave the soldiers twelve [772] months' provision allowance (*rizq*).

When the commanders, soldiers, and children of Hārūn who had received Muḥammad's letters in Ṭūs read them, they took counsel together about joining Muḥammad.[51] Al-Faḍl b. al-Rabīʿ said, "I will not foresake a present king for another whose future position is unknown." He ordered the men to depart, and they did so out of a desire to rejoin their families and homes in Baghdad. Thus they abandoned their obligations to al-Ma'mūn.

---

46. A *farsakh*, from Persian *farsang*, originally was the distance that could be covered on foot in an hour's march. In Islamic times it was standardized at three Arab miles—5.985 km or 3.717 miles. See *EI*[2] s.v. (Hinz).

47. Samarqand (modern Samarkand in the Uzbek S.S.R.) was the chief city of the district of Sughd (ancient Sogdiana), which included the fertile lands between the Oxus (Jayḥūn, modern Amu Darya) and Jaxartes (Sayḥūn, modern Syr Darya) rivers. See Le Strange, *Lands*, 460–67; *EI*[1] s.v. Samarḳand (Schaeder).

48. Al-ʿAbbās b. al-Musayyab b. Zuhayr al-Ḍabbī commanded a group of *shurṭah* troops. See Crone, *Slaves on Horses*, 187.

49. The *Dār al-Imārah*, or "House of the Government," on the central square of Marw had been built by Abū Muslim, the great partisan of the ʿAbbāsids. See Le Strange, *Lands*, 399.

50. The text of al-Ma'mūn's words on the occasion is given in Dīnawarī, 388.

51. Parallel versions: Ibn al-Athīr, V, 153; *Fragmenta*, 320–21.

When word of their action reached al-Maʾmūn in Marw, he gathered his father's military commanders who were with him. They included ʿAbdallāh b. Mālik, Yaḥyā b. Muʿādh, Shabīb b. Ḥumayd b. Qaḥṭabah,[52] al-ʿAlāʾ the *mawlā* of Hārūn,[53] al-ʿAbbās b. al-Musayyab b. Zuhayr (who was in charge of his police [*shurṭah*]), and Ayyūb b. Abī Sumayr[54] (who was in charge of his correspondence). Of the members of his household ʿAbd al-Raḥmān b. ʿAbd al-Malik b. Ṣāliḥ[55] and Dhū al-Riʾāsatayn[56] were with him—the latter was one of the men most in his esteem and closest to him. He asked their advice and told them the news. They urged him to overtake the men with a detachment of 2,000 horsemen and turn them back. Men were named for this.[57] Then Dhū al-Riʾāsatayn came before him and said to him, "If you do what they have urged upon you, you will have made these men a gift to Muḥammad.[58] The wisest plan is for you to write them a letter and send them a messenger, reminding them of the oath of allegiance, asking them to fulfill it, and warning them about oath breaking and its consequences for them in the present world and the hereafter." [Continuing, al-Faḍl b. Sahl] said: I said to him, "Your letter and your messengers will stand in your stead, so that you will search out what the people think. You
[773] should send Sahl b. Ṣāʿid"—he was his chief steward. "He puts his hope in you and expects to attain his hope, and so he will never flag in his loyalty to you. You should also send Nawfal the eunuch (*khādim*), the *mawlā* of Mūsā [al-Hādī], the

52. He was the grandson of Qaḥṭabah b. Shabīb al-Ṭāʾī, next to Abū Muslim the most important general of the ʿAbbāsid revolution. See Crone, *Slaves on Horses*, 189.

53. He held the post of chamberlain (*ḥājib*). See Ibn al-Athīr, V, 153.

54. See Sourdel, *Vizirat ʿabbāside*, I, 184, 198.

55. ʿAbd al-Raḥmān b. ʿAbd al-Malik b. Ṣāliḥ b. ʿAlī b. ʿAbdallāh b. ʿAbbās was a member of the ʿAbbāsid family.

56. That is, al-Faḍl b. Sahl. The title means "possessor of two primacies"—i.e., primacy in civil affairs and primacy in military affairs. It is an anachronism here, for it was not conferred on al-Faḍl b. Sahl by al-Maʾmūn until 196/812. See pp. 101–2, below.

57. That is, to stop al-Faḍl b. al-Rabīʿ by force. Cf. *Fragmenta*, 321: "He acted in accordance with this opinion and named men to travel with him." In other words, the first plan was for al-Maʾmūn himself to accompany the detachment.

58. Cf. *Fragmenta*, 321, and Ibn al-Athīr, V, 154: "these men will make you a gift to Muḥammad." The word for "gift" (*hadiyyah*) can also mean "sacrificial animal."

Commander of the Faithful, who is judicious." So he wrote a letter and sent the two messengers, who overtook the men in Naysābūr.[59] They had already traveled three stages.

According to al-Ḥasan b. Abī Saʿīd—Sahl b. Ṣāʿid, who said: When I delivered his letter to al-Faḍl b. al-Rabīʿ, he said to me, "I am one of them."[60] [Continuing, al-Ḥasan] said: Sahl said to me: ʿAbd al-Raḥmān b. Jabalah assaulted me with a spear and made it pass along my side. Then he said, "Tell your master [al-Maʾmūn], 'By God, if you were present, I would put the spear into your mouth!' This is my answer." Then he defamed al-Maʾmūn. I returned with the news.

According to al-Faḍl b. Sahl: I said to al-Maʾmūn, "Enemies—now you have been relieved of them! But mark what I am saying to you. This dynasty (*dawlah*)[61] was never more powerful than it was in the days of Abū Jaʿfar;[62] yet al-Muqannaʿ rebelled against him, claiming divinity.[63] Some said he was seeking vengeance for Abū Muslim.[64] The army was shaken by his revolt in Khurāsān, but God averted the trouble from (Abū Jaʿfar). After him Yūsuf al-Barm[65] rebelled—in the sight of some

---

59. Naysābūr (Persian Nīshāpūr) was the chief city of the westernmost of the four quarters into which Khurāsān province was divided. See Le Strange, *Lands*, 382–88.

60. Cf. Ibn al-Athīr's gloss (V, 156): "I am only one of the soldiers (*jund*)."

61. *Dawlah* literally means "turning" or "revolution" (in its etymological sense). The ʿAbbāsid caliphs used the term to make an ideological claim justifying their rule as "a turn of fortune which had eliminated the Umayyad usurpers, avenged the Prophet's family, restored the rightful dynasty, and filled the earth with justice"; Crone, *Slaves on Horses*, 65.

62. That is, al-Manṣūr, the second ʿAbbāsid caliph, who ruled from 136/754 to 158/775. See *EI*[2] s.v. al-Manṣūr (Kennedy).

63. Hāshim b. Ḥakīm, known as al-Muqannaʿ ("the Veiled One") because he wore a green cloth over his face continuously and asserted that mere mortals could not bear the light of his countenance, led a revolt in Khurāsān that had extended into the reign of al-Mahdī. He is said to have declared himself an incarnation of the deity and to have preached the transmigration of souls. See Ṭabarī, III, 484, 494, and 499 (A.H. 161 and 163); Barthold, *Turkestan down to the Mongol Invasion*, 199–200.

64. Abū Muslim, the architect of the ʿAbbāsid revolution, was executed by Abū Jaʿfar al-Manṣūr in a move to consolidate his own power. See *EI*[2] s.v. Abū Muslim (Moscati).

65. Yūsuf b. Ibrāhīm al-Barm led a rebellion in Khurāsān in 160/776–77 against al-Mahdī. He was defeated by troops led by Yazīd b. Mazyad and sent back to al-Ruṣāfah, where al-Mahdī had him executed. See Ṭabarī, III, 470–71; Yaʿqūbī, II, 478–79.

Muslims, he was an infidel (*kāfir*)—but God averted the trouble. Then Ustādhsīs[66] rebelled, calling people to infidelity (*kufr*). Al-Mahdī[67] marched from al-Rayy[68] to Naysābūr and took care of the trouble. But what I do will be more for you! Tell me, how do you think the troops were, when they received the news of Rāfiʿ [b. Layth]?"[69] He said, "I think they were greatly disturbed." I said, "How will they be regarding you, when you are lodged among your maternal uncles,[70] with the oath of allegiance to you binding them? What will the disturbance of the Baghdad troops be? Be patient, and I will guarantee you the caliphate!" I placed my hand on my heart. He said, "I will. I put the matter into your hands. Carry it out!"

Then I said, "By God, I will speak the truth to you. ʿAbdallāh b. Mālik, Yaḥyā b. Muʿādh, and the leading commanders we have named—if *they*[71] undertake the matter for you, they will
[774] be more advantageous for you than I, with their renowned leadership and because of the strength they possess for fighting. Whoever undertakes the matter, I will be his servant until you attain your desire and decide as you think best about me." So I met them in their lodgings. I reminded them of the oath of allegiance binding them and their obligation to fulfill it. It was as if I had brought them carrion on a plate. One of them said, "This is not lawful; go away!" Another of them said, "Who would

---

66. The revolt of Ustādhsīs during the reign of al-Manṣūr in 150/767 involved elements from Harāt, Bādghīs, Sijistān, and parts of Khurāsān. See Ṭabarī, III, 354–58; Yaʿqūbī, II, 457; Kennedy, *Early Abbasid Caliphate*, 183–84.

67. Al-Mahdī, the third ʿAbbāsid caliph, ruled from 158/775 to 169/785. See EI^2 s.v. (Kennedy).

68. Al-Rayy, or Ray (ancient Rhages), was a major city in northeastern Jibāl province. The modern city of Tehran began as a suburb of it. See Le Strange, *Lands*, 214–17; EI^1 s.v. Raiy (Minorsky).

69. The revolt of Rāfiʿ b. Layth b. Naṣr b. Sayyār (apparently the grandson of the last Umayyad governor of Khurāsān) was the occasion for al-Rashīd's expedition to Khurāsān. The revolt had begun in 190/805–6 as an expression of discontent against the misrule of ʿAlī b. ʿĪsā b. Māhān as governor of Khurāsān, developed considerable local support, and was still continuing when al-Rashīd died. See Ṭabarī, III, 707–8; Yaʿqūbī, II, 528; Barthold, *Turkestan down to the Mongol Invasion*, 200–1.

70. This alludes to al-Maʾmūn's mother, Marājil, who was of Iranian extraction.

71. Correcting the reading of ed. Leiden ("it will be . . .") on the basis of ed. Cairo and Maqrīzī (see ed. Leiden, *Addenda*, DCCLXIV).

interfere between the Commander of the Faithful and his brother?" So I came and informed (al-Ma'mūn). He said, "Undertake the matter!"

I said (to al-Ma'mūn), "You have read the Qur'ān, heard traditions,[72] and become learned in religion. The wisest plan is for you to send to the learned men in your entourage, summoning them to justice and its performance, and to reviving the Sunnah.[73] You should sit on felt mats[74] and relieve injustices." We did this. We sent to the men learned [in religious matters]. Also we treated the military commanders, kings, and descendants of kings generously. To the Tamīmī[75] we would say, "We set you in the place of Mūsā b. Ka'b"; to the Raba'ī[76] we would say, "[We set you] in the place of Abū Dāwūd Khālid b. Ibrāhīm"; and to the Yemenī, "We set you in the place of Qaḥṭabah and Mālik b. al-Haytham."[77] We summoned each tribe to the greatest of their heads. We gained the favor of the heads and said things like this to them.[78] We reduced the land tax (*kharāj*) from

---

72. *Aḥādīth*, pl. of *ḥadīth*: reports of sayings or actions of the Prophet, transmitted by reliable intermediaries and serving as precedents for action. See *EI*[2] s.v. On al-Ma'mūn's religious education, see the biography of al-Ma'mūn in Ṣafadī, *al-Wāfī bi-al-wafayāt*, XVII, 654–61 (repeated in Kutubī, *Fawāt al-wafayāt*, II, 235–39); and Ya'qūbī, II, 571–72.

73. *Sunnah* (from *sanna*, to institute) originally meant "a way of acting or conduct . . . instituted by former people, and . . . pursued by those after them"; Lane, *Lexicon*, IV, 1438. Before Islam *sunnah* referred to the practice of an ancestor handed down from one generation of a tribe to another as worthy of praise and emulation. The Islamic community applied the word to the normative actions and sayings of Muḥammad handed down within the community. See also Bravmann, *The Spiritual Background of Early Islam*, 123–98.

74. That is, as a sign of humility. Ibn al-Athīr, V, 155, reads "wool."

75. That is, a member of the powerful tribe of Tamīm.

76. That is, from the tribe of Rabī'ah.

77. Cf. Ibn al-Athīr, VI, 155: "All these men had been *naqībs* ('supervisors, chiefs') of the 'Abbāsid revolution." Mūsā b. Ka'b had fought in the revolution and headed al-Manṣūr's *shurṭah* (Kennedy, *Early Abbasid Caliphate*, 79; Crone, *Slaves on Horses*, 186). Abū Dāwūd Khālid b. Ibrāhīm had been Abū Muslim's second in command and became governor of Khurāsān after Abū Muslim's execution (Kennedy, ibid., 62–63). Qaḥṭabah b. Shabīb al-Ṭā'ī had been the most important military commander of the revolution next to Abū Muslim (Crone, ibid., 188). Mālik b. al-Haytham al-Khuzā'ī had been the head of Abū Muslim's *shurṭah* (Crone, ibid., 181).

78. The manuscript followed by ed. Leiden has a lacuna at this point, and the translation follows the text of ed. Cairo, which may itself be corrupt. Two groups of "heads" seem to be involved: the Arab tribal leaders who had been

Khurāsān by one-fourth. They were favorably impressed and gladdened by this. They said, "The son of our sister and the son (i.e., descendant) of the paternal uncle of the Prophet, may God bless him and grant him peace!"[79]

According to ʿAlī b. Isḥāq: When the caliphate devolved upon Muḥammad [al-Amīn] and the people of Baghdad became calm, he arose on Saturday morning, a day after allegiance had been sworn to him, and ordered the building of a parade ground (*maydān*) around the Palace of Abū Jaʿfar in the city for polo and games.[80] Concerning this, a poet from the people of Baghdad said:

God's *Amīn*[81] built a parade ground,
    and he turned the tract into a garden.
[775] The gazelles in it were ben trees
    that were brought to him in it as gazelles.

Various Items of Information

In the month of Shaʿbān[82] of this year, Umm Jaʿfar[83] left al-Raqqah,[84] taking all the treasures and other things she had there.

---

active in the ʿAbbāsid revolution, and the Persian elite, which was favorably impressed by the reduction in the land tax and by references to al-Maʾmūn's Persian descent on his mother's side.

79. Cf. *Fragmenta*, 321: "The Persians said, 'The son . . . , the learned, just, and pious!" "Son of our sister" refers to the fact that al-Maʾmūn's mother, Marājil, was Persian and sometimes said to have been the captured daughter of Ustādhsīs, the Khurāsānian rebel. See Kennedy, *Early Abbasid Caliphate*, 124; *EI*[2] s.v. al-Maʾmūn.

80. Parallels: Ibn al-Athīr, VI, 155; *Fragmenta*, 321.

81. There is a pun on the meaning of the name *al-Amīn*, "the trustworthy one." The second verse of the couplet is textually uncertain (see ed. Leiden note). I take it to mean that the gazelles in the garden were beautiful maidens (ben trees, because of their shapeliness, were a typical poetic comparison for women) that were brought to a place where wild gazelles once had roamed.

82. Shaʿbān 193 began on May 20, 809.

83. Umm Jaʿfar is the *kunyah* (agnomen) of Zubaydah, the niece of al-Manṣūr and mother of al-Amīn. See *EI*[2] s.v. al-Amīn; also Abbott, *Two Queens of Baghdad*.

84. Al-Raqqah, on the Euphrates river, was the main town of the Diyār Muḍar district of al-Jazīrah province (see note 96). The ʿAbbāsids established a major garrison adjoining the town, and al-Rashīd used al-Raqqah as a residence when the climate of Baghdad was too hot. See Le Strange, *Lands*, 101–3.

Her son, Muḥammad al-Amīn, met her at al-Anbār[85] with all the dignitaries who had been in Baghdad. Al-Ma'mūn established himself in charge of that to which he had been appointed —that is, the governorship of Khurāsān and its districts as far as al-Rayy. He wrote to al-Amīn and sent him many gifts. Al-Ma'mūn's letters to Muḥammad arrived one after the other, extolling the latter's greatness, and accompanied by gifts of Khurāsānian rarities—furniture, vessels, musk, beasts, and weapons.

In this year, Harthamah[86] entered the wall of Samarqand.[87] Rāfiʿ [b. Layth] took refuge in the inner city and sent a message to the Turks, who came to him. Harthamah was caught between Rāfiʿ and the Turks, but the Turks withdrew, and Rāfiʿ grew weaker.

In this year, Niqfūr,[88] the king of the Romans, died fighting the Bulgars.[89] His reign is said to have lasted seven[90] years. Istabrāq,[91] the son of Niqfūr, became king after him, but he had been wounded and survived only two months and then died. Istabrāq's brother-in-law, Mīkhā'īl[92] the son of Jūrjis, then became king.

In this year, Dāwūd b. ʿĪsā b. Mūsā b. Muḥammad b. ʿAlī,[93] the governor of Mecca, led the pilgrimage.[94]

---

85. Al-Anbār, an important city on the left bank of the Euphrates, was about 12 *farsakh*s (44.6 miles) west and slightly north of Baghdad. It was the terminus of an important canal, the Nahr ʿĪsā, connecting the Euphrates and the Tigris at Baghdad. See Le Strange, *Lands*, 65–67; *EI*[2] s.v.

86. On Harthamah b. Aʿyan, see *EI*[2] s.v. Har<u>th</u>ama (Pellat); Crone, *Slaves on Horses*, 177.

87. Parallel: Yaʿqūbī, II, 528.

88. That is, Nicephorus I, Byzantine emperor from 802 to 811, who died in battle against the khan of the Bulgars on July 26, 811 (Ṭabarī's date for his death is incorrect). For an account of his origins, see Ṭabarī, III, 695. Cf. Vasiliev, *History of the Byzantine Empire*, 271; and Ostrogorsky, *Geschichte des byzantinischen Staates*, 151–60.

89. *Al-Burjān* (Bulgars) were a Turkish people who had moved into the Balkans.

90. The reading "nine years," noted in ed. Cairo, is probably correct. The words for "seven" and "nine" are easily confused in Arabic script.

91. That is, Stauracius.

92. That is, Michael I Rhangabe, who ruled from 811 to 813.

93. Dāwūd b. ʿĪsā was an ʿAbbāsid family member, a distant cousin of al-Rashīd.

94. Yaʿqūbī, II, 526, reports that Zubaydah, the mother of al-Amīn, also made the pilgrimage this year.

In this year, Muḥammad b. Hārūn confirmed[95] his brother al-Qāsim b. Hārūn in the governorship of al-Jazīrah[96] to which his father had appointed him. He appointed Khuzaymah b. Khāzim[97] to be (al-Qāsim's) agent for al-Jazīrah, and he also confirmed al-Qāsim over Qinnasrīn[98] and the frontier strongholds.[99]

---

95. I understand the text to mean that al-Amīn confirmed his younger brother in his titular governorships, but appointed an agent to administer the districts as deputy. Note, however, that the parallel in Ibn al-Athīr, VI, 155, reads: "Al-Amīn *removed* his brother al-Qāsim al-Mu'taman from al-Jazīrah and appointed him over Qinnasrīn and al-ʿAwāṣim. As governor of al-Jazīrah he appointed Khuzaymah b. Khāzim." Cf. the report below, p. 22, about al-Qāsim's being removed in 194/809–10.

96. Al-Jazīrah ("the island" or "peninsula") was the Arabic name for Upper Mesopotamia. Al-Mawṣil, al-Raqqah, and Āmid were the main towns of its three districts. See Le Strange, *Lands*, 85–114; *EI*[2] s.v. al-Djazīra (Canard).

97. Khuzaymah b. Khāzim b. Khuzaymah al-Tamīmī was of Khurāsānian origin and the son of a *naqīb* of the ʿAbbāsid revolution. He was prominent among the *Abnā'*, military leaders of Khurāsānian origin who had come to Baghdad with the revolution. See Crone, *Slaves on Horses*, 180.

98. Qinnasrīn was a city in Syria south of modern Aleppo (Ḥalab). It was considered one of the *ʿAwāṣim* (see note 99, below). See *EI*[2] s.v. Ḳinnasrīn (Elisseeff).

99. *ʿAwāṣim* (pl. of *ʿāṣimah*, a defending city): This was the new line of garrisons that al-Rashīd had established in Syria to defend the Byzantine border and provide a base for launching attacks. Manbij was the main town. See *EI*[2] s.v. al-ʿAwāṣim (Canard); Shaban, *Islamic History*, II, 29; Kennedy, *Early Abbasid Caliphate*, 130. For other actions by al-Amīn at the beginning of his reign, see Yaʿqūbī, II, 526–28, as well as p. 103, below (the release of the ʿAbbāsid ʿAbd al-Malik b. Ṣāliḥ from prison).

The Events of the Year

194

(October 15, 809–October 3, 810)

Among these events was the disobedience of the people of Ḥimṣ[100] against their governor, Isḥāq b. Sulaymān,[101] whom Muḥammad had appointed as governor.[102] When they disobeyed him, he moved to Salamyah.[103] Muḥammad removed him from them and appointed ʿAbdallāh b. Saʿīd al-Ḥarashī,[104] with whom was ʿĀfiyah b. Sulaymān. He imprisoned a number of their prominent people and set fire to their city from its outer parts. When they asked him for quarter (*amān*), he agreed, and they became quiet. Later, they rioted; so he cut off the heads of a number of them.[105] [776]

---

100. Ḥimṣ (modern Ḥomṣ) is about 135 km north of Damascus in Syria, approximately halfway between Damascus and Aleppo. See *EI*[2] s.v. (Elisséeff).

101. Isḥāq b. Sulaymān b. ʿAlī b. ʿAbdallāh b. al-ʿAbbās was a member of the ʿAbbāsid family.

102. Parallel: Ibn al-Athīr, VI, 156.

103. Salamyah (modern Salamiyyah) is about 50 km northeast of Ḥimṣ. A number of members of the Hāshimī family had settled in it, and therefore it would be a more congenial residence for the governor in the face of hostility in Ḥimṣ. See *EI*[1] s.v. Salamīya (Kramers).

104. He is probably to be identified as the grandson (not son) of Saʿīd b. ʿAmr al-Ḥarashī, a Qaysī military commander from Qinnasrīn who had served the Umayyads. See Crone, *Slaves on Horses*, 144–45.

105. This notice about a rebellion in Ḥimṣ is repeated almost verbatim at the end of the year's events (p. 45, below).

In this year, Muḥammad removed his brother al-Qāsim from everything over which his father, Hārūn, had given him charge—the districts of Damascus (*al-Sha'm*), Qinnasrīn, the frontier strongholds (*ʿawāṣim*), and the border regions (*thughūr*).[106] He replaced him with Khuzaymah b. Khāzim and commanded (al-Qāsim) to live in Madīnat al-Salām.[107]

In this year, Muḥammad ordered prayers to be offered from the pulpits on behalf of his son Mūsā for the office of commander.[108]

In this year, Muḥammad al-Amīn and ʿAbdallāh al-Ma'mūn practiced deceit against each other, and a falling out became apparent between the two.

Reasons for the Falling out between Muḥammad al-Amīn and ʿAbdallāh al-Ma'mūn

It has been mentioned: After he had come to Muḥammad in Iraq, leaving Ṭūs and breaking the promises that al-Rashīd had made him give to his son ʿAbdallāh [al-Ma'mūn], al-Faḍl b. al-Rabīʿ took thought.[109] He realized that, if the caliphate ever devolved upon al-Ma'mūn in his own lifetime, the latter would not allow him to survive; if he gained power over him, it would be his downfall. So he strove to incite Muḥammad against ʿAbdallāh. He urged him to depose him and to divert the succession to his own son Mūsā. This had not been Muḥammad's plan or intention. His intention, according to what has been mentioned about him, was to carry out for his brothers ʿAbdallāh and al-Qāsim the promises and stipulations that his father had caused him to make to them. Al-Faḍl kept on disparaging
[777] al-Ma'mūn in his eyes and recommending that he be deposed. Finally, al-Faḍl said, "What are you waiting for in the matter of

106. On the *thughūr*, see Shaban, *Islamic History*, II, 28–29.

107. I.e., Baghdad, which had been named "City of Peace" by its founder, al-Manṣūr. For discussion of the name, see Lassner, *Topography of Baghdad*, p. 45 and note.

108. The action indicated official recognition of Mūsā as successor to the office of Commander of the Faithful. See Dozy, *Supplément*, I, 445, for a discussion of the idiom.

109. Parallels: Yaʿqūbī, II, 529; Dīnawarī, 389; *Fragmenta*, 321–23; Ibn al-Athīr, VI, 156; Masʿūdī, VI, 419.

ʿAbdallāh and al-Qāsim, your brothers? The oath of allegiance was to you first, before the two of them; they were only brought into it after you, one after the other." Al-Faḍl brought into the affair those whose opinion was on his side—ʿAlī b. ʿĪsā b. Māhān,[110] al-Sindī, and others in his entourage—and he caused Muḥammad to change his mind. The first thing that Muḥammad did in conformity with the counsel of al-Faḍl b. al-Rabīʿ in the affair was to write ordering all the governors in all the garrison cities to offer prayers on behalf of his son Mūsā for the office of commander after the prayers for himself, al-Maʾmūn, and al-Qāsim b. al-Rashīd.[111]

According to al-Faḍl b. Isḥāq b. Sulaymān:[112] When al-Maʾmūn learned what Muḥammad had commanded, that his own son Mūsā should be prayed for [as an heir], and that he had removed al-Qāsim from the districts that al-Rashīd had assigned him and had made him come to Madīnat al-Salām (i.e., Baghdad), he realized that Muḥammad was plotting against him to depose him. He cut off the post[113] from Muḥammad and dropped his name from the embroidered decorations on official garments.[114]

---

110. ʿAlī b. ʿĪsā b. Māhān, the son of a *naqīb* (deputy) and *dāʿī* in Marw during the ʿAbbāsid revolution, was from a prominent family of *Abnāʾ* in Baghdad. He had been active in service to the dynasty since the reign of al-Mahdī. Under al-Rashīd he had served as governor of Khurāsān, where he had become highly unpopular because of his methods. His disastrous expedition against al-Maʾmūn's commander Ṭāhir b. al-Ḥusayn will be narrated in detail on pp. 49ff., below. See also *EI*² s.v. Ibn Māhān (Sourdel); Crone, *Slaves on Horses*, 181–82; Kennedy, *Early Abbasid Caliphate*, 80–81.

111. Note that this account says that Mūsā's name was added after the names of al-Maʾmūn and al-Qāsim, but did not replace them. The next account (from another source apparently; there is a textual problem) has al-Amīn demanding that al-Maʾmūn give Mūsā precedence (p. 25, below). Finally, Ṭabarī, p. 27, below (apparently the same source, but this is not certain) has al-Faḍl b. al-Rabīʿ forbidding any mention of ʿAbdallāh and al-Qāsim as heirs. The exact sequence of events is anything but clear.

112. Probably to be identified as the son of the ʿAbbāsid prince Isḥāq b. Sulaymān, who held various governorships under al-Rashīd. See Bosworth, *ʿAbbāsid Caliphate in Equilibrium*, 15n.

113. That is, he stopped sending reports to the central government in Baghdad. On the post (*barīd*), see note 5.

114. Ms. A (cited in ed. Cairo) adds: "and from the coinage." The calligraphic motifs embroidered on robes worn by rulers and persons of high rank were called *ṭirāz*. Such garments were produced in state workshops, and the wording of the embroidered band was carefully controlled. It normally mentioned the reigning caliph and sometimes his minister or the official in charge of the workshops.

When Rāfiʿ b. al-Layth b. Naṣr b. Sayyār received news about al-Ma'mūn and his good behavior toward the people of his province and good treatment of them, he sent asking quarter (*amān*) for himself. Harthamah promptly granted it.[115] Rāfiʿ came out and joined al-Ma'mūn; Harthamah remained established at Samarqand. Al-Ma'mūn treated Rāfiʿ generously. Ṭāhir b. al-Ḥusayn[116] had been with Harthamah at the siege of Rāfiʿ. After quarter had been granted to Rāfiʿ, Harthamah asked al-Maʿmūn for permission to come to him. He took his army across the Balkh River[117] while it was frozen, the people met him, and al-Ma'mūn put him in charge of the guard (*ḥaras*). Muḥammad took a dim view of all this and began plotting against al-Ma'mūn. As part of the plotting, he wrote to al-ʿAbbās b. ʿAbdallāh b. Mālik,[118] who was al-Ma'mūn's financial agent for al-Rayy, commanding him to send him some
[778] exotic plants from al-Rayy, wishing to test him by this. Al-ʿAbbās sent him what he had commanded him to send and concealed the matter from al-Ma'mūn and Dhū al-Ri'āsatayn. Word of what he had done reached al-Ma'mūn. He sent out al-Ḥasan b. ʿAlī al-Ma'mūnī,[119] as whose subordinate he ap-

---

Thus, omitting al-Amīn's name could be considered a very serious act. The Meccan documents fixing the succession to al-Rashīd granted control of the *ṭirāz* workshops of Khurāsān to al-Ma'mūn (cf. Ṭabarī, III, 655). An example of *ṭirāz* from the reign of al-Amīn, dated A.H. 197, mentioning both al-Amīn and al-Faḍl b. al-Rabīʿ, is in the Museum of Islamic Art in Cairo, along with one from the reign of al-Ma'mūn (A.H. 216). See Day, "Dated Ṭirāz," 422; texts in *REA*, I, No. 93, 208A. On *ṭirāz* more generally, see *EI*[1] and *EI*[1] Supplement, s.v. (Grohmann); Ibn Khaldūn, *Muqaddimah* (trans. Rosenthal), II, 65–67; and Sergeant, *Islamic Textiles*.

115. Cf. Yaʿqūbī, II, 529, where the capitulation of Rāfiʿ is dated in Muḥarram 194.

116. This is the first mention of the commander who would lead al-Ma'mūn's forces to victory in the coming civil war. His family, apparently of Arab origin, had been settled at Būshang, near Harāt, since late Umayyad times. See *EI*[1] s.v. (Barthold); Kennedy, *Early Abbasid Caliphate*, 138–39; and Kaabi, "Les Origines ṭāhirides dans la *daʿwa* ʿabbāside," 145–64.

117. I.e., the Oxus (Jayḥūn), which lies on the route between Samarqand and Marw.

118. He was a grandson of the early ʿAbbāsid military leader who has already been mentioned (note 77). See Crone, *Slaves on Horses*, 182.

119. As his name indicates, he was a *mawlā* of al-Ma'mūn. A native of Bādghīs, he later became governor of Armenia for al-Ma'mūn. See Ṭabarī, III, 985; Yaʿqūbī, II, 566; and Crone, *Slaves on Horses*, 257 n. 599.

pointed al-Rustumī to be in charge of the post, and he removed al-ʿAbbās b. ʿAbdallāh b. Mālik. It is reported on al-Rustumī's authority that, as soon as he dismounted, a thousand men of the inhabitants of al-Rayy rallied to him.

Muḥammad sent three people to al-Ma'mūn as messengers.[120] One was al-ʿAbbās b. Mūsā b. ʿĪsā;[121] the second was Ṣāliḥ, the keeper of the prayer rug;[122] and the third was Muḥammad b. ʿĪsā b. Nahīk.[123] To be taken with them, he wrote a letter [to al-Ma'mūn, asking him to give his son Mūsā precedence over himself and to come to him, as he felt loneliness because of his being far away. When the message reached al-Ma'mūn, the latter wrote][124] to the master of al-Rayy, saying, "Receive them in full panoply and with weapons visible." He wrote similarly to the governor[s] of Qūmis,[125] Naysābūr, and Sarakhs,[126] and they did it. When the messengers arrived in Marw, weapons and various equipment and supplies had been prepared because of them. They went to al-Ma'mūn and de-

---

120. Note that there is a second, somewhat different account of what is apparently the same embassy to al-Ma'mūn, see pp. 65–74, below, under the events of the year 195, but with the notice that "this took place in the year 194." For a discussion of the two accounts, see Gabrieli, "La successione di Hārūn al-Rašīd," 356ff.

121. He was a member of the ʿAbbāsid family; full name: al-ʿAbbās b. Mūsā b. ʿĪsā b. Mūsā b. Muḥammad b. ʿAlī b. ʿAbdallāh b. al-ʿAbbās.

122. On the caliph's prayer rug (*muṣallā*) and its significance in ʿAbbāsid court etiquette, see D. Sourdel, "Questions de cérémonial ʿabbaside," 131–32; Bosworth, *ʿAbbāsid Caliphate in Equilibrium*, 53 n. 210.

123. Three members of this family are known to have fought for al-Amīn: ʿUthmān b. ʿĪsā b. Nahīk, Muḥammad b. ʿĪsā b. Nahīk, and ʿAlī b. Muḥammad b. ʿĪsā b. Nahīk. See Crone, *Slaves on Horses*, 189.

124. There is a lacuna in the manuscript, which ed. Leiden (but not ed. Cairo) restores on the basis of the parallel text in Ibn al-Athīr, VI, 157–58. The restoration should be treated with caution, because Ibn al-Athīr does not always follow the exact wording of his sources and sometimes conflates accounts to form a smoother narrative. Note that the demand that al-Ma'mūn give Mūsā precedence as heir can be deduced from the next few sentences in Ṭabarī. However, the demand that al-Ma'mūn return to Baghdad plays no further role in this account, although it is important in the second account of the embassy (pp. 65–74, below). See Gabrieli, "La successione di Hārūn ar-Rašīd," 357n.

125. Qūmis was a small province lying along the Khurāsān road between al-Rayy (in al-Jibāl province) and Naysābūr (in Khurāsān). See Le Strange, *Lands*, 364–68; EI^2 s.v. Ḳūmis (Bosworth).

126. Sarakhs, in Khurāsān province, was located about midway between Ṭūs and Marw. See Le Strange, *Lands*, 395–96.

livered Muḥammad's letter to him. It asked him to give Mūsā precedence over himself, and said that Muḥammad had given Mūsā the title *al-Nāṭiq bi-al-Ḥaqq* ("Speaker of the Truth"). The person who had counseled Muḥammad to do this was ʿAlī b. ʿĪsā b. Māhān, who used to tell him that the people of Khurāsān would obey him. Al-Ma'mūn rejected [the request] and refused [to give Mūsā precedence].

[Continuing, al-Faḍl b. Isḥāq] said: Dhū al-Ri'āsatayn said to me: Al-ʿAbbās b. Mūsā b. ʿĪsā b. Mūsā said (to al-Ma'mūn), "What do you have to fear, commander, from this? Behold, my grandfather, ʿĪsā b. Mūsā, was deprived (of the succession), and it did not harm him."[127] "Be silent," I cried to him. "Your grandfather was a prisoner in their hands, whereas this man is among his maternal uncles and his partisans." So the messengers went away, and each of them was lodged in a lodging.

Dhū al-Ri'āsatayn [continued his report to me,] saying: What I saw of the acuteness of al-ʿAbbās b. Mūsā pleased me; so I
[779] met with him in private and said, "Will you, with your understanding and your age, neglect an opportunity to obtain your good fortune from the imām?" (At that time, al-Ma'mūn was called "the imām"; he was not called by the title of caliph. His being called "the imām" caused what came to pass—namely Muḥammad's removing him [from the succession]. Muḥammad had said to those whom he had sent, "Al-Ma'mūn has named himself 'the imām.'") Al-ʿAbbās said to me, "*You* have called him 'the imām.'" I said to him, "He may well become the imām of the mosque and the nation.[128] If you keep faith, he will not hurt you; but, if you betray, that's it!" Then I said to al-ʿAbbās, "You can ask me for the governorship of the pilgrimage feast, for there is no governorship more prestigious than that; or you can have one of the places of office in Egypt, if you wish." Before al-

---

127. ʿĪsā b. Mūsā, the nephew of the caliphs al-Saffāḥ and al-Manṣūr, had been appointed by al-Saffāḥ to be next in the line of succession after al-Manṣūr. After al-Manṣūr succeeded to the caliphate, he replaced ʿĪsā with his own son, who later reigned as al-Mahdī. ʿĪsā finally renounced his rights in 146/746. See Kennedy, *Early Abbasid Caliphate*, 91–93.

128. *Qabīlah*: In modern usage the word means "tribe," but here it has the less specific sense of an ethnic group, descendants of one father. Cf. *Lisān*, s.v. The phrase *imām al-qabīlah* recalls the phrases *imām al-ummah* and *imām al-qawm*. Amending it to *imām al-qiblah* is unnecessary.

ʿAbbās b. Mūsā departed, I received from him the oath of allegiance to al-Maʾmūn for the caliphate. Afterward, he used to write us reports [from Baghdad][129] and provide us with advice.

[Continuing, al-Faḍl b. Isḥāq] said: ʿAlī b. Yaḥyā al-Sarakhsī said (to me): Al-ʿAbbās b. Mūsā visited me on his way to Marw. I described to him al-Maʾmūn's policy, the excellent management of Dhū al-Riʾāsatayn, and his suitability for the position; but he did not accept this from me. When he came back, he visited me (again), and I said to him, "What do you think now?" He said, "Dhū al-Riʾāsatayn is more than you have described!" I asked him, "Did you shake hands with the imām?" "Yes," he said. I said, "Stroke your hand over my head!"

[Continuing, al-Faḍl b. Isḥāq] said: The men went to Muḥammad and informed him of al-Maʾmūn's refusal. Al-Faḍl b. al-Rabīʿ and ʿAlī b. ʿĪsā urged Muḥammad about the oath of allegiance to his son and the deposition of al-Maʾmūn—he gave al-Faḍl money [as a reward for this]—until (Muḥammad) had the oath of allegiance rendered to his son Mūsā and named him *al-Nāṭiq bi-al-Ḥaqq* ("Speaker of the Truth"). He made ʿAlī b. ʿĪsā his tutor and made him governor of Iraq. The first person to administer an oath of allegiance to Mūsā was Bishr b. al-Samaydaʿ al-Azdī, the governor of Balad.[130] Then the governor of Mecca and the governor of Medina administered the oath to a few dignitaries, but not to the populace. Al-Faḍl b. al-Rabīʿ
forbade the mention of ʿAbdallāh and al-Qāsim and prayer for [780]
them [as heirs] on any pulpit. He intrigued to have ʿAbdallāh mentioned disparagingly. He sent a letter to Mecca—the messenger was one of the doorkeepers of the Kaʿbah,[131] a man named Muḥammad b. ʿAbdallāh b. ʿUthmān b. Ṭalḥah—saying that the two documents that Hārūn had written and placed in the Kaʿbah on behalf of ʿAbdallāh and as binding upon Muḥammad should be taken. The messenger brought the two documents to al-Faḍl. The other doorkeepers spoke about this, but they were not heeded, and they feared for their lives. When

129. Cf. Ibn al-Athīr, VI, 158.

130. Balad was a town on the Tigris, 7 *farsakh*s (41.9 km/26 miles) north of al-Mawṣil. See Le Strange, *Lands*, 99, 125; Yāqūt, *Muʿjam*, s.v.

131. That is, a holder of the office of *ḥājib* (doorkeeper or guardian) of the Kaʿbah.

he brought the two documents to Muḥammad, the latter took possession of them and rewarded him with a large reward. Muḥammad tore up the two documents and nullified them.

According to what has been mentioned: Muḥammad wrote to al-Ma'mūn before al-Ma'mūn openly disobeyed him, asking al-Ma'mūn to relinquish to him some districts (*kuwar*) of Khurāsān that he named. Financial agents were to be sent to these districts to act on behalf of Muḥammad, and al-Ma'mūn was to allow al-Amīn to send a man to be in charge of the post (*barīd*) over his head and to write letters to al-Amīn with reports about him. When the letter to this effect reached al-Ma'mūn, it was grievous and distressing to him. He summoned al-Faḍl b. Sahl and the latter's brother al-Ḥasan and asked their advice. Al-Faḍl said, "The matter is dangerous. You have a retinue of your supporters and members of your household. They are put at ease by consultation; but, if matters are settled without them, it will cause uneasiness among them and the appearance of mistrust. So it would be best for the commander to do this (i.e., consult them)." Al-Ḥasan said, "It used to be said, 'In seeking the right view, consult those whose advice you trust; but, when an affair cannot be concealed, conciliate your foe by consulting him.'" So al-Ma'mūn summoned his intimates—the chiefs and notables—and read the letter to them. They all said to him, "Commander, you are asking counsel in a dangerous matter. Give our first intuition a chance for deliberate reflection." "That is the prudent thing to do," said al-Ma'mūn, and he gave them three days. When they assembled afterward, one of them said, "Commander, you have been urged to do two things displeasing
[781] to you. I do not think it a mistake to repel by the inconvenience of the first of them the fear of the inconvenience of the second of them." Another said, "Commander—may God grant you happiness—people say that, if a matter is dangerous, it is better for you to give your rival part of what he wants than to come to an open falling out with him by refusing." Another said, "It is said, 'If knowledge of [future] matters is hidden from you, hold to the proper course[132] for today as much as you can; for you run the

132. For *hidyah*, "[proper] course," ed. Cairo, following Ms. A, reads *hudnah*, "tranquillity, peace."

risk that today's disorder may bring on tomorrow's disorder for you.'" Another said, "If you fear that yielding voluntarily will have consequences, the breach that will be caused if we do not avoid a split will surely be even more serious."[133] Another said, "I do not think one should abandon a state of peace, for with it I may perchance be given health and safety." Al-Ḥasan [b. Sahl] said, "You all deserve [thanks] for your effort, although I differ from you in opinion." Al-Ma'mūn said, "Argue with them." He said, "The assembly was for that purpose." So al-Ḥasan approached them and said, "Do you know that Muḥammad has overstepped the bounds to ask for something that is not his by right?" "Yes," they said, "and it should be tolerated because of the harm we fear that refusing it [would cause]."[134] He said, "Are you confident that he will stop after (al-Ma'mūn) gives him these (districts), and will not go on to ask for others?" "No," they said, "but perhaps peace will transpire before what you fear and expect." He said, "But if, after asking for these districts, he asks for more, do you not think that al-Ma'mūn will have become weak because of what he has given up willingly?" They said, "We shall ward off what may befall him later by putting off the danger[135] that lies immediately at hand." "This," he said, "is contrary to the maxim we have heard of the sages who lived before us. They said, 'Seek to make your future affairs thrive by bearing whatever hardship befalls you today, but do not seek peace[136] today at the cost of exposing yourself to danger tomorrow.'" Al-Ma'mūn said to al-Faḍl, "What do you say about the issue on which they differ?" He said, "Commander, may God grant you happiness! Can one avoid fearing [782]
that Muḥammad may be asking you for your excess strength in order to gain backing to oppose you in the future? Does a prudent man pursue an excess of present ease at the cost of

133. Ed. Cairo, following Ms. A, reads: "the breach that a *refusal* will cause will surely be even more serious."

134. The translation follows ed. Cairo. The Leiden text reads, "it should be tolerated for him the harm of whose refusing we fear."

135. The translation follows the reading of ed. Cairo (*maḥdhūr*), instead of the Leiden editor's conjectural emendation (*mā tunjizūn*, "what you will achieve").

136. Following the reading of ed. Cairo (*hudnah*), rather than that of ed. Leiden (*hidyah*), "(proper) course of action."

danger that will befall him later? The sages advised that inconvenience should be borne for the sake of future benefit they hoped would come thereby." So al-Ma'mūn said, "Indeed, by preferring the immediate present, many a man has spoiled the consequences in this world and the next." The men said, "We have spoken all the opinion that is necessary. May God assist the commander with success!" So al-Ma'mūn said, "Write to him, Faḍl!" Al-Faḍl wrote [in the name of al-Ma'mūn]:[137]

> I have received the letter of the Commander of the Faithful in which he requests the relinquishment of certain specified places—part of what al-Rashīd established in the agreement and whose command he granted to me. No one will transgress the greater part of what the Commander of the Faithful has thought best. However, he who gave me the region where I am[138] was neither to be suspected of carelessness toward his populace nor ignorant in entrusting to me those of his affairs that he entrusted. Even if that had not been confirmed by oaths and sworn covenants, not to mention my being in my present situation of looking down on an enemy of fearful strength, with a populace not to be conciliated from its unruliness and soldiers whose obedience can be obtained only by money and a good deal of largesse, the Commander of the Faithful's interest in his populace and his desire to unite his domains would be enough to cause him to devote much of his attention to the matter and promote it by spending much of his wealth. How much more so in a matter that right has made an obligation and that a sworn promise has confirmed? I am certain that, if the Commander of the Faithful had known what I know about the situation, he would not have communicated the request that he wrote to me. I am confident of approval after this explanation, God willing.

137. Italian translation and discussion in Gabrieli, "Documenti," 206.

138. For "where I am" (*ana bihi*), ed. Cairo reads the same consonants as a single word (*unābuhu*), "of which I am made to be agent."

Al-Ma'mūn had sent a garrison to the border.[139] As soon as any messenger from Iraq crossed, they would send him with trusted agents; the messenger would not be allowed to ask about any news or exert any influence, induce anyone to follow by enticement or fear, or deliver a verbal or written message to anyone. Thus al-Ma'mūn prevented the people of Khurāsān from being swayed by enticement, having fear lodged in their breasts, or being led to a state of disobeying or abandoning [him]. He placed trusty guards over the lookouts of the roads. No one might pass them except those whose business caused no suspicion—one who came bearing a passport allowing him to return to his home or a well-known merchant trusted in his person and in his religion. Lone travelers without baggage[140] were prevented from traveling the roads, passing through markets, or infiltrating towns in the guise of unexpected wayfarers. Letters were searched. The first people—[it is reported][141]—to come from Muḥammad to contest al-Ma'mūn's refusal of the demands were a group who were sent only so that (Muḥammad) might know that they had seen and taken note, and that he might then ask them to give freely or[142] withhold; thus from what they said there would be an argument he might allege or an excuse for what he sought. When they came to the border of al-Rayy, they found strong management and a military command well established and confirmed. The guards held them on all sides, so that even when they unsaddled and took up lodging, they were kept from imparting or asking for news. Letters were sent ahead with a report about them. Permission came for them to be given mounts. They were conveyed under guard; no news reached them, and no news slipped out from them to others. They had been prepared to spread the news among the populace, make known the argument for abandoning [al-Ma'mūn], and call on the powerful to disobey, bestowing [783]

---

139. Parallels: Ibn al-Athīr, VI, 159; *Fragmenta*, 323.

140. *Ashtātāt* is thus interpreted by ed. Leiden, *Glossarium*, CCCV, but the root from which the word is derived frequently implies disorderliness. The exact meaning is uncertain.

141. The parenthetical remark is from ed. Cairo.

142. Following ed. Cairo; ed. Leiden reads "and." The text may be corrupt.

money and guaranteeing them most of the governorships
[784] (*wilāyāt*), land grants (*qaṭā'i'*), and positions. However, they found that all this had been prevented and stopped. Finally, they came to al-Ma'mūn's gate. The following was the letter delivered to al-Ma'mūn [from al-Amīn]:[143]

> To proceed: Although the Commander of the Faithful, al-Rashīd, assigned the province [of Khurāsān] to you alone and attached to you certain districts of al-Jabal[144] to strengthen you and protect your province, that does not give you a claim to the excess money above your need. This province and its land tax (*kharāj*) have been sufficient for its circumstances. You, however, go beyond what is sufficient to the excess of its revenue. In addition to the province, he joined to you certain major revenue-producing districts that you do not need. [The revenues from] them ought to be returned to their people and the places to which they belong. I wrote asking you to return the districts in question to their former status, so that their excess revenue would be sent back where it belongs, and that you should allow an information officer to be in your court to send us information of interest to us about the news of your province. However, you wrote refusing to grant this, saying things which, if you were to act upon them, justice would lead us to make a demand upon you. Turn from your intention, and I will turn from making a demand upon you, God willing!

When al-Ma'mūn read the letter, he wrote in reply to him:[145]

> To proceed: The letter of the Commander of the Faithful has reached me. As he writes about what he does not

143. Italian translation and discussion in Gabrieli, "Documenti," 207.

144. Al-Jabal ("the Mountain," often in the plural form *al-Jibāl*) was the region known earlier as Māh or Media, roughly the northwestern quarter of the Iranian plateau. Its main cities were Qirmasīn (Kirmānshāh), Hamadhān, Rayy, and Iṣbahān (Isfahān). Khurāsān lay to the east, separated from al-Jibāl by the province of Qūmis. See EI^2 s.v. Djibāl (Lockhart); Le Strange, *Lands*, 185 ff.

145. Italian translation and discussion in Gabrieli, "Documenti," 207–8.

know, I will reveal to him the true state of affairs; as he asks for something to which he has no claim, he obliges me to justify my forbearing to comply.[146] Two rivals go beyond a state of equal sharing only when equal sharing [785] is insufficient for those who hold to it. When did someone ever depart from it while it was enough for everyone and the departure from it resulted only in breaking with it and suffering what lay in its abandonment? Son of my father, do not cause me to oppose you, when I willingly grant you obedience; nor to become estranged from you, when I want to be on friendly terms with you. Be satisfied with what justice has assigned to you, and I will be in the place where justice has set me as regards relations between us. Peace!

Then he summoned the messengers and said, "I have written a reply to the Commander of the Faithful in a matter about which he wrote to me. Deliver the letter to him, and tell him that I shall remain obedient to him until he forces me, by departing from binding right, to disobey him." So they went to deliver the message. He said, "Take exactly the same attitude as we took in speaking with you, and convey carefully what you have heard; for, as regards the letter to us, you have imparted to us what I hope you did not want to say to us." So the messengers departed; they had not carried any of their argument, nor did they bear a [favorable] report to convey to their master. They had seen a serious intention, not mixed with jest, to refuse them what they alleged to be their due.

When al-Ma'mūn's letter reached Muḥammad, he found its contents distressing. He burst into rage at whatever of it was repeated [in his hearing].[147] It was then that he commanded what we have mentioned—that prayers should cease being made for (al-Ma'mūn) on the pulpits—and he wrote to him:[148]

146. Ed. Cairo differs somewhat: "He has not written about what he does not know, that I should reveal to him the true state of affairs; nor has he asked me for something to which he has a right, that I should be obliged to justify my forbearing to comply."

147. The bracketed words are from ed. Cairo.

148. Italian translation and discussion in Gabrieli, "Documenti," 208.

To proceed: I have received your letter, in which you show ingratitude for God's favor toward you in enabling you to enjoy the protection of His favor, and where you expose yourself to the burning of a fire you cannot control. Indeed, your disinclination to obey [me] was more tolerable [than your ingratitude toward God]. If some previous request proceeded from me, its grounds were
[786] none other than your benefit, as it was to the advantage of the majority of your subjects; moreover, it would establish you in a position of safety and assure for you a condition of peace. Let me know your view, and I will act in accordance with it, God willing.

According to Sahl b. Hārūn—al-Ḥasan b. Sahl: Al-Ma'mūn said to Dhū al-Ri'āsatayn, "My children, my family, and my wealth that al-Rashīd set aside for me—a hundred million [dirhams][149]—are at Muḥammad's court. I need them, but they are with him. What do you advise?" He consulted him several times. Dhū al-Ri'āsatayn said to him, "Commander, you need to have the remainder of your wealth and your family in your residence and beside you; but, if you write a commanding letter and he refuses you, it will lead to his breaking his oath; and, if he does so, he will force you, even against your will, to go to war with him. I would not want you to be the first to open the door of estrangement, as long as God has closed it before you. Instead, you should write a letter appealing for your due and the coming of your family, in such a way that his refusal will not oblige him to break his oath to you. If he obeys, well and good; if he refuses, you will not have gotten yourself into a war. Write to him." So (Dhū al-Ri'āsatayn) wrote on his behalf:[150]

To proceed: The regard of the Commander of the Faithful for the populace is the regard of one who does not limit himself to giving an equal share with himself; rather, he goes beyond that for them with his kindness and benevolence. This being his view concerning his

149. Cf. p. 57, below, where a sum of a million dirhams is said to have been confiscated.

150. Italian translation and discussion in Gabrieli, "Documenti," 208–9.

populace, how fitting it is for him to go beyond that with his brother and kinsman! Surely you know, Commander of the Faithful, in what state I am, encamped in the uttermost parts of frontier regions, with armies who are always certain to show their indiscipline and disloyalty, and with little revenue at my disposal—my family, children, and wealth being with the Commander of the Faithful. As for my family, although they are adequately provided for out of the kindness of the Commander of [787]
the Faithful, who has become a father to them, they cannot help desiring and yearning for my protection. [You know, too,] the strength and help the money would give me to set things in order in my court. I have sent [someone] to convey my family and the money. May it please the Commander of the Faithful to allow him to proceed to al-Raqqah to convey this money and to command that he be given assistance in the matter, not causing him therein to fall into such difficulty as would happen by his disobedience or moving him to a decision that would be disapproved.[151] Peace.

Muḥammad then wrote to him:[152]

To proceed: I have received your letter, in which you spoke of how the Commander of the Faithful views his populace, not to mention the obligation due to one of his own family and his copartner; how you are encamped in the uttermost parts of the frontier regions; how, being encamped there, you need extra money to strengthen your position and the money from the public treasury that was assigned to be yours; finally, how you have sent someone to convey it and your family from the presence of the Commander of the Faithful. Assuredly, the Commander of the Faithful does not deny his view of his populace as you mentioned and the attachment that it

151. The translation of the last clause is uncertain. Gabrieli makes it a separate sentence: "Con ciò peraltro non si vuole spingerlo in un imbarazzo contro sua voglia, nè indurlo a una decisione contro il suo beneplacito."

152. Italian translation and discussion in Gabrieli, "Documenti," 209–10.

> obliges him to have to his closest relations and his populace. He needs the money you mentioned to strengthen the affairs of the Muslims. Thus, it is more appropriate for him to spend it on his obligations and return it to those who are entitled to it. Neither will what brings benefit to your subjects as a whole fail to benefit you. As for what you mentioned about conveying your family, it is the intention of the Commander of the Faithful to assume responsibility for their affairs, notwithstanding the right of close relationship in which you stand. As for sending them on a journey as you have thought best to
> [788] do, I do not think it wise to expose them to becoming separated by a journey. If I decide so for my part, I will send them to you with trusted messengers of my own, God willing. Peace.

When the letter came to al-Ma'mūn, he said, "Refusing to grant what is our due, he wants us to become weakened by his withholding of our forces. Then, because of our weakness, he will gain a chance to oppose us." Dhū al-Ri'āsatayn said to him, "Is it not known that al-Rashīd gave that money to al-Amīn to be kept together, and that al-Amīn took possession of it in the sight of the leading men of his populace on the basis that he would hold it for administration and would not touch it? So do not leave him with no way out of this. Write to him something whose consequence will not force you to show him open hostility over it. It is best to hold fast to the rope of trust and prevent estrangement. [If he abstains, well and good.][153] If he casts covetous eyes on it, he will lay himself open to [punishment from] God for his opposition; you, by forbearance, stand to receive God's help and assistance."

Al-Ma'mūn and al-Faḍl knew that after his letter some incident would occur that would require his knowledge,[154] and some report that would require that he deal with it through his trusty companions. He knew that (Muḥammad) would cause no incident without the concurrence of men of eminence and power

153. The bracketed text is added in ed. Cairo from Ms. A.
154. Ed. Cairo: "that would require his rectification."

among the partisans [of the ʿAbbāsids] and those with long service [to the ʿAbbāsid cause].[155] So he decided to choose a man to carry letters addressed to the leading figures of the army in Baghdad. If Muḥammad caused al-Ma'mūn to be deposed, the man would go and deliver[156] the letters and would feel out the inclinations of the addressees. If Muḥammad did none of this, the man would keep [the letters] in his box and withhold [789]
delivery of them. He ordered the man to travel quickly. When he arrived, he delivered the letters.[157] (Al-Ma'mūn's) letter with the messenger whom he sent to find out news was as follows:[158]

> To proceed: In regard to their affairs, the faithful are like the members of the body.[159] If disease occurs in one of them, the misfortune is painful to all of them. So it is with the Muslims: an incident occurs regarding one of them, but the misfortune of it reaches the others because of the law (*sharīʿah*) of their religion that unites them and the sanctity of their brotherhood[160] that binds them. As regards the imāms, this is an even more serious matter because of the position in which the imāms stand in relation to the rest of their peoples. There has been such a report as I cannot but believe will clearly express its distressing nature and uncover what has been hidden of its real meaning.[161] Never did two disputants dispute, one of them being on the side of God's command,[162] but that the Muslims' first help and assistance were with God Himself. You—may God have mercy upon you—

155. Arabic: *al-shīʿah wa-ahl al-sābiqah.*

156. Reading, with ed. Cairo, *dafʿihā*, rather than the conjectural emendation of ed. Leiden, *dhawīhā*, "the owners, i.e., addressees" of the letters.

157. The translation follows ed. Cairo. The Leiden text reads: "When he arrived, he continued the letters."

158. Italian translation and discussion in Gabrieli, "Documenti," 210–11.

159. The translation follows the emended reading of ed. Leiden. Ed. Cairo keeps the original reading, which yields a loose, but not impossible sentence: "The *Commander* [reading *amīr*, not *amr*] of the Faithful is like the members of the body."

160. The translation follows ed. Cairo (*ukhuwwatihim*). Ed. Leiden reads *ākhiratihim*: "the sanctity of their Hereafter."

161. The translation follows ed. Cairo. Ed. Leiden reads: "such a report as I believe will return from its coming and uncover what was hidden."

162. Ed. Cairo fills the lacuna found in ed. Leiden.

are in sight and hearing of the affair and are so situated that, if you speak, what you say will be listened to.[163] If you, finding it impossible to speak, refrain from something fearful, your example in the matter will be followed. The reward for good action will not be neglected by God, in addition to the obligation to you that we shall incur by your good action. A lot that obtains for you both parts, or one of them, is better than eagerly desiring one of the parts, while exposing oneself to the loss of both. Write to me with your view. Tell it to my messenger, that he may convey it to me from you, God willing.

He wrote similarly to the eminent military men.

The messenger's arrival in Baghdad coincided with the command to cease praying for al-Ma'mūn in the Friday sermon. (The messenger) was in a position of trust vis-à-vis all those to whom letters had been sent through him. Some of them refrained from replying, but clearly told the messenger what they thought; others replied to the letter. One of them wrote:[164]

[790] To proceed: I have received your letter. Truth has a proof that is self-evident, whereby it carries the argument against all who depart from it. What a bad bargain it is to lose a share of future good fortune because of present good fortune for which one hopes![165] It is even more clearly a bad bargain to lose future good fortune along with becoming subject to [present] misfortune and contingencies. I have such knowledge of where my fortune[166] lies that I hope thereby to take good care of myself and that this will spare me the trouble of seeking more, God willing.

163. The vocalization of ed. Cairo, followed here, seems more likely than that of ed. Leiden, which reads: "if you speak, *I* will listen to what you say."

164. Italian translation and discussion in Gabrieli, "Documenti," 211.

165. The translation follows ed. Cairo.

166. Following ed. Cairo's *ḥaẓẓī*, "my fortune," instead of ed. Leiden's *khaṭar*, "danger."

The messenger who had been sent to Baghdad wrote to al-Ma'mūn and Dhū al-Ri'āsatayn:[167]

> To proceed: I have come to the city. Your copartner has publicly shown his alteration.[168] He has put forward a sign of his opposition and separation [and has ceased from what is his duty to mention and discharge][169] in his court. I delivered your letters and found most of the people to be friends of secrecy, rejecters of publicity. I found those who are eminent among the populace[170] to care only for it and to be unconcerned about what they have borne in it. [Your] opponent is in a quandary, neither finding anyone to repel him from his design, nor anyone desiring it in its entirety. Those who disengage themselves consider the completion of the innovation to be lawful, so that they may become safe from the defeat of their innovation. The [fighting] men are in a state of earnestness. Do not give languor [a part in your affair],[171] God willing. Peace!

When Sa'īd b. Mālik b. Qādim, 'Abdallāh b. Ḥumayd b. Qaḥṭabah,[172] al-'Abbās b. al-Layth (the *mawlā* of the Commander of the Faithful),[173] Manṣūr b. Abī Maṭar, and Kathīr b. Qādirah came to Muḥammad from al-Ma'mūn's camp, he showed them kindness and drew them close. For those of them

---

167. Italian translation and discussion in Gabrieli, "Documenti," 210–11. Gabrieli's comment on the obscurity and probable corruptness of the text should be noted.

168. The translation follows ed. Cairo: *tanakkur*, "change, alteration," usually in a pejorative sense.

169. The bracketed words are from ed. Cairo.

170. The text is difficult and almost certainly corrupt. Ed. Leiden notes a lacuna in the manuscript and conjectures an original reading, "those who were swayed by desire." Ed. Cairo reads, *al-mushrifīn* or *al-musharrafīn bi-al-ra'iyyah*, "those who are eminent (or honored) among the populace." *Mushrifīn* might also mean "those who desire vehemently."

171. The bracketed words are from ed. Cairo.

172. He was the grandson of Qaḥṭabah b. Shabīb al-Ṭā'ī, next to Abū Muslim the most important general of the 'Abbāsid revolution. See Kennedy, *Early Abbasid Caliphate*, 79–80; Crone, *Slaves on Horses*, 188–89.

173. See Crone, *Slaves on Horses*, 192.

who had collected [pay] for six months, he ordered twelve months' allowance (*rizq*), and he increased their special and general stipends (*al-khāṣṣah wa-al-ʿāmmah*); for those who had not yet collected, he ordered eighteen months' [pay].

When Muḥammad resolved to depose al-Ma'mūn, he summoned Yaḥyā b. Sulaym and consulted him about it.[174] Yaḥyā
[791] said, "Commander of the Faithful, how can you do such a thing, given the oath of allegiance to him that al-Rashīd confirmed, binding himself in the matter by his promise and by taking oaths and stipulating conditions in the document that he wrote?" Muḥammad said to him, "Al-Rashīd's decision was a whim that Jaʿfar b. Yaḥyā [al-Barmakī],[175] with his beguilement, represented to him as good; he swayed him with his charms and spells, so that he planted for us a hateful shoot. Never will our situation benefit us unless that shoot is cut down; never will our affairs run straight unless it is uprooted and we have relief from it." (Yaḥyā) said, "Then if the Commander of the Faithful thinks that he should be deposed, do not announce it openly, lest [important] people disapprove and the ordinary troops regard it as unseemly. Rather, summon one body of troops after another and one commander after another, pacifying each with kindnesses and gifts. Separate his confidants and those who are on his side. Entice them with money, and sway them with hopes of gain. When you have sapped his strength and drawn away his men, you will command him to come to you. If he comes, it will turn out as you wish with regard to him; if he refuses, you will take him with his force dulled, his wing broken, his support weakened, and his strength cut off." Muḥammad said, "Nothing settles an affair like a firm decision. You are a garrulous speechmaker, not a man of counsel. Turn from this view to [that of] 'the fortunate old man and wise vizier.'[176] Up, and get back to your ink and your pens." [Yaḥyā] said: [I said,—it was anger][177] mixed with truth and good counsel—"You have alluded to a

174. Parallel: Ibn al-Athīr, VI, 161.

175. For the career of this member of the famous family of viziers, see *EI*² s.v. al-Barāmika (Sourdel). Note that Jaʿfar b. Yaḥyā had served as tutor to al-Ma'mūn.

176. I.e., al-Faḍl b. al-Rabīʿ.

177. The bracketed words are from ed. Cairo. The text seems to be unreliable.

view that is mixed with deceit and ignorance." By God, before many days had passed, he remembered what he had said and it tormented him with his error and stupidity.[178]

According to Sahl b. Hārūn: Al-Faḍl b. Sahl had infiltrated chosen men, commanders and prominent people whom he trusted in Baghdad, to write him reports on a daily basis.[179] When Muḥammad was about to depose al-Ma'mūn, al-Faḍl b. [792]
al-Rabīʿ sent to one of these men to consult him about what he thought in the matter. The man made al-Faḍl see the gravity of breaking the promise to al-Ma'mūn and the loathsomeness of treachery toward him. Al-Faḍl said to him, "You are right, but ʿAbdallāh has already caused an incident[180] that makes it necessary to break what al-Rashīd caused to be sworn to him." The man said, "Has the argument of his well-known incident become as firmly fixed in the mind of the populace as is the argument of the promise to him that has been renewed?" "No," he replied. "Then," said the man, "does this man's incident regarding you necessitate from the point of view of the populace the breaking of your promise, as long as his incident has not been a well-known one such as requires the annulment of the promise to him?" "Yes," said al-Faḍl. Raising his voice, the man said, "By God, never have I seen—as I have today—a man's judgment leading him to look into a matter, where he consults about removing a kingdom that is in his hand by argument, and then proceeds to demand it from him with stubbornness and contention!"

Al-Faḍl fell silent for a moment; then he said, "You have given me honest advice and have kindly transmitted confidential information.[181] Tell me, however: if we disregard[182] what the populace (*al-ʿāmmah*) say and find helpers from our partisans (*shīʿatinā*) and our soldiers, what would you say?" "God keep you!" said the man. "Don't your soldiers belong to

178. Following ed. Cairo's *wa-qarraʿahu bi-khaṭa'ihi wa-khurqihi,* rather than ed. Leiden's "and he fled from him (*wa-farra ʿanhu*) with his error and ill-fatedness (*ḥurfihi*)."

179. Parallel: Ibn al-Athīr, VI, 161.

180. *Aḥdatha al-ḥadath* can also mean "has innovated an innovation."

181. Ed. Cairo: "and have sustained the burden of trustworthiness."

182. Reading *aghmaḍnā* (ed. Cairo), instead of *aʿaḍnā* (ed. Leiden).

your populace in their having sworn the oath of allegiance and in the power that a true argument has in their hearts? Even if they give you their outward obedience, will they not be on the side of the covenant documents about which they have assured knowledge?" [Al-Faḍl b. al-Rabīʿ said, "And what if they give us obedience nevertheless?"][183] The man said, "There is no obedience unless one has firm inner conviction." Al-Faḍl said, "We will awaken their desire by improving their fortunes." "Then," said he, "they will accept[184] at first, but then abandon you when you need their loyalty." Al-Faḍl said, "What is your opinion about ʿAbdallāh's soldiers?" "They are men," he said, "Who have enthusiasm for their enterprise because of their longstanding effort and the important affair in which they are engaged together."[185] Al-Faḍl said, "What is your opinion of their common people?" "They are men," he said, "who were in
[793] great distress because of mistreatment. Because[186] they in their property and persons have come through him to their desire[187] as regards property and to easy circumstances of life, they are defending prosperity that is newly come to them, and they remember tribulation to which they fear a return." (Al-Faḍl) asked,[188] "Is there no way to corrupt the loyalty of the great men of the land to rebel against him, so that our battle with him could be by the intrigue of his side, not by marching toward him to do battle with him?" [He replied,][189] "As for the weak, they have come to love him because of the security and fair treat-

183. The translation follows ed. Cairo. The words in brackets were omitted in the manuscript used for the Leiden text. The Leiden editor made an unnecessary conjectural emendation to preserve the sense of his defective text.

184. Following ed. Cairo's *taqabbul*. Ed. Leiden's reading (*thiqal*, "heaviness, indolence") is a conjectural emendation of an incompletely written word in the manuscript.

185. Ed. Cairo: "their longstanding oath of allegiance and their fortune in which they are engaged together."

186. Ed. Cairo reads *wulātihim* ("their governors"), where ed. Leiden reads *wa-liʾannahum* ("and because they"). The Cairo text may be translated: "who were in great distress because of their governors' mistreatment of their property and even their persons, and who came through him. . . ."

187. Alternate translation: "to security." See ed. Leiden, *Glossarium*, p. CXX.

188. Following ed. Cairo; the manuscript used by ed. Leiden was defective at this point.

189. The bracketed text is from ed. Cairo.

ment they have obtained from him, while the powerful have found nothing to censure and no ground for argument; and the weak are the great majority." Al-Faḍl said, "I think you have left us no room to believe that we should go [to fight] his soldiers or that concern about our soldiers has taken hold on his side.[190] Even stronger is what you have said about the weakness of our soldiers and the strength of his soldiers in a conflict with him. But the Commander of the Faithful is not content to abandon what he knows to be his right, nor am I satisfied with peace, given the progress that has occurred in his enterprise. Sometimes matters approach threatening danger, but in the aftermath they reveal peace and profit." The two then parted.

Because al-Faḍl b. al-Rabīʿ had set up observation points so that letters might not cross the border, the messenger wrote by way of a woman, depositing the letter in the hollowed-out board of a packsaddle, and writing to the postmaster to speed the news on. The woman passed among the border posts (*masāliḥ*) unmolested and unsearched, as if she were traveling from village to village. The news reached al-Ma'mūn, agreeing with the other letters that came to him; the letters corroborated each other. So al-Ma'mūn said to Dhū al-Ri'āsatayn, "These are matters whose substance judgment foretold. These are harbingers that portend what is to come. It is enough for us that we are on the [794]
side of the truth. Perhaps what is hateful will bring good in its wake."

The first action that al-Faḍl b. Sahl took after prayer for al-Ma'mūn was omitted and the report of this was confirmed was to gather the troops he had prepared in the vicinity of al-Rayy, along with troops he had garrisoned there and [other] troops to undertake their enterprise. Because the country was too barren to support them, he supplied the troops with goods brought in by pack animals over every mountain pass and road, so that they lacked nothing they needed. They stayed at the border, not crossing it and not laying violent hands on anyone coming in or passing through.[191] Then he dispatched Ṭāhir b. al-Ḥusayn,

190. The text seems disturbed.

191. Following ed. Cairo's *ʿāmid*, rather than ed. Leiden's *ʿāmmah* ("ordinary person"), which makes less sense.

along with the commanders and soldiers he attached to him. Ṭāhir marched quickly, turning aside for nothing, until he arrived at al-Rayy and encamped there. He assigned men to its districts, established his garrisons, and sent out his spies and scouts. One of the poets of Khurāsān said:[192]

The imām of justice and right-guided king
has launched against the people of Iraq and its ruler
The man who of all who walk [the earth] is most resolute in judgment, prudence,
and effective stratagem in what he devises:
A calamity[193] oppressive[194] and swift,
whose fearful assault turns the newborn babe's hair white.

It has been mentioned: Muḥammad [al-Amīn] sent ʿIṣmah b. Ḥammād b. Sālim to Hamadhān[195] with a thousand men and put him in charge of military affairs of the districts (*kuwar*) of al-Jibāl. He commanded him to stay at Hamadhān and to send his vanguard to Sāwah.[196] (ʿIṣmah) appointed his brother ʿAbd al-Raḥmān b. Ḥammād to be his deputy over the guard (*ḥaras*). Al-Faḍl b. al-Rabīʿ and ʿAlī b. ʿĪsā began inflaming Muḥammad and urging him to depose al-Maʾmūn and have allegiance sworn to his own son Mūsā.

Various Items of Information

In this year, in the month of Rabīʿ I,[197] Muḥammad b. Hārūn confirmed his son Mūsā over everything for which he had made
[795] him his deputy and made ʿAlī b. ʿĪsā b. Māhān master of all

---

192. Parallel: Ibn al-Athīr, VI, 162.

193. *Dāhiyah* can mean both "calamity, misfortune," and "a man who is very cunning, or very intelligent." See Lane, *Lexicon*, III, 928.

194. The translation follows ed. Cairo (*naʾādin*), rather than ed. Leiden (*taʾaddu*, "that comes").

195. Hamadhān (modern Hamadān, ancient Ecbatana), a major city of western Jibāl province, lay on the Khurāsān road, approximately 250 miles northeast of Baghdad. See Le Strange, *Lands*, 194–96, 227–30; *EI*[2] s.v. Hamadhān (Frye).

196. Sāwah (modern Sāveh) lay approximately midway between Hamadhān and al-Rayy on the great Khurāsān road (ca. 175 km east of Hamadhān). See Le Strange, *Lands*, 211–12, 228–30. A more detailed account of the mission of ʿIṣmah b. Abī ʿIṣmah al-Sabīʿī is given in Yaʿqūbī, II, 530. See p. 50, below.

197. Rabīʿ I 194, corresponds to December 13, 809–January 11, 810.

his affairs. Muḥammad b. ʿĪsā b. Nahīk was in charge of (Muḥammad's) police (*shurat*); ʿUthmān b. ʿĪsā b. Nahīk was in charge of his personal guard (*ḥaras*); ʿAbdallāh b. ʿUbaydah was in charge of his tax [bureau] (*kharāj*); and in charge of his correspondence bureau (*dīwān al-rasāʾil*) was ʿAlī b. Ṣāliḥ the keeper of the prayer rug (*muṣallā*).

In this year, the Romans rose against Mīkhāʾīl,[198] the ruler of the Romans. He fled and became a monk. His reign is said to have lasted for two years.

In this year, Leon the General[199] became king of the Romans.

In this year, Muḥammad b. Hārūn removed Isḥāq b. Sulaymān from [the governorship of] Ḥimṣ and appointed as its governor ʿAbdallāh b. Saʿīd al-Ḥarashī, with whom was ʿĀfiyah b. Sulaymān. He killed a number of their prominent people and imprisoned a number, and he set fire to their city from its outer parts. When they asked him for quarter (*amān*), he agreed, and they became quiet. Later, they rioted; so he cut off the heads of a number of them.

---

198. That is, Michael I Rhangabe. See note 92.

199 That is, Leon V, the Armenian, who ruled from 813 to 820. See Ostrogorsky, *Geschichte des byzantinischen Staates*, 163–65.

The Events of the Year 195

(October 4, 810–September 22, 811)

Among the events taking place this year was Muḥammad b. Hārūn's order to invalidate the dīnārs and dirhams that had been struck for his brother ʿAbdallāh al-Maʾmūn in Khurāsān in the year 194, because al-Maʾmūn had ordered that Muḥammad's name should not be recorded on them.[200]

---

200. Parallel: Ibn al-Athīr, VI, 164–65. The conflict over coinage raises many questions: What was the established practice as to inscriptions upon al-Amīn's accession in 193? What changes did each brother make in coins issued in his territory, and would these changes cause offense? First, it needs to be said that no dīnārs have been discovered from any Iranian mint before the reign of al-Muʿtaṣim, so the information in the text seems to project the circumstances of Ṭabarī's time back into the earlier period. As for dirhams, there was no established practice at the time of al-Rashīd's death as to whose name might appear on them. Al-Amīn's coins for 193 used the inscription *Rabbī Allāh* ("God is my Lord"), without naming anyone. In the same year, the mints under al-Maʾmūn's control introduced dirhams inscribed *mimma amara bihi al-Amīr al-Maʾmūn walī ʿahd al-muslimīn ʿAbd Allāh b. Amīr al-Muʾminīn* ("By order of the Commander al-Maʾmūn, heir to the rule of the Muslims, the Servant of God, son of the Commander of the Faithful"), and this continued throughout 194 and into 195, with the addition of the name of al-Faḍl sometime during 194. In 194, al-Amīn added to his dirhams the inscription *mimma amara bihi ʿAbd Allāh al-Amīn Muḥammad Amīr al-Muʾminīn al-ʿAbbās* ("By order of the Servant of God al-Amīn Muḥammad, Commander of the Faithful, Family of ʿAbbās"). Al-Amīn might at this point have objected to al-Maʾmūn's refusal to accept the new caliphal inscription or identify himself as anything

These dīnārs and dirhams were called *rubāʿiyyah*. For a time they were not allowed [as currency].

Al-Amīn Forbids Prayer for al-Maʾmūn and al-Qāsim as Heirs

In this year, al-Amīn forbade prayer from the pulpits in his entire domain for al-Maʾmūn and al-Qāsim. He commanded that there should be prayer for himself on them, and after him for his son Mūsā. This took place in Ṣafar[201] of this year. His [796] son Mūsā was a child at the time. He named him, "*al-Nāṭiq bi-al-Ḥaqq*" ("Speaker of the Truth"). He acted in the matter on the advice of al-Faḍl b. al-Rabīʿ. Concerning this, a poet said:[202]

The caliphate has been brought to ruin by the vizier's malice,
the commander's (*amīr*) dissoluteness, and the counselor's ignorance.
Faḍl is a vizier and Bakr[203] a counselor
who desire what will bring about the commander's death.

When word of this reached al-Maʾmūn, he took for himself the name "*Imām al-Hudā*" ("Imām of Right Guidance"), and he was addressed by this name in letters.[204]

---

else than the heir of the previous caliph. Al-Maʾmūn, for his part, could point out that many governors in previous reigns had put their names on the coinage without any reference to the reigning caliph. A more serious offense took place in 195, when al-Maʾmūn introduced the inscription *al-Imām al-Maʾmūn*, openly claiming the imāmate and by implication the caliphate. About *rubāʿiyyah* one can only guess. It does not seem to be the name of a denomination or to refer to the year 194 (from *arbaʿ* "four"). It is possible that an author or copyist at some point confused the words *rubāʿiyyah* and *rabbāniyyah* (very similar in Arabic script) and that the passage had originally added information about al-Amīn's coins, which may have been called *rabbāniyyah* because of the inscription *Rabbī Allāh*—but this is speculation. (I am indebted to Dr. Michael L. Bates of the American Numismatic Society for this information.)

201. I.e., between November 3 and December 1, 810.

202. The poem is quoted again, with additional lines, on pp. 58–59, below. See note 252.

203. I.e., Bakr b. al-Muʿtamir.

204. Cf. Kennedy, *Early Abbasid Caliphate*, 136–37: "No Abbasid caliph had officially used this title [sc. *imām*] before, and he himself refrained from taking the title of caliph at this time. It was probably a deliberately ambiguous gesture,

ʿAlī b. ʿĪsā b. Māhān Assigned Command of al-Jabal

In this year, on Wednesday, the first day of the month of Rabīʿ II (January 1, 811), Muḥammad gave ʿAlī b. ʿĪsā b. Māhān governance of all the districts (*kuwar*) of al-Jabal—Nahāwand, Hamadhān, Qumm, and Iṣfahān—both their military command and their taxes.[205] He attached to him a group of commanders and ordered that he should be given—according to what has been mentioned—200,000 dīnārs, and that his sons[206] should be given 50,000 dīnārs. He gave much money to the army and ordered for it 2,000 ornamented swords and 6,000[207] garments as robes of honor. Muḥammad had the people of his household, his *mawālī*, and his military commanders come to the *maqṣūrah* [of the mosque] in al-Shammāsiyyah[208] on Friday, the 8th day of Jumādā II (March 7, 811). Having led the Friday worship, Muḥammad went into [the *maqṣūrah*]; his son, Mūsā, held an audience for them in the *miḥrāb*—with him were al-Faḍl b. al-Rabīʿ and all who had been summoned. He read them a letter from al-Amīn. It informed them of his good opinion of them, his right over them, how they had previously sworn allegiance to him as having priority and as having none to share in the allegiance with him, and how this was binding for them. It informed them also of the innovations ʿAbdallāh had caused: styling himself imām, having prayers made on his behalf, cutting off the post, and omitting mention (of al-Amīn) in the mints and workshops for embroidered garments (*ṭirāz*);

---

to announce his defiance of his brother without providing an excuse for attack. It also shows that Ma'mun was pursuing the policy, begun by Mahdi and continued by the Barmakids, of developing the religious nature of Abbasid authority and seeking a reconciliation with the Alids and their supporters."

205. Parallels: Ibn al-Athīr, VI, 165; *Fragmenta*, 323.

206. At least four sons of ʿAlī b. ʿĪsā are known. ʿĪsā b. ʿAlī had already died fighting the rebel Rāfiʿ (Ṭabarī, III, 712). Al-Ḥusayn b. ʿAlī commanded his father's right wing (p. 52, below) and after his father's death was sent by al-Amīn to Syria to recruit troops. Afterward, he switched his allegiance to al-Ma'mūn, attempted a coup in Baghdad, and was killed. Also mentioned are ʿAbdallāh b. ʿAlī and Yaḥyā b. ʿAlī (p. 82, below). See Crone, *Slaves on Horses*, 179.

207. *Fragmenta*, 323: "seven thousand."

208. The quarter of East Baghdad lying to the northeast of al-Ruṣāfah; see Le Strange, *Baghdad*, 199–216.

(ʿAbdallāh) had no right to such innovations, nor were the stipulations that he claimed had been made in his favor valid. [797]
It urged them to obey (al-Amīn) and maintain allegiance to him. After the letter had been read, Saʿīd b. al-Faḍl, the preacher, rose and spoke in the same vein, seconding it and saying things similar to what it had said. Then al-Faḍl b. al-Rabīʿ spoke while seated; he spoke energetically and at length. He mentioned how no one but the Commander of the Faithful, Muḥammad al-Amīn, had any right to the imāmate and caliphate; God had given neither ʿAbdallāh nor anyone else any share or portion therein. As for Muḥammad's household or the others, none of them said anything, except Muḥammad b. ʿĪsā b. Nahīk and a group of important persons from the caliph's personal guard (*ḥaras*). In his speech, al-Faḍl b. al-Rabīʿ said, "Prince Mūsā, the son of the Commander of the Faithful, has ordered that you be given, people of Khurāsān,[209] from his very own money 3 million dirhams to be divided among you." Then the people departed. ʿAlī b. ʿĪsā came to Muḥammad [al-Amīn] and told him that the people of Khurāsān had written him a letter saying that if he marched forth, they would obey him and be led by him.

In this year, ʿAlī b. ʿĪsā went to al-Rayy to fight al-Maʾmūn.[210]

ʿAlī b. ʿĪsā b. Māhān Goes to al-Rayy to Fight the Forces of al-Maʾmūn

According to al-Faḍl b. Isḥāq: ʿAlī b. ʿĪsā left the City of Peace[211] the evening of Friday, the 15th of Jumādā II of the year

209. Note that the people addressed must be troops of Khurāsānian origin resident in Baghdad, i.e., the so-called *Abnāʾ al-Dawlah*. On the other hand, Ibn al-Athīr, VI, 195, interprets the letter mentioned in the next sentence as having actually come from the province of Khurāsān ("if he came to them, they would obey him . . ."). In view of ʿAlī b. ʿĪsā's record as governor of Khurāsān, al-Amīn should have been aware of potential problems. See the report given on p. 63, below, explaining the appointment of ʿAlī b. ʿĪsā as having been cunningly engineered by an agent of Dhū al-Riʾāsatayn, knowing that the people of Khurāsān hated their former governor.

210. Parallels: Yaʿqūbī, II, 530; *Fragmenta*, 323.

211. I.e., Baghdad. See note 15. A second account of the expedition can be found on pp. 75 ff., below, with different dates.

195 (March 14, 811). He left in the late afternoon of that day, between the Jumʿah prayer and the afternoon (*ʿaṣr*) prayer, for his camp on the Bīn Canal.[212] There he stayed with about
[798] 40,000 men. He carried with him a silver shackle with which to bind al-Maʾmūn—so he asserted. Muḥammad al-Amīn went with him as far as al-Nahrawān on Sunday, six days before the end of Jumādā II (March 23, 811); there he reviewed the troops who had been attached to ʿAlī b. ʿĪsā. He remained the rest of that day in al-Nahrawān and then returned to the City of Peace. ʿAlī b. ʿĪsā stayed at al-Nahrawān for three days. Then he marched quickly in the direction he had been ordered to take. When he reached Hamadhān, he appointed ʿAbdallāh b. Ḥumayd b. Qaḥṭabah to be in charge of it. Muḥammad had written to ʿIṣmah b. Ḥammād, instructing him to return with his closest companions, and had attached the rest of his army, including its funds and other things, to ʿAlī b. ʿĪsā.[213] He had also written to Abū Dulaf al-Qāsim b. ʿĪsā,[214] instructing him, along with his companions who were with him, to join (ʿAlī b. ʿĪsā). He sent with him Hilāl b. ʿAbdallāh al-Ḥaḍramī and commanded that soldiers with stipends (*farḍ*) [be assigned] to him. Then he assigned to ʿAbd al-Raḥmān b. Jabalah al-Abnāwī[215] the command over Dīnawar[216] and commanded him to travel with the best[217] of

212. The Bīn Canal (*Nahr Bīn*) branched from the Nahrawān Canal at the town of Jisr Nahrawān (about 10 miles northeast of Baghdad, where the Khurāsān road crossed the Nahrawān Canal) and flowed west and south to join the Tigris at Kalwādhā. See Le Strange, *Lands*, 59–60, 174.

213. According to Yaʿqūbī, II, 530, al-Amīn had earlier sent out ʿIṣmah b. Abī ʿIṣmah al-Sabīʿī, but ʿIṣmah, calling attention to the Meccan agreement, had refused to cross into al-Maʾmūn's territory without the latter's permission. Cf. p. 44, above, and p. 74, below; neither of these reports, however, mentions ʿIṣmah's reluctance to breach the Meccan agreement as a motive for his replacement.

214. Abū Dulaf al-Qāsim b. ʿĪsā b. Idrīs al-ʿIjlī was an important Arab landowner in the area southeast of Hamadhān and leader of the Banū ʿIjl tribal group. See Kennedy, *Early Abbasid Caliphate*, 139.

215. The name is corrected in ed. Cairo to "al-Abnāwī"; ed. Leiden reads "al-Anbārī" throughout.

216. The city of Dīnawar in western Jibāl province lay about 60 miles west of Hamadhān, north of the main Khurāsān road. See Le Strange, *Lands*, 189; *EI*[2] s.v. (Lockhart).

217. *Baqiyyah* often has this meaning; cf. ed. Leiden, *Glossarium*, CXXXIX. An alternative translation would be "with the remainder of his companions."

his companions; with him he sent 2 million dirhams that had been conveyed to him previously. ʿAlī b. ʿĪsā left Hamadhān for al-Rayy before ʿAbd al-Raḥmān reached him; he traveled until he reached al-Rayy in full battle readiness. Ṭāhir b. al-Ḥusayn met him with fewer than 4,000 men—it has been reported that he was with 3,800 men.

Three persons left Ṭāhir's army for ʿAlī b. ʿĪsā, seeking thereby to gain his favor.[218] He asked them who they were and from which country. One of them told him that he was from the army of (ʿAlī's) son ʿĪsā, whom Rāfiʿ [b. Layth] had killed.[219] "Then," he said, "you are one of my soldiers!"[220] He [799]
gave orders concerning him, and the man was flogged two hundred strokes; the [other] two men he treated with contempt. The report of this reached the companions of Ṭāhir, and they became more eager to fight ʿAlī and more hostile toward him.

According to Aḥmad b. Hishām, who was in charge of Ṭāhir's police (*shurṭah*), who said:[221] The letter from al-Maʾmūn saying that he should be addressed as caliph had not reached them when we met [in battle]. I said to Ṭāhir, "ʿAlī b. ʿĪsā has come with those whom you see. If we show ourselves to him and he says, 'I am the agent of the Commander of the Faithful,' and we concede that to him, we shall not be in a position to fight him."[222] Ṭāhir said to me, "I have received nothing concerning this." So I said, "Leave me to what I intend to do." "As you will," he said. I ascended the pulpit, cast off [allegiance to] Muḥammad, and offered prayers for al-Maʾmūn as caliph. We set out that day or the next, a Saturday—it was in Shaʿbān[223] of the year 195. We encamped at Qusṭānah, which is the first stage from al-Rayy toward Iraq. ʿAlī b. ʿĪsā reached a desert tract called Mushkuwayh.[224] Between him and us was a distance

---

218. Parallels: Ibn al-Athīr, VI, 168; *Fragmenta*, 324.

219. For the death of ʿĪsā b. ʿAlī b. ʿĪsā fighting the rebel Rāfiʿ b. Layth in 191/806–7, see Ṭabarī, III, 712.

220. That is, you had no business remaining with al-Maʾmūn.

221. His father had suffered at the hands of ʿAlī b. ʿĪsā. See Kennedy, *Early Abbasid Caliphate*, 140. Parallel: Ibn al-Athīr, VI, 167.

222. See Gabrieli, "La successione di Hārūn ar-Rašīd," 368, for a discussion of Aḥmad b. Hishām's advice.

223. I.e., between April 29 and May 27, 811.

224. According to Yāqūt, *Muʿjam*, this was a small town two stages from al-Rayy on the road to Sāwah.

of seven *farsakhs* (26 miles). We set our vanguard at a distance of two *farsakhs* (7.4 miles) from Qusṭānah.[225] ʿAlī b. ʿĪsā thought that when Ṭāhir saw him, he would hand over the administrative district [of al-Rayy] to him. When he saw that Ṭāhir was serious [in his intention to fight], he said, "This is a desert place, not a place for encampment." He therefore turned left, toward a district called Rustāq Banī al-Rāzī.[226] The Turks were with us. We encamped by a river, and he encamped near us; between him and us there were sand flats (*dakādik*) and hills. In the last part of the night, a man came to me and told me that ʿAlī b. ʿĪsā had entered [the territory of] al-Rayy; he had sent a letter to the people, and they had responded to him. I went out onto the road with the man and said to him, "This is
[800] their road, but there are no hoof-prints here and nothing to indicate his passage." I went to Ṭāhir and awakened him. "Are you going to pray?" I asked. "Yes," he said, and he called for water and made ready. Then I told him the report. We prayed the morning prayer. Then he told me to mount. We stopped on the road. He said to me, "Would you like to cross these flats?" So we looked down on ʿAlī b. ʿĪsā's army. They had girded on their swords. "Go back," he said. "We have made a mistake." So we went back. He said to me, "Go forth."[227] So I summoned al-Ma'mūnī, al-Ḥasan b. Yūnus al-Muḥāribī, al-Rustumī, and Muḥammad b. Muṣʿab. All of them went forth. Al-Ma'mūnī was in charge of the right wing. Al-Rustumī and Muḥammad b. Muṣʿab were in charge of the left wing.

ʿAlī [b. ʿĪsā] approached with his army. The desert was filled with white and yellow from the swords and the gold.[228] Over his right wing he set al-Ḥusayn b. ʿAlī [b. ʿĪsā]. With him was Abū Dulaf al-Qāsim b. ʿĪsā b. Idrīs. Another person was in charge of his left wing. They charged and drove us back, until they entered the army, which with great difficulty rose and drove them off.

225. The translation follows ed. Cairo (note), rather than the conjecture of ed. Leiden.

226. That is, he entered the administrative district (*ʿamal*) of al-Rayy by a road other than the main road.

227. Ed. Cairo: "Make our companions depart."

228. Alternative reading: "from the gilded swords."

When he saw ʿAlī b. ʿĪsā, Ṭāhir said, "This is something we cannot stand up to, but let us do it like the Khārijites!"[229] So he decided to attack the main part of the army. He gathered 700 men from the Khwārazmians, among them Mīkā'īl, Saysal,[230] and Dāwūd Siyāh.

According to Aḥmad b. Hishām:[231] We said to Ṭāhir, "We should remind ʿAlī b. ʿĪsā of the oath of allegiance that was sworn and the oath of allegiance that he himself received specifically on behalf of al-Ma'mūn from the people of Khurāsān." He agreed. So we attached the two [texts] to two spears. I stood between the battle lines and said, "Truce! Do not shoot at us, and we will not shoot at you." ʿAlī b. ʿĪsā said, "You have it." I then said, "ʿAlī b. ʿĪsā, do you not fear God? Isn't this the text of the oath of allegiance that you yourself had people swear? Fear God, for you have reached the door [801]
of your grave!" "Who are you?" he asked. "Aḥmad b. Hishām," I said. (ʿAlī b. ʿĪsā had once given him 400 lashes.[232]) ʿAlī b. ʿĪsā cried out, "People of Khurāsān, whoever fetches him shall have 1,000 dirhams!"

There were people from Bukhārā with us. They shot at (ʿAlī), saying, "We will kill you and take your money." From (ʿAlī's) army, al-ʿAbbās b. al-Layth, the *mawlā* of al-Mahdī, came forth; also, a man called Ḥātim al-Ṭā'ī came forth. Ṭāhir attacked him, grasped the hilt of the sword with both hands, struck him, and felled him.[233] Dāwūd Siyāh attacked ʿAlī b.

---

229. This appears to be the meaning of *najʿalhā khārijiyyatan*. That is, "Let us make an attack on a vastly more numerous foe," an attack such as the notoriously ferocious Khārijite rebels might make.

230. Saysal is the correction suggested by ed. Leiden, *Addenda*, DCCLXIV; the manuscript and ed. Cairo read "Sabsal." Ed. Leiden also suggests that "Mīkā'īl" may be a mistake for "Mīkāl."

231. Parallel: Ibn al-Athīr, VI, 168.

232. Presumably this had occurred during ʿAlī's term as governor of Khurāsān under al-Rashīd.

233. Ed. Cairo adds, "and killed him." Cf. Ibn al-Athīr, VI, 168: "And for that reason, Ṭāhir was named *Dhū al-Yamīnayn* ('Possessor of Two Right Hands')." Masʿūdī, VI, 423, adds that Ṭāhir's two-handed blow killing al-ʿAbbās b. al-Layth caused the defeat of ʿAlī's army and earned him this nickname. An astrological derivation of the name is given in Ibn Khallikān (trans. de Slane), II, 472.

ʿĪsā and felled him, not recognizing him.[234] ʿAlī b. ʿĪsā was on a white-backed destrier[235] that Muḥammad [al-Amīn] had given him as a mount. Such a horse is thought unlucky in battle and presages defeat. Dāwūd said, "Let us sport with them."[236]

[Continuing, Aḥmad b. Hishām] reported: Ṭāhir the Younger—i.e., Ṭāhir b. al-Tājī—said, "Are you ʿAlī b. ʿĪsā?" "Yes," he replied, "I am ʿAlī b. ʿĪsā." (ʿAlī) thought that he would be held in awe and that no one would advance against him; but (Ṭāhir) attacked him and slaughtered him with the sword.[237] Muḥammad b. Muqātil b. Ṣāliḥ attempted to wrest the head from them; he tore out a tuft of his beard and took it to Ṭāhir [b. al-Ḥusayn], announcing the good news to him. Ṭāhir's blow[238] was the victory, and for that reason he was given the name *Dhū al-Yamīnayn* ("Possessor of Two Right Hands") that day, because he had grasped the sword with his two hands. The companions (of ʿAlī b. ʿĪsā) took up arrows to shoot us. I did not know about ʿAlī's death until someone said, "By God, the commander has been killed." We followed them for two *farsakh*s. Twelve times they stood their ground against us, but we kept driving them back. Ṭāhir b. al-Tājī came up to me with the head of ʿAlī b. ʿĪsā. (The latter had sworn that he
[802] would set up Aḥmad's head on the pulpit on which Muḥammad had been deposed and had ordered the morning meal to be prepared for him in al-Rayy.)

I went back and found a leather bag that had belonged to ʿAlī. It contained a tunic (*durrāʿah*), a coat (*jubbah*), and an

---

234. Cf. Ibn al-Athīr, VI, 169: "Some accounts say that Dāwūd Siyāh shot him with an arrow and killed him." Cf. Masʿūdī, VI, 423.

235. *Birdhawn*, a war horse capable of carrying a man in full armor, not the lighter-limbed and fleeter Arabian horse. See Lane, *Lexicon*, I, 186.

236. The words of Dāwūd Siyāh (the name means "Black David" in Persian) seem to be Persian, but the copyist has so corrupted them that they are unintelligible. Ed. Leiden reads: "*nārī a??nān katabtum*. Ed. Cairo reads: "*nārī asnān katabtum*." In Arabic, this would mean, "My fire teeth you have written." Ed. Leiden, *Addenda*, DCCLXIV, proposes reading "*bāzī-yi īnān kunīm*," which is what I have translated.

237. Note that Yaʿqūbī, II, 531, conflates Ṭāhir al-Tājī and Ṭāhir b. al-Ḥusayn.

238. Cf. Masʿūdī, VI, 423: "which he inflicted with both hands on al-ʿAbbās b. al-Layth was the reason for the army's defeat."

undershirt (*ghilālah*). I put them on and prayed two prostrations of prayer in thanksgiving to God, who is exalted and blessed. In his camp we found 700 bags, with 1,000 dirhams in each. In the hands of the men from Bukhārā who had taunted him, saying that they would take his money, we found a number of mules carrying chests. They thought that it was money, but when they broke open the chests, lo and behold it was wine from the Sawād.[239] They divided up the bottles and said, "We have worked hard in order to drink!"

According to Aḥmad b. Hishām: I came to Ṭāhir's tent. He had become worried because I had been away from him so long. "Good news!" he said to me. ["This is a tuft from ʿAlī's beard!" "Good news!" I said to him.] "This is ʿAlī's head."[240] In thanksgiving to God, Ṭāhir freed those of his slaves who were in his presence. Then they brought [the body of] ʿAlī—the aides had tied his hands to his feet—carried on a beam, as a [dead][241] donkey would be carried. Ṭāhir gave orders concerning him: he was wrapped in a felt cloth and thrown into a well. Ṭāhir wrote a letter to Dhū al-Riʾāsatayn with the news. The mail pouch traveled the night of Friday, the night of Saturday, and the night of Sunday—there are about 250 *farsakh*s between Marw and that place. It arrived with them on Sunday.[242]

According to Dhū al-Riʾāsatayn: We had given directions to Harthamah and furnished him with supplies of weapons.[243] He set out that day, and al-Maʾmūn saw him off. I said to al-Maʾmūn, "Do not stop on any account until you are saluted as caliph, for it has become your due. We cannot be sure that someone may not propose a truce between the two brothers; but if you are saluted as caliph, it will not be possible for you to

239. The Sawād (literally, "the black," sc. earth) is the fertile plain of Mesopotamia.

240. The bracketed words are from ed. Cairo. The manuscript used for ed. Leiden became abbreviated through homoioteleuton. The version in Masʿūdī, VI, 423–24, adds that the page of Aḥmad b. Hishām was carrying the head in a horse's nosebag, which he set before Ṭāhir on cue from his master.

241. The addition is from ed. Cairo.

242. This implies an astonishing average daily speed of 400 km (248 miles) over the ca. 1,150 km (713 miles) between al-Rayy and Marw. See Kennedy, *Early Abbasid Caliphate*, 33.

243. That is, to reinforce Ṭāhir. Cf. Ibn al-Athīr, VI, 169.

retreat." I came forward, along with Harthamah and al-Ḥasan b. Sahl, and we saluted him as caliph. Al-Maʾmūn's supporters hastened [to do the same]. Then I went back tired and weary; I had not slept for three days while outfitting Harthamah. The servant said to me, "Here comes ʿAbd al-Raḥmān b. Mudrik." The latter was in charge of the postal service, and we were awaiting the mail pouch [to learn whether matters had turned out] for us or against us. He came in, but remained silent. I said, "Alas, what are you hiding?" "Victory!" he said. Lo, Ṭāhir's letter to me was:[244]

> May God lengthen your life, subdue your enemies, and make those who hate you your ransom! I write to you with the head of ʿAlī b. ʿĪsā before me and his ring on my finger. Praise be to God, the Lord of the worlds!

I rushed to the residence of the Commander of the Faithful, and the slave lad (*ghulām*) followed me with black clothing.[245] I went before al-Maʾmūn, announced the good news to him, and read him the letter. He ordered that the people of his family, the commanders, and important people be summoned. They came in and saluted him as caliph. The head of ʿAlī arrived on Tuesday and was sent around Khurāsān [to be displayed].

According to al-Ḥasan b. Abī Saʿīd, who said: We appointed Ṭāhir to a military command in the year 194, and his command has continued uninterrupted until the present time.[246]

According to Muḥammad b. Yaḥyā b. ʿAbd al-Malik al-Naysābūrī, who said:[247] When news of the death of ʿAlī b. ʿĪsā reached Muḥammad b. Zubaydah, who at the time was by the riverside, fishing, he said to the man who announced it

---

244. Parallels: Ibn al-Athīr, VI, 169; Masʿūdī, VI, 424.

245. *Sawād*: black clothing was the court dress of officials. See ed. Leiden, *Glossarium*, CCCI; Dozy, *Supplément*, I, 699.

246. The original significance of this truncated report is unclear. It may be connected to the report in Ibn Khallikān (trans. de Slane), II, 473, that, at the time Ṭāhir was assigned his command, al-Faḍl b. Sahl predicted that his standard would not be "untied" (i.e., defeated) for 56 years, and that this prediction proved true.

247. Parallels: Ibn al-Athīr, VI, 169; *Fragmenta*, 325.

to him, "Woe to you! Leave me. Kawthar[248] has already caught two fishes, and I haven't caught anything yet."

[Continuing,] he said: A certain man who was envious used to say, "Ṭāhir thinks that ʿAlī is superior to him."[249] He also said, "When will Ṭāhir arise to fight ʿAlī, given the large size of his army and the obedience of the people of Khurāsān to him?" When ʿAlī was killed, he backed down and said, "By God, had Ṭāhir met him by himself, he would have fought him with his army until he prevailed or was killed in the attempt."

One of ʿAlī's companions, a man of strength and courage, said concerning the death of ʿAlī:[250]

With him we met the lion when it breaks the neck of its prey;
and we were such as never to be frightened away by an encounter.
From of old we have rushed into death and adversities;
when (death) bears down, there is nowhere to hide!
He brought low our riders when we met:
death came, and the covering was removed.[251]
He killed our ram, our head, [804]
as if destiny had been in his hand.

When news of the death of ʿAlī b. ʿĪsā reached Muḥammad and al-Faḍl [b. al-Rabīʿ], the latter sent on Muḥammad's authority to Nawfal, al-Maʾmūn's eunuch (*khādim*)—he was al-Maʾmūn's agent in Baghdad, his treasurer, and his caretaker for his family, children, estates, and money—and took from him the million dirhams that al-Rashīd had given to al-Maʾmūn. He seized his estates and the income from them in the Sawād and put his own agents in charge of them. He sent out ʿAbd

248. Kawthar was al-Amīn's favorite eunuch.

249. Following ed. Cairo; ed. Leiden reads, "A certain man who was envious of Ṭāhir used to say that ʿAlī was superior to him."

250. Ed. Cairo adds: "and the encounter with Ṭāhir."

251. "Covering" is a metaphor for ignorance. Cf. Qurʾān 50:21–22 (describing the Day of Judgment): "And the Trumpet shall be blown; that is the Day of the Threat. And every soul shall come, and with it a driver and a witness. 'Thou wast heedless of this; therefore We have now removed from thee thy covering, and so thy sight today is piercing.'"

al-Raḥmān al-Abnāwī with strength and armaments. The latter encamped at Hamadhān.

Someone mentioned having heard ʿAbdallāh b. Khāzim say at that time: Muḥammad [al-Amīn] wants to remove mountains and rout armies with his management and ill-fated heedlessness. How far he is from doing that, by God! As the former man said: "God has caused the flock you were herding to perish."

When Muḥammad had the oath of allegiance sworn to his son Mūsā and sent out ʿAlī b. ʿĪsā, a poet from Baghdad, seeing Muḥammad's preoccupation with his own diversion and his idleness and how he neglected to oversee ʿAlī and al-Faḍl b. al-Rabīʿ, said:[252]

The caliphate has been brought to ruin by the vizier's malice,
    the imām's dissoluteness, and the counselor's ignorance.
Faḍl is a vizier and Bakr a counselor
    who desire what will bring about the commander's death.
This is nothing but a path of delusion:
    the worst of roads are the paths of delusion.
The caliph's active homosexuality (*liwāṭ*) is a marvel,
    even more marvelous than it is the vizier's passive homosexuality (*ḥulāq*).[253]
One of them buggers; the other gets buggered:
    such, by my life, is the difference of the cases.
[805] If only the two would make use of each other,
    they could manage to keep the affair quiet.
But one of them plunged into [the eunuch] Kawthar,
    and being covered by donkeys did not satiate the other.

---

252. Masʿūdī, VI, 438, quotes eight lines of the poem and identifies the author as the blind poet ʿAlī b. Abī Ṭālib. Ibn al-Athīr, VI, 170, quotes the first three verses, but says that he has omitted the remaining verses "because of the foul slander in them. I am amazed that Abū Jaʿfar [al-Ṭabarī], Godfearing man that he was, recorded them!"

253. Both printed editions misread the word *ḥulāq* as *khalāq* "portion, share"; the two words differ by a single diacritical dot. The parallelism of the verse points to a sexual meaning. In *Lisān*, II, 970, one finds two sexual meanings for *ḥulāq*: either an infectious venereal disease of horses and donkeys, causing inflammation of the skin of the penis, and treated by gelding the infected animal; or the condition of a female ass constantly in heat but never conceiving despite being covered many times. See also al-Khafājī, *Shifāʾ al-ghalīl*, s.v. *ḥalaqī*.

So they themselves brought their deeds into scorn,
and they were at odds, like a camel's way of urinating.[254]
More wondrous than the one and the other is that we
swear allegiance to the small child among us:
One who does not know how to wash his buttocks,
and whose back[255] has not left the bosom of a nurse.
This has happened only because of Faḍl and Bakr,
who want to abrogate the Book that gives light.
Were it not for time's vicissitudes, would these two
be either in the caravan or in the company going forth to fight?[256]
But these are disorders[257] like mountains
on which the lowly and contemptible have risen aloft.
Patience! In patience there is great good,
even if the long-suffering man's patience has already worn thin.
Lord, take them quickly
to Thyself; bring them to the punishment of hellfire.
Make an example of Faḍl and his party,
and crucify them around these bridges.[258]

It has been mentioned: When Muḥammad sent to al-Ma'mūn concerning the oath of allegiance to his son Mūsā, and sent out messengers to him about the matter, al-Ma'mūn wrote in reply to his letter:[259]

> To proceed: The letter of the Commander of the Faithful has reached me, criticizing my rejection of a

254. Arabic lexicographers explain the proverb "More contrary than a camel's urinating," as arising from the ability of the camel (and also the lion, according to Arab naturalists) to direct the stream of its urine backward. See Freytag, *Proverbia*, I, 456; Maydānī, *Amthāl*, I, 447.

255. Another reading: "And from whose urine the nurse's breast is not free."

256. The line alludes to the proverb "Such a one is neither in the caravan nor in the company going forth to fight," applied to one not regarded as fit for a difficult undertaking. See Lane, *Lexicon*, VIII, 2825; Freytag, *Proverbia*, II, 500; Maydānī, *Amthāl*, III, 168–69.

257. Following the reading (*fitan*) in ed. Leiden, *Addenda*, DCCLXIV, instead of the original Leiden reading (*qunan*), "hills."

258. This is probably meant to recall the unhappy fate of al-Rashīd's disgraced vizier Ja'far b. Yaḥyā al-Barmakī in 187/803. See Ṭabarī, III, 667 ff.

259. Italian translation and discussion in Gabrieli, "Documenti," 212.

position wherein he has wronged me and has desired me to be in a state contrary to what he knows to be right. By my life, had the Commander of the Faithful brought things to a state of fairness, demanding only it, and not provoking disapproval by its abandonment, his very first words would have been clearly persuasive, and I would have been convicted if I abandoned rightful obedience to him. However, as I am quick to render what is rightful, while he is ceasing to act in accordance with it, it rather behooves him to act in accordance with what is right in his own affair. He should adhere to it
[806] and give of his own accord. Then, if I do what is right, I shall have freed him from worry; whereas if I reject what is right, he will be justified [in what he does]. As for the beneficence he has promised in exchange for obedience to him and the punishment he has threatened for disobedience to him, has anyone ever departed from the right in his action, and yet left the considerate man room to trust his word? Peace!

[Continuing,] he said: He wrote to ʿAlī b. ʿĪsā, when he learned of what the latter had resolved to do:[260]

To proceed: You are in the [protective] shadow of a mission (*daʿwah*) whose sanctum you and your forebears have always been ready to defend, whose preservation you have sought, and whose right you have upheld. Making this your duty to your imāms, you have clung to the rope of your community (*jamāʿah*), giving willing obedience, joining together against your opponents, and being partisans and brethren[261] to those who agree with you. You have preferred them before fathers and children, and gone through thick and thin with them.[262] You have considered nothing more advantageous to you than that which unites your fellow-

---

260. Italian translation and discussion in Gabrieli, "Documenti," 213–15.

261. Ed. Cairo: "helpers."

262. Literally: "comporting yourselves in whatever tribulation or prosperity they comported themselves."

ship, and nothing more damaging to you than that which dissolves your unity. Anyone averse to this you have held to be astray from the goal and from following the path of truth; and against them you have been swords of God's vengeance. How many of them have been left lying in a land of rending beasts, lifeless limbs, with the winds blowing dust in their faces, and the beasts of prey summoning each other to the place where they fell unbedded and unpillowed, having gone to a nation . . .[263] and whose good fortune is not quick to come! The imāms have therefore accorded you the trust in their affairs and precedence in their traditions that you have earned. You yourself have been more zealous than many of their trusted agents and close associates, so that God has made you the hero of the people of your mission (*da'wah*) and the chief who undertakes the main part of the business of your community.[264] If you tell them to draw near, they draw near; if you give the sign to proceed, they proceed; and if you hold back, they stop and stand still from faith in you[265] and seeking counsel. You increase in fortune with the increase in yourself [of obedience to them], and they increase in [807]
fortune with the increase for you of [their] obedience to you. Now you have arrived at a position in which you have approached your day (i.e., your end), a position for which the greater part of your lifetime was expended. Only the seal of your work remains to be awaited. If it is good, your earlier good deeds will be accepted because of it; if it is the opposite, your earlier effort will be lost because of it. Abū Yaḥyā, you now see a state of affairs in which you have dislodged the people who favored you and the rulers who upheld the right of your imāmate by thrusting at a knot that you yourself undertook to

263. There is a lacuna in the manuscript.

264. Ed. Cairo: "your imāms."

265. Following the emendation (*īmānan bika*) proposed by ed. Leiden, *Addenda*, DCCLXIV. The original Leiden reading, followed by ed. Cairo, was *wi'āman laka*, "in harmony with you."

tighten and by [violating][266] covenants whose ratification you oversaw. These affected first the inner circle, but then the matter reached the generality of Muslims, with binding oaths and confirmed pacts. What has arisen is something that will cause unanimity to be disrupted, a community to be split, and a unity to be dispersed. You thereby expose yourself to an alteration of favor and the disappearance of the path that former imāms have trodden. When favor departs from those who govern your affairs, its departure will extend to you in your own persons. God will not change [His favor] toward a people until they change their own state.[267] Anyone who labors to disperse it labors therein not so much against himself as against those who sustain it[268] and are in charge of its defense, having exposed them to becoming prey to their enemies and food for a people whose claws will immerse themselves in their blood. Your position is such that if you speak, your words will be regarded; if you advise, you will not be impugned for your counsel. By favoring the right, you will have favor with the people of right. How different the man who obtains present gain by abandoning the right, bringing ruin upon himself in his last state, and the man who backs the right, attaining to a good last state along with abundant good fortune in his present life! That to which you are being summoned is not your advantage; that to which you are being asked to incline is not his disadvantage. It is a duty that your merits demand, something that will deserve reward from your Lord and from the people of your imāmate whose right you will have maintained. If it is impossible for you to speak or act,

266. The word is supplied from ed. Cairo, reading *khatr* for *khathr*.

267. Cf. Qur'ān 8:53 and 13:11. Cf. the paraphrase of the verse in Ṭabarī, *Jāmiʿ al-bayān*, XIII, 81: "God does not change the favor and well-being that are among a people, removing these and destroying the people, until they exchange their state for mutual injustice and aggression; that is when God's punishment and indignation alight upon them."

268. Following the reading of ed. Cairo (*ḥamalatihā*). Ed. Leiden reads *jumlatihā*, "the totality of it." The meaning is unclear.

go to an abode where you will be free from fear for your person and where you will rule by your judgment. Cross over to someone who will favorably receive your good action and who will restore you to your post and your wealth.[269] God will be with you in this; and God suffices as a guarantor. If that is not feasible for you for reasons of your own safety, then withhold your hand, and speak the truth as long as you[270] do not fear that it will entail harm to you. Perhaps, someone will emulate you and be content with your prohibition! Inform me of your opinion, that I may know it, God willing. [808]

ʿAlī [b. ʿĪsā] brought the letter to Muḥammad. The people who were for abrogation among the aides aroused the latter's ardor and fueled his fires. His intoxication with power and his base nature assisted in this. He turned over judgment in the matter to al-Faḍl b. al-Rabīʿ, for the latter used to act as his helper. Meanwhile, the letters of Dhū al-Riʾāsatayn were reaching the spy he was consulting in his affair, saying: "If the people insist on deciding for conflict, use subtle means so that they entrust the matter to ʿAlī b. ʿĪsā." Dhū al-Riʾāsatayn specified ʿAlī for this because the latter had left a bad impression on the people of Khurāsān, who were united in their opposition to him, and because the populace held that he should be fought.[271] Al-Faḍl consulted the spy he used to consult, and the man said, "ʿAlī b. ʿĪsā—if he does it, you cannot hit them with anyone like him in terms of his wide renown,[272] generosity of spirit, and his position of having long governed in the terri-

---

269. This may be an offer to restore ʿAlī to the governorship of Khurāsān.

270. Reading with ed. Cairo *takhaf* ("you do not fear") for ed. Leiden's *nakhaf* ("we do not fear").

271. Cf. Ṭabarī, III, 702 (year 189/804–5): "When ʿAlī b. ʿĪsā went off to Khurāsān, he tyrannized over its people and treated them harshly. He gathered an immense sum of money, and out of it sent to Hārūn presents, including horses, slaves, clothing, musk, and wealth, whose like had never been seen before." (Translation, Bosworth, *ʿAbbāsid Caliphate in Equilibrium*, 250–51.)

272. Reading *ṣawtihi*, as suggested by ed. Leiden, *Addenda*, DCCLXIV. Ed. Leiden originally read *ṣawmihi* ("his fasting"). The reading of ed. Cairo (*ṣawbihi*, "his rain") may be preferable. Rain is sometimes used as a metaphor for generosity. "Extensiveness or abundance of rain" would form a parallel to "generosity of spirit."

tory of Khurāsān and done many good works among its people. Furthermore, he is the elder statesman (*shaykh*) of the mission (*daʿwah*) and the best[273] of those who are its partisans." So they decided to send ʿAlī, and events took their course. Two armies rallied to al-Maʾmūn when ʿAlī was sent: his soldiers with whom he made war on the enemy, and the common people of Khurāsān, who were a party[274] against ʿAlī because of the bad impression he had left with them. This (sc. the appointment of ʿAlī b. ʿĪsā) was a policy in which there was great risk, except in the minds of men of weak judgment, both
[809] because of ʿAlī's own nature and because of what he and his forebears had done previously. So events took their course and he was killed.

Sahl [b. Hārūn] mentioned that ʿAmr b. Ḥafṣ, the *mawlā* of Muḥammad, said: I went in to see Muḥammad in the middle of the night—I was one of his inner circle and could come to him when none of his [other] *mawālī* and entourage could. I found him with a candle before him, thinking. I greeted him, but he did not reply to me; so I realized that he was planning some affair of his. I remained standing in his presence until most of the night had passed. Then he raised his head to me and said, "Bring me ʿAbdallāh b. Khāzim." I went to ʿAbdallāh and brought him, and (ʿAbdallāh) continued arguing with (Muḥammad) until the night ended. I heard ʿAbdallāh saying, "I beseech you for God's sake, Commander of the Faithful; do not be the first of the caliphs who broke his promise, violated his covenant, made light of his oath, and rejected the judgment of the caliph who preceded him." "Be silent," he said. "What a man you are![275] ʿAbd al-Malik[276] was wiser than you and

---

273. Perhaps to be translated, "the remnant of those who were its partisans."

274. Ed. Cairo reads, "who made war against him."

275. Literally, "To God [be attributable] your father!" For an explanation of the idiom, see Lane, *Lexicon*, I, 11.

276. The parallel accounts disagree about which ʿAbd al-Malik is meant. Dīnawarī, 389, identifies him as the Umayyad caliph ʿAbd al-Malik b. Marwān (ruled from 65/685 to 86/705). Masʿūdī, VI, 419–20, identifies him as ʿAbd al-Malik b. Ṣāliḥ, a prominent member of the ʿAbbāsid family who had been imprisoned by al-Rashīd on suspicion of aspiring to the caliphate and who was released by al-Amīn. See Ṭabarī, III, 688–94. Ibn al-Athīr, VI, 156, places the episode in 194.

saw things more fully when he said, 'Two stallions cannot be together in one camel herd.'"

ʿAmr b. Ḥafṣ [continued,] saying: I heard Muḥammad saying to al-Faḍl b. al-Rabīʿ, "Alas, Faḍl, life is impossible while ʿAbdallāh remains and resists. He must be deposed." Al-Faḍl was supporting him in this and promising him that he would do it. (Al-Amīn) was saying, "When will that be, if he gains control of Khurāsān and the adjacent territory?"

One of Muḥammad's eunuchs (*khadam*) mentioned: When Muḥammad set about deposing al-Ma'mūn and having allegiance sworn to his son, he gathered the chief military commanders and proposed [the matter] to them one by one.[277] They refused him; scarcely any people backed him. Finally, he reached Khuzaymah b. Khāzim and asked him for his advice about it. The latter said, "Commander of the Faithful, anyone who lies to you is not giving you sincere advice, and anyone who speaks the truth to you is not deceiving you. Do not embolden the military commanders to depose, lest they depose you; and do not induce them to break the compact, lest they break their compact with you and their allegiance to you; for the treacherous man is abandoned, and the perfidious man is defeated." ʿAlī b. ʿĪsā b. Māhān approached. Muḥammad [810] smiled and said, "But the elder statesman (*shaykh*) of this regime, the eyetooth of this dynasty (*dawlah*) will not oppose his imām and will not obey halfheartedly." Then he raised him to a place to which I had never seen him raise him before. People therefore say that he was the first of the military commanders who agreed to depose ʿAbdallāh and followed Muḥammad in his opinion.

According to Abū Jaʿfar [al-Ṭabarī]:[278] When Muḥammad resolved to depose ʿAbdallāh, al-Faḍl b. al-Rabīʿ said to him, "Will you not excuse him, Commander of the Faithful? After all, he is your brother. Perhaps he will concede this matter peacefully, and you will have been spared the trouble of dealing

277. Cf. the parallel account in Dīnawarī, 391, where the issue is not the deposition of al-Ma'mūn, but his being asked to return to Baghdad to serve as vizier, while Mūsā was to be made governor of Khurāsān.

278. Parallel: Ibn al-Athīr, VI, 159.

with him and will have escaped from having to fight and oppose him." "What should I do?" he said. "You should write a letter to him," he said, "trying to placate him, allaying his apprehension, and asking him to yield to you what he has under his control. That is a more effective way of managing the affair and will be better spoken of than trying to subdue him with troops and forestall him with trickery." Muḥammad said to him, "I[279] will do as you think best in the matter." When Ismāʿīl b. Ṣubayḥ came to write the letter to ʿAbdallāh, he said, "Commander of the Faithful, your asking him to yield what he has under his control will engender doubt, strengthen suspicion, and put him on guard. Write to him telling him that you need him and that you would like to have him close to you and profit from his counsel. Ask him to come to you; that will be more effective and more likely to lead to making him obey and comply." Al-Faḍl said, "What he has said is right, Commander of the Faithful." "Then," he said, "let him write as he thinks best." So he wrote to him:[280]

From al-Amīn Muḥammad, Commander of the Faithful, to ʿAbdallāh, the son of the Commander of the Faithful Hārūn:

To proceed: The Commander of the Faithful has considered your situation, your location in your frontier region, and the help and assistance he hopes to obtain
[811] in his God-given burden and responsibility for the affairs of God's worshipers and lands from your closeness. He has pondered the governorship that the Commander of the Faithful, al-Rashīd, assigned to you and what he commanded—that you alone should be in charge of what was assigned to you. The Commander of the Faithful hoped that no offense toward his religion or violation of his oath would be introduced, as his sending for you was in a matter whose benefit affects the Muslims and whose advantage and merit extends to

279. Following ed. Cairo; ed. Leiden has "Do as you think best."

280. Italian translation and discussion in Gabrieli, "Documenti," 204–5. The letter is paraphrased in Dīnawarī, 389–90.

> them all. The Commander of the Faithful has realized that your being close to him will be a more solid defense for the frontier regions and better for the armies. It will render the income from captured lands (*fay'*)[281] more secure and will be more profitable for the populace than your staying in the province of Khurāsān, separated from your family, and absent from the Commander of the Faithful and from the advice and counsel from you that he wishes to enjoy. In investing Mūsā, the son of the Commander of the Faithful, as your deputy, the Commander of the Faithful has thought it wise to give him responsibility for any of your commands or prohibitions that shall reach him.[282] Come to the Commander of the Faithful with God's blessing and assistance, bringing the amplest hope, the broadest expectation, the most praiseworthy result, and the most penetrating intelligence; for you are the most worthy person for the Commander of the Faithful to ask for help in his affairs and to relieve his toil in matters involving the good of the people of his household[283] and those under his protection. Peace!

He gave the letter to al-ʿAbbās b. Mūsā b. ʿĪsā b. Mūsā b. Muḥammad b. ʿAlī, ʿĪsā b. Jaʿfar b. Abī Jaʿfar,[284] Muḥammad b. ʿĪsā b. Nahīk, and Ṣāliḥ, the keeper of the prayer rug, and commanded them to take it to ʿAbdallāh al-Maʾmūn. They were to spare no manner of softness and gentleness and were to make the matter easy for him. One of

---

281. *Fay'* ("permanent booty") was the tribute or tax income from captured lands from which the stipends of Muslim soldiers were paid. See *EI*[2] s.v.

282. This seems to imply that Mūsā is to assume nominal responsibility for Khurāsān (doubtlessly under an elder tutor to carry out the actual administration) as al-Maʾmūn's *khalīfah* (deputy). Cf. Dīnawarī, 389; Gabrieli, "La successione di Hārūn ar-Rašīd," 357.

283. Following ed. Leiden in reading *ahl baytihi*. Ed. Cairo reads *ahl millatihi* ("people of his religious community," i.e., Muslims), contrasting with *dhimmatihi* ("those under his protection," i.e., non-Muslims). The Cairo reading may be preferable. Note that on p. 69, below, both editions agree on a similar phrase, *ahl al-millah wa'l-dhimmah* ("people of the [Muslim] community and protected [non-Muslims]").

284. That is, the grandson of al-Manṣūr.

them carried money, favors, and gifts. This was in the year 194. So they took his letter. When they reached ʿAbdallāh, he
[812] admitted them, and they gave him Muḥammad's letter and the money, favors, and gifts he had sent with them.

Then al-ʿAbbās b. Mūsā b. ʿĪsā spoke. Having praised and extolled God, he said, "Commander, your brother has taken upon himself in the caliphate a great weight and in attending to the affairs of men an enormous burden. He has been truly intent on good, so that he has needed ministers, aides, and assistants in what is just. He has little fellowship with the members of his family. You are his brother, his like; he has turned to you in his affairs, and has hoped for your help and assistance. Not because we doubt your sincerity toward him do we deem you to be slow in devotion to him, nor is it because we fear you will disobey him that we urge you to obedience. In your coming to him lies great fellowship and benefit for his dynasty (*dawlah*) and reign. Answer, commander, the call of your brother. Choose obedience to him, and help him in those of his affairs in which he has called upon you for help; for therein lies the performance of what is right, kindness toward kindred, the welfare of the dynasty (*dawlah*), and the strength of the caliphate. May God make the commander resolute to follow the right course in his affairs, and may He grant him goodness and righteousness in the outcome of his judgment."

ʿĪsā b. Jaʿfar b. Abī Jaʿfar spoke, saying, "Multiplying words to the commander, may God assist him,[285] would be foolishness, and frugality[286] in acquainting him with his duty toward the Commander of the Faithful would be deficiency. The commander, may God grant him honor, has been absent from the Commander of the Faithful, and the latter has not been able to dispense with his presence. In the presence of other members of his family he finds that he has no one adequate, and he finds no substitute or replacement for him. The com-

---

285. The translation follows ed. Cairo's *ayyadahu Allāh*. Ed. Leiden's *Allāh Allāh* is a probably a copyist's error based on the similar ductus of the two words.

286. Following ed. Cairo's *iqtiṣād*, which is preferable to ed. Leiden's *iqtiṣār* ("limitation, abbreviation").

mander is the person whom it most behooves to show piety toward his brother and to obey his imām. Let the commander do as the Commander of the Faithful has written to him, as will be most pleasing and closest to the approval and affection of the Commander of the Faithful. Coming to him will be an act of merit and good fortune; slowness in coming to him will be an offense to religion and a damage and harm to the Muslims."

Muḥammad b. ʿĪsā b. Nahīk spoke, saying, "Commander, we will not give you even more multiplication of words and [813] long-windedness about what you already know concerning the right of the Commander of the Faithful, nor will we[287] with stories and sermons sharpen your intention about the attention and concern required of you in the affairs of the Muslims. The Commander of the Faithful has needed aides and advisors in his presence. He has tried to place you under obligation, turning to you to help and strengthen him in his affairs. If you respond to the Commander of the Faithful in his invitation to you, it will be a great blessing and to the advantage of your subjects and family. If you stay put, God will enable the Commander of the Faithful to dispense with you; but that will not cause him to be any less devoted to you or to rely less on your obedience and sincere advice than he does now."

Ṣāliḥ, the keeper of the prayer rug, spoke, saying, "Commander, the caliphate is weighty, and aides are few. The people of strife and disobedience who plot against this dynasty (*dawlah*) and harbor deceit toward it and recalcitrance toward its friends are many. You are the brother of the Commander of the Faithful and his like. Whether matters go well or badly depends on you and on him; for you are his heir by virtue of a covenant, and the sharer in his authority and governorship. The Commander of the Faithful has tried to lay you under obligation by his letter. He has trusted that you will assist in those of his affairs in which he has asked you to help. Your agreeing to come to him will entail great benefit for the caliphate and joy and ease of mind for people of the [Muslim] community and protected aliens. May God grant the commander success in his affairs and

287. Following ed. Cairo's *nashḥadhu*; ed. Leiden's *yushḥadhu* is unlikely on grammatical grounds.

decree for him that which will be most pleasing and profitable to him."

Al-Ma'mūn then praised and extolled God and said, "You have informed me of what I do not deny as regards the right of the Commander of the Faithful, may God grant him honor. You have called me to what I choose and do not reject—namely, to help and assist. I am ready to obey the Commander of the
[814] Faithful and eager to hasten to do what will please him and be agreeable to him. But in deliberateness lies clarification of judgment, and in using good judgment lies sincere resolution. The matter to which the Commander of the Faithful has called me is one from which I will not hang back by way of delaying or resisting, but I will not embark on it haphazardly or hastily. I am in one of the frontier regions of the Muslims. Its enemy is rabid with fury; his vehemence is intense. If I neglect him, I fear that damage and harm will befall both soldiers and subjects. Yet, if I stay to deal with him, I fear that I shall fail to do what I would like—namely, help and assist the Commander of the Faithful and freely give him obedience. Depart until I consider my affair and [obtain] sincere advice about what I should decide as regards going, if God so wills." He then commanded that they should be lodged, given hospitality, and treated well.

According to Sufyān b. Muḥammad: When al-Ma'mūn read the letter, he wrung his hands.[288] What came to him in it was distressing to him, and he did not know what to reply to it. So he called al-Faḍl b. Sahl, had him read the letter, and said, "What do you think about this matter?" He replied, "I think you should hold fast to your position and not make a way against us,[289] while you can avoid it." "How," he asked, "can I hold fast to my position and defy Muḥammad, when the greater part of the commanders and troops are with him, and when most of the money and stores have gone to him, not to mention the favors and benefits that he has distributed among the people of Baghdad? People incline toward money and are led by it; if they find it, they do not care about maintaining allegiance or desire to fulfill a covenant or a trust." Al-Faḍl

288. Parallels: Dīnawarī, 390; Ibn al-Athīr, VI, 159–60.
289. Ed. Cairo: "against yourself."

said to him, "When suspicion has arisen, caution is in order. I fear Muḥammad's treachery and am apprehensive that he may covet what you have in your hands. It is better for you to be with your soldiers and your strength, residing amid the people of your governorate. If something befalls you from him, you shall gather forces against him and strive to overcome him in battle and by strategy. Either God will give you victory over [815]
him in reward for your loyalty [to the Meccan agreement] and good intention, or the other will happen, and you will have died steadfast, with your honor intact; you will not have sat idle and enabled your enemy to have his way with your person and your blood."

Al-Ma'mūn said, "Had this affair come upon me while I was in a position of strength and while my affairs were in good order, it would have been of minor importance, and it would have been possible to repel it by stratagem. But it has come upon me after Khurasan has been stirred up. Its inhabited lands and waste lands are in a state of disturbance. Jabghūyah[290] has abandoned obedience; Khāqān, the ruler of Tibet,[291] is acting up; the king of Kābul is preparing to raid the lands of Khurāsān that border on him; the king of Abrāzbandah[292] is withholding the tribute (*ḍarībah*) that he used to render; and I have no strength for even one of these matters. I know that Muḥammad has asked me to come only for some evil that he plans. I see nothing else to do than abandon my position and join Khāqān, the king of the

---

290. Barthold identifies *jabghū* or *yabghū* as a Turkish title and identifies the ruler in question as "the jabghū of the Qarluq [Turks]" (cf. *Turkestan down to the Mongol Invasion*, 173, 202). Kennedy, *Early Abbasid Caliphate*, 138, freely renders, "the *jabghū* of the Turks." Gabrieli, "La successione di Hārūn ar-Rašīd," 358 n., calls him "Jabghūyah the king of Ṭukhāristān," following Ṭabarī, II, 1206.

291. Arabic *Tubbat*, from which the word "Tibet" comes, referred to the lands around the headwaters of the Oxus River, in the west of modern Sinkiang province of China, rather than Tibet proper. See Le Strange, *Lands*, 435, 437; Yāqūt, *Mu'jam*, s.v. Tubbat.

292. Or, Barāzbandah: The original reading, amended on the basis of references given in ed. Leiden, *Addenda*, DCCLXIV, was Utrārbandah, apparently a compound of the place name Utrār or Uṭrār, a town on the Sayḥūn (Jaxartes, Syr Darya) River, earlier known as Bārāb or Fārāb, with the Persian word *band*, dam or weir. Cf. Yāqūt, *Mu'jam*, s.v. Uṭrār; Le Strange, *Lands*, 484–85. Barthold, *Turkestan down to the Mongol Invasion*, 202, accepts the reading Utrārbandah.

Turks, asking him for protection in his country. It is better for me to be safe in my person and out of reach of someone who wants to subdue me and use treachery against me."

Al-Faḍl said to him, "Commander, the end of treachery is disaster, and one cannot be safe from the evil consequence of injustice and tyranny. Many a man disesteemed has again become powerful; many a man subdued has again become an overpowering subduer. Victory is not by small or great numbers. The anguish of death is less grievous than the anguish of humiliation and injury. I do not think you should leave your position and go to obey Muḥammad, stripped of your commanders and soldiers, like a head separated from its body, for him to pass judgment over you, so that you become one of his subjects without exerting yourself in striving and fighting. Rather, write to Jabghūyah and Khāqān. Give them charge over their lands. Promise them that you will strengthen them in fighting the kings. Send to the king of Kābul some gifts and precious things from Khurāsān, and ask him for a treaty; you
[816] will find him eager for it. Remit to the king of Abrāzbandah his tribute for this year; make it a gift from yourself that you grant to him. Gather your outlying provinces to yourself, and attach to yourself those of your troops who have become separated. Then strike cavalry with cavalry and infantry with infantry. If you win, [well and good]; if not, you will be able to join Khāqān as you wish."

ʿAbdallāh realized that what he had said was right. "Do as you think best," he said, "in this and in my other affairs." (Al-Faḍl) sent letters to those rebels. They became satisfied and yielded. He wrote to the commanders and soldiers who had left Marw, and made them come to him. He wrote to Ṭāhir b. al-Ḥusayn, who was then ʿAbdallāh's agent in charge of al-Rayy. He commanded him to secure his area, gather his outlying districts to himself, and be in a state of alert and preparation for an army if it invaded him or a foe[293] if it attacked him. So the latter readied himself for war and prepared to repel Muḥammad from the province of Khurāsān.

---

293. Reading *aw ʿadūw*, with ed. Cairo, rather than *wa-ʿadad* ("and a number") as in ed. Leiden.

It is said: ʿAbdallāh sent to al-Faḍl b. Sahl and asked his advice in the matter of Muḥammad. "Commander," he replied, "give me a respite today, and I will bring you an opinion tomorrow." He spent that night considering what was best to do. In the morning, he came to (ʿAbdallāh) and told him that he had considered the stars and had seen that he would win and that the result would be in his favor.[294] So ʿAbdallāh remained in his place and made up his mind to fight and contend with Muḥammad. Having finished consolidating matters in Khurāsān as he wished, ʿAbdallāh wrote:[295]

> To the Servant of God Muḥammad, Commander of the Faithful, from ʿAbdallāh b. Hārūn:
>
> To proceed: I have received the letter of the Commander of the Faithful. I am merely one of his governors and aides. Al-Rashīd, may God's blessings be upon him, commanded me to stay in this frontier region and oppose any enemy of the Commander of the Faithful who seeks to ensnare its people. Upon my life, my remaining here will be more profitable for the Com- [817]
> mander of the Faithful and more useful to the Muslims than my going to the Commander of the Faithful, although I would be happy to be in his presence and glad to see God's favor toward him. Therefore, if he thinks it wise to confirm me over my district and excuse me from going to him, he will do so, God willing. Peace.

Then he summoned al-ʿAbbās b. Mūsā, ʿĪsā b. Jaʿfar, Muḥammad [b. ʿĪsā], and Ṣāliḥ and gave them the letter. He gave them generous gifts for the way and conveyed to Muḥammad a gift to Khurāsānian delicacies that he had prepared for him. He asked them to speak well of him in Muḥammad's presence and to excuse him.

According to Sufyān b. Muḥammad: When Muḥammad read ʿAbdallāh's letter, he realized that al-Maʾmūn would not

294. On al-Faḍl b. Sahl's knowledge of astrology, see Ibn Khallikān (trans. de Slane), II, 472–73; also Dīnawarī, 390.

295. Parallels: Dīnawarī, 390–91; Ibn al-Athīr, VI, 160; Italian translation and discussion in Gabrieli, "Documenti," 205–6.

submit and come to him. He therefore dispatched ʿIṣmah b. Ḥammād b. Sālim, the master of his guard (*ṣāḥib ḥarasihi*), and commanded him to establish a garrison (*maslaḥah*) between Hamadhān and al-Rayy. He was to prevent merchants from carrying any provisions into Khurāsān. He was to search travelers, so that they would have no letters with them containing reports about him and what he intended to do. This was in the year 194. Then he resolved to fight him. He summoned ʿAlī b. ʿĪsā b. Māhān and assigned him the command of 50,000 horsemen and foot soldiers from the people of Baghdad.[296] He handed him the army registers (*dafātir al-jund*) and commanded him to select and choose those who pleased him. He was to give special treatment to whomever he liked and raise those he wanted to [a salary of] 80 [dīnārs]. He gave him access to the [stores of] weapons and treasuries. Then they were dispatched against al-Ma'mūn.

According to Yazīd b. al-Ḥārith, who said: When ʿAlī [b. ʿĪsā] was about to set out for Khurāsān, he rode to the door of Umm Jaʿfar and said goodbye to her.[297] She said, "ʿAlī, although the Commander of the Faithful is my child for whom I feel the utmost affection and greatest anxiety, I sympathize
[818] with ʿAbdallāh and feel pity for him because of the adversity and harm that are befalling him. My son is merely a king who has competed with his brother for his power and who has envied what the latter has in his hand. The generous [among his followers] will devour his flesh; the others will kill him![298] Show ʿAbdallāh the respect due to him because of his father and because of his being a brother. Do not speak roughly to him, for you are not his peer. Do not compel him as slaves are compelled, and do not weaken him with a shackle or fetter. Do

296. *Ahl Baghdād*: This normally does not mean the general population of the city, but rather the soldiers registered on the military rolls at Baghdad. See Lassner, *The Shaping of ʿAbbāsid Rule*, 280 (note 61) for a discussion of the term.

297. That is, to the residence of al-Amīn's mother, Zubaydah. Parallels: Dīnawarī, 392; Ibn al-Athīr, VI, 165–66.

298. Cf. the somewhat freer translation of Nabia Abbott: "The better sort among his followers devour his worldly substance and the rest would be the death of him." (*Two Queens of Baghdad*, 213–14). "Eat the flesh of someone" can mean either devour his wealth or defame him. See Lane, *Lexicon*, I, 71, s.v. *akala*.

not deprive him of a maidservant or servant. Do not be harsh with him in journeying. Do not go beside him or ride before him. Do not mount your horse until you have held his stirrup. If he reviles you, bear with him. If he uses many words[299] to you, do not dispute with him." Then she gave him a silver shackle and said, "If he comes to be in your hand, bind him with this shackle."[300] He said to her, "I accept your command and will act in obedience to you in this."

Muḥammad published the deposition of al-Ma'mūn and had allegiance sworn to his two sons, Mūsā and ʿAbdallāh, in all regions except Khurāsān. When they swore allegiance, he gave the Banū Hāshim, the military commanders, and the army money and gifts. He gave Mūsā the name *al-Nāṭiq bi-al-Ḥaqq* ("Speaker of the Truth"), and he gave ʿAbdallāh the name *al-Qā'im bi-al-Ḥaqq* ("Upholder of the Truth"). ʿAlī b. ʿĪsā departed from Baghdad on 7 Shaʿbān 195 (May 5, 811) and encamped at al-Nahrawān.[301] Muḥammad escorted him out, and the commanders and soldiers also rode forth. Provision wagons[302] were gathered, and craftsmen and workers were dispatched with him. It is said that his army was a *farsakh* [in length], with its tents, equipment, and baggage. One of the people of Baghdad said they had never seen an army with more men, livelier mounts, brighter swords, fuller equipment, or in more perfect array than his army.

According to ʿAmr b. Saʿīd: After Muḥammad had passed the Khurāsān Gate,[303] [ʿAlī][304] dismounted and went on foot. (Muḥammad) approached to impart a commission to him.[305] He said, "Forbid your soldiers to harass the populace, or raid the [819]

299. Ed. Cairo reads, "If he behaves foolishly." The same reading is suggested in ed. Leiden, *Glossarium*, CCXCII.

300. The parallel in Yaʿqūbī, II, 530, has al-Amīn give ʿAlī the shackle.

301. The date has previously been given as 15 Jumādā II 195 (p. 49, above). Arguments in favor of the earlier date are given in Gabrieli, "La successione di Hārūn ar-Rašīd," 366 (note 3).

302. *Aswāq*: see ed. Leiden, *Glossarium*, CCCII, for this meaning.

303. The Khurāsān Gate (*Bāb Khurāsān*), one of the four gates in the walls of the original Round City of Baghdad, faced northeast and led to the main floating bridge over the Tigris and the great Khurāsān highway. See Le Strange, *Baghdad*, p. 15.

304. The bracketed text is present only in ed. Cairo.

305. Parallel: Dīnawarī, 391.

people of the villages, or cut trees, or rape women. Put Yaḥyā b. ʿAlī in charge of al-Rayy. Attach to him a large body of troops. Command him to pay his troops their salaries (*arzāq*) from income from the land tax (*kharāj*) [of al-Rayy]. Put one of your companions in charge of every district you leave. If any of the soldiers or notables of the people of Khurāsān comes out to you, honor him openly and give him a generous gift.[306] Do not punish a brother for his brother. Remit from the people of Khurāsān one-fourth of the land tax (*kharāj*). Grant no quarter to anyone who shoots an arrow at you or who thrusts at one of your companions with a spear. Do not allow ʿAbdallāh to remain more than three days from the day you capture him. When you send him forth, let him be with your trustiest companion. If Satan beguiles him, so that he shows himself hostile to you, be careful to bind him well. If he escapes from you into one of the districts of Khurāsān, take charge yourself of going after him. Have you understood all I have charged you?" "Yes," he said, "may God preserve the Commander of the Faithful." "Go," he said, "with God's blessing and help."

It has been mentioned: His astrologer came to him and said, "May God preserve the commander! If you delayed your journey until the moon is good,[307] bad luck would be in the ascendant for him, and good luck would be declining and departing from him." He, however, said to one of his slaves, "Saʿīd, tell the commander of the vanguard to strike his drum and advance his banner. We know no difference between a bad moon and a good moon. If anyone fights us, we fight him; if anyone makes peace with us, we make peace with him and leave him alone. If anyone makes war on us and fights us, there is nothing for us to do than slake the swords with his blood. We take no account

306. Contrast ʿAlī's behavior toward the three deserters from Ṭāhir's camp mentioned on p. 51, above.

307. *Ṣalāḥ al-qamar*: this may mean the full moon, although I have not found the phrase in any dictionary. Since ʿAlī left Baghdad on the seventh day of the lunar month, this would have meant a week's delay. The phrase *fasād al-qamar* ("a bad, imperfect moon") also is not recorded in the dictionaries. Another possibility is that *ṣalāḥ* ("becoming better") and *fasād* ("deteriorating") refer to waxing and waning phases of the moon or to its location in auspicious or inauspicious signs of the zodiac.

of a bad moon. We have set our minds on bravery in the encounter and on fighting the enemy."

According to Abū Jaʿfar [al-Ṭabarī]: One of (those in the army of ʿAlī b. ʿĪsā) was mentioned as having said: I was among those who went out in the army of ʿAlī b. ʿĪsā b. Māhān. When he passed Ḥulwān,[308] caravans from Khurāsān met him.[309] He asked them about the news, seeking inform- [820]
ation about the troops of Khurāsān. He was told that Ṭāhir was staying at al-Rayy, reviewing his forces and mending his equipment. He laughed and said, "What is Ṭāhir? By God, he is a mere thorn, compared to my branches; or a spark, compared to my fire. Someone like Ṭāhir does not take charge of armies and deal with battles." Then he turned to his companions and said, "By God, all that stands between you and his being snapped like a tree in a tempest is that word reach him of our crossing the pass of Hamadhān. Lambs are not strong enough to butt with their horns, neither do foxes have the endurance to encounter lions. If Ṭāhir stays in his place, he will be the first to be subjected to the edges of swords and the points of spears!"

According to Yazīd b. al-Ḥārith: When ʿAlī b. ʿĪsā reached the pass of Hamadhān, he met a caravan that had come from Khurāsān. He asked them about the report. They said that Ṭāhir was established at al-Rayy; he had prepared for fighting and had obtained battle gear; reinforcements were flowing to him from Khurāsān and the adjacent districts; he was growing stronger by the day and his forces more numerous; and he was, they thought, the master of the army of Khurāsān. ʿAlī said, "Has anyone [of account][310] from the people of Khurāsān come?" "No," they said, "but matters there are confused, and the people are frightened." So he ordered that they should journey on without stopping. He said to his companions, "The enemy's farthest point is al-Rayy. Once we have put it behind our backs,

308. The town of Ḥulwān (east of modern Qaṣr-e Shīrīn) lay on the great Khurāsān road in a mountain pass that marked the border between Iraq and al-Jibāl province (the Iranian highlands). See Le Strange, *Lands*, pp. 63, 191, 227–28; *EI*² s.v. (Lockhart).

309. Parallels: Dīnawarī, 392–93; Masʿūdī, VI, 420–24; Ibn al-Athīr, VI, 166–67.

310. The words in brackets are from ed. Cairo.

that will break their strength; they will become disorganized, and their forces will scatter." Then he sent letters to the kings of Daylam[311] and the Ṭabaristān mountains[312] and to the kings friendly to them, promising them favors and gifts. He made them presents of crowns, bracelets, and gold-ornamented swords, and he commanded them to cut the Khurāsān road and stop anyone who intended to reach Ṭāhir to reinforce him. They agreed to do this. Then he marched until he reached the
[821] beginning of the district of al-Rayy. The commander of his vanguard came to him and said, "God save the commander! If you were to send spies, dispatch scouts, and look for a place where you could encamp and make a trench for your forces so that they would be safe, that would be a better plan and more pleasing to the soldiers." "No," he replied, "one does not prepare for someone like Ṭāhir by stratagems and caution. Ṭāhir's condition will result in one of two things: either he will fortify himself in al-Rayy, and its inhabitants will fall upon him unexpectedly, saving us the trouble of dealing with him; or he will vacate the city and retreat, if our horsemen and soldiers approach him." Yaḥyā b. ʿAlī came to him and said, "Pull the army together; take care that your troops are not attacked by night; and do not send the horses out to pasture without men to protect them: for armies are not managed by negligence, neither are wars conducted by being unprepared. The sure way is for you to be on guard. Do not say, 'My opponent is Ṭāhir'; for a hidden spark has often become a blaze, and a trickle has often been disregarded and dismissed, only to become a great flood. Our armies have drawn near to Ṭāhir; had his intention been to flee, he would not have waited until today." "Be silent," he replied, "for Ṭāhir is not of the rank that you think him to be. Men use caution only when they meet their match; they make preparations only if their foe is their peer or their equal."

---

311. Daylam, a small mountainous area between the Safīd Rūd River and the Caspian Sea in Gīlān province of northwestern Iran, was inhabited by warlike tribesmen who had served the Sasanians as mercenaries and maintained their autonomy after the Iranian plateau came under Arab rule. See Le Strange, *Lands*, 172–74; EI^2 s.v. (Minorsky).

312. Ṭabaristān was the region of high mountains (the Alburz chain) south of the Caspian Sea. See Le Strange, *Lands*, 368–76.

According to ʿAbdallāh b. Mujālid, who said: ʿAlī b. ʿĪsā advanced until he encamped ten *farsakh*s from al-Rayy. Ṭāhir was in the city; he had shut its gates and placed garrisons on the roads leading to it, and had made ready to fight ʿAlī. Ṭāhir consulted his companions, and they advised him to remain in the city of al-Rayy and delay fighting as long as possible, until reinforcements of cavalry came to him from Khurāsān and a military commander to take charge of the matter instead of him. They said, "Your staying in the city of al-Rayy will be easier on your forces and on you.[313] It will render them better able to obtain supplies and find shelter from the cold. Better, if a fight [822] befalls you suddenly, that they[314] take refuge in houses and that you[315] have strength to procrastinate and hold out until reinforcements reach you or a force comes to you from behind you."

Ṭāhir replied, "Yours is not the best plan. The people of al-Rayy are in awe of ʿAlī and fearful of his depredation and violence. On his side are those you have heard about: Bedouins from the desert, brigands from the mountains, and rabble from the villages. I am worried that if he attacks the city while we are in it, fear of him may lead its people to rise against us and help him fight us. Also, never have fighters been threatened in their homes, with the army of the foe coming against them, but that they lost courage and became submissive; their strength departed, and their foe became emboldened against them. The only plan is for us to set the city of al-Rayy behind our backs. If God gives us victory, [well and good]; if not, we shall rely upon the city, fighting in its streets, and taking refuge in its impregnability, until reinforcements or a force from Khurāsān comes to us." "Yours is the best plan," they said. So Ṭāhir issued orders among his forces, and they went out and encamped five *farsakh*s from al-Rayy, at a village called Kalwāṣ. Muḥammad b. al-ʿAlāʾ came to him and said, "Commander,

313. Ed. Cairo omits the words, "and on you." They may be the result of dittography.

314. That is, "your forces." The translation follows the text of ed. Cairo. The Leiden text (*naʿtaṣimū*, "we take refuge") is grammatically anomalous.

315. The translation follows the Cairo reading. The Leiden reading (*naqwū*, "we have strength") is grammatically anomalous.

your soldiers have become awed by this army; their hearts have filled with fear and terror of it. You should stay in your place and put off fighting, until your men sniff out the foe, become at ease with them, and know the way to take in fighting them." "No," he replied, "I will not be destroyed by inexperience and irresoluteness. My men are few; the enemy's army is great, and their numbers are many. If I put off fighting and delay the conflict, I fear they will learn how few in number we are and how exposed. They may seek to win over those on my side by enticement or intimidation, so that most of my forces may turn
[823] away from me, and the men of steadfastness and endurance may abandon me. Instead, I will make infantrymen fight hand to hand with infantrymen, and horsemen join battle with horsemen. I will rely on obedience and loyalty. I will be steadfast, like one who reckons on a good reward and is eager to gain the merit of martyrdom. If God bestows victory and success, that is what we want and hope; if the other happens, I shall not be the first to have fought and been killed! What is in God's presence is greater and better."

ʿAlī [b. ʿĪsā] said to his companions, "Hasten toward the enemy, for their number is small. If you advance toward them, they will have no courage to endure the heat of swords or the thrust of spears." He arranged his troops into a right wing, left wing, and center. He assigned ten banners, with a thousand men under each, and sent the banners forward one by one, putting a bowshot between each. He gave orders to the commanders: when the first banner had fought, held out, and defended [those behind], and the battle had become too protracted for it, the next banner was to be brought forward; the one that had fought was to be moved back, until its men regained their spirits, rested, and had energy to fight again. He put men with coats of mail, chest armor, and helmets in front of the banners; he himself stayed in the center with his companions—men of strength, constancy, and courage.

Ṭāhir b. al-Ḥusayn arranged his troops, divided his squadrons of horsemen, and set his ranks in order. He passed by each commander and each group and said, "You friends of God and people who are loyal and give Him thanks, you are not like these whom you see—people of perfidy and treachery. They

have neglected what you have preserved; they have scorned what you have honored; they have violated the oaths to which you have been faithful; they are seeking only what is false and are fighting in a state of treachery and ignorance—men of plunder and pillage! If you avert your eyes and make firm your feet, God will fulfill His promise and will open to you the gates of His strength and help. Fight for your religion against tempters to civil strife and lords of hellfire! Repel their falsehood by your [824]
truth, for it is but a single hour until God will judge between you—and He is the best of judges!"[316] He became very anxious and began saying, "People of loyalty and sincerity, be steadfast, be steadfast! Defend [your honor], defend [your honor]!"

The people [in the two armies] advanced toward each other. The inhabitants of al-Rayy gathered[317] and locked the city gates.[318] Ṭāhir proclaimed, "Friends of God, attend to those in front of you, rather than to those behind you, for only effort and valor will save you." They joined and fought fiercely with each other; both sides showed endurance. ʿAlī's right wing overcame and badly broke Ṭāhir's left wing, and his left wing dislodged (Ṭāhir's) right wing from its position. Ṭāhir said, "Set your strength and your effort against the squadrons of horsemen in the middle! If you break one of their banners, those in front will turn back upon those in the rear." So his forces showed true bravery; they attacked the foremost of the center banners, put them to flight, and killed many among them. The banners turned back upon each other, and ʿAlī's right wing collapsed. The men in Ṭāhir's right wing and his left wing saw what his companions had done. They turned against those who were opposite them and put them to flight. The rout reached ʿAlī, and he began calling to his companions, "Where are the wearers of bracelets and crowns? You Sons [of the Dynasty],[319] come to

316. Qur'ān 7:87.

317. Ed. Cairo: "rose up."

318. Parallels: Dīnawarī, 393; Ibn al-Athīr, VI, 168.

319. The *Abnā' al-Dawlah* ("Sons of the Mission or Dynasty") were Arabs and Iranians of Khurāsānian origin, who had come to Iraq with the ʿAbbāsid revolution, settled in Baghdad, and formed the dominant force in the army of al-Amīn. See Kennedy, *Early Abbasid Caliphate*, 104; Crone, *Slaves on Horses*, 66; Lassner, *The Shaping of ʿAbbāsid Rule*, 133–36; and Bosworth, *The ʿAbbāsid Caliphate in Equilibrium*, pp. xvii and 4.

me! Rally after retreat! Returning[320] to the battle is part of endurance in it!" One of Ṭāhir's men shot him with an arrow and killed him. They set their swords on them, killing them and taking them prisoner, until night fell and separated them from their quarry. They took many spoils. Ṭāhir proclaimed among ʿAlī's forces that anyone who laid down his weapons would be safe. So they threw away their weapons and dismounted from their horses. Ṭāhir returned to the city of al-Rayy and sent the prisoners and heads to al-Ma'mūn.

It has been mentioned: ʿAbdallāh b. ʿAlī b. ʿĪsā threw
[825] himself down on that day among the slain. He had received many wounds. He remained among the dead, pretending to be one of them, that day and that night, until he felt safe from pursuit. Then he got up, attached himself to a group of refugees from the army, and went to Baghdad. He was one of ʿAlī's oldest sons.

According to Sufyān b. Muḥammad: When ʿAlī [b. ʿĪsā] set out toward Khurāsān, al-Ma'mūn sent to the commanders who were on his side, proposing to each one of them individually that he should fight him. All of them showed fear and made excuses in order to find a way to be released from encountering him and fighting him.

According to one of the people of Khurāsān: When al-Ma'mūn received Ṭāhir's letter with the news about ʿAlī [b. ʿĪsā] and what God had inflicted upon him, he gave audience to the people. They came before him, congratulated him, and wished him strength and victory. On that day, he proclaimed that Muḥammad was deposed. He himself[321] was mentioned as caliph in prayers in all the districts of Khurāsān and neighboring areas.[322] The people of Khurāsān were delighted. Preachers there gave sermons, and poets recited verses. On that subject, a poet [from the people of Khurāsān][323] said:

---

320. Following the Cairo reading (*muʿāwadah*), which makes better sense than the Leiden reading (*muʿāwanah*, "assistance").

321. Following ed. Cairo; ed. Leiden reads: "and mentioning [himself] as caliph in prayers," which is syntactically strained.

322. Yaʿqūbī, II, 531, gives a sermon reportedly preached by al-Ma'mūn on this occasion.

323. The bracketed words are from ed. Cairo.

The community has come to be in a state of happiness
regarding its worldly affairs and religion:
For it has kept the compact of the Imām of Right Guidance,
the best of Eve's sons, its Trusted One (*ma'mūnihā*).[324]
It was on the brink [of destruction]; but when it kept faith,
it escaped the evil that would have destroyed it.
It upheld God's truth, when there were written
among his children the books of its registers.
Do you not see the community—how, after ruin,
God has brought it good fortune to adorn it?

The [rest of the] poem is many verses long.

According to ʿAlī b. Ṣāliḥ al-Ḥarbī: When ʿAlī b. ʿĪsā was killed, people in Baghdad became very agitated and spread wild rumors.[325] Muḥammad regretted his own perfidy and treachery. The military commanders met among themselves. This took place on Thursday, the middle of Shawwāl 195 (July 10, 811). They said, "ʿAlī has been killed, and we do not doubt that Muḥammad needs men and must employ people who have skills. Men are advanced only by their own selves; they are [826] raised by their valor and boldness. Let each of you command his troops to riot and demand pay and gifts. Perhaps, given this state of affairs, we shall obtain from him what is to our advantage and to the advantage of our troops." They agreed upon this. The next morning they went to Bāb al-Jisr.[326] They shouted, "*Allāhu akbar!*"[327] and demanded pay and gifts. News of this reached ʿAbdallāh b. Khāzim, and he rode toward them with his men and with the forces of other commanders of Bedouin Arabs. The two sides shot arrows at each other, threw stones, and fought fiercely. Muḥammad heard the shout of "*Allāhu akbar!*" and the noise. He sent one of his *mawālī* to bring him a report. The man returned to him and informed him

324. The line alludes to the title *Imām al-Hudā* taken by al-Ma'mūn (see p. 47, above) and puns on the meaning of al-Ma'mūn's name, "he who is trusted or trustworthy."

325. Parallels: Ibn al-Athīr, VI, 170; *Fragmenta*, 325.

326. Bāb al-Jisr (Gate of the Floating Bridge) was at the eastern end of the northernmost of the three floating bridges linking Baghdad with the districts on the east bank of the Tigris. See Le Strange, *Baghdad*, p. 178.

327. "God is most great!"—used here as a rallying cry.

that the troops had assembled and had rioted to demand their pay. "And are they demanding anything except their pay?" he asked. "No," the man replied. "How small a thing they have demanded!" he said. "Go back to ʿAbdallāh b. Khāzim, and command him to turn away from them." Then he ordered that they should be given four months' pay. He raised those who had been under eighty [dīnārs] to eighty.[328] He ordered that the commanders and inner circle (*khawāṣṣ*) should be given presents and gifts.

Al-Amīn Sends ʿAbd al-Raḥmān b. Jabalah to Fight Ṭāhir

In this year, Muḥammad the Deposed[329] sent ʿAbd al-Raḥmān b. Jabalah al-Abnāwī to Hamadhān to fight Ṭāhir.[330]

According to ʿAbdallāh b. Ṣāliḥ: When news that ʿAlī b. ʿĪsā b. Māhān had been killed and that Ṭāhir had extirpated his army reached Muḥammad, he dispatched ʿAbd al-Raḥmān
[827] al-Abnāwī with 20,000 men from the *Abnā'*.[331] He sent money with him, strengthened him with weapons and horses, gave him gifts, and appointed him governor of Ḥulwān in addition to whatever territory of Khurāsān he might conquer. With him he assigned skilled horsemen of the *Abnā'* and men of valor, vigor, and ability from them. He commanded him to travel quickly, with little tarrying or resting, so that he would arrive at the city of Hamadhān before Ṭāhir. He was to dig a trench around himself and his forces, gather to himself [war][332] equipment, and hasten to fight Ṭāhir and his forces. ʿAbd al-Raḥmān exerted himself and carried out al-Amīn's command in all that the latter wanted him to do. He advanced toward Ṭāhir cautiously and warily, avoiding the negligence and slug-

328. On military salaries for the period, see Kennedy, *Early Abbasid Caliphate*, 78.

329. Henceforth, the reports in Ṭabarī frequently designate al-Amīn as "Muḥammad the Deposed (*al-Makhlūʿ*)."

330. Parallels: Yaʿqūbī, II, 532; Dīnawarī, 393–94; Ibn al-Athīr, VI, 170; *Fragmenta*, 325–26.

331. See note 319 on *Abnā' al-Dawlah* ("Sons of the Mission or Dynasty").

332. The addition is from ed. Cairo.

gishness of ʿAlī [b. ʿĪsā]. ʿAbd al-Raḥmān went and took up quarters at the city of Hamadhān. He secured the roads leading to it, fortified its wall and its gates, and repaired the breaches in them. He gathered provision wagons and laborers into the city, collected equipment and provisions in it, and prepared to meet Ṭāhir and fight him.

After his father was killed, Yaḥyā b. ʿAlī escaped with a group of his companions and established himself between al-Rayy and Hamadhān. Whenever any refugee from his father's army passed him, he retained him. He thought that Muḥammad would appoint him in his father's stead and would send him cavalry and infantry. He intended to gather the remnants of the army until reinforcements and help reached him. He wrote to Muḥammad, asking him for help and assistance. Muḥammad wrote back, informing him that he had sent ʿAbd al-Raḥmān al-Abnāwī and commanding him to stay where he was and encounter Ṭāhir with the men he had with him; if he needed strength and men, he was to write to ʿAbd al-Raḥmān, and the latter would strengthen and help him.

Having received the news, Ṭāhir headed toward ʿAbd al-Raḥmān and his forces. When he drew near Yaḥyā, Yaḥyā said to his companions, "Ṭāhir has drawn near us. He has with him those whom you know—foot soldiers and horsemen of Khurāsān. [828]
He was your master only yesterday. If I encounter him with the remnants of the army that I have with me, I fear he will scatter us, causing those behind us to lose courage. ʿAbd al-Raḥmān will use this as an excuse and thereby clothe me with shame, cowardice, and weakness in the eyes of the Commander of the Faithful. On the other hand, if I appeal to him for assistance and remain waiting for his help, I fear that he may hold back from us, clinging to his men, preserving them, and trying to avoid having them killed. Let us march toward the city of Hamadhān and encamp near ʿAbd al-Raḥmān. If we appeal to him for help, his help will be close to us. If he needs us, we will help him; we shall be in his vicinity and fight on his side." "Yours is the best plan," they replied. So Yaḥyā departed; but when he approached the city of Hamadhān, his companions abandoned him, and most of those who had gathered around him dispersed.

Ṭāhir proceeded to the city of Hamadhān and came within

sight of it. ʿAbd al-Raḥmān called up his forces, and they came out in battle order; he drew up his ranks[333] against Ṭāhir, and they fought fiercely. Both sides held out steadfastly, and there were many killed or wounded among them. Then ʿAbd al-Raḥmān was driven back. He entered the city of Hamadhān and remained there some days, until his forces became stronger and the wounded recuperated. He then ordered preparations and marched out to fight Ṭāhir. When Ṭāhir saw his banners and the first of his forces come into sight, he said to his companions, "ʿAbd al-Raḥmān wants to present himself to your sight. If you approach him, he will fight you. If you drive him back, he will hurry to the city, enter it, and fight you by its trench, making himself secure by means of the gates and wall of the city. If he drives you back, they will have wide room to maneuver against you: the breadth of the battlefield will enable them to fight you and kill any of you who are driven back and flee. So take a stand close to our trench and our camp: if he approaches us, we will fight him; if he goes far from their trench, we will
[829] close in on him." So Ṭāhir halted where he was. ʿAbd al-Raḥmān, thinking that fear was making him slow to encounter him and attack him, hastened to fight with him. They fought fiercely. Ṭāhir held out resolutely and killed many of ʿAbd al-Raḥmān's men. ʿAbd al-Raḥmān kept saying to his forces, "People of the *Abnāʾ*! Sons of kings, and men familiar with swords![334] These are Persians; they are not men who can last for long or show endurance. So hold out against them—may my father and my mother be your ransom!" He would pass by each banner, saying, "Show endurance, for we need to endure only a little while. This [hour] is the beginning of endurance and victory!" With his own hands he fought hard and made fierce charges; with every charge he inflicted much slaughter upon Ṭāhir's forces, but no one withdrew or moved from his place. Then one of Ṭāhir's men attacked ʿAbd al-Raḥmān's standard bearer and killed him, and Ṭāhir's forces made a bold rush

333. Ed. Cairo reads: "he encountered Ṭāhir."

334. The translation follows the emendation (*ālāf*, "those who are familiar with," instead of manuscript *alfāf*, "groves") proposed in ed. Leiden, *Glossarium*, CDLXX.

against their foe. The latter turned to flee, and Ṭāhir's forces put their swords to them and continued killing them until they had driven them back to the gate of the city of Hamadhān. Ṭāhir stayed at the gate of the city besieging him and the inhabitants. ʿAbd al-Raḥmān would come out every day and fight at the gates of the city; his men would throw stones and shoot arrows from on top of the wall. The siege tightened around them. The inhabitants of the city suffered harm at the hands of (ʿAbd al-Raḥmān's) men and loathed the fighting and the war. Ṭāhir cut off their supplies from every direction. When ʿAbd al-Raḥmān saw this—seeing that his men had perished or were in distress and fearing that the people of Hamadhān would rise against him—he sent to Ṭāhir and asked him for safe conduct (*amān*) for himself and those on his side. Ṭāhir granted it to him and fulfilled [the agreement]. ʿAbd al-Raḥmān withdrew with his forces and those forces of Yaḥyā b. ʿAlī for whom he had requested safe conduct.

Ṭāhir b. al-Ḥusayn Named Dhū al-Yamīnayn

In this year, Ṭāhir b. al-Ḥusayn was given the name Dhū al-Yamīnayn ("He Who Has Two Right Hands"). The report of the reason why he was thus named has already been given;[335] now the person who gave him that name will be mentioned.[336] [830]

It is mentioned that after Ṭāhir had defeated the army of ʿAlī b. ʿĪsā b. Māhān and had killed ʿAlī b. ʿĪsā, he wrote to al-Faḍl b. Sahl:

> May God lengthen your life, subdue your enemies, and make those who hate you your ransom! I write to you with the head of ʿAlī b. ʿĪsā on my lap and his ring on my hand. Praise be to God, the Lord of the Worlds!

Al-Faḍl arose and saluted al-Maʾmūn as Commander of the Faithful. Al-Maʾmūn reinforced Ṭāhir b. al-Ḥusayn with men and commanders and named him Dhū al-Yamīnayn and Ṣāḥib

---

335. See p. 54, above, and note 233.
336. Ed. Cairo, "now we shall mention the person . . ."

Ḥabl al-Dīn.[337] He raised those with him who were at [a salary] under eighty [dīnārs] to eighty [dīnārs].

The Rebellion of al-Sufyānī in Syria

In this year, al-Sufyānī[338] (ʿAlī b. ʿAbdallāh b. Khālid b. Yazīd b. Muʿāwiyah) appeared in Syria and pressed his claim to power. This took place in the month of Dhū al-Ḥijjah.[339] He expelled Sulaymān b. Abī Jaʿfar from there, after having besieged him in Damascus. Sulaymān was Muḥammad's governor of Damascus, and he made his escape only after he had despaired.[340] Muḥammad the Deposed dispatched al-Ḥusayn b. ʿAlī b. ʿĪsā b. Māhān to [fight] him. Al-Ḥusayn did not reach him; instead, when he reached al-Raqqah,[341] he remained there.

Ṭāhir Expels al-Amīn's Agents from al-Jibāl Province

In this year, Ṭāhir expelled Muḥammad's agents from Qazwīn[342] and the other districts of al-Jibāl province.[343] The reason for this was as follows.

---

337. The title means "Master of the Rope of Religion," i.e., the bond or covenant of the Islamic religion, and thus commemorates Ṭāhir's upholding of the Meccan agreement. Its wording is modeled on Qur'ān 3:103, "Hold fast to God's rope, together, and do not scatter."

338. The name identifies him as a descendant of Muʿāwiyah b. Abī Sufyān, the founder of the Umayyad dynasty overthrown by the ʿAbbāsids. He was one of the few survivors of the Umayyad family. His grandfather, Khālid b. Yazīd, had played a prominent role in Umayyad family politics during the reigns of Marwān and ʿAbd al-Malik. His mother was a descendant of ʿAlī. Parallels: Yaʿqūbī, II, 532; Ibn al-Athīr, VI, 172. Further references in Crone, *Slaves on Horses*, 253, note 549.

339. That is, the last month of the year, between August 25 and September 22, 811.

340. Accepting the emendation (*al-ya's*) proposed by ed. Leiden, *Addenda*, DCCLXV, which also is the reading of ed. Cairo. The original Leiden reading (*al-ba's*) would mean "after valor," i.e., after a fight.

341. The city of al-Raqqah was located on the upper Euphrates River in the province of al-Jazīrah. The ʿAbbāsids made it the center of a large military garrison. See Le Strange, *Lands*, 101–3.

342. Qazwīn (modern Qazvīn), about 100 miles northwest of al-Rayy and 125 miles northeast of Hamadhān, was heavily garrisoned to defend the Iranian heartland against the only partially pacified Daylamī tribesmen to the north. See Le Strange, *Lands*, 218–20; *EI*[2] s.v. Ḳazwīn (Hillenbrand).

343. Parallel: Ibn al-Athīr, VI, 171.

According to ʿAlī b. ʿAbdallāh b. Ṣāliḥ: When Ṭāhir headed toward ʿAbd al-Raḥmān al-Abnāwī in Hamadhān, he became afraid that Kathīr b. Qādirah, who was in Qazwīn as one of Muḥammad's agents, along with a large army, would fall upon him if he left him behind his back. After Ṭāhir had drawn near to Hamadhān, he commanded his forces to encamp, and they did so. He then rode with a thousand horsemen and a thousand [831] foot soldiers and headed toward Kathīr b. Qādirah. When he drew near him, Kathīr fled with his men and abandoned Qazwīn. Ṭāhir stationed a large garrison of soldiers there. He put one of his companions in charge of the city and commanded him to fight any of the forces of ʿAbd al-Raḥmān al-Abnāwī or any others who tried to enter the city.

The Death of ʿAbd al-Raḥmān b. Jabalah al-Abnāwī

In this year, ʿAbd al-Raḥmān b. Jabalah al-Abnāwī was killed at Asadābādh.[344]

According to ʿAbd al-Raḥmān b. Ṣāliḥ: When Muḥammad the Deposed dispatched ʿAbd al-Raḥmān al-Abnāwī to Hamadhān, he had the two sons of al-Ḥarashī, ʿAbdallāh and Aḥmad, follow him with a large body of horsemen from the people of Baghdad. He commanded the two to encamp at Qaṣr al-Luṣūṣ.[345] They were to heed and obey ʿAbd al-Raḥmān and reinforce him if he needed their help. After ʿAbd al-Raḥmān had come out to Ṭāhir on a guarantee of safety, ʿAbd al-Raḥmān remained to show Ṭāhir and his forces that he was peaceably intentioned and satisfied with their promises and oaths. But then he took them off guard. He rode with his men—Ṭāhir and his forces sensed nothing—and attacked them; and they laid their swords to them. The foot soldiers among Ṭāhir's forces held their ground against them by means of swords,

344. The town of Asadābādh was located on the great Khurāsān road about 30 miles east of Hamadhān, on the eastern side of a mountain pass. See Le Strange, *Lands*, 195–96; EI^2 s.v. (Streck). Parallels: Dīnawarī, 394; Ibn al-Athīr, VI, 171; *Fragmenta*, 326.

345. Qaṣr al-Luṣūṣ ("Robbers' Castle") was the Arabic name for the town of Kanguvār, about 120 miles east of Ḥulwān on the Khurāsān Road, and 60 miles west of Hamadhān. See Le Strange, *Lands*, 20, 188.

shields, and arrows; they knelt down on their knees[346] and fought him as fiercely as possible. The foot soldiers held off the attackers until the horsemen had taken up their equipment and gear and advanced boldly in battle. The two sides fought fiercely, until swords became ragged and spears broke in two. Then ʿAbd al-Raḥmān's forces fled. He himself dismounted with some of his companions and fought until he was killed. His companions said to him, "You can escape; do so! The foe has wearied of fighting. The battle has tired them out. They have no energy or strength to pursue." He kept saying, "I will
[832] never retreat! The Commander of the Faithful shall never see the face of me defeated." There was great slaughter among his companions, and his army was destroyed. Those of his forces who escaped reached the camp of ʿAbdallāh and Aḥmad, the sons of al-Ḥarashī. The forces of the latter became overcome by apprehension[347] and faintheartedness; their hearts were filled with fear and terror, so that they turned back in defeat, turning aside for nothing, without anyone encountering them until they reached Baghdad. The country having become open to him, Ṭāhir advanced, passing[348] town by town and district by district, until he encamped in one of the villages near Ḥulwān, called Shalāshān. He dug a trench there, fortified his camp, and gathered his forces around him.

One of the *Abnāʾ*, elegizing ʿAbd al-Raḥmān al-Abnāwī, said:

Verily, eyes are weeping only for a horseman
who banished shame from himself with swords and spear shafts.
When the dust of death[349] cleared away, revealing the surface of his face,
he had attained the highest glory and made it his own.

---

346. This was a defensive position used by infantry being attacked by cavalry.

347. Ed. Cairo reads, "weakness."

348. Ed. Cairo reads, "taking," which is also the reading of the parallel texts in Ibn al-Athīr and *Fragmenta*.

349. *Ghubār al-mawt* can be interpreted in a number of ways. Because dust is a frequent attribute of battles in Arabic poetry, it could mean "the death-bringing dust of battle." Because *ghubār* can be a synonym for *ghubrah*, "dusty color," the phrase could also mean "the dusty color or paleness of death."

He was a young man who, as long as he was close to manliness, cared not
whether this afflicted the citadel of his soul or scattered his wealth;
One who made for spearheads a marketplace,[350]
and who did not fear appointed death when it drew near.

Various Items of Information

In this year, the governor of Mecca and Medina for Muḥammad b. Hārun was Dāwūd b. ʿĪsā b. Mūsā b. Muḥammad b. ʿAlī b. ʿAbdallāh b. ʿAbbās. It was he who led the pilgrimage in this year and in the two years preceding—193 and 194. Al-ʿAbbās b. Mūsā al-Hādī was governor of al-Kūfah for Muḥammad. Manṣūr b. al-Mahdī was governor of al-Baṣrah for Muḥammad. [833]
Al-Maʾmūn was in Khurāsān; his brother Muḥammad was in Baghdad.[351]

---

350. The word *sūq* ("market") is frequent in military metaphors. Al-Zamakhsharī, *Asās al-Balāghah*, 314, explains the phrase *sūq al-ḥarb* ("the war's marketplace") as "the thick of the battle and its center." In other words, ʿAbd al-Raḥmān was always in the place where the spears were thickest.

351. Cf. Yaʿqūbī, II, 532–33 for additional reports for this year, especially two pro-Maʾmun disturbances, one in the Sawād of Iraq, the other among the *Abnāʾ* in al-Ḥarbiyyah quarter of Baghdad. Yaʿqūbī also has a report of trouble in Egypt when al-Amīn's governor there omitted al-Maʾmūn's name as heir from the oath of allegiance.

The Events of the Year 196

(September 23, 811–September 11, 812)

Among the events taking place this year was Muḥammad b. Hārūn's imprisonment of Asad b. Yazīd b. Mazyad and his dispatching of Aḥmad b. Mazyad and ʿAbdallāh b. Ḥumayd b. Qaḥṭabah to Ḥulwān to fight Ṭāhir.

Al-Amīn Imprisons Asad b. Yazīd and Dispatches Aḥmad b. Mazyad to Fight Ṭāhir

According to ʿAbd al-Raḥmān b. Waththāb: Asad b. Yazīd b. Mazyad related to him that al-Faḍl b. al-Rabīʿ had sent to him after the death of ʿAbd al-Raḥmān al-Abnāwī.[352] [Asad b. Yazīd continued,] saying: So I came to him. When I went in to him, I found him sitting in the courtyard of his house, with a piece of paper he had read in his hand. His eyes were red, and he was very angry. He was saying, "He sleeps like a polecat, [and he wakes up like a wolf whose only concern is its belly and that tries to deceive the herdsman, while the dogs lie in wait for it.][353] He does not consider how happiness comes to an end,

---

352. Parallels: Ibn al-Athīr, VI, 174; *Fragmenta*, 327.

353. The bracketed words are restored from ed. Cairo. A line of text has dropped out of the manuscript used by ed. Leiden.

and he does not set his mind on carrying out a plan or strategy. His cup diverts him; his goblet distracts him. He runs after his pleasure, while the days approach stealthily[354] for his destruction. ʿAbdallāh already has set to work to deal with him. He has notched for him his most accurate arrow, to hit him, despite the remoteness of his dwelling, with a lethal blow that penetrates, with death that strikes home. He has marshalled doom for him on horseback and has hung tribulation for him on spearheads and sword blades." Then he exclaimed, "Surely we belong to God, and to Him we return!"[355] and quoted from the poetry of al-Baʿīth:[356]

I remember a slender girl, tight-knit as a rein, bashful,
with curly hair and a beautiful face;
With a mouth clear-colored and sweet-tasting—
on account of it, the darkness brightens when she smiles—
With breasts like two [perfume] boxes, a stomach lean [834]
and slender, and beauty[357] whose fire burns vehemently.
I sported with her the longest night of the year, Ibn Khālid,[358]
while at Marw al-Rūdh[359] in anger you abstain from sin.[360]
I keep speaking tenderly to her, while under Ibn Khālid
Umayyah is a strong [horse] with large flanks.
Charging against cavalry in many an attack has made it lean;
it has a cheek by which spearheads resound.

354. Ed. Cairo: "while the days hasten."

355. Qur'ān 2:156, traditionally said in times of misfortune.

356. Al-Baʿīth (Khidāsh b. Bishr b. Khālid al-Mujāshiʿī) was a poet and orator of the tribe of Tamīm who died ca. 134/751 in al-Baṣrah. He was involved in exchanges of satires with the poet Jarīr. See Sezgin, *GAS*, II, 363–64; *EI*[2] s.v. al-Baʿīth (Pellat). The text of the poem in Ibn al-Athīr, VI, 174, contains some variants.

357. Reading *juhr*, the emendation proposed in the Leiden note. The manuscripts and Ibn al-Athīr (followed by the Cairo edition) read *jahm*, "a frowning, or austere look."

358. This may refer to Umayyah (b. ʿAbdallāh) b. Khālid b. Asīd, a member of the Umayyad family who served as governor of Khurāsān under ʿAbd al-Malik between 74/693 and 78/697.

359. Marw al-Rūdh (Marv-ar-Rūd, Marrūd), called Upper or Little Marv to distinguish it from the larger city of Marw, was located about 160 miles south of its namesake on the same river, the Murghāb, in the province of Khurāsān. See Le Strange, *Lands*, 404.

360. Following ed. Cairo's *wa-anta* ("while you"); ed. Leiden reads *ʿalayya* ("against me").

He battles Ibn Khāqān's Turks by night,
    not wavering until dawn becomes visible.
The next day from the long chase his body is
    emaciated; but I in the morning devote myself to pleasure.
[Early in the morning I take something that is ruddy, whose
    odor is like musk;
    when you sniff it in its jug it has a sweet fragrance.][361]
What a difference there is between me and Ibn Khālid
    Umayyah in the sustenance that God allots!

Then he turned to me and said, "Abū al-Ḥārith,[362] you and I are running toward a goal such that if we fail to reach it, we shall be blamed; yet if we exert ourselves to attain it, we shall be cut off. We are branches from a [single] root: if it thrives, we thrive; if it weakens, we weaken. This fellow[363] has abandoned himself to fate like a foolish slave girl. He takes counsel with women and pursues dreams. The pleasure seekers and reckless men who are with him have gained his ear. They promise him
[835] victory and make him expect a good outcome, while destruction is coming toward him faster than a torrent toward a sandy plain. I fear, by God, that we shall perish when he perishes and be destroyed when he is destroyed. You are the outstanding horseman of the Arabs and the son of their outstanding horseman.[364] He has turned to you to confront this man. Two things on your part have given him hope: one is the sincerity of your obedience and the merit of your advice; the other is the good fortune that attends on your counsel and the firmness of your courage. He has commanded me to remove any excuse you might have and give you whatever you desire, although moderation is the beginning of good counsel and the key to good fortune and blessing. So take whatever you need, and hasten quickly toward your enemy. I hope that God will grant you the honor of this victory and that through you He will set in order the muddled affairs of this caliphate and dynasty (*dawlah*)."

---

361. The bracketed line, which refers to wine, is found only in ed. Cairo and in the parallel text in Ibn al-Athīr.

362. "Abū al-Ḥārith" is the *kunyah* (agnomen) of Asad b. Yazīd.

363. That is, al-Amīn. The Arabic implies contempt.

364. See note 38.

I said, "I will be bold to obey the Commander of the Faithful, may God strengthen him, and to obey you, and eager to do everything that will bring weakness and humiliation upon his enemy and your enemy. However, a warrior does not act without preparation, nor does he begin his business with inadequacy and deficiency. There can be no warrior without soldiers, and there can be no soldiers without money. The Commander of the Faithful—may God strengthen him—has filled the hands of his soldiers who are present in the camp [sc. at Baghdad]; he has continually given them ample salaries and generous gifts and benefits. If I lead my men forth while their hearts are fixed on their brethren who remain behind, they will be of no use to me in confronting him who is in front of me. Indeed, he has preferred men [of peace][365] to men of war; he has elevated men of repose above men of exertion and toil. What I ask is that a year's salary be ordered for my men and that salaries for a year be carried with them. He should give extra salary (*khāṣṣah*) to those men of ability and valor among them who do not have it now. I will replace those among them who are chronically ill or weak and give horses to a thousand of the men who are with me. I will not be asked to give an account of the cities and districts I have captured for myself." "You have demanded a great deal," he said. "The matter must [836]
be discussed with the Commander of the Faithful." Then he mounted, and I rode with him. He went in to Muḥammad before me and announced me; then I was given admittance and entered. Scarcely had two words been exchanged between us before (Muḥammad) became angry and ordered me to be imprisoned.

According to one of Muḥammad's courtiers (*khāṣṣah*): Asad said to Muḥammad, "Give me the two sons of ʿAbdallāh al-Maʾmūn, to be prisoners in my hands. If he gives me obedience and submits to me, [well and good]; if not, I will deal with them according to my judgment and carry out my command upon them." (Muḥammad) replied, "You are a mad Bedouin![366]

365. The words in brackets are from ed. Cairo.

366. *Aʿrābī* means a Bedouin, as opposed to a sedentary Arab, but as ed. Leiden, *Glossarium*, CCCLV, notes, it often is used abusively ("rustic"). Cf.

I call upon you to lead the Arabs and the Persians; I assign you the tax revenue of the districts of al-Jibāl province as far as Khurāsān; I raise your rank above your peers among the sons of military commanders and kings—and you call upon me to kill my children and spill the blood of my family! Truly, this is folly and insanity!" Two of the sons of ʿAbdallāh al-Maʾmūn were in Baghdad. They were with their mother, Umm ʿĪsā, the daughter of Mūsā al-Hādī, living in al-Maʾmūn's palace in Baghdad. When al-Maʾmūn gained control of Baghdad, they went out with their mother to join him in Khurāsān, where they remained until they [all] came to Baghdad. They were his oldest sons.

According to Ziyād b. ʿAlī, who said: When Muḥammad became angry with Asad b. Yazīd and ordered his imprisonment, he said, "Is there among the family of this man anyone who can take his place? For I do not want to render them disaffected, given their priority in service[367] and their past obedience and loyalty." He was told, "Yes, among them there is Aḥmad b. Mazyad.[368] He is the best of them in manner of conduct and the soundest of them in intention to obey. In addition to this, he possesses strength, valor, and skill in managing soldiers and confronting battles." So Muḥammad sent a post rider to him to command him to come to him.

According to Bakr b. Aḥmad, who said: Aḥmad was heading toward a village called Isḥāqiyyah. With him were a group of
[837] his family members, his *mawālī*, and his entourage. After he had crossed the Abān River,[369] he heard the voice of the post rider in the middle of the night. "This is very strange," he said, "a post rider at a time like this and a place like this! Surely, he is about some business."[370] Presently, the post rider halted and

---

Ṭabarī, II, 590: *mā ahlu Makkata illā aʿrāb* ("The people of Mecca are nothing but rustics").

367. That is, the early attachment of their family to the ʿAbbāsids.

368. Aḥmad b. Mazyad was the uncle of Asad b. Yazīd b. Mazyad.

369. The Abān or Bān River was one of the watercourses through which the Tigris flowed into the Great Swamp between Wāsiṭ and al-Baṣrah in southern Iraq. See Le Strange, *Lands*, 40–41.

370. The translation follows the emendation proposed by ed. Leiden, *Addenda*, DCCLXV. The earlier emendation proposed by ed. Cairo was, "Surely, this business is strange."

called to the boatman, "Is Aḥmad b. Mazyad with you?" "Yes," he said. So the rider dismounted and handed him Muḥammad's letter. Aḥmad read it; then he said, "I have reached my estate—between me and it there is only a mile.[371] Let me visit it and give what orders I wish to give concerning it. I will come with you tomorrow morning." "No," he replied, "the Commander of the Faithful commanded me not to let you delay or allow you to rest, but to make you set out at whatever hour of night or day I met with you." So Aḥmad went back with him. When he reached al-Kūfah, he stayed there for a day, until he had outfitted himself and had taken provisions for the journey; then he went to Muḥammad.

According to Aḥmad [b. Mazyad], who said: When I entered Baghdad, I went first to al-Faḍl b. al-Rabīʿ. I said, "I will greet him and make use of his position and influence with Muḥammad." Having been given admittance, I went in to him. With him was ʿAbdallāh b. Ḥumayd b. Qaḥṭabah, whom he was trying to induce to go to [fight] Ṭāhir. ʿAbdallāh was making large demands upon him for money and men. When (al-Faḍl) saw me, he greeted me and took me by the hand. Then he led me up until he had brought me with him onto the elevated part of the sitting room. He turned toward ʿAbdallāh, jesting and joking with him. With a smile on his face, he said:

I tell you, when your cord became frayed,[372] we found
a mother and a father from the tribe of Shaybān instead of you.[373]
If one were to count the stones, the Shaybānīs would be even more numerous;
and they are more closely related to us than you.

ʿAbdallāh replied, "They are indeed so. By them the breach will be filled, the enemy defeated, and obedient subjects de- [838]

371. An Arabic mile (*mīl*) was one-third of a *farsakh*, or about 2 km (1.08 miles). See Hinz, *Islamische Masse und Gewichte*, 63.

372. The frayed tent rope is a metaphor for a relationship or obligation that is weakening or unraveling.

373. Asad b. Yazīd b. Mazyad and Aḥmad b. Mazyad were from the tribe of Shaybān. See Crone, *Slaves on Horses*, 169–70. A pun may be involved: *dūnakum* ("instead of you") may also mean "cheaper than you."

fended from the violence of rebels." Al-Faḍl then turned toward me and said, "The Commander of the Faithful mentioned you; so I described you to him as being very obedient, excellent in counsel, severe against rebels, and outstanding in judgment. He therefore has decided to choose you for a mission and make your name famous. He will raise you to a rank that no member of your family has ever attained." He turned to his servant and said, "Saddler, order my horses!" Horses were saddled for him without delay; he went, and I went with him. When we went in to Muḥammad, he was in the courtyard of his residence, with a cloak.[374] He kept ordering me to come closer, until I was almost touching him. He said, "Your nephew's confused ideas and bad manners became too much for me. His contrariness went on too long for me. Finally it alienated me from him and engendered suspicion about him in my heart. By his misconduct and disobedience he caused me to impose on him such correction and imprisonment as I did not wish to impose on him. But you have been described to me as a fine man, and a good character has been imputed to you; so I have decided to raise your status, exalt your rank, and give you precedence over the other members of your family. I will put you in charge of making war on this miscreant, perfidious company of men, and I will give you pay and reward for encountering them in battle. Consider how you will act. Make firm your intention, and help the Commander of the Faithful according to your goodness. Make him rejoice over his enemy, and your joy and honor shall be abundant." I replied, "In obedience to the Commander of the Faithful—may God strengthen him!—I will give my heart's blood. In making war on his enemy, I will accomplish the best he has hoped from me and the strength and skill he expects from me, God willing."

Muḥammad said, "Faḍl!" "At your service, Commander of the Faithful," he replied. "Give him," he said, "the registers
[839] of Asad's men, and attach to him the men of al-Jazīrah and the Bedouin Arabs who are present in the camp." [To me] he said, "Hurry about your business, and hasten your journey toward

374. *Lahu sāj* "with, i.e., wearing a cloak," is problematic. See ed. Leiden, *Glossarium*, CCC.

him." I went out, selected the men, and reviewed the registers. The number of men whose names I certified came to 20,000. Then I set out for Ḥulwān with them.

It has been mentioned that when Aḥmad b. Mazyad was about to depart, he went before Muḥammad and said, "Give me your charge—may God bestow honor upon the Commander of the Faithful!" Muḥammad said, "I commend a number of good traits to you. Beware of envy, for envy is the shackle of aid [from God].[375] Take no step forward without asking God's blessing. Unsheathe the sword only after doing what excuses.[376] If you can accomplish something by mildness, do not go beyond it to roughness and sharpness.[377] Be a good companion to the regular soldiers (*jund*) who are with you. Inform me of your news every day. Do not endanger yourself in the pursuit of favor with me, and do not bestir yourself in anything that you fear may redound to my disadvantage. Be a sincere brother and good comrade to ʿAbdallāh [b. Ḥumayd]; do your best to join with him, accompany him, and be on good terms with him.[378] Do not let him down, if you asks you for help; do not delay, if he calls on you to aid. Let your hands be one and your word be in agreement." Then he said, "Ask for what you need, and set out as soon as possible toward your enemy." Aḥmad invoked blessings upon him and said, "Pray often for me. Do not believe what the envious say about me. Do not reject me before learning where my foot stands for you, [and do not contravene my considered judgment. Grant me the pardon of my nephew." "It is granted to you," he said.][379] He then sent to Asad, loosed his bonds, and

375. The expression is proverbial. From an original sense of "strong desire," the word *baghy* developed the negative connotation of "desiring that someone else's happiness be transferred to oneself," and then the even more negative meaning of "acting wrongfully, injuriously, or tyrannically." See Lane, *Lexicon*, I, 231.

376. That is, only after giving a warning. Cf. the proverbial expression, *aʿdhara man andhara*, "He who warns has an excuse," i.e., cannot be blamed for his action. See Lane, *Lexicon*, V, 1983–84.

377. Reading *shirrah* ("evil, inordinate desire, sharpness, anger") with ed. Cairo, rather than ed. Leiden's *sharah* ("vehement desire, greed").

378. That is, do not allow friction to develop between your Bedouin troops and ʿAbdallāh b. Ḥumayd's regular troops (*Abnāʾ*) from Baghdad.

379. The translation follows the longer text of ed. Cairo. In place of the words in brackets, ed. Leiden reads, "Send to Asad, loose his bonds, and set him free."

set him free. [Praising Aḥmad, and mentioning his condition and rank,][380] Abū al-Asad al-Shaybānī[381] said concerning this:

Let the decision of his imām give joy to Abū al-ʿAbbās;
  what he has in mind concerning him is the bestowing of more and more.
The Commander of the Faithful summoned him to a thing
  from which the shadow of every pillar[382] falls short.
He hastened to do it with judgment, resolution, and skill:
  the judgment of Abū al-ʿAbbās is strong and true.
[840] You rose to a task that [other] men could not shoulder,
  and you [shouldered it] with ready success and good fortune.
You thereby restored to the seekers the person most dear to them:
  one who is like you links newly acquired with inherited honor.
He saved Asad from the constraint and pain of shackles,
  and to him he was as kind as Yazīd.[383]
He fetched him out like an enormous lion,
  the sire of cubs, with brawny arms, and tall of stature.

According to Yazīd b. al-Ḥārith: Muḥammad [al-Amīn] dispatched Aḥmad b. Mazyad with 20,000 men of the Bedouin Arabs, and ʿAbdallāh b. Ḥumayd b. Qaḥṭabah with 20,000 men of the *Abnāʾ*. He commanded the two of them to encamp at Ḥulwān and repel Ṭāhir and his forces from it. If Ṭāhir stayed at Shalāshān, they were to head toward him with their forces, so as to push him back and make war on him. He also charged them to maintain unity, be on friendly terms with each other, and love one another in obedience [to him].

The two of them set out and encamped near Ḥulwān, at a

---

380. The text in brackets is from ed. Cairo.

381. See *Aghānī*, XII, 174–79 (ed. Cairo, XIV, 5005–15) for a biography of this poet, whose full name was Abū al-Asad Nubātah b. ʿAbdallāh al-Ḥimmānī al-Shaybānī.

382. *ʿAmīd* ("pillar, stay") also means "a person on whom one relies," and hence, "military commander." In modern Arabic the word means "brigadier general."

383. That is, he was like a father to his nephew Asad b. Yazīd.

place called Khāniqīn.[384] Ṭāhir stayed in place and entrenched himself and his forces. He smuggled spies and scouts into the camps of the two men; these brought false rumors to the men and told them that Muḥammad had assigned military pay (*ʿaṭāʾ*) to his companions and had commanded such and such salaries (*arzāq*) for them. Ṭāhir kept working surreptitiously to stir up dissent and sedition among the men. Finally, they fell out with each other, and their affairs became disorganized. They fought each other, evacuated Khāniqīn, and retreated without having encountered Ṭāhir and without any fighting having transpired between them and him. Ṭāhir advanced and encamped at Ḥulwān. Having entered Ḥulwān, Ṭāhir remained only a short time, until Harthamah b. Aʿyan brought him a letter from al-Maʾmūn and al-Faḍl b. Sahl, commanding him to hand over to him the cities and districts he had taken and go to al-Ahwāz.[385] Ṭāhir handed them over to him. Harthamah established himself in Ḥulwān and fortified it. He placed his garrisons and observation posts on its roads [841]
and its mountains. Ṭāhir went to al-Ahwāz.

Al-Maʾmūn Raises the Rank of al-Faḍl b. Sahl

In this year, al-Maʾmūn raised the rank and standing of al-Faḍl b. Sahl.[386]

It has been mentioned: After al-Maʾmūn received the news that Ṭāhir had killed ʿAlī b. ʿĪsā and had seized his camp and that he had named him "Commander of the Faithful"; when, furthermore, al-Faḍl b. Sahl saluted him with this title; and when he became convinced that the report about Ṭāhir's having killed ʿAbd al-Raḥmān b. Jabalah al-Abnāwī and overcome his army was true, he summoned al-Faḍl b. Sahl and in Rajab[387] of this year gave him the governance of the East, from

384. Khāniqīn, on the Khurāsān road, was six *farsakh*s (22.3 miles) before Qaṣr Shīrīn, which in turn was six *farsakh*s before Ḥulwān. See Le Strange, *Lands*, p. 62; *EI*[2] s.v. Khānikīn (Schwarz).

385. Al-Ahwāz was a city in Khūzistān, about 260 miles southeast of Ḥulwān and about 70 miles northeast of al-Baṣrah. See *EI*[2] s.v. (Lockhart).

386. Parallels: Ibn al-Athīr, VI, 177; *Fragmenta*, 327–28.

387. That is, between March 18 and April 16, 812.

the mountains of Hamadhān to the mountains of Siqīnān[388] and Tibet in longitude, and from the Sea of Persia and India to the Sea of Daylam and Jurjān[389] in latitude. He gave him a salary (*ʿumālah*) of 3 million dirhams. He bound his banner on a two-pronged spearhead, gave him a flag, and named him "Dhū al-Riʾāsatayn."[390]

Someone has mentioned that he saw his sword at the house of al-Ḥasan b. Sahl. On one side it was inscribed in silver, *Riʾāsat al-Ḥarb* ("Leadership of War"), and on the other side, *Riʾāsat al-Tadbīr* ("Leadership of Administration"). ʿAlī b. Hishām carried the banner; Nuʿaym b. Ḥāzim carried the flag. He appointed al-Ḥasan b. Sahl to be in charge of the tax bureau (*dīwān al-kharāj*).

ʿAbd al-Malik b. Ṣāliḥ Appointed Governor of Syria

In this year, Muḥammad b. Hārūn appointed ʿAbd al-Malik b. Ṣāliḥ b. ʿAlī[391] to be in charge of Syria and commanded him to travel there. He recruited soldiers for him from its inhabitants

---

388. *Siqīnān* is the Leiden editor's conjectural emendation for the manuscript's *Sufyān*. Ed. Cairo reads *Siqīnān*, but does not say whether Ms. A confirms this reading. The Leiden editor based his emendation on De Goeje's edition of al-Istakhrī's *Kitāb Masālik al-mamālik*, 290. De Goeje originally read this Central Asiatic place-name as *al-Safīnah*, but in the glossary and addenda volume (p. 426) he corrected the reading to *al-Saqīnah*, citing an 1873 article on Central Asiatic place-names preserved in a contemporary Chinese travel account (H. Yule, "Notes on Hwen Thsang's Account of the Principalities of Tokháristán," 92–120). Yule connected the Chinese form *Shikhini* with the Arabic *Shighnān*. De Goeje apparently thought that *Siqīnān* was an alternate form of the same name. In any case, a mountainous area on the upper headwaters of the Oxus River seems to fit the context as the northeastern boundary of the area assigned to al-Faḍl b. Sahl.

389. I.e., the Caspian Sea. Jurjān was the province and city of the same name at the southeastern corner of the Caspian Sea (approximately the modern Iranian province of Astarābād). See Le Strange, *Lands*, 376–81; *EI*[2] s.v. Gurgān (Hartmann).

390. See note 56.

391. ʿAbd al-Malik's father was an uncle of al-Manṣūr. ʿAbd al-Malik had been imprisoned by al-Rashīd at the time of the fall of the Barmakids, but was released by al-Amīn after al-Rashīd's death. Cf. Ṭabarī, III, 692; Yaʿqūbī, II, 526–27; Ibn al-Athīr, 177–79; *Fragmenta*, 327; Gabrieli, "La successione di Hārūn ar-Rašīd," 372. For a history of this branch of the ʿAbbāsid family and its power in Syria, see Kennedy, *Early Abbasid Caliphate*, 74–75, 142.

to fight Ṭāhir and Harthamah. A report of the reason for this appointment follows.

According to Dāwūd b. Sulaymān: After Ṭāhir had become strong, after his cause had advanced, and after he had defeated those of Muḥammad's commanders and armies that he de- [842]
feated, ʿAbd al-Malik b. Ṣāliḥ came before Muḥammad. ʿAbd al-Malik had been imprisoned in al-Rashīd's prison. After al-Rashīd died and Muḥammad succeeded to power, the latter commanded that ʿAbd al-Malik should be released. This took place in Dhū al-Qaʿdah 193.[392] ʿAbd al-Malik felt grateful to Muḥammad for this and considered it his obligation to obey him and give him sincere advice in return. So he said, "Commander of the Faithful, I see that the people have become emboldened against you. The men of the two armies have acted in this way. You have given free rein to your generosity. If you keep doing this, you will make them unruly and insolent; and if you stop giving and being generous, you will irritate and anger them. One does not retain soldiers by economizing; on the other hand, fiscal stability cannot last in the face of expenditure and extravagance. Furthermore, the defeats have frightened your army. Fighting and battles have unnerved and weakened them, and their hearts have become filled with awe of their enemy and aversion to meeting them and fighting them. If you send them against Ṭāhir, he with his few troops will overcome their large numbers; with his strength of resolve, he will defeat their weak loyalty and resolve. The Syrians, on the other hand, are men tested in war and disciplined by hardships. Most of them are submissive to me and quick to obey me. If the Commander of the Faithful dispatches me, I will get him an army of them who will do great damage to his enemy and through whom God will aid His friends and the people who obey Him."

Muḥammad said, "I will put you in charge of them and strengthen you with whatever money and equipment you ask. Set out as soon as possible. With your judgment and insight, act so that the effect of the action will become apparent and its benefit will be praised, God willing!" He put him in charge

392. That is, between August 16 and September 14, 809.

of Syria and al-Jazīrah and strongly urged him to depart. He sent with him a garrison (*kanaf*) of soldiers and *Abnā'*.

ʿAbd al-Malik b. Ṣāliḥ Recruits Troops in Syria for al-Amīn

In this year, ʿAbd al-Malik b. Ṣāliḥ traveled to Syria. When he reached al-Raqqah, he established himself there. [He dispatched his messengers and letters to the heads of the armies of the Syrians, saying that men should be assembled there and Muḥammad should be supplied with them for the war against
[843] Ṭāhir.][393] A report of this follows. (I have already mentioned the reasons why Muḥammad sent him to do this.)

According to Dāwūd b. Sulaymān: When ʿAbd al-Malik reached al-Raqqah, he dispatched his messengers and wrote to the heads of the armies of Syria and the chiefs of al-Jazīrah. There remained not one of them of whom hopes were entertained and whose valor and ability were commended to whom he did not make promises and whose hopes and expectations he did not enlarge. So they came to him chief after chief and group after group. Whenever anyone came before him, he would give him a gift, bestow a robe of honor upon him, and give him a horse. So the people of Syria—*Zawāqil*[394] and Bedouin Arabs—came to him from every direction. They assembled in his presence until they became very numerous. Then someone from the army of the people of Khurāsān[395] sighted a horse that had been taken from him at the battle of Sulaymān b. Abī

---

393. The bracketed text is from ed. Cairo.

394. Ed. Leiden, *Glossarium*, CCLXXVIII, wrongly suggests the translation, "non-Arab soldiers of Syria and Mesopotamia," for *Zawāqil*. Note the unambiguously Arab (Qaysi) names of the three *Zawāqil* leaders mentioned on p. 108, below: Naṣr b. Shabath [al-ʿUqaylī], ʿAmr al-Sulamī, and al-ʿAbbās b. Zufar. According to Ibn Durayd (quoted in *Lisān al-ʿArab*), *Zawāqil* was the name of a tribe in and adjacent to al-Jazīrah. The Leiden glossary quotes this passage and adds (on the authority of al-Jāḥiẓ), "they seem not to have been of good reputation, because highwaymen were designated by the same name." The *Zawāqil* were probably a group of Qaysī tribesmen known for brigandage. See discussions in Kennedy, *Early Abbasid Caliphate*, 143; Ayalon, *The Military Reforms of Caliph al-Muʿtaṣim*, 18–20.

395. That is, from the *Abnā'* who had come from Baghdad; they were of Khurāsānian origin.

Jaʿfar[396] being ridden by one of the *Zawāqīl*. He pursued[397] it, and a quarrel ensued between the two men. A group of *Zawāqīl* and [Khurāsānian] soldiers gathered. They joined battle. Each group helped its man. They clashed and fought hand to hand. The *Abnā'* consulted with each other and assembled before Muḥammad b. Abī Khālid.[398] "You are our shaykh," they said, "our chief and our hero. You have seen how the *Zawāqīl* have treated us. Unite us; or else they will despise us, embolden themselves against us, and behave like this every day." He replied, "I am not going to get into a fight or be present with you in such a situation." The *Abnā'* then prepared themselves and made ready. They took the *Zawāqīl* by surprise, attacked them with swords, killed large numbers of them, and slaughtered them in their dwellings. The *Zawāqīl* assembled, mounted their horses, and girded on their swords. A battle broke out between them. Word of this reached ʿAbd al-Malik b. Ṣāliḥ. He sent a messenger to them, commanding them to stop and lay down their arms, but they threw stones at him. They fought fiercely all day, and the *Abnā'* killed many of [844]
the *Zawāqīl*. When ʿAbd al-Malik, who was seriously ill, was told of the large number who had been killed, he struck his hands together and said, "Oh my humiliation! The Arabs are being mistreated in their own dwelling, their own place, and their own land."

The *Abnā'* who had held back from the violence became

---

396. This does not refer to the Battle of Fakhkh (169/786), at which al-Manṣūr's son, Sulaymān b. Abī Jaʿfar, put down an ʿAlid revolt at Mecca (cf. Ṭabarī, III, 551–68), which would make the horse over thirty years old! The chronicle of Michael the Syrian records that soon after his accession, al-Amīn sent Sulaymān b. al-Manṣūr to govern Ḥimṣ, Damascus, and Palestine, but that his forces were badly defeated by a certain rebel named ʿAmr and returned covered with shame to Baghdad. The same chronicle mentions that the fighting on this later occasion broke out when a "Persian" (i.e., a soldier from the regular army sent from Baghdad) saw one of the "Ṭaiyayê" (Bedouins) passing Callinice (al-Raqqah) riding a horse "that had belonged to his father, who had been killed by the Ṭaiyayê at Saroug." This makes it clear that the reference here is to Sulaymān b. Abī Jaʿfar's activity in Syria no more than three years earlier, not to the battle of Fakhkh. See Michel le Syrien, *Chronique*, III, 21–22, 26.

397. *Taʿallaqa bihā* could also mean "he grabbed hold of it."

398. On Muḥammad b. Abī Khālid al-Marwazī, see Kennedy, *Early Abbasid Caliphate*, 105, 144–45.

angry. The situation worsened. Al-Ḥusayn b. ʿAlī b. ʿĪsā b. Māhān led the *Abnāʾ*. The next morning, the *Zawāqīl* gathered in al-Raqqah; the *Abnāʾ* and Khurāsānians gathered in al-Rāfiqah.[399] One of the men of Ḥimṣ[400] stood up and said, "People of Ḥimṣ, flight is a lesser evil than destruction, and death is a lesser evil than humiliation.[401] You have gone far from your lands and have left your regions, seeking abundance after having experienced dearth, and esteem after having been despised—and now you have fallen into disaster and dismounted in the place where death rages most fiercely! Death is in the moustaches and the high hats of the black-robed ones.[402] To arms! To arms!—before the way is cut off, and trouble alights; before the time of seeking passes, and the way of departure becomes difficult; before action becomes impossible, and the appointed time draws near!"[403] A man from [the tribe of] Kalb stood up in the stirrups of his camel and recited:[404]

A war so vehement that whoever suffers it comes to grief!
 A war whose horsemen have leveled their spear shafts!
God has brought a blaze—the blaze of war!
 If Kalb plunges into it, He will cover them with shame!

Then he said, "Men of Kalb, it is the black banner![405] By God, it has never turned back or turned aside. Its upholder[406] has never submitted, and its keeper has never become weak. You know the blows that the Khurāsānians' swords have inflicted on your

---

399. Al-Rāfiqah ("the Companion") was the new garrison town built on the outskirts of al-Raqqah by the caliph al-Manṣūr in 155/772. See Le Strange, *Lands*, 101–2.

400. The men from Ḥimṣ, identified later as belonging to the tribe of Kalb, are a group separate from the *Zawāqīl* (Qays). See Kennedy, *Early Abbasid Caliphate*, 143.

401. The meaning seems to be "death from famine" is better than humiliation.

402. That is, the partisans of the ʿAbbāsids, who wore black as their color. See Lane, *Lexicon*, s.v. *musawwid*. On the high hat (*qalansuwah*), see note 482.

403. The end of the speech is in rhymed prose (*sajʿ*), suggesting the gravity of the speaker's words and his excitement.

404. The meter is *rajaz*, often used for such spontaneous battlefield poems.

405. Black was the color of the ʿAbbāsids.

406. Reading, with ed. Cairo, *nāṣiruhā*, instead of ed. Leiden, *naṣruhā* ("its help, victory").

necks and the marks of their spears on your breasts. Withdraw from evil, before it grows great; pass it by, before it flames up. To Syria! [To Syria!][407] To your home! To your home! A Palestinian death is better than a life in al-Jazīrah.[408] I for one [845]
am going back. Whoever wants to depart, let him depart with me." So he went, and most of the Syrians went with him.

The *Zawāqīl* went and burned most of the fodder that the merchants had gathered. Al-Ḥusayn b. ʿAlī b. ʿĪsā b. Māhān with a group of Khurāsānian troops stayed at the gate of al-Rāfiqah for fear of Ṭawq b. Mālik. A man from the Banū Taghlib went to Ṭawq and said, "Don't you see what the Arabs have suffered at the hands of these men? Arise! You are not the kind of man to hold back from this affair. The people of al-Jazīrah have turned their eyes to you. They hope for your help and assistance." Ṭawq replied, "By God, I do not belong to al-Jazīrah's Qays or to its Yemen.[409] I was not involved in the beginning of this affair, that I should be present to witness its end! I care too much for my men and my people to expose them to death on account of these fools from the army and ignorant men from Qays. I see safety only in keeping clear."

Naṣr b. Shabath [al-ʿUqaylī][410] came with the *Zawāqīl*. He was riding a chestnut horse with a blaze on its forehead and was wearing a black tunic (*durrāʿah*) that he had tied behind his back. In his hand he had a spear and shield, and he was reciting:

Horsemen of Qays, be steadfast unto death!
[My soul],[411] do not frighten me away from meeting sudden death.

---

407. The second "Syria" is supplied from ed. Cairo. One must understand an imperative or hortatory verb, such as "let us go toward," or "take care for."

408. After the preceding reference to abundance and dearth, the intention seems to be, "Death by starvation in Palestine is better than a livelihood in al-Jazīrah."

409. Qays and Kalb (or Yemen) were the two parties into which the Bedouins of al-Jazīrah were divided.

410. His full name is given in Ibn al-Athīr, VI, 179.

411. The verbs in this line and the next are in the feminine. They must be understood as addressed to something feminine, such as *yā nafsī*, "O my soul." Ed. Cairo incorrectly vocalizes the verb in the second line as *turhibunī* ("you [m. sg.] do not frighten me"), which is metrically impossible. The vocalization of ed. Leiden (*turhibinnī*, second energetic mood) is correct.

Cease hoping[412] with [thoughts of] "it might be" and "would that it were."

He and his companions then attacked. He fought fiercely, but the army held firm against them, and there was great slaughter among the *Zawāqīl*. Then the *Abnāʾ* made attacks, killing and wounding in each of them. Most of the killing and bravery in that charge were the work of Kathīr b. Qādirah, Abū al-Fīl, and Dāwūd b. Mūsā b. ʿĪsā al-Khurāsānī. The *Zawāqīl* were defeated. Their line of defense that day had been led by Naṣr b. Shabath, ʿAmr [b. ʿAbd al-ʿAzīz] al-Sulamī, and al-ʿAbbās b. Zufar [al-Kilābī].[413]

[846] In this year, ʿAbd al-Malik b. Ṣāliḥ died.[414]

In this year, Muḥammad b. Hārūn was deposed and made to swear allegiance to his brother, ʿAbdallāh al-Maʾmūn, in Baghdad.

The Abortive Coup of al-Ḥusayn b. ʿAlī b. ʿĪsā b. Māhān against al-Amīn in Baghdad

In this year, Muḥammad b. Hārūn was imprisoned in the Palace of Abū Jaʿfar with Umm Jaʿfar, the daughter of Jaʿfar b. Abī Jaʿfar.[415] A report of the reason for this follows.

According to Dāwūd b. Sulaymān: After the death of ʿAbd al-Malik b. Ṣāliḥ at al-Raqqah, al-Ḥusayn b. ʿAlī b. ʿĪsā b. Māhān summoned the army. He put the foot soldiers into boats and had the horsemen mount. He gave them gifts; those who were weak he strengthened and mounted on horses, until he brought them out of the territory of al-Jazīrah. This was in the year 196.

Aḥmad b. ʿAbdallāh mentioned that he was one of those present in al-Jazīrah with ʿAbd al-Malik when al-Ḥusayn b. ʿAlī led them back and that this was in Rajab of 196.[416]

412. The reading of ed. Cairo (*tamannī*) is superior to the conjecture of ed. Leiden (*taḥannī*, "bending, being compassionate").

413. Full names from Ibn al-Athīr, VI, 179.

414. Cf. Yaʿqūbī, II, 534, on the anarchy in Syria.

415. Parallels: Yaʿqūbī, II, 534; Ibn al-Athīr, VI, 179–80; *Fragmenta*, 328–30.

416. I.e., between March 18 and April 16, 812.

He mentioned that the *Abnā'* and people of Baghdad met al-Ḥusayn with honor and exaltation. They erected tents for him,[417] and the commanders, chiefs, and nobles (*ashrāf*) went out to meet him. He entered his home in the highest honor and making a very fine figure.

In the middle of the night, Muḥammad sent to him, commanding him to ride to him. Al-Ḥusayn said to the messenger, "By God, I am not a singer, an evening companion, or a jester. I have not taken charge of any province for him, nor have I collected money for him. Why does he want me at this hour? Go away! When it is morning, I will come early to him, God willing." The messenger went away. In the morning, al-Ḥusayn went to Bāb al-Jisr.[418] Troops gathered around him, and he ordered that the gate leading out to the Palace of ʿAbdallāh[419] b. ʿAlī should be locked, along with the gate of the Market of Yaḥyā.[420] He said, "Men of the *Abnā'*, God's caliphate gives [847] no license for arrogant behavior, nor do His favors consort with insolence and pride. Muḥammad wants to corrupt the usages of your religion. He would violate [the terms of] your oath of allegiance, break up your unity, and transfer your strength to others. Only yesterday, he was the master of the *Zawāqīl*! By God, if his term lasts long and he regains strength, the unwholesome consequences of this will return upon you, and the harm and adversity he causes to your dynasty (*dawlah*) and regime (*daʿwah*) will become evident. Cut off his influence, before he cuts off yours! Bring down his strength, before he brings down yours! By God, none of you has aided him but that he has been abandoned, and no one has protected him but that he has been killed. No one finds indulgence with God, nor does

417. Ed. Leiden, *Glossarium*, CDX, suggests that the phrase *ḍarabū lahu al-qibāb* may mean "they decorated the squares in his honor with garlands and wreaths," or "they set up a triumphal arch for him."

418. Gabrieli, on the basis of other indications of location in the passage, locates this Bāb al-Jisr (Bridge Gate) at the end of the second or main bridge over the Tigris. See "La successione di Hārūn ar-Rašīd," 374 (note 3); but cf. note 326 earlier.

419. Corrected from the manuscript reading ʿUbaydallāh by the editor of ed. Leiden, who suggests that this is the Palace of ʿAbdallāh b. ʿAlī b. ʿĪsā b. Māhān. See ed. Leiden, *Addenda*, DCCLXV.

420. On the Market of Yaḥyā (*Sūq Yaḥyā*), see Le Strange, *Baghdad*, 199–201.

God have regard for him, if he violates his promises and breaks his oaths."

Then he ordered the people to cross the bridge. They crossed it and came to the Khurāsān Gate Road.[421] [Meanwhile, the people of] al-Ḥarbiyyah[422] and the people of the suburbs near the Syrian Gate, [al-Anbār Gate, and the bank of the Ṣarāt Canal near al-Kūfah Gate][423] gathered. Some of Muḥammad's horsemen—Bedouin Arabs and others—hurried to [fight] al-Ḥusayn b. ʿAlī. They fought fiercely for part of the day. Al-Ḥusayn ordered his commanders and close companions who were with him to dismount. They dismounted to fight their foe with swords and spears, fighting with true valor, and pushing them back until they dispersed from the gate of al-Khuld [Palace].

On Sunday, the 11th of Rajab, 196 (March 28, 812), al-Ḥusayn b. ʿAlī declared Muḥammad to be deposed and received the oath of allegiance for ʿAbdallāh al-Maʾmūn from the morning of Monday until the evening. On Tuesday, after the battle between al-Ḥusayn and the forces of Muḥammad, al-ʿAbbās b. Mūsā b. ʿĪsā al-Hāshimī went early to Muḥammad and seized him. He went in to him and forced him to leave al-Khuld Palace for the Palace of Abū Jaʿfar. There he imprisoned him until
[848] the time of the midday prayer. Then al-ʿAbbās b. Mūsā b. ʿĪsā seized Umm Jaʿfar and ordered her to leave her palace for the City of Abū Jaʿfar.[424] She refused; so he summoned a chair for her and ordered her to sit on it. He lay about her head with a whip, abused her, and spoke coarsely to her; so she sat in it. Then he gave orders concerning her and she was taken into the city, [to be] with her son and her [other] children.

The next day, the men demanded their pay (*arzāq*) from al-Ḥusayn b. ʿAlī and became unruly. Muḥammad b. Abī Khālid stood up at the Syrian Gate and said, "Men! By God, I do not know why al-Ḥusayn b. ʿAlī is acting as if he were our com-

---

421. That is, the road near the Khurāsān Gate of the Round City. See Kennedy, *Early Abbasid Caliphate*, 144.

422. Al-Ḥarbiyyah quarter was located to the northwest of the Round City, beyond the Syrian Gate. It was populated mainly by people who had accompanied the ʿAbbāsids from Khurāsān. See Le Strange, *Baghdad*, 107 ff.

423. The bracketed text is from ed. Cairo.

424. That is, the Round City of Abū Jaʿfar al-Manṣūr.

mander and taking charge of this affair instead of us. He is not the oldest among us, nor the one among us with the greatest claim to honor, nor the highest among us in rank. Among us there are those who will not accept base action and will not be led by deception. I am the first of you to break his compact. I openly rebuke him and condemn his action. Whoever thinks as I do, let him stand aside with me."

Asad al-Ḥarbī stood up and said, "People of al-Ḥarbiyyah, this is a day of great consequence. You have been asleep, and your sleep has lasted a long time. You have lagged behind, and others have been given precedence over you. Some people have taken the position that Muḥammad should be deposed and imprisoned; as for you, go and take the position that he should be released and set free."

Then came an aged shaykh on a horse, one of the "abstainers."[425] He shouted to the men to be quiet, and they did so. He said, "Men, are you assailing Muḥammad because he has cut off your pay?" "No," they said. "Has he fallen short," he said "in what is due to any of you, or your chiefs, or your eminent men?" "We know of no such case," they said. "Has he removed any of your leaders?" he said. "God forbid that he should have done that!" "Then why have you abandoned him," he said, "and helped his enemy oppress him and take him captive? I swear to God, never have people killed their caliph [849]
but God has set upon them the power of the slaying sword and violent death. Arise and defend your caliph. Fight against whoever wants to depose and murder him."

[The troops from] al-Ḥarbiyyah arose, and with them arose most of the people of the suburbs, with drawn swords[426] and

425. *Abnā' al-kaffiyyah* (the original, unamended Leiden reading, which is recommended in *Addenda*, DCCLXV) is explained thus in ed. Leiden, *Glossarium*, CDLIV: "In Iraq in Umayyad times, those who, although dissatisfied with the death of ʿUthmān, refrained from taking up arms, saying..., 'Better that you should be ʿAbdallāh the slain than ʿAbdallāh the murderer,' were called *ahl al-kaff*. In Khurāsān, this name was given to those who dedicated themselves and their possessions to the cause of the house of the Prophet.... In Ṭabarī, III, 848, they are called *al-kaffiyyah*, which seems to refer to abstaining from stipends—i.e., that they would accept no stipends." Ed. Cairo prefers Guyard's original emendation: *abnā' al-kifāyah*, "men of capability, skill, or intelligence."

426. Reading *mushahharāt*, with ed. Cairo, rather than ed. Leiden's *mushtaharāt*, "holiday garments."

good equipment. They fought fiercely against al-Ḥusayn b. ʿAlī and his forces from mid-morning until the rays of the sun grew weak, inflicting many wounds upon his forces. Al-Ḥusayn b. ʿAlī was taken prisoner. Asad al-Ḥarbī went in to Muḥammad, broke his fetters, and seated him in the caliph's seat. Muḥammad noticed some men who were not wearing military or army clothing and who were not carrying weapons; he gave them orders, and they took what they needed from the weapons that were in the storerooms. He made them promises and raised their hopes; as a result the rabble (*ghawghā'*) looted many weapons, silken goods, and other things. Al-Ḥusayn b. ʿAlī was brought, and Muḥammad rebuked him for his disobedience, saying, "Did I not advance your father over people? Did I not give him charge of cavalry troops and fill his hand with money? Did I not give you positions of honor among the people of Khurāsān and raise your ranks above those of other commanders?" "Yes," he replied. "Then how have I deserved your repudiating obedience to me," he asked, "your inciting the people against me, and your urging them to fight me?" Al-Ḥusayn said, "I trust the pardon of the Commander of the Faithful and hope for his forgiveness and favor." (Muḥammad) said, "The Commander of the Faithful hereby does so for you and puts you in charge of avenging yourself[427] and the slain members of your family." He then called for a robe of honor for him and put it on him. He gave him mounts, commanded him to go to Ḥulwān, and put him in charge of whatever was beyond its pass.

[850] According to ʿUthmān b. Saʿīd al-Ṭā'ī, who said: I used to enjoy special favor with al-Ḥusayn b. ʿAlī. After Muḥammad pardoned him and restored to him his command and rank, I crossed over to him along with the well-wishers. I found him standing at Bāb al-Jisr. I congratulated him and wished him well. Then I said to him, "You have become master of the two armies and the confidant of the Commander of the Faithful. Be thankful for the pardon and forgiveness!" Then I jested and joked with him. I recited some verses to him, saying:

---

427. Perhaps one should read, "avenging your father," as in *Fragmenta*, 329, and Ibn al-Jawzī [Leiden note].

They slew him when his perfection had become complete,
and he had become renowned for generosity and nobility.
He was bright faced, as if the full moon were the form of his face,
when he came walking in a coat of mail.
When the coward's soul was sick with fear and recoiled,
he marched forward, with a Mashrifī sword of Indian steel.
He was grave in the council chamber, but impetuous in the fray:
often turning back to fight the foe, not speaking in excess.
Then avenge yourself upon the enemy, for they
intentionally have assailed you with a foul and ignoble deed.

He laughed and said, "How eager I am for that, if time helps me, and if I am aided by conquest and victory!" Then he halted at the foot of Bāb al-Jisr.[428] He fled with a group of his servants and *mawālī*. Muḥammad summoned troops, and they rode in pursuit of him. They overtook him at the Mosque of Kawthar. When he saw the horsemen, he dismounted and tied his horse. He prayed two prostrations and placed himself in a state of dedication.[429] Then he encountered them, charging at them, driving them back with each charge, and killing some of them. Then his horse stumbled and he fell off. The people hastened [851]
to strike him with spears and swords, and they took his head. Concerning this, ʿAlī b. Jabalah (some say al-Khuraymī) said:[430]

Yea, may God assail those who disbelieved in Him,
and took[431] the head of Ḥusayn al-Harthamī.
In him they brought down a firm spear [of a man],
with a Yemeni sword and Rudayni spear.

428. The fuller text in Ibn al-Athīr, VI, 181, is probably original and may have been shortened in the Ṭabarī manuscript by a copyist's error (homoioteleuton): "People were congratulating him. When the people departed from him, he cut the bridge and fled."

429. The Arabic *taḥarrama* can mean either to assume the simple garment (*iḥrām*) of a pilgrim, or to pronounce the words *Allāhu akbar* ("God is most great!"). The latter seems appropriate here as a preparation for death.

430. ʿAlī b. Jabalah al-ʿAkawwak (160/776–213/828) was a poet of Khurāsānian origins active in Baghdad. See Sezgin, *GAS*, II, 572–74; *EI*[2] s.v. al-ʿAkawwak (Blachère). On al-Khuraymī (corrected from manuscript al-Khuzaymī), see note 462.

431. The translation follows ed. Cairo, *fāzū*, rather than ed. Leiden, *fādaw* ("they ransomed").

In opposition to right he expected honor and authority,
but his desire brought him only the boot of Ḥunayn to wear.[432]

It has been said: When Muḥammad pardoned al-Ḥusayn, he appointed him vizier and gave him his ring.

Al-Ḥusayn b. ʿAlī b. ʿĪsā b. Māhān was killed on the middle day of Rajab of this year,[433] in the Mosque of Kawthar, one *farsakh* from Baghdad on the road to Nahr Bīn.[434] Allegiance was renewed to Muḥammad on Friday, the 16th of Rajab of this year (April 2, 812). Al-Ḥusayn's imprisonment of Muḥammad in the Palace of Abū Jaʿfar had lasted two days. During the night in which Ḥusayn b. ʿAlī was killed, al-Faḍl b. al-Rabīʿ fled.

The Death of Muḥammad b. Yazīd al-Muhallabī and Ṭāhir's Entry into al-Ahwāz

During this year, Ṭāhir b. al-Ḥusayn, when Harthamah had come to him, went from Ḥulwān to al-Ahwāz and killed Muḥammad's governor of the city, Muḥammad b. Yazīd al-Muhallabī.[435] This happened after Ṭāhir sent armies ahead of himself toward the city, and before he himself set out toward him to fight him. A report of this follows.

[852] According to Yazīd b. al-Ḥārith, who said: After Ṭāhir had encamped at Shalāshān, he dispatched al-Ḥusayn b. ʿUmar al-Rustumī to al-Ahwāz. He commanded him to travel at a moderate pace: he was not to travel without sending out scout-

---

432. "Coming back wearing the boots of Ḥunayn" was a proverbial expression for coming back empty-handed or not achieving one's hopes. The source of the proverb is explained in Lane, *Lexicon*, II, 770.

433. I.e., the fifteenth day of the month, April 1, 812.

434. The Bīn Canal (Nahr Bīn) was a subsidiary canal east of Baghdad. It left the main Nahrawān Canal a short distance above the town of Nahrawān and flowed into the Tigris about 2 *farsakh*s below Baghdad. See Le Strange, *Baghdad*, 174–76.

435. Parallels: Yaʿqūbī, II, 534; Ibn al-Athīr, VI, 181–83; *Fragmenta*, 330. On the Muhallabī family, to which the governor Muḥammad b. Yazīd b. Ḥātim b. Qabīṣah b. al-Muhallab belonged, and its importance among the Azd tribesmen of al-Baṣrah, see Kennedy, *Early Abbasid Caliphate*, 82–83; Crone, *Slaves on Horses*, 135.

ing parties, and he was to encamp only in a secure location, where he could feel safe about his forces. After al-Ḥusayn had set out, Ṭāhir's spies came and informed him that Muḥammad b. Yazīd al-Muhallabī, Muḥammad's governor of al-Ahwāz, had set out with a large host, intending to encamp at Junday Sābūr,[436] which was the boundary between [the provinces of] al-Ahwāz and al-Jabal, to protect al-Ahwāz and ward off any of Ṭāhir's forces who wanted to enter it. They said that he was with a numerous and powerful force. Ṭāhir summoned a number of his companions, including Muḥammad b. Ṭālūt, Muḥammad b. al-ʿAlāʾ, al-ʿAbbās b. Bukhārākhudhāh, al-Ḥārith b. Hishām, Dāwūd b. Mūsā, and Hādī b. Ḥafṣ. He ordered them to travel quickly, until their foremost forces made contact with the rearmost forces of al-Ḥusayn b. ʿUmar al-Rustumī. If he needed reinforcement, they were to reinforce him; if an army encountered him, they would back him up.

Ṭāhir sent out these armies, but no one encountered them until they were close to al-Ahwāz. Word of them reached Muḥammad b. Yazīd. He reviewed his forces, strengthened those of them who were weak, and mounted the foot soldiers on mules. He advanced and encamped at the market of ʿAskar Mukram,[437] setting the inhabited area and the water behind his back. Ṭāhir became fearful that (Muḥammad) would hasten toward his forces; so he reinforced them with Quraysh b. Shibl, and he himself set out until he was close to them. He dispatched al-Ḥasan b. ʿAlī al-Maʾmūnī and commanded him to join up with Quraysh b. Shibl and al-Ḥusayn b. ʿUmar al-Rustumī. These armies traveled until they drew close to Muḥammad b. Yazīd at ʿAskar Mukram. Muḥammad gathered his forces and [853]
said, "What do you think best? Should I delay fighting and put off the encounter with enemy, or should I fight it out with them, regardless of whether it is to my advantage or against it?

436. Junday Sābūr, or Jundī Shāpūr, about seventy miles north of al-Ahwāz, was an important city. Under the Sasanians, it had been the capital of Khūzistān province and was famous for its medical school. See Le Strange, *Lands*, 238, 247; *EI*[2] s.v. Gondē<u>sh</u>āpūr (Huart).

437. The town of ʿAskar Mukram, on the Masruqān Canal in Khūzistān, was about halfway between al-Ahwāz and Junday Sābūr. See Le Strange, *Lands*, 233, 236–37, 242, 246–47; *EI*[2] s.v. (Streck).

By God, I do not think that I should go back [to the Commander of the Faithful or leave al-Ahwāz." They said to him, "The best plan is for you to return] to al-Ahwāz, fortify yourself there, and avoid fighting Ṭāhir. You should send to al-Baṣrah and enroll troops there, summoning an army from those of your tribesmen over whom you have authority and who have sworn allegiance to you."[438] He accepted their advice. His men followed him, and he turned back until he came to Sūq al-Ahwāz.[439] Ṭāhir commanded Quraysh b. Shibl to follow him and deal quickly with him, before he could fortify himself in Sūq al-Ahwāz. He commanded al-Ḥasan b. ʿAlī al-Maʾmūnī and al-Ḥusayn b. ʿUmar al-Rustumī to travel on the heels of (Quraysh); if he needed their help, they were to help him. Quraysh b. Shibl closely followed Muḥammad b. Yazīd: whenever Muḥammad b. Yazīd departed from a village, Quraysh encamped in it, until they came to Sūq al-Ahwāz. Muḥammad b. Yazīd arrived at the city first and entered it. He relied on the inhabited area for support, setting it to his rear; he mustered his forces and resolved to fight the enemy. He called for money, and it was poured out before him. He said to his companions, "Whoever among you wants reward and rank, let him show me his mettle." Quraysh b. Shibl advanced until he was close to him and said to his companions, "Remain in your position and your battle lines. Let most of your fighting with them be done while you are on foot. Fight them with energy and strength." There was not one of his men who did not gather for himself as many stones as he could. Before Muḥammad b. Yazīd could pass over toward them, they weakened his men with stones and inflicted many injuries on them with arrows. A group of Muḥammad b. Yazīd's forces came over. Quraysh ordered his forces to dismount to fight them, and they did so, fighting them fiercely, until they went back, retreating one group after the

438. The translation of the three preceding sentences follows the Cairo text, which is clearly superior to that of ed. Leiden, with the exception of one word (*tughādiya*, "hasten," sc. to fight), where I prefer the Leiden reading (*nuʿādiya*, "we should avoid," sc. fighting). The bracketed words are not found in ed. Leiden. The Cairo text itself may contain corruptions.

439. Sūq al-Ahwāz ("Market of al-Ahwāz") is the longer form of the name of the city of al-Ahwāz. See Le Strange, *Lands*, 232.

other. Muḥammad b. Yazīd turned to a group of his *mawālī* [854] who were with him and said, "What do you think best?" They said, "Regarding what?" He said, "I see that those on my side have been routed. I fear they will abandon me. I do not expect them to return. I have decided to dismount and fight by myself, until God decrees what He wants. Whoever of you wishes to depart, let him depart. By God, I would rather that you survive than that you perish and be destroyed!" They replied, "Then we would be treating you unjustly, by God! You freed us from slavery, raised us up from humiliation, enriched us after we were poor—and then we abandon you in this condition! No, we will advance before you and die beside the stirrup of your horse. May God curse this world and life after your death!" Then they dismounted, hamstrung their horses, and attacked Quraysh's forces fiercely, killing many of them, and crushing their heads with rocks and other things. But one of Ṭāhir's men reached Muḥammad b. Yazīd, struck him with a spear, and felled him. The men rushed to strike him and thrust at him, until they killed him.

Lamenting the death of Muḥammad b. Yazīd, one of the people of al-Baṣrah said:

Whoever tastes slumber's savor of joy—
as for me, sleeplessness has pressed me hard.
A generous man of right action has passed away; I have lost, in him,
my heart and my hearing, and my eyes have overwhelmed me [with tears].
He was succor in time of drought:
and now the spring rainclouds have passed away.
Al-ʿUyaynī[440] was faithful to the imām:
the blow of the ridged, iridescent one[441] did not frighten him.
He would have assailed time's vicissitude with his skill,
were it not that mankind is subject to the Decree.

---

440. I.e., al-Muhallabī [Leiden note].

441. I.e., the sword: a well-tempered sword had ridges in the metal of its blade and an iridescence.

Then depart praised; for everyone with an allotted term of life
strives for what you strove for at the end of life.

A Muhallabī clansman who was wounded many times in the battle and whose hand was cut off said:[442]

[855] I reproached myself only that I was incapable
of agility, and that I had been weakened by wounds.
Had my two hands been sound, I would have fought to defend him,
and I would have warded off from him Ṭāhir's accursed one.
He was a hero never seen to abandon the sword in the fray,
when he entered battle with its dust and earned fame.[443]

According to al-Haytham b. ʿAdī, who said: When Ibn Abī ʿUyaynah[444] went before Ṭāhir, he recited to him his poem [that begins with the verse]:

He whom a country delights does not depart
from it, but he whom it displeases does not abide.

Finally, he came to his verse:

My thought was grieved only because of one thing
concealed in the breast from speech.

Ṭāhir smiled and said, "By God, what grieved you regarding him grieved me also, and what pained you pained me. I disliked what happened, but death will occur and destiny will descend. Ties of kindred are inevitably cut and one becomes estranged from relatives for the sake of upholding the caliphate and performing the duty of obedience." We supposed that he was referring to Muḥammad b. Yazīd b. Ḥātim.

---

442. Parallel: Ibn al-Athīr, VI, 182.

443. Literally, "and became known by a by-name."

444. Two poets, brothers from the al-Muhallabī family, both sometimes called simply "Ibn Abī ʿUyaynah," were active at this time, and the poem sometimes is attributed to one and sometimes to the other. The elder was Abū Jaʿfar ʿAbdallāh b. Muḥammad b. Abī ʿUyaynah b. al-Muhallab b. Abī Ṣufrah; the younger was Abū al-Minhāl Abū ʿUyaynah b. Muḥammad b. Abī ʿUyaynah. The poem can be found in *Aghānī*, XVIII, 17 (ed. Cairo, 7742). Its theme is disappointment over kinsmen who do not maintain family solidarity—thus its appropriateness to the present context. See also Sezgin, *GAS*, II, 605–6.

According to ʿUmar b. Asad, who said: Ṭāhir established himself at al-Ahwāz after he had killed Muḥammad b. Yazīd b. Ḥātim.[445] He sent out his agents into its districts and took charge of al-Yamāmah,[446] al-Baḥrayn, and ʿUmān—what was adjacent to al-Ahwāz and what was adjacent to the district of al-Baṣrah. Then he turned inland, heading toward Wāsiṭ.[447] At that time, al-Sindī b. Yaḥyā al-Ḥarashī and al-Haytham, the [856] deputy of Khuzaymah b. Khāzim, were in the city. The garrisons and agents began to collapse, garrison by garrison, and agent by agent. As soon as Ṭāhir approached them, they left their districts and fled from them, until Ṭāhir was close to Wāsiṭ. Al-Sindī b. Yaḥyā and al-Haytham b. Shuʿbah summoned their forces, gathered them to themselves, and were about to fight. Al-Haytham b. Shuʿbah ordered the master of his horses to saddle his horses for him. So the man brought him a horse, but al-Haytham kept shifting his eyes from one horse to another—there were a number of them before him. The master of horses saw the disturbance and fear in his face. "If you are going to flee," he said, "this is the one for you. She gallops farther and is stronger for traveling." Al-Haytham laughed and said, "Bring the escape horse here! It is Ṭāhir; there is no shame for us in fleeing from him!" So both of them left Wāsiṭ and fled.

Ṭāhir entered Wāsiṭ. He became fearful that al-Haytham and al-Sindī would reach Fam al-Ṣilḥ[448] before him and fortify themselves there. So he dispatched Muḥammad b. Ṭālūt and commanded him to reach Fam al-Ṣilḥ before the two and prevent them from entering it, if they tried. He also dispatched one of his commanders, a man called Aḥmad b. al-Muhallab, toward al-Kūfah, which was then being governed by al-ʿAbbās b. Mūsā al-Hādī. When the report about Aḥmad b. al-Muhallab reached al-ʿAbbās, he threw off his allegiance to Muḥammad and wrote to Ṭāhir that he would obey and swear allegiance to

445. Parallels: Ibn al-Athīr, VI, 183–84; *Fragmenta*, 330.

446. Al-Yamāmah was a part of the Najd area in central Arabia. See Yāqūt, *Muʿjam*, s.v.

447. Wāsiṭ was a major city on the lower Tigris. It was called "Wāsiṭ" (central, middle) because it was roughly equidistant from Baghdad, al-Kūfah, and al-Baṣrah. See Le Strange, *Lands*, 39.

448. Fam al-Ṣilḥ ("Mouth of the Ṣilḥ Canal") was a town seven *farsakh*s (26 miles) upstream from Wāsiṭ. See Le Strange, *Lands*, 38.

al-Ma'mūn. Ṭāhir's horsemen encamped at Fam al-Nīl,[449] and Ṭāhir took control of everything between Wāsiṭ and al-Kūfah. Al-Manṣūr b. al-Mahdī, who was Muḥammad's governor of al-Baṣrah, wrote to Ṭāhir announcing his obedience. Ṭāhir moved on and encamped at Ṭarnāyā.[450] He stayed there for two days, but did not think it a suitable location for the army. He ordered a floating bridge, and it was thrown across the river.
[857] He secured his camp with a trench, and he sent his letters of appointment to the governors. Al-Manṣūr b. al-Mahdī in al-Baṣrah, al-ʿAbbās b. Mūsā al-Hādī in al-Kūfah, and al-Muṭṭalib b. ʿAbdallāh b. Mālik in al-Mawṣil swore allegiance to al-Ma'mūn and cast off their allegiance to Muḥammad in Rajab of the year 196.[451] Some have said that the man who was governing al-Kūfah for Muḥammad when Ṭāhir arrived was al-Faḍl b. al-ʿAbbās b. Mūsā b. ʿĪsā. After the men I have just mentioned wrote to Ṭāhir announcing their allegiance to al-Ma'mūn and their repudiation of Muḥammad, Ṭāhir confirmed them over their districts. He appointed Dāwūd b. ʿĪsā b. Mūsā b. Muḥammad b. ʿAlī al-Hāshimī to govern Mecca and Medina, and Yazīd b. Jarīr al-Bajalī to govern Yemen, and he dispatched al-Ḥārith b. Hishām and Dāwūd b. Mūsā to Qaṣr Ibn Hubayrah.[452]

Ṭāhir Takes al-Madā'in and Marches toward Ṣarṣar

In this year, Ṭāhir b. al-Ḥusayn took al-Madā'in[453] from the forces of Muḥammad [al-Amīn]. From there he went toward

---

449. Fam al-Nīl ("Mouth of the Nīl Canal"), where the Nīl Canal flowed into the Tigris, was a few miles above Fam al-Ṣilḥ. See Le Strange, *Lands*, 72–73.

450. The location and vocalization are unknown. The manuscript may be corrupt. Ibn al-Jawzi and Ibn al-Athīr read "at Jarjarāyā," which is on the Tigris River about halfway between Wāsiṭ and Baghdad.

451. That is, between March 18 and April 16, 812. Yaʿqūbī, II, 534, dates Ṭāhir's entry into Wāsiṭ on 3 Rajab 196.

452. Qaṣr Ibn Hubayrah was located just east of the Sūrā branch of the Euphrates River, on the main road halfway between Baghdad and al-Kūfah. Under the name al-Hāshimiyyah, which never succeeded in displacing the original name, the town had served briefly as the first capital of the ʿAbbāsids in Iraq. See Le Strange, *Lands*, 70–71; *EI*[2] s.v. Ḳaṣr ibn Hubayrah (Lassner).

453. Al-Madā'in ("the cities," so named because it consisted of a number of separate towns linked by a floating bridge across the Tigris) was the former Sasanian winter capital about 20 miles south of Baghdad. See *EI*[2] s.v. (Streck).

Ṣarṣar,[454] constructed a floating bridge, and proceeded to Ṣarṣar. A report of the reason for his entering al-Madā'in and going to Ṣarṣar follows.

It has been mentioned: After Ṭāhir had sent al-Ḥārith b. Hishām and Dāwūd b. Mūsā to Qaṣr Ibn Hubayrah, and after word had reached Muḥammad that his governor in al-Kūfah had cast off allegiance to him and had sworn allegiance to al-Ma'mūn, Muḥammad dispatched the commander Muḥammad b. Sulaymān and Muḥammad b. Ḥammād al-Barbarī.[455] He commanded them to attack al-Ḥārith and Dāwūd by night at Qaṣr [Ibn Hubayrah]. They were told, "If you follow the main road, it will not escape their notice; instead, take the shortest route to Fam al-Jāmiʿ,[456] which is the site of a market and a camp. Encamp there, and make a night attack upon them, if you want to do that, for you will be near enough to them." So the two of them sent the foot soldiers from al-Yāsiriyyah[457] to Fam al-Jāmiʿ. Word of this reached al-Ḥārith and Dāwūd. They rode with a detachment of horsemen and prepared to deal with the foot soldiers. They crossed over to them by a ford in the [858] Sūrā',[458] beside which they had encamped, and inflicted a heavy blow on them. Ṭāhir dispatched Muḥammad b. Ziyād and Nuṣayr b. al-Khaṭṭāb to reinforce al-Ḥārith and Dāwūd. The armies assembled at al-Jāmiʿ and marched until they encountered Muḥammad b. Sulaymān and Muḥammad b.

---

454. Ṣarṣar, on the canal of the same name, which joined the Tigris a few miles above al-Madā'in, was only 5 miles south of Baghdad, on the main north-south road to al-Kūfah. See Le Strange, *Lands*, 32, 35, 67.

455. Muḥammad's father, Ḥammād al-Barbarī ("the Berber" or "the Nubian"), had been a slave and *mawlā* of the caliph. He had been freed by al-Rashīd at the opening of his reign. See Yaʿqūbī, II, 498–99; Crone, *Slaves on Horses*, 191.

456. Location uncertain: Fam al-Jāmiʿ (the mouth of the Jāmiʿ canal) is perhaps to be connected with the town of al-Ḥillah, sometimes called al-Jāmiʿayn (the Two Mosques), on the east branch of the Euphrates, south of Qaṣr Ibn Hubayrah. The road to al-Ḥillah passed east of Qaṣr Ibn Hubayrah. See Le Strange, *Lands*, 71; Gabrieli, "La successione di Hārūn ar-Rašīd," 376 n. 2.

457. Al-Yāsiriyyah, on the ʿĪsā Canal 2 miles west of Baghdad, was considered either the westernmost quarter of the city or a separate village. See Le Strange, *Baghdad*, 74, 76, 151–52.

458. That is, the Sūrā (eastern) branch of the Euphrates. See Le Strange, *Lands*, 70.

Ḥammād between the Durqīṭ Canal[459] and al-Jāmiʿ. The two sides fought each other fiercely. The forces from Baghdad were defeated. Muḥammad b. Sulaymān fled and reached the village of Shāhī.[460] He crossed the Euphrates and took the desert road to al-Anbār.[461] Muḥammad b. Ḥammād returned to Baghdad. Concerning this, Abū Yaʿqūb al-Khuraymī[462] said:

The two of them transgressed with breach of promise, that they might split thereby
the rock of truth; so they (themselves) were broken, with scattered host.
A lean one, O Ibn al-Barbarī, allowed us to escape—
a horse that goes forth for a long march and finds the way.

According to Yazīd b. al-Ḥārith: When Muḥammad b. Ḥammād al-Barbarī entered Baghdad, Muḥammad the Deposed sent al-Faḍl b. Mūsā b. ʿĪsā al-Hāshimī to al-Kūfah and appointed him governor of it. He joined to him Abū al-Salāsil, Iyās al-Ḥirābī, and Jumhūr al-Najjārī and commanded him to travel quickly. Al-Faḍl set out. After he crossed the ʿĪsā Canal,[463] his horse stumbled and fell. He therefore switched from it to another, regarding it as an evil omen, and said, "O God, I ask you for blessing on this journey!" Word of this reached Ṭāhir, and he sent Muḥammad b. al-ʿAlā' and wrote to al-Ḥārith b. Hishām and Dāwūd b. Mūsā that they should obey him. Muḥammad b.

---

459. For the Durqīṭ (or Darqīṭ) Canal, see Le Strange, *Lands*, 80.

460. Yāqūt, with some uncertainly, places Shāhī near al-Qādisiyyah, which was west of al-Kūfah on the road to Mecca. The text here implies a location on the east side of the Euphrates.

461. Al-Anbār, on the left bank of the Euphrates, was about 12 *farsakh*s (44.6 miles) west of Baghdad. It was an important crossing point on the Euphrates near the northernmost navigable canal connecting the Euphrates with the Tigris. See EI^2 s.v. (Streck).

462. Abū Yaʿqūb Isḥāq b. Ḥassān b. Qūhī al-Khuraymī was a poet of Sogdian origin who settled in Iraq and became a *mawlā* of the Khuraym family. A eulogist of al-Rashīd and the Barmakids, he supported al-Amīn in the civil war and died ca. 214/829. See *GAL*, S I, 111–12; Sezgin, *GAS*, II, 550–51; EI^2 s.v. Abū Yaʿqūb al-Khuraymī (Pellat). His poems have been collected and edited by ʿAlī Jawad al-Ṭāhir and Muḥammad Jabbār al-Muʿaybid, *Dīwān al-Khuraymī* (Beirut, 1971). The following poem is not included in their collection.

463. The ʿĪsā Canal flowed in a semicircle around the southern limits of Baghdad. See Le Strange, *Baghdad*, 49–56.

al-ʿAlāʾ encountered al-Faḍl at Qaryat al-Aʿrāb.[464] Al-Faḍl sent word to him, saying, "I will heed and obey Ṭāhir. My departure was merely a deception on my part upon Muḥammad [al-Amīn]; so leave me free to go to (Ṭāhir)." Muḥammad [b. al- [859]
ʿAlāʾ] said to him, "I do not know of what you are speaking; I neither accept it nor reject it. If you want the commander Ṭāhir, turn around and take the easiest and most direct way." So he went back. Muḥammad [b. al-ʿAlāʾ] said to his companions, "Be careful, for I fear this man's trickery." Thinking that Muḥammad b. al-ʿAlāʾ felt himself safe from him, al-Faḍl without delay cried out, "God is most great!"[465] However, he found Muḥammad ready and prepared. They fought very fiercely. Al-Faḍl's horse fell, but Abū al-Salāsil defended him until he mounted, and he said, "I will mention this stand to the Commander of the Faithful." The forces of Muḥammad b. al-ʿAlāʾ attacked those of al-Faḍl and defeated them: they continued killing them all the way to Kūthā.[466] Ismāʿīl b. Muḥammad al-Qurashī and Jumhūr al-Najjārī were taken prisoner in that battle.

Ṭāhir headed toward al-Madāʾin, where there was a large force of Muḥammad's cavalry under al-Barmakī, who had fortified himself there and was receiving reinforcements, gifts, and robes of honor from Muḥammad every day.[467] When Ṭāhir had drawn near to al-Madāʾin, but was still two *farsakh*s away, he dismounted, prayed two prostrations, and added many extra prayers to God, saying, "O God, we ask for help, as Thou didst help the Muslims at the Battle of al-Madāʾin."[468] He dispatched al-Ḥasan b. ʿAlī al-Maʾmūnī and Quraysh b. Shibl. He dispatched al-Hādī b. Ḥafṣ in charge of his vanguard, and

---

464. Qaryat al-Aʿrāb seems to be a proper name; however, it may simply mean "the village of the Bedouin Arabs."

465. *Allāhu akbar*, i.e., as the signal for an attack.

466. The town of Kūthā, on the canal of the same name, was located on the main north-south road from Baghdad to al-Kūfah, about 35 miles south of Baghdad, and 18 miles north of Qaṣr Ibn Hubayrah. See Le Strange, *Lands*, 68–69; *EI*² s.v. (Plessner).

467. Parallel: Ibn al-Athīr, VI, 184.

468. That is, the battle in which the capital of the Sasanian Empire fell to Muslim forces led by Saʿd b. Abī Waqqāṣ in Ṣafar 16 (March 637). See *EI*² s.v. al-Madāʾin (Streck).

he marched. When al-Barmakī's forces heard the sound of his drums, they saddled the horses. They began to draw up their ranks and make those in the forefront of the men join those in the rear. Al-Barmakī began setting the ranks into good order; but as soon as he set a line in order, it would break up and fall into disorder. "O God," he said, "we take refuge in Thee from desertion!" Then he turned to the commander of his rear and said, "Let the men go, for I see an army that is worthless." So they followed one another closely, heading toward Baghdad. Ṭāhir encamped at al-Madā'in and sent Quraysh b. Shibl and al-ʿAbbās b. Bukhārākhudhāh ahead to al-Darzījān.[469] Aḥmad
[860] b. Saʿīd al-Ḥarashī and Naṣr b. Manṣūr b. Naṣr b. Mālik were encamped at the Diyālā River,[470] and they prevented al-Barmakī's forces from crossing to Baghdad. Ṭāhir advanced until he reached al-Darzījān, opposite Aḥmad [b. Saʿīd] and Naṣr b. Manṣūr. He had the foot soldiers go over to them. Not much fighting took place between the two sides before [al-Barmakī's forces] were defeated. Ṭāhir turned left, toward the Ṣarṣar Canal, constructed a floating bridge, and encamped there (sc. at Ṣarṣar).

The Governor of Mecca Casts off Allegiance to al-Amīn

In this year, Dāwūd b. ʿĪsā, the governor of Mecca and Medina, cast off his allegiance to Muḥammad, whose governor he was for the two cities.[471] He swore allegiance to al-Ma'mūn and received the oath of allegiance to him from the people. He wrote announcing this to Ṭāhir and al-Ma'mūn. Then he himself departed to go to al-Ma'mūn. A report of how this happened follows.

It has been mentioned: After the caliphate had devolved upon al-Amīn, he sent to Mecca and Medina Dāwūd b. ʿĪsā b. Mūsā b. Muḥammad b. ʿAlī b. ʿAbdallāh b. ʿAbbās and

---

469. Al-Darzījān was a large village located close to Baghdad on the west side of the Tigris. See Yāqūt, *Muʿjam*, s.v.

470. The Diyālā River flowed into the Tigris from the east 3 miles below Baghdad. See Le Strange, *Lands*, 59–60; *EI*[2] s.v. (Longrigg).

471. Parallels: Ibn al-Athīr, VI, 184–85; *Fragmenta*, 330–31.

removed al-Rashīd's governor of Mecca, Muḥammad b. ʿAbd al-Raḥmān b. Muḥammad al-Makhzūmī, who had been responsible for public worship, the police (*aḥdāth*), and the administration of justice among the people. Muḥammad [b. ʿAbd al-Raḥmān] was replaced in all of these things by Dāwūd b. ʿĪsā, save for the administration of justice, for al-Amīn retained (Muḥammad b. ʿAbd al-Raḥmān) in the latter office. Dāwūd resided as governor of Mecca and Medina on behalf of Muḥammad [al-Amīn]. He led the pilgrimage in the years 193, 194, and 195. After the year 196 began, word reached him about how ʿAbdallāh al-Maʾmūn had deposed his brother and what Ṭāhir had done to Muḥammad's commanders. Muḥammad had written to Dāwūd b. ʿĪsā, commanding him to cast off allegiance to ʿAbdallāh al-Maʾmūn and swear allegiance to al-Amīn's son, Mūsā. Muḥammad sent for the two documents [861]
that al-Rashīd had written and hung in the Kaʿbah and took them.[472] After Muḥammad had done this, Dāwūd assembled the doorkeepers of the Kaʿbah, the people of Quraysh, the jurists, and the witnesses who had attested to the contents of the two documents—Dāwūd himself had been one of them. Dāwūd said, "You know the promise and covenant that al-Rashīd received from us and from you at the Sacred House of God, when we swore allegiance to his two sons, that you[473] would be on the side of the wronged against the wrongdoer, the injured against the injurer, and the betrayed against the betrayer. Now we have seen, and you have seen too, how Muḥammad has initiated the wronging, injuring, and betrayal of his brothers ʿAbdallāh al-Maʾmūn and al-Qāsim al-Muʾtaman. He has deposed the two of them and has had allegiance sworn to his infant son, a babe not yet weaned. He has disobediently [and wrongfully][474] had the two contracts removed from the Kaʿbah and has burned them with fire. I have decided to cast him off

472. The chronology is unclear. Ibn al-Athīr, VI, 162, places al-Amīn's action in 194, before al-Maʾmūn's sending of Ṭāhir to al-Rayy. In any case, Dāwūd's anger over the destruction of the Meccan documents was not the immediate cause of this change of allegiance. See Kimber, "Hārūn al-Rashīd's Meccan Settlement," 58.

473. Ed. Cairo: "we."

474. The bracketed text is from ed. Cairo.

and swear allegiance to ʿAbdallāh al-Maʾmūn as caliph, because he has been wronged and injured." The people of Mecca said to him, "Our judgment is as your judgment. We will cast him off with you." He set them a time—the midday prayer—and sent a crier into the roads between the mountains of Mecca, announcing, "To prayer! In congregation!" When the time for the midday prayer came—it was Thursday,[475] the 27th day of Rajab 196—Dāwūd b. ʿĪsā came out [of his residence] and led the people in the midday prayer. The pulpit had been placed for him between the Corner and the Standing Place.[476] He climbed up and sat on it. He gave orders for the dignitaries and nobles (*ashrāf*) of the people, and they drew near to the pulpit. Dāwūd was an eloquent preacher with a strong voice. The people having assembled, he rose to preach, saying:

> Praise be to God, the Possessor of dominion, who gives dominion to whom He will, and withdraws dominion from whom He will; who exalts whom He will, and abases whom He will; in whose hand is the good;
> [862] and He is powerful over everything.[477] I bear witness that there is no god but God alone, who has no partner, and who upholds justice; there is no god but He, the Almighty, the Wise.[478] And I bear witness that Muḥammad is His servant and His messenger, whom He sent to bring the religion [of Islam], through whom He sealed the prophets, and whom He made a mercy for all beings.[479] May God bless him among the ancients and those of later times.

---

475. The 27th of Rajab (April 13, 812) fell on a Tuesday, and the 29th fell on Thursday. The numbers *sabʿ* (seven) and *tisʿ* (nine) are very similar in Arabic script and are often confused. The correct reading is probably "Thursday, the 29th of Rajab" (April 15, 812).

476. That is, between the eastern corner (*rukn*) of the Kaʿbah's main façade, where the Black Stone kissed by pilgrims is affixed to the building, and the Standing Place (*maqām*) of Abraham, located in front of the main façade, which also contains the door of the building. According to Qurʾān 2:125 and 3:97, the Kaʿbah stands at the place where Abraham had once prayed. See von Grunebaum, *Muhammadan Festivals*, 19.

477. Cf. Qurʾān 3:26.

478. Ibid., 3:18.

479. Ibid., 21:107.

> To proceed: People of Mecca, you are the root and the branch, tribesmen and kin, partners in the blessing. To your land have God's visitors[480] come, and toward your *qiblah*[481] the Muslims turn. You know the promise and covenant that al-Rashīd Hārūn—may the mercy and blessing of God be upon him—enjoined upon you when he received the oath of allegiance to his two sons, Muḥammad and ʿAbdallāh, in your midst: that you would help the wronged against the wronger, the injured against the injurer, and the betrayed against the betrayer. Now you have learned, and we have learned also, that Muḥammad b. Hārūn has initiated wronging, injuring, and betrayal. He has violated the conditions that he voluntarily granted in the interior of the Sacred House. Now it has become lawful for us and for you to depose him from the caliphate and to transfer it to him who has been wronged, injured, and betrayed. Behold, I make you witnesses that I have cast off Muḥammad b. Hārūn from the caliphate, even as I have cast off this *qalansuwah*[482] from my head.

He removed his *qalansuwah* from his head and threw it to one of the servants at his feet. It was made of red striped Yemeni cloth.[483] A black Hāshimī *qalansuwah* was brought, and he put it on. Then he said: "I swear allegiance to the Servant of God ʿAbdallāh al-Maʾmūn, the Commander of the Faithful, for the caliphate! Arise to swear allegiance to your caliph!" A group of dignitaries ascended the pulpit to him, one after the other, swore to him the oath of allegiance to ʿAbdallāh al-Maʾmūn for the caliphate, and repudiated Muḥammad [al-Amīn]. Then

---

480. That is, the participants in the annual pilgrimage, who are called "visitors" (*wafd*) of God.

481. The *qiblah* is the direction of the Kaʿbah. Muslims face it during prayer.

482. The *qalansuwah* was a tall, conical hat, a symbol of high rank in Sasanian Iraq, later worn by the Abbasid caliphs, their viziers, and judges. See Dozy, *Supplément*, II, 409, and *Dictionnaire détaillé des noms des vêtements*, 365–71; Sourdel, "Questions de cérémonial ʿabbaside," 133–34; Morony, *Iraq after the Muslim Conquest*, 186.

483. *Burūd ḥibarah musalsalah*: Cf. Dozy, *Dictionnaire détaillé des noms des vêtements*, 133–36.

[863] he descended from the pulpit. The time for the midafternoon prayer had arrived, so he led the people in worship and then sat down at one end of the mosque. People began to swear the oath of allegiance to him, one group after another. He would read to them the document of allegiance, and they would clasp his hand. He did this for several days. He also wrote to [his son,][484] Sulaymān b. Dāwūd b. ʿĪsā, who was his deputy in Medina, commanding him to do with the people of Medina as he had done with the people of Mecca—cast off Muḥammad and swear allegiance to ʿAbdallāh al-Maʾmūn.

As soon as he received a [favorable] reply from Medina about the swearing of allegiance [to al-Maʾmūn], Dāwūd, who was in Mecca, set out—he and a group of his children—to go to al-Maʾmūn in Marw. He went by way of al-Baṣrah, Fārs, and Kirmān. When he reached al-Maʾmūn in Marw, he told him how he had sworn allegiance to him and had cast off Muḥammad and how the people of Mecca and of Medina had hastened to do the same. Al-Maʾmūn was delighted by this. He took the fact that the people of Mecca and Medina were the first to swear allegiance to him as a good omen, and he wrote them a gentle and amiable letter, promising them good things, and raising their hopes. He ordered that a writ be drawn up appointing Dāwūd to be in charge of Mecca, Medina, and their districts—public worship, special exactions,[485] and taxes (*jibāyah*). In addition, he was given the governorship of ʿAkk.[486] Three brigades (*alwiyah*) of troops were assigned to him to deal with these. Al-Maʾmūn wrote on his behalf to al-Rayy authorizing a special grant (*maʿūnah*) of 500,000 dirhams.

Dāwūd b. ʿĪsā left in haste, journeying quickly, striving to arrive in time for the pilgrimage. With him was his nephew, al-ʿAbbās b. Mūsā b. ʿĪsā b. Mūsā b. Muḥammad b. ʿAlī b. ʿAbdallāh b. al-ʿAbbās. Al-Maʾmūn had appointed al-ʿAbbās

---

484. The bracketed words are from ed. Cairo.

485. *Maʿāwin*, pl. of *maʿūnah*, probably refers to levies for the police force. *Ṣāḥib al-maʿūnah* often means "chief of police." See Dozy, *Supplément*, II, 192.

486. ʿAkk was a tribe with territory in the Tihāmah, the coastal plain of Yemen. See *EI*[2] s.v. (Caskel).

b. Mūsā b. ʿĪsā to be in charge of the pilgrimage festival. He and his uncle Dāwūd traveled and stayed at Baghdad as guests of Ṭāhir b. al-Ḥusayn, who honored them, showed them favor, and gave them generous support. He dispatched with the two of them Yazīd b. Jarīr b. Yazīd b. Khālid b. ʿAbdallāh al-Qasrī, [864] whom Ṭāhir had appointed to be governor of Yemen, and with whom he sent a large body of horsemen. Yazīd b. Jarīr b. Yazīd b. Khālid b. ʿAbdallāh al-Qasrī guaranteed them that he would induce his family and tribesmen, the kings and nobles of the people of Yemen, to cast off Muḥammad and swear allegiance to ʿAbdallāh al-Maʾmūn. They all traveled until they reached Mecca. When the pilgrimage arrived, al-ʿAbbās b. Mūsā b. ʿĪsā led the people who came for the festival. After they had completed the pilgrimage, al-ʿAbbās returned to Ṭāhir b. al-Ḥusayn, who was besieging Muḥammad. Dāwūd b. ʿĪsā remained in his district of Mecca and Medina, and Yazīd b. Jarīr went on to Yemen. He called on its people to cast off Muḥammad and swear allegiance to ʿAbdallāh al-Maʾmūn. He read them a letter from Ṭāhir b. al-Ḥusayn, promising them justice and equity, encouraging them to obey al-Maʾmūn, and telling them of the just treatment al-Maʾmūn had extended to his subjects. The people of Yemen agreed to swear allegiance to al-Maʾmūn. They were delighted with this, swore allegiance to al-Maʾmūn, and cast off Muḥammad. Yazīd b. Jarīr b. Yazīd conducted himself very well among them, showing justice and equity. He wrote to al-Maʾmūn and to Ṭāhir b. al-Ḥusayn about their acquiescence and swearing of allegiance.

Harthamah b. Aʿyan Defeats al-Amīn's Forces

In this year, during the months of Rajab and Shaʿbān,[487] Muḥammad [al-Amīn] placed about 400 companies (*liwāʾ*) of troops under the command of various leaders and appointed ʿAlī b. Muḥammad b. ʿĪsā b. Nahīk commander over them all.[488] He commanded them to march against Harthamah b.

487. I.e., between March 18 and May 15, 812.
488. Parallels: Yaʿqūbī, II, 534–35; Ibn al-Athīr, VI, 186–87; *Fragmenta*, 332.

Aʿyan. They did so, and the two sides met at Jalultā, a few miles from al-Nahrawān, during the month of Ramaḍān.[489] Harthamah defeated them and captured ʿAlī b. Muḥammad b. ʿĪsā b. Nahīk. Harthamah sent him to al-Maʾmūn. Harthamah advanced and encamped at al-Nahrawān.

Some of Ṭāhir's Men Go over to al-Amīn

[865] In this year, a large group of men left Ṭāhir and went over to Muḥammad on a promise of safety (*amān*), and the army mutinied against Ṭāhir. Muḥammad distributed a large sum of money among Ṭāhir's men who had come to him. He appointed men to be commanders and daubed their beards with perfume.[490] People therefore called them "the perfume commanders." A report of the reason and consequences of this follows.

According to Yazīd b. al-Ḥārith, who said: Having reached [Ṣarṣar], Ṭāhir established himself by the Ṣarṣar Canal and energetically prosecuted the war against Muḥammad and the people of Baghdad. He defeated every army that came against him. But the money and clothing that Muḥammad was giving were too much for Ṭāhir's men, and about 5,000 Khurāsānians and others who joined them left his army. Muḥammad was delighted with them. He made promises to them, raised their hopes, and registered their names among [those who received pay of] eighty [dīnārs].

They continued at this for months. (Muḥammad) appointed commanders from al-Ḥarbiyyah and others—men who presented themselves and sought the position. He gave them appointments and sent them to Daskarat al-Malik[491] and al-Nahrawān. He sent to them Ḥabīb b. Jahm al-Namarī the Bedouin Arab with his forces. There was not much fighting between them

489. I.e., between May 16 and June 14, 812.

490. *Ghāliyah* was a perfume containing musk, ambergris, camphor, and oil of ben. See Lane, *Lexicon*, VI, 2289.

491. Daskarat al-Malik ("King's Daskarah," so named because of the ruins of a Sasanian palace), 16 *farsakh*s northeast of Baghdad on the Khurāsān highway, was the stage beyond Nahrawān and before Jalūlā. See Le Strange, *Lands*, 62; *EI*^{2} s.v. Daskara (Duri).

[and the enemy]. Muḥammad summoned some of the Baghdad commanders and sent them to al-Yāsiriyyah,[492] al-Kawthariyyah, and the Double [Bridge of] Boats.[493] He supplied them with food, strengthened them with pay allowances (*arzāq*), and made them a buttress for those behind them. He scattered spies among Ṭāhir's forces and smuggled letters to the heads of the army, raising their hopes, and exciting their desires, so that they mutinied against Ṭāhir. Many of them went over to Muḥammad on a promise of safety. Each group of ten had a drum; they thundered and stormed and raised a clamor. They advanced until they were close to the Ṣarṣar Canal. Ṭāhir [866]
arranged his forces in phalanxes (*karādīs*). Then he passed by each phalanx and said, "Do not let the multitude of those you see deceive you, and do not let the fact that some of them went over on a promise of safety inhibit you; for victory lies with true bravery and constancy, and conquest lies with steadfastness. 'How often a little company has overcome a numerous company, by God's leave; and God is with the steadfast'."[494] Then he commanded them to advance, and they did so. They fought the enemy with swords for a time. Then God made the people of Baghdad turn their backs; they retreated in defeat and evacuated their campsite. Ṭāhir's forces plundered all the weapons and money it contained.

When news of this reached Muḥammad, he commanded that pay (*ʿaṭā'*) [be distributed], and it was done.[495] He brought out his chests and treasuries and distributed gifts. He gathered the people of the suburbs and reviewed the men with his own eyes. Whenever he saw someone handsome and good-looking, he gave him a robe of honor and appointed him commander. Whenever he appointed someone a commander, he had the man's beard daubed with perfume. They were the ones that

492. See note 457.

493. *Al-Safīnatayn* apparently refers to the fourth bridge of boats, described as "double," that al-Amīn added to the three that already crossed the Tigris. Located downstream from the Lower Bridge, it crossed the river to a point near the palace that al-Amīn built at Kalwādhā, on the east bank. See Le Strange, *Baghdad*, 179, 296–97.

494. Qur'ān 2:249.

495. Parallels: Yaʿqūbī, II, 534; Masʿūdī, VI, 446–47.

people called "perfume commanders." To each of his new commanders he distributed 500 dirhams and a flask of perfume, but he gave nothing to the army of the commanders and their forces. When Ṭāhir's scouts and spies brought him word of this, he sent messengers and letters to the men, made them promises, and sought to win them over to his side. He set the lower ranks among them against the higher ranks. They mutinied against Muḥammad on Wednesday, the 6th of Dhū al-Ḥijjah 196 (August 18, 812). One of the *Abnā'* of the people of Baghdad said concerning this:

Say to al-Amīn, "By God Himself,
  it was only the perfume that dispersed the army."
And Ṭāhir—my soul, fear Ṭāhir,
  with his deliberateness and ample provisions!
The reins of the kingdom have come to be in his hand,
  while he fights the company who commit injustice.
[867] O perfidious one, delivered [to destruction] by your own perfidy,
  the disgrace of your wickedness has been revealed.
The chief lion has come upon you with his assaults,
  raging, among ravenous lions.
Flee! But there is no place of refuge from one like him,
  except to the Fire [of Hell] or the Pit.

When the army mutinied and matters became difficult for Muḥammad, he consulted his commanders. He was told, "Make amends to the men, and correct your affairs; for in them is the stay of your kingdom. It was they, after God, who took it away from you in the days of al-Ḥusayn [b. ʿAlī b. ʿĪsā]; it was they who returned it to you; and you have learned their valor and bravery." But he was stubborn about them and commanded that they should be fought. He sent al-Tanūkhī to deal with them, along with others of those who had come over on a promise of safety (*musta'minah*) and soldiers who were on his side, and the latter hastened to fight the men. Ṭāhir sent the men messages, and they sent messages to him. He took [persons who were] their pledges for obedience to him and wrote to the men. He gave them a guarantee of safety (*amān*) and bestowed money on them generously. On Tuesday, the 12th of Dhū al-Ḥijjah (August 25, 812), Ṭāhir advanced as far as the garden at the foot of al-Anbār Gate.[496] He encamped at the garden with his commanders, soldiers, and forces. Muḥammad's commanders and soldiers who had joined Ṭāhir on a guarantee of safety also encamped in the garden and in the suburbs. He increased the pay (*arzāq*) of all of them to eighty [dīnārs], doubled the special bonuses (*khawāṣṣ*) for commanders and the sons of commanders, and caused the money to be paid regularly to them and many of their men.

The prisoners breached the prisons and came out. There was civil disorder. Rogues and scoundrels (*al-duʿʿār wa'l-shuṭṭār*) assaulted decent people. Sinners became powerful, believers were humiliated, and decent people were disturbed. Conditions among the people deteriorated, except for those who were in Ṭāhir's camp, for he kept check on the situation, restrained unruly and immoral people, and was severe with them. He went out to fight both early and late, until the two sides grew sluggish and populated areas became ruinous.

In this year, al-ʿAbbās b. Mūsā b. ʿĪsā b. Mūsā b. Muḥammad [868]
b. ʿAlī led the pilgrimage on behalf of Ṭāhir. He mentioned al-Ma'mūn as caliph in the prayers. This was the first pilgrimage festival at which prayers were offered for him as caliph at Mecca and Medina.

---

496. Ṭāhir's position was to the northwest of the city, outside the suburb of al-Ḥarbiyyah, and controlling the main road that, leaving the Round City through the Syrian Gate, went west to the city of al-Anbār. The al-Anbār Gate (*Bāb al-Anbār*) was located where this road crossed the canal known as the Trench of Ṭāhir, approximately 1 mile west of the Syrian Gate. See Le Strange, *Baghdad*, 110–11.

The Events of the Year 197

(September 12, 812–August 31, 813)

In this year, al-Qāsim b. Hārūn al-Rashīd and Manṣūr b. al-Mahdī joined al-Ma'mūn from Iraq. Al-Ma'mūn sent al-Qāsim to Jurjān. Also in this year, Ṭāhir, Harthamah, and Zuhayr b. al-Musayyab besieged Muḥammad b. Hārūn in Baghdad.[497]

Details and Results of the Siege of Baghdad

According to Muḥammad b. Yazīd al-Tamīmī and others: Zuhayr b. al-Musayyab al-Ḍabbī encamped at the Palace of Raqqat Kalwādhā.[498] He set up siege engines—*manjanīqs* and *'arrādahs*[499]—and dug ditches. He would go out during

497. Parallels: Ya'qūbī, II, 535; Mas'ūdī, VI, 447–72; Ibn al-Athīr, VI, 188–94; *Fragmenta*, 332–34.

498. This palace (the name means "the palace of the plain or marsh of Kalwādhā") was built by al-Amīn on the east bank of the Tigris, near the town of Kalwādhā, about 6 miles south of the Lower Bridge of Baghdad. See Le Strange, *Baghdad*, 295, 307.

499. The *manjanīq* and the *'arrādah* were stone-hurling machines of the traction trebuchet type. An asymmetrically positioned beam was rotated swiftly around a fulcrum by several men pulling ropes attached to the beam's shorter end. The projectile was attached to a sling on the beam's longer end. The *manjanīq* was the larger machine, with two trestles supporting a horizontal

the days, when the army was occupied with the fight against Ṭāhir, and with the *ʿarrādah*s would shoot at people who were coming and going. He collected a tithe on merchants' money, taxed boats, and harassed the people greatly. What he was doing was reported to Ṭāhir: the people came and complained to him of what had befallen them at the hands of Zuhayr b. al-Musayyab. Word of this also reached Harthamah. (Ṭāhir) reinforced him[500] with soldiers, for he had almost been taken. The troops then desisted from [attacking] him.

An anonymous poet from the East Bank said concerning Zuhayr and how he killed people with *manjanīq*s:[501]

Do not come near the *manjanīq* and the stones.
You saw this slain man, how he was buried:
He went out early, that no news might escape him; [869]
he came back a slain man and left the news behind!
What energy he had,
and what bodily health when he went out early!
He did not want it to be said, "There took place involving so-and-so
some affair," while he did not know who had commanded it.[502]
O master of the *manjanīq*, what have your hands wrought?
They have not spared or left alone.[503]
His desire was other than what was decreed:
Alas, desire will never overcome fate!

Harthamah encamped at the Bīn Canal, surrounded himself with a wall and a ditch, and set up *manjanīq*s and *ʿarrādah*s.

---

beam that served as fulcrum for the arm. In the *ʿarrādah*, a single upright with a U-shaped socket attached to its upper end supported the arm. I am indebted to an unpublished paper by Dr. Paul Chevedden for details about the operation of the two engines. See also *EI*² s.vv. ʿArrāda (Cahen) and Mandjanīḳ (Hill).

500. The reference appears to be to Harthamah—cf. the incident narrated on pp. 164 ff., below.

501. Masʿūdī, VI, 454, quotes six lines with variants and identifies the author as the blind poet ʿAlī b. Abī Ṭālib.

502. The line puns on two words from the same root: *amr*, affair, and *amara*, he commanded.

503. Cf. Qurʾān 74:28.

He had ʿUbaydallāh b. al-Waḍḍāḥ encamp at al-Shammāsiyyah. Ṭāhir encamped at the garden by al-Anbār Gate.

According to al-Ḥusayn al-Khalīʿ,[504] who said: When Ṭāhir took possession of the garden at al-Anbār Gate, Muḥammad felt very afraid that he would enter Baghdad. He distributed whatever money he had at hand. Distressed and with burning heart, he commanded that whatever property was in the storerooms should be sold and that the gold and silver vessels should be minted into dīnārs and dirhams; these were to be brought to him for his forces and expenses. It was at this time that he commanded that al-Ḥarbiyyah should be bombarded with naphtha and fire and by *manjanīq*s and *ʿarrādah*s; people coming and going there were killed as a result of them. Concerning this, ʿAmr b. ʿAbd al-Malik al-ʿItrī al-Warrāq[505] said:

[870] O shooters of the *manjanīq*,
all of you are without compassion.
You do not care whether one is a friend,
or is not a friend.
Alas, do you know what you are shooting?
Passers-by on the road!
Many a tender girl, flirtatious,
like a leafy bough,
Was expelled from her world
and from a goodly life.
She found no way to avoid it:
she was forced into public view on the day of the fire.

According to Muḥammad b. Manṣūr al-Bāwardī, who said: After Ṭāhir's strength had become too strong for Muḥammad, so that the latter's troops were defeated and his commanders scattered, one of those who went over to Ṭāhir on a promise of safety was Saʿīd b. Mālik b. Qādim. He joined Ṭāhir, and the latter put him in charge of the district of al-Baghiyyīn[506] and

---

504. See note 512.

505. Further information about ʿAmr b. ʿAbd al-Malik al-Warrāq in Sezgin, *GAS*, II, 524. Masʿūdī, VI, 455, ascribes the verses (with an additional fifth verse) to the blind poet ʿAlī b. Abī Ṭālib.

506. Al-Baghiyyīn district was on the west bank of the Tigris, at the foot of the Upper Bridge, north and east of al-Ḥarbiyyah. See Le Strange, *Baghdad*, 108.

the markets there, and the bank of the Tigris, with what adjoins it and faces it, up to the Tigris bridges. He commanded him to dig trenches and build walls in all the [areas of] houses and streets he took. He provided him with money, workers, and weapons. He commanded [the people of] al-Ḥarbiyyah to accompany him on patrols. He assigned someone to Dār al-Raqīq[507] Road and someone to the Syrian Gate, giving orders similar to those he had given to Saʿīd b. Mālik. There was so much ruin and destruction that the beauties of Baghdad were effaced. Concerning this, al-ʿItrī says:[508]

Who has smitten you, Baghdad, with the [evil] eye? [871]
 Were you not for a long time the delight of the eye?
Were there not in you people whose dwelling
 and whose friendship were a great adornment?
The raven[509] cried to them of departure, so they separated.
 Oh the pain of departure I felt because of them!
I commend to God people whom I never remember
 but that tears flow from my eye.
They once were; then a fate separated and dispersed them:
 for fate it is that separates the two sides.

Muḥammad [al-Amīn] assigned ʿAlī Farāhmard, along with the fighters (*muqātilah*) he joined to him, to the Palace of Ṣāliḥ (*Qaṣr Ṣāliḥ*) and the Palace of Sulaymān b. Abī Jaʿfar,[510] up to the palaces of the Tigris and adjoining areas. He diligently burned houses and streets and destroyed them with *manjanīq*s and *ʿarrādah*s at the hands of a man who was known as al-Samarqandī, who used to shoot with the *manjanīq*. Ṭāhir

507. Dār al-Raqīq ("Slaves' House") was not far from the Upper Bridge, off the main road between al-Baghiyyīn and al-Ḥarbiyyah. It originally was a barracks for slaves brought from the Turkish borderlands to serve in the caliphal household. See Le Strange, *Baghdad*, 123. Gabrieli, "La successione di Hārūn ar-Rašīd," 382 (note 1) discusses this front of the siege.

508. For more lines of the poem, see pp. 213–14, below. Masʿūdī, VI, 456, quotes the poem with variants.

509. In Arabic poetry, the raven is a harbinger of separation.

510. The Palace of Prince Ṣāliḥ (*Qaṣr Ṣāliḥ*) and the Palace of Prince Sulaymān (*Qaṣr Sulaymān*), named after sons of the caliph Manṣūr, were located on the west bank of the Tigris not far upstream from the Main Bridge, which carried the Khurāsān Road across the river. See Le Strange, *Baghdad*, 108.

acted similarly. He sent messages to the people of the suburbs—al-Anbār Road, al-Kūfah Gate, and adjoining areas. Whenever the people of an area yielded to him,[511] he dug a trench around them and positioned his garrisons and banners. If any people refused to yield and become obedient to him, he opened hostilities, fought them, and burned their houses. Thus he came
[872] and went with his commanders, horsemen, and foot soldiers, until Baghdad became desolate, and people feared that it would remain a ruin. Concerning this, al-Ḥusayn al-Khalīʿ says:[512]

Are the men hurrying with rapid pace
  from both sides of Baghdad, or what is it?
Have you not seen how strife has joined
  to men of strife men who are strangers [to strife].[513]
Baghdad—its buildings have been pulled to pieces,
  according to the decision of neither that man nor this one.
By destruction and fire her people have been annihilated;
  a punishment has encompassed whoever sought refuge.
How good time's changes will be, if *Baghdād*,
  for lack of people, does not again become *Baghdādh*![514]

Ṭāhir gave the name "Abode of Promise-Breaking"[515] to the suburbs whose inhabitants disobeyed him, the eastern City of

---

511. Variant in Ibn al-Athīr, VI, 189: "assailed him."

512. The poet al-Ḥusayn b. al-Ḍaḥḥāk, called al-Khalīʿ ("the Profligate") or al-Ashqar ("the Blond"), was a courtier of al-Amīn. The first of these nicknames seems to have been acquired through feats of wine drinking. See *Aghānī*, VI, 170ff., for a biography; also Sezgin, *GAS*, II, 518–19; *EI*[2] s.v. (Pellat).

513. *Shudhdhādh*, here rendered "strangers," can have a variety of meanings derived from a basic meaning of "to be apart, to fall out of the common mass of things." It sometimes means "deviant." See Lane, *Lexicon*, s.v. I read the verb in the line as active, rather than passive as vocalized by ed. Leiden. The meaning seems to be that the fighting has affected not only those normally affected by war—soldiers—but also those who should be strangers to it—either irregular troops or civilian casualties.

514. That is, if the city whose Arabic name is *Baghdād* does not return to bearing the name of the Persian village *Baghdādh* that occupied the site before the caliph al-Manṣūr constructed his capital. Ed. Leiden, *Addenda*, DCCLXVI, lists other Arabic authors who note (and condemn) the pronunciation *Baghdādh* as "pagan" and "non-Arab."

515. *Dār al-Nakth*: Cf. the expression *Dār al-Ḥarb* ("Abode of War") used to designate territory occupied by people who resisted the advance of Islam and rejected its call, thereby becoming legitimate objects of war.

Abū Jaʿfar,[516] and the markets of al-Karkh[517] and al-Khuld[518] and adjacent areas. He seized the estates and commercial properties (*ghallāt*) of any members of the Hāshimī family, military commanders, and *mawālī* who did not come out promptly to him, wherever these properties were to be found in the area under his control; so they became submissive, broken in spirit, and obedient. [On al-Amīn's side,] the soldiers became submissive and too sluggish to fight—except for the street vendors, naked ones, people from the prisons, riffraff, rabble, cutpurses, and people of the market, to whom Ḥātim b. al-Ṣaqr had given permission to plunder.[519] Al-Hirsh[520] and the Africans (*Afāriqah*) went forth; Ṭāhir fought them without letup, without wearying, [873]
and without tiring. Mentioning Baghdad, and describing what took place in it, al-Khuraymī said:[521]

They said, when Time had not yet made sport with Baghdad,
 when her misfortunes had not yet caused her to fall;
When she was like a bride, whose hidden part[522]
 was as enticing to the young man as her visible part:

516. Perhaps the text should be corrected to "the City of Abū Jaʿfar *and* al-Sharqiyyah." Al-Sharqiyyah was a suburb southeast of the Round City. See Le Strange, *Baghdad*, 188.

517. Al-Karkh was the quarter located to the southwest of the Round City. It became the market center for the entire city. See Le Strange, *Baghdad*, 65–68.

518. I.e., the markets near al-Khuld Palace, to the east of the Round City, near the foot of the Main Bridge. See Le Strange, *Baghdad*, 101–2.

519. Naked ones (*ʿurāh*): the word can mean unclothed or unarmed (see Dozy, *Supplément*, II, 123)—either paupers who fought in their rags or people who fought with makeshift weapons. The accounts of al-Amīn's irregulars use a colorful vocabulary—*ʿurāh* (naked ones), *awbāsh* (riffraff), *riʿāʿ* (rabble), *ghawghāʾ* (mob), *ṭarrārūn* (cutpurses), and *ʿayyārūn* (vagrants). Masʿūdī, VI, 452–53, gives a detailed description of them. Cf. Gabrieli, "La successione di Hārūn ar-Rašīd," 383–84; Kennedy, *Early Abbasid Caliphate*, 145–46.

520. For the identity of al-Ḥasan al-Hirsh, a leader of irregular troops, see *Fragmenta*, 412 note b [Leiden note].

521. The text of this 135-verse poem was badly preserved in the manuscript available to the Leiden editor: not only did many places require emendation, but there were a number of lacunae. In many of these places the Cairo edition is superior. The text may also be found in the modern *Dīwān*, 27–37 (poem number 24), which is based on the text from Ṭabarī.

522. The Cairo reading (*bāṭinuhā*, "her hidden part") is logically and grammatically preferable to the conjectural Leiden reading (*bādiyuhā*, "her apparent part").

"A paradise on earth![523] The abode of happiness!"
    Of distressing calamities there were few.
The world's breasts yielded abundantly to her inhabitants;
    there were few of them who were debtors or creditors.
Her residents enjoyed a life of ease;
    they pastured there on her pleasures.
Her people were in a pleasing garden,
    whose flowers shone brightly after the raindrops.[524]
[They were] people whom a life in pleasure and ease beguiled—
    if only the prosperous places of this world endured!
It was the abode of kings whose foundations were anchored
    there, and whose pulpits were established in it:
People of eminence and wealth,[525] epitomes
    of glory,[526] if one were to count their exploits;
Fortune's favorites,[527] in the inheritance of a kingdom
    whose stays were tied firmly by its elders.
But then—time is full of change—
    their younger successors kept injuring their kingdom,
Until they gave each other an intoxicating cup to drink
    of strife whose destructiveness cannot be told.
Once there had been fellowship, but now they separated into parties,
    with the bonds between them severed.
Have you seen the kings, what they did
    when no rebuker restrained them with counsel?
Our kings made themselves fall
    into a pit of perdition from which they could not emerge.
How would it have harmed them if they had fulfilled their pact,
    and if their zeal for righteousness had been strong;
[874] If they had not competed to shed the blood of their partisans,

---

523. Ed. Cairo: "A paradise of immortality (*khuld*)," with a pun on al-Khuld Palace.

524. The translation follows ed. Cairo.

525. Ed. Cairo: "eminence and generosity"—reading *nadā* instead of ed. Leiden's *tharā*.

526. Literally, "gathering places of glory," i.e., people in whom all titles to glory came together, as if assembling in a "club" (*nādī*).

527. Literally, "the chicks of happiness" (*afrākhu nuʿmā*)—happiness being compared to a hen nurturing its brood.

and sent out[528] warriors to contend for superiority against each other;
And if the goods of this world that had been gathered for them had satisfied them?
But the soul's voraciousness harms the soul!
The pool of the kings—they kept digging it,
those of them who were filled with desire and those who filled them [with it].[529]
They kept desiring[530] the luxuries of this world, seeking to surpass each other,
until their treasures were plundered by force.
They kept selling what the fathers had gathered
for the sons—may their traffickings bring no profit!
Have you seen the gardens in flower,
when their blossoms delight the eye of the beholder?
Have you seen the palaces rising into view,
their chambers concealing women like statues?
Have you seen the villages the kings have planted,
when their fields are green,
Surrounded by vineyards, palm trees,
and fragrant herbs from which their birds take seeds?[531]
Now they have become devoid of
people. Their gardens[532] have been defiled with blood—
Desolate and empty! Dogs howl in them.
He who visits[533] them does not recognize the vestiges of them.
Now misery never leaves them;
it is their companion, while joy has forsaken them.

528. The translation follows ed. Cairo (*tabta'ith fityatan*).

529. That is, both kings and their counselors dug a pit for themselves.

530. The translation follows ed. Cairo (*tabghī*), rather than ed. Leiden (*tubqī*), "preserving."

531. The translation follows ed. Cairo for the second part of this line. The copyist of the manuscript used for ed. Leiden replaced the line's second hemistich with the corresponding hemistich of the following line.

532. A double meaning is involved: *maḥājir* means both "enclosed gardens" and "cheeks."

533. The translation follows ed. Cairo (*zā'iruhā*).

At Zandaward[534] and al-Yāsiriyyah,[535]
    and on the two river banks, where the ferries have ceased,
At the mills[536] and Upper al-Khayzurāniyyah,[537]
    whose bridges were lofty,
And at the Palace of ʿAbdūyah, there is a lesson and guidance
    for every soul whose inner thoughts have become pure.
Where are their guards,[538] and where is their guardian?
    Where is he upon whom benefits were bestowed, and where is their bestower?
Where are their eunuchs and their servants?
    Where are their inhabitants and their builder?
Where have the Slavic *al-Jarādiyyah*[539] guards gone,
    and the Abyssinians, with their pendulous lips?
[875] The army disperses from its parades;
    its lean [horses] run there at random—
Carrying men from Sind and India, Slavs,
    and Nubians with whom Berbers have been mixed—
Like birds in flights,[540] they have been sent forth to no avail,
    their fair-skinned troops preceding their blacks.
Where are the virgin gazelles in the garden
    of the kingdom—the young ones who walked so gracefully?
Where are their comforts and their pleasures?

---

534. At Zandaward, on the east bank of the Tigris, south of Baghdad, there was a monastery famous for its orchards. See Le Strange, *Baghdad*, 210–11.

535. See note 457.

536. The conjectured reading *bi'l-ruḥiyyi* is metrically difficult, and the manuscripts have *ya t.r.l.ḥ.y*, which makes no sense. The mills might be Ruḥā al-Baṭrīq, "the Patrician's Mill," a large grain milling complex at the southern end of a very fertile tract of land west of the city. See Le Strange, *Baghdad*, 142–44.

537. Al-Khayzurāniyyah, named for the wife of the caliph al-Mahdī, was north of Ruṣāfah on the east bank of the Tigris and contained a cemetery where the imām Abū Ḥanīfah was buried. See Le Strange, *Baghdad*, 190–92.

538. Instead of *ḥurrās*, "guards," I conjecture an original reading of *maḥrūs*, "the one who is guarded." This would make the first hemistich parallel in construction with the second.

539. The Jarādiyyah corps of guards may have been given this name in reference to the pale color of the locust (*jarād*) or to a species of falcon (*ṣaqr al-jarād* or *al-jarādī*). See ed. Leiden, *Glossarium*, CLXII; also the explanation given on p. 225, below.)

540. The unusual word *abābīl* echoes Qur'ān 105:3, a passage evoking the flight of an army.

Where are they who were adorned, and he who adorned them?
With musk, Yemeni ambergris,
and aloes wood their censers were kindled.
They glided in silk, in garments saffron-colored and embroidered, with their lyres strung.
Where is their dancer and their piper,
to whom they responded until their throats were tired?
People's ears were utterly captivated,
when their flutes vied with their lutes.
Now it has become as empty as the belly of a wild ass,[541]
and he who burns it burns it with blazing fire.
One would think that in their courts had dwelt
the people of ʿĀd,[542] and that roaring winds had smitten them.
No soul knows what will assail it by night—
what accident of Fortune—or what will come upon it in the morning.
Morning and evening it is a target and a butt,
wherever its inclination leads it,
For the arrows that Fortune shoots—
those that draw blood and those that rip open.
Oh the misfortune of Baghdad, the capital of a kingdom
whose calamities have fallen on its people!
God granted her a respite; then he punished her,
when her grievous sins encompassed her,
With leveling to the ground, bombardment, and fire,
and with war that came to assail her.

---

541. The comparison of a deserted place to the belly of a wild ass goes back to pre-Islamic poetry, e.g., verse 49 of the *Muʿallaqah* of Imru al-Qays. Commentators gave various explanations: that the wild ass is an emblem of poverty because it finds little fodder, that it is useless because it cannot be ridden or milked, or that there was a desert place named *Jawf al-Ḥimār* ("Ḥimār's Hollow") whose inhabitant, a man named *Ḥimār* ("Ass"), was punished by God.

542. The people of ʿĀd are mentioned in the Qurʾān. They were people of old, perhaps giants, and builders of buildings still to be seen. The prophet Hūd was sent to them to warn them to mend their ways, but they disbelieved and were destroyed by a wind that below for seven nights and days. See Bell, *Introduction to the Qurʾān*, 127–28; Qurʾān, Suras 7, 11, 26, 46, 54, and 69.

[876] How many transgressions have we seen in Baghdad!
Will the Lord of Majesty forgive her?[543]
Upon Baghdad, while she was at peace, descended
a disaster she had not anticipated.
Evil rose over her from its places of rising,
and her people were overtaken by their offenses.
Religion was weak in her: there was no respect
for the virtuous, and her unrighteous overpowered the devout.
The slave humiliated his master,
and her freeborn[544] were enslaved.
He who was most wicked became lord of his neighbors,
and robbers gained control over the gates of the streets.
He who has seen Baghdad, with the armies by it,
with the soldiers having thrown a cordon around it,
With many a numerous troop, well armed and courageous,
their shrieks causing unborn babes to be aborted,
Throwing its gentle girls into the perdition of death,
with Ṭāhir bearing down to attack it,
With the "shaykh"[545] passing with his troops collected,
sending forward their rear, attacking by turns,
While Zuhayr at al-Firk[546] has a band of lions—
distinguished ones, who bear up under adversity—
Squadrons of death, under banners
whose victor and helpers bring trouble:
[He who has seen these things] knows that things foreordained
must surely take place as their Ordainer desires.
Behold Baghdad! No nest is built
in its houses by its sparrows from bewilderment.
Behold it surrounded by destruction, encircled
with humiliation, its proud men besieged.

---

543. The translation of the second hemistich follows ed. Cairo. The manuscript used by ed. Leiden was illegible at this point.

544. Following ed. Cairo; ed. Leiden reads, "her women living in seclusion."

545. The reference is unclear. Perhaps one of the leaders of street gangs or irregular troops is intended.

546. Following ed. Cairo: al-Firk was a village near Kalwādhā on the east bank of the Tigris south of Baghdad (Yāqūt, *Muʿjam*). Ed. Leiden has *bi-l-qawli* ("according to report"), a *lectio facilior.* On Zuhayr b. al-Musayyab's encampment near Kalwādhā, see p. 134, above.

From the shore of the Euphrates up to
the Tigris, where its ferries have stopped,
Fire, like the neck of a red-maned horse, stampedes, [877]
while its ruddy ones gallop around it.[547]
This one burns [the city], and that one demolishes it;
and the scoundrel (*shāṭir*) sates himself with plunder.
The markets of al-Karkh are deserted;
its vagrant (*ʿayyār*) and wayward prance about.[548]
From the vilest of her men war has brought forth
mighty lions from their lairs to assail them.
Their shields are of reed mats;
their neck protectors,[549] when they put them on, are of palm leaves.
Early to the battle in their coats of mail
made of wool, when their "horsemen" are numbered,[550]
Go the battalions of al-Hirsh, under whose banner
the cutpurse aids the gambler.
They get neither pay (*rizq*) nor salary (*ʿaṭāʾ*),
nor does their gatherer assemble them for the encounter.[551]
In every gated street and on every side
there is a siege engine[552] whose moving beam[553] raises its voice.

---

547. The text of this verse is corrupt in the two available manuscripts. The Leiden editor marks the line "*non certum*." The Cairo text is metrically possible, but incomprehensible. The *Dīwān*, 32, restores the line based on a quotation in *Muḥāḍarāt al-Udabāʾ* by Rāghib al-Iṣfahānī. Its reading (*nārun ka-hādi l-shaqrāʾi nāfiratun*) turns the line into a striking metaphor based on the fact that the adjective *ashqar* ("ruddy") is applied both to horses with red manes and to fire (cf. Lane, *Lexicon*, s.v.).

548. This and the next two verses are quoted in Masʿūdī, VI, 462.

549. The *mighfar* was a piece of fine mail worn under the helmet and extending downward to cover the shoulders. See Lane, *Lexicon*, s.v.

550. That these are not regular troops is emphasized by describing their makeshift armor: shields made of reed mats, neck protectors made of palm leaves, and armor made of wool. The word used for "horsemen" (*asāwir*, pl. of *iswār*) normally refers to heavily armored Persian cavalrymen and may be ironic, as these irregulars had no war horses.

551. Variant: "with difficulty."

552. The word used, *khaṭṭārah*, is derived from the verb *khaṭara*, "it (an animal) lashed its tail up and down or from side to side." The seesaw action of the beam of the *manjanīq* suggested the name, which was also given to a rotating-beam irrigation machine. See ed. Leiden, *Glossarium*, CCXXVI; Lane, *Lexicon*, s.v.; Dozy, *Supplément*, I, 382.

With [projectiles] like men's heads [taken] from pieces
of stone the evil man loads the sling.
It is as if over their heads there were flocks
of dusky sand grouse taking flight in commotion.[554]
The shouts of the men come from beneath them,
while the swinging beams hurl [their missiles].
Have you seen the unsheathed swords
that men are brandishing in the markets?
Horses are prancing in its lanes,
carrying Turks with sharpened daggers.
Naphtha and fire are in its roads;
its inhabitants are fleeing because of the smoke.
[878] Men run carrying plunder,
while the city's wellborn women have exposed their ankle bracelets,[555]
Having gathered in the lanes:
their Concealer[556] has caused them to emerge into view.
Each is a woman who used to lie abed until midmorning, concealed from view,
her visage not visible among her family.
The hidden damsel of the curtained chamber has emerged
into public with her hair loose.
She trips over her gown; urging her to haste
is a charge of horses whose hooves are being spurred on.
Distraught, she asks where the way is;
behind her the flames strive to reach her.
The sun has never unveiled her fair beauty,
but now war has unveiled her to touch her.
Have you seen the woman bereft of her child, wailing
in the streets, running, overcome by fatigue,

---

553. The Leiden glossary suggests that the participle *khāṭir* is used to describe the operator of the *manjanīq*: "and its operator raises his voice." It is more likely that the term describes the beam of the machine and that the line refers to the sound it makes as it is fired.

554. The stones flung by the *manjanīq* are like the swift flight of flocks of desert sand grouse (*qaṭā*).

555. That is, as they run, their ankle bracelets become visible.

556. *Sātir*, the Concealer or Protector, is an epithet for God. A woman in danger of being seen in a state of undress would call out, "*yā Sātir!*" See Dozy, *Supplément*, I, 633.

Following a bier on which her only son,
in his breast a spear wound, assails her [with grief]?
Wide [the wound]: its spacious place purges away dishonor;
he that pierced it shook it with the head of the spear.[557]
She looks at his face and cries of
bereavement, while a flood of tears covers her.
The breath rattled in his throat, then he gave up the ghost,
slain for naught, with no avenger to be feared.
I have seen the young men on the field
of battle, their noses defiled in the dust.
Each was a young man who defended those he was honor-bound to protect:
kindlers of strife experienced distress in the fray because of him.
The dogs have spent the night by him, mangling him,
their claws stained with blood.
Have you not seen the horses wheeling round
with the men, their hindquarters wounded?
The horses trip over the handsome faces
of the dead, and the skin around their hooves is smeared with blood.
They trample the livers of courageous young men,
and their hooves split their skulls.
Have you not seen the women under the *manjanīq*s,
striving with each other in running, their hair dissheveled:
Noble women, aged women, [879]
and middle-aged spinsters; the young girls among them have had no experience?[558]

557. The text is uncertain and its meaning unclear to me. For ed. Leiden's *murīduhā* ("its desirer"), which is metrically impossible, ed. Cairo reads *mirbaduhā* ("its spacious place"), which is metrically possible but problematic in meaning. The line may describe the wound of the only son referred to in the previous verse. The Leiden editor's suggested emendation for the first hemistich, *tulqī n-nuthāra min yadiha*, "she (the distraught mother) scatters coins from her hand," hardly seems appropriate, even if such a funeral custom existed. In any case, the vocabulary of the line points to a context of spears and wounds. For the possibility of a spear's metaphorically "desiring" to make a wound, see Lane, *Lexicon*, III, 1184.

558. The text and meaning of the second hemistich are uncertain. The reading of ed. Leiden, *lam tukhayyar* ("have not been chosen") is impossible on metrical

They carry food made of flour on their
shoulders, their headcloths bound tightly.
Both she who lived in poverty and she who was wealthy:
a stone crushes the head now of one, now of the other.
One asks about her family, having been despoiled;
even the rag on her head has been stripped away.
Would that I knew[559]—for fortune is full of changes,
some desirable, and others whose occurrence is to be feared—
Will our land ever again be rich as once it was,
now that its events have brought us to this end?
Who will deliver to Dhū al-Ri'āsatayn
messages whose author has occupied himself with good counsel?—
That the best of rulers men have ever known,
when their noble qualities are enumerated,
Is God's caliph among mankind, al-Ma'mūn,
their rescuer[560] and restorer.
Toward him have aspired the hopes of his nation
submissively, both the righteous and the sinner.
They expect an abundant rain of justice from his indications,
and the evidences of them reveal godliness.
They have praised policy on your part which has removed doubt,
and other policy whose justifications are sound.[561]
They have joined together in obedience, through your gentleness,
to al-Ma'mūn, those in the highlands and those in the lowlands.
You [Dhū al-Ri'āsatayn] are his ear among mankind,

grounds. Ed. Cairo reads *lam tuḥtabar*, a form not attested in the dictionaries. Perhaps one should read *lam takhtabir*, which is what I have translated.

559. The translation follows ed. Cairo, *yā layta shiʿrī*, rather than the emendation proposed by Leiden to make sense of an unintelligible manuscript reading.

560. The reading of ed. Cairo (*muntāshuhā*, "their rescuer, savior [from destruction]) is superior to that of ed. Leiden (*sā'isuhā*, "their manager, governor").

561. The parallelism of the line implies that the first "policy" or "behavior" (*sīrah*) refers to benefits bestowed, whereas the second reference is to punishments imposed. For this use of *maʿdhirah* ("justification, excuse") to refer to heavy-handed actions, see Lane, *Lexicon*, V, 1984.

and an eye whose sight never weakens;
So give thanks to Him who is Enthroned for the favor of His blessing:
whoever is thankful for favor becomes deserving of even more favor.[562]
Be on guard—ransom for you be your subjects
and the armies, both those who are commanded in them and those who command.
Do not bring yourself into deep waters
from which no one can emerge by skill.
Keep to the shallow water; do not embark upon
the deep when its floods are in tumult.
Moderation! The road is full of branchings:
the most unlucky of them are those where [feet sink into] soft sand and that deviate.
You are now in a nation [880]
whose latter-day [rulers] have departed from the guidance of its earliest [rulers].
But you are its skilled manager and guide:
will you compel it to the right?
Chastise men whose behavior you have seen,
who by their actions have violated the ordinance of the Book;
And extend to the people the hand of mercy,
thereby rendering them free from want.
You are in a position to act with justice, for that is your intent,
and destiny agrees with its extension.
People have seen that toward which their faces turn,
and its best men have been made to rule the nation.
Our[563] necks are turned toward you,
whenever the nobles of the tribes assemble.
How many sincere counsels we have for you,
for the sake of God and kinship whose props are strong!—
And a claim whose bonds have drawn [me] close
to you, and another one—do you remember it?

---

562. The repetition of *faḍl* ("favor") in each hemistich evokes the name of al-Faḍl b. Sahl ("Dhū al-Riʾāsatayn").

563. Ed. Cairo reads, "its," i.e., the nation's.

Men's striving for knowledge causes them to make requests;
both those of them who travel in the evening and those who travel in the morning hasten.[564]
Receive something [viz. a poem] bright as a mirror:
as it travels it will not become lost in any country.[565]
I have not composed it from greed or insolence:
every soul is subject to the command of its ruling passion.
God has caused it to travel bringing sincere advice
and reverence; and its strands have been tightly woven.
It has come to you to relate matters to you,
as one might unroll a merchant's bolt of cloth.
I have caused it to be conveyed by a friend who is trustworthy,
one who, because of admiration for it, will continually recite it.

The Battle at Qaṣr Ṣāliḥ

In this year, those who had been put in charge of Qaṣr Ṣāliḥ (the Palace of Ṣāliḥ) by Muḥammad [al-Amīn] went over [to Ṭāhir] on a promise of safety. In this year the battle that went against Ṭāhir's forces at Qaṣr Ṣāliḥ took place. The account of this battle follows.

According to Muḥammad b. al-Ḥusayn b. Muṣʿab: Ṭāhir
[881] continued to vie in endurance with Muḥammad and his army, as I have described, until the people of Baghdad grew weary of fighting him. ʿAlī Farāhmard, who had been assigned to the Palaces of Ṣāliḥ and Sulaymān b. Abī Jaʿfar by Muḥammad [al-Amīn], wrote to Ṭāhir, asking him for a promise of safety, and guaranteeing him that he would give him what was in his possession from that area to the bridges, including the *manjanīq*s and *ʿarrādah*s that were there. (Ṭāhir) accepted this from him and responded favorably to his request. By night he sent to him[566] Abū al-ʿAbbās Yūsuf b. Yaʿqūb al-Bādhaghīsī,

564. The sense is not clear. I vocalize the last word of the first hemistich as *muṭlibuhum*, following Lane, *Lexicon*, V, 1846.

565. The idea may be that the fame of the poem will spread far and wide, reaching all lands.

566. Possibly "to the palace"; the Arabic is ambiguous.

the commander of his police, along with those of his commanders and valiant horsemen whom he had joined to the latter. On the eve of Saturday, the middle day of Jumādā II of the year 197,[567] (ʿAlī Farāhmard) handed over everything that Muḥammad had put him in charge of. Muḥammad b. ʿĪsā [b. Nahīk], Muḥammad's chief of police, also asked for a promise of safety from [Ṭāhir]. He had been fighting along with the Africans (*Afāriqah*), men from the prisons, and rabble (*awbāsh*). Muḥammad b. ʿĪsā had not been in any way insincere in regard to Muḥammad and was redoubtable in war. When these two went over to Ṭāhir on a promise of safety, Muḥammad was on the brink of destruction. So disquieted that he could not remain at rest, he resigned himself [to his fate] and went to the gate of [the palace of] Umm Jaʿfar[568] to await what would happen. Irregulars (*ghuwāt*) consisting of vagrants (*ʿayyārūn*), street vendors, and soldiers came, and the two sides fought each other inside and outside Qaṣr Ṣāliḥ until the day became advanced.

Abū al-ʿAbbās Yūsuf b. Yaʿqūb al-Bādhaghīsī was killed inside Qaṣr [Ṣāliḥ], along with the important commanders and chiefs who were with him. Farāhmard and his forces fought outside Qaṣr [Ṣāliḥ], until he was defeated and withdrew to Ṭāhir. No battle before or after was more difficult for Ṭāhir's forces than this one; none resulted in more dead, injured, and [882]
disabled among Ṭāhir's forces than this battle. The factions[569] composed a great deal of poetry about it, mentioning the intense fighting that occurred in the war. The mob (*ghawghāʾ*) and

567. According to Wüstenfeld-Mahler, the middle day of Jumādā II (the 14th day of a month of twenty-nine days) in 197 fell on Sunday, February 14, 813. Possibly, the previous thirty-day month was ended a day early, so that the 14th fell on Saturday, February 13. In any case, ʿAlī Farāhmard surrendered during the night between Friday and Saturday.

568. This palace, named after al-Amīn's mother, Zubaydah ("Umm Jaʿfar"), was also called al-Qarār Palace. It was on the west bank of the Tigris, about half a mile south of al-Khuld Palace, between the Main Bridge and the Lower Bridge. See Le Strange, *Baghdad,* 102–3.

569. Accepting the reading *ḥizab* of ed. Leiden and interpreting it as a plural of *ḥazbah,* which is attested by Dozy, *Supplément,* I, 281, in this meaning. The reading is suspect. Ed. Cairo reads *al-shuʿarāʾ,* "the poets."

rabble (*riʿāʿ*) composed [poetry] about it. Among what was said about it were the verses of [al-Ḥusayn] al-Khalīʿ:[570]

God's *Amīn*, trust in God,[571]
and you shall be granted endurance and help.
Entrust the matter to God,
and God the Almighty will protect you.
Victory will be ours with God's help—
the attack, and not the retreat;
Whereas for the renegades, your enemies,
will come a day of evil and defeat.
Many a cup that spews forth death,
hateful its taste and bitter,
Have we been made to drink, and we have made them drink of it;
but the thirst was with them.[572]
Thus it is with war—sometimes
it is against us, and sometimes for us.

According to one of the *Abnāʾ*: Ṭāhir dispersed his messengers and wrote to the commanders, Hāshimītes, and others, after he had taken their estates and properties, inviting them to a promise of safety (*amān*) and to join in repudiating Muḥammad and in swearing allegiance to al-Maʾmūn. A group went over to him, including ʿAbdallāh b. Ḥumayd b. Qaḥṭabah al-Ṭāʾī and his brothers, the children of al-Ḥasan b. Qaḥṭabah, Yaḥyā b. ʿAlī b. Māhān, and Muḥammad b. Abī al-ʿĀṣ.[573] Some of the commanders and Hāshimites corresponded with him in secret, and their hearts and inclinations came to be on his side.

After the battle of Qaṣr Ṣāliḥ, Muḥammad turned to diversion and drink. He entrusted matters to Muḥammad b. ʿĪsā b.

570. This poem, which was recited in al-Amīn's presence to celebrate the victory over Ṭāhir at Qaṣr Ṣāliḥ, is said to have earned the poet a reward of 10,000 dirhams. It is quoted in *Aghānī*, VI, 202; also Masʿūdī, VI, 458–59.

571. The hemistich puns on the meaning of al-Amīn's name, "the trustworthy one." One might translate "Trustworthy one of God, trust in God."

572. That is, they were the ones who drank deeply of the drink of death. Variant in Masʿūdī: "but the last [draught] of it was for them."

573. Ibn al-Athīr, VI, 190, reads, "Muḥammad b. Abī al-ʿAbbās al-Ṭāʾī."

Nahīk and al-Hirsh. From the streets and gates near them, the two of them placed their agents in the city gates, suburbs, al-Karkh market, the Tigris quays, al-Muḥawwal Gate,[574] and al-Kunāsah.[575] The thieves and criminals of these areas despoiled anyone they were able to lay hands on—men, women, and infirm people from the [Muslim] community and non-Muslims.[576] They did things the likes of which we have never heard to have happened in any other countries at war. [883]

When this had gone on a long time for the people and Baghdad had become oppressive for its inhabitants, those who had the strength to do so left the city after the oppressive exactions, painful affliction, and great danger. Ṭāhir admonished his forces to behave quite differently: he was strict in this and treated suspicious characters roughly. He commanded Muḥammad b. Abī Khālid to protect the weak and women and to give them gifts and relief. When a man or a woman escaped from the hands of al-Hirsh's forces and reached Ṭāhir's forces, their fear would depart and they would feel secure. The woman would display whatever gold and silver, goods, or fine clothing she had. People therefore said that [the situation of] Ṭāhir's forces, the forces and companions of al-Hirsh, and the people who had escaped was like the parable of the wall, concerning which God, whose Name is exalted, said:[577] "And a wall shall be set up between them, having a door on whose inward side is mercy, and on whose outward side is chastisement." After the people's tribulation had gone on a long time, their condition became very bad and they were unable to endure it any longer. Concerning this, one of the young men of Baghdad said:[578]

I wept blood over Baghdad, when
    I lost the ease of a pleasant life.

574. Al-Muḥawwal Gate was located about three-quarters of a mile from the al-Kūfah Gate of the Round City, on the southwest. See Le Strange, *Baghdad*, 146.

575. Al-Kunāsah ("Place of Sweepings") was an open space about 2 miles west of al-Muḥawwal Gate on the main road. See Le Strange, *Baghdad*, 150.

576. *Ahl al-dhimmah*: protected monotheists, Jews and Christians.

577. Qur'ān 57:13.

578. Ibn al-Athīr, VI, 190–91, quotes fourteen verses of the poem with variants; Mas'ūdī, VI, 460, quotes twelve verses with variants.

We have been given sorrow in exchange for joy,
and in exchange for plenty we have been given scarcity.
[884] The [evil] eye of the envious has afflicted Baghdad,
and has caused its people to perish by the *manjanīq*.
Here are people who have been overcome and burned by the fire,
and here a woman is mourning for a drowned man.
Here a woman is shouting, "Alas the day!"
and here one is crying over the loss of someone dear.
Here a dark-eyed woman, pleasing of mien,
in a shift anointed with perfume,
Is fleeing from the fire into the looting,
while her father is fleeing [from the looting] into the fire.
One who stole [the beauty of] her eyes from the gazelle,
and whose teeth are like the flash of lightning—
[All these], as bewildered as beasts being led to the sacrifice, pensive,
wearing necklaces around their throats,
Call on someone to take pity, but there is none to take pity:
brother has lost brother.
Here are people who have been expelled from the shade of this world:
their property is being sold in every market.
[885] Here a stranger, whose home is close,[579] lies
headless in the middle of the road.
He was caught in the middle of all their fighting,
and people do not know to which party [he belonged].
Child does not remain to care for his father,
and friend has fled without friend.
Whatever I may forget of the past,
I will always remember [the battle of] Dār al-Raqīq.[580]

It has been mentioned: One of Ṭāhir's Khurāsānian commanders, a man of courage and strength, went out one day to fight. Seeing some unclothed[581] men without weapons, he said to his companions in scorn and contempt, "Are only these

579. The sense is uncertain. The variant in Mas'ūdī, "far from home," makes more sense.
580. See note 507. This may refer to the battle described on p. 176, below.
581. See note 519.

whom I see fighting us?" "Yes," he was told, "these whom you see are the plague!" "Fie on you," he said, "shrinking from them and holding back, when you have splendid weapons, equipment, and strength, as well as your bravery and courage! What could the devices of these I see accomplish, when they have no weapons, no equipment, and no armor to protect them?" So he strung his bow and went forward. One of the men [on the other side] saw him and went toward him with a pitch-covered reed mat in his hand and a horse's nose bag full of stones under his arm. Whenever the Khurāsānian shot an arrow, the vagrant (*ʿayyār*) covered himself, and the arrow fell on his mat or near him. He would then take it and put it into a part of his reed mat he had prepared for that purpose and had fashioned like a quiver. Whenever an arrow fell, he would take it and cry [886]
out, "A dāniq!"—that is to say, he had obtained the value of the arrow, which was a dāniq.[582] The Khurāsānian and the vagrant continued at this until the Khurāsānian exhausted his arrows. He then rushed at the vagrant to strike him with his sword. The latter took a stone out of his bag, put it into a sling, hurled it, and did not miss the man's eye. Then he hurled another and would have knocked the man off his horse, had he not dodged it. The man wheeled round and retreated, saying, "These people are not human beings!"[583]

[Continuing, the narrator of this account] said: It has been related to me that when the story of the man was told to Ṭāhir, he was moved to laughter and excused the Khurāsānian from going out to fight. One of the poets of Baghdad said concerning this:[584]

These wars have brought out men
who belong neither to war's Qaḥṭān nor to its Nizār:[585]
A company in woolen coats of mail

---

582. The dāniq or dānaq was a small coin, one-sixth of a dirham.

583. That is, they fight like demons (*jinn*), rather than men (*ins*). Cf. *Fragmenta*, 334: "These people are not men; they are *jinn*."

584. Masʿūdī identifies the author as the blind poet ʿAlī b. Abī Ṭālib.

585. That is, they belong to none of the famous lineages of the Arabs—Qaḥṭān being the ancestor of the South Arabian tribes, and Nizār an ancestor of the North Arabian tribes.

who go into battle like ravenous lions.
Upon them are neck protectors made of palm fronds,
which serve instead of helmets, and shields of reed mats.
They do not know what flight is, when
even heroes seek refuge from the spears in flight.
One of them rushes to attack
two thousand—naked, not having even a waist wrapper.
They young fellow says, when he strikes
a spear thrust, "Take that from the vagrant lad (*ʿayyār*)!"
[887] How many a noble (*sharīf*) has war rendered of no repute!
How many a gambler and cutpurse has it exalted!

Ṭāhir Forbids Boatmen to Bring Anything to Baghdad[586]

According to Muḥammad b. Jarīr [al-Ṭabarī]: In this year, Ṭāhir forbade boatmen and others to bring anything to Baghdad, except to the people who were in his camp. He established surveillance over them for this purpose. A report of what took place between him and the forces of Muḥammad the Deposed in this and Ṭāhir's reason for doing so follows.

The reason for this, according to what has been related, was as follows: When so many of his forces were killed or wounded at Qaṣr Ṣāliḥ, Ṭāhir was pained and troubled. Never had he had a battle that had not gone in his favor, rather than against him. Feeling troubled, he ordered razing and burning. He tore down the houses of those who opposed him between the Tigris, Dār al-Raqīq, and the Syrian Gate, and [from] al-Kūfah Gate to the Ṣarāt Canal, the mills of Abū Jaʿfar,[587] the suburb of Ḥumayd, the Karkhāyā Canal, and al-Kunāsah.[588] He began to make

586. The following paragraph and the accompanying heading are not in the manuscript on which the Leiden edition was based. The translation follows ed. Cairo.

587. Apparently, this was another name the Patrician's Mill (*Raḥā al-Baṭrīq*), on the Ṣarāt Canal close to al-Kūfah Gate on the southwest side of the Round City. See Le Strange, *Baghdad*, 142, and note 536, above.

588. The suburb of Ḥumayd, named after a fief granted to Ḥumayd b. Qaḥṭabah, was located along the Muḥawwal Road, going west from al-Kūfah Gate. The Karkhāyā Canal paralleled this road, and al-Kunāsah (see note 575) lay farther west along it. See Le Strange, *Baghdad*, 147–48.

attacks on Muḥammad's forces during the night and just before daybreak. Every day he gained possession of one district after another, dug trenches around them, [and set] watchposts of soldiers [in them]. Muḥammad's forces also began to demolish, adding [to the destruction]. Ṭāhir's forces would wreck a house and depart, whereupon Muḥammad's forces would pull off its doors and roofing and would be even more damaging in their depredations upon their own people than Ṭāhir's forces were. One of their poets—some say he was ʿAmr b. ʿAbd al-Malik al-Warrāq al-ʿItrī—said about this:[589]

Every day we have a breach we cannot close;
they increase in regard to what they seek, and we decrease.
Whenever they tear down a house, we take its roofing, [888]
and wait for yet another one [to be torn down].
Whenever they strive their utmost in evil,
our mob strives even more than they to do evil.
They have hemmed in every broad place of our land;
they have come to have people in it and have stayed.
They start the quarry with drums; if there appears
to them the face of game nearby, they hunt it down.
They have destroyed the lands east and west
for us, and we do not know where to go.
When they are present, they speak of what they know;
and if they see nothing ugly, they conjecture.[590]
No one kills brave men like an experienced man,
a messenger of death, who roves as a thief by night.
You see the hero famous in every town,
if he ever sees an "unclothed one,"[591] show his fear.
If a vigorous man sees him, limping
back on his heels for fear he retreats.
He will sell you the head of a young man for a dirham;
if he says, "I will get it cheaper," he will do it.
How many among us who slay one of them [889]

589. Ibn al-Athīr, VI, 192, quotes the first eight verses with variants; Masʿūdī, VI, 464, quotes ten verses with variants.

590. The text may be corrupt. The sense is difficult. The word translated "conjecture" (*takharraṣū*) can also mean "speak falsehood."

591. I.e., one of the irregular troops.

will, in recompense for his death, have his sins purged away!
You see him, if he proclaims a truce (*amān*), coming forth to single combat;
sometimes he signs at us, and sometimes he singles [us] out.
Our Qur'ān readers have given authorization to fight them,
so that any man killed has been killed only by someone who has received authorization.

He also said about this:[592]

People are in the midst of destruction and movement from place to place;
they have spoken allusively, spreading rumors.
You who ask about their condition,
your eye will suffice you instead of asking.
Once they said "*Allāhu akbar!*" referring to the Merciful One;
now they say "*Allāhu akbar!*" for battle.[593]
Cast your eyes upon their host;
wait for relief, and count the nights.
No one remains in Baghdad but he
to whom poverty clings, who has many children to support.[594]
No mother protects her home, nor
does her brother protect it, nor anyone else.
He has no wealth but a spear;
his spear in his hand is his capital.
[890] It was the lesser [of evils] to God, so He provided for
his hands, because of his misery, the killing of men [as a means of support].
If this condition comes upon anyone,
his end is to be killed, in any event!

---

592. Mas'ūdī, VI, 465–66, quotes eight verses, attributing them to the blind poet 'Alī b. Abī Ṭālib.

593. That is, they use the slogan "God is most great!" as a battle cry. Literally, "Once their *takbīr* was for *al-Raḥmān*; now their *takbīr* is for fighting."

594. Mas'ūdī adds after this line: "Or a man who has escaped from prison, who is neither an Arab nor one of the *mawālī*." The line, "He has no wealth but a spear" seems to continue the sense of this line that Ṭabarī omits.

Why are we being killed for their sake?
Praise be to Thee, O God of glory!

He also said:

I will never leave Baghdad,
no matter who departs or who stays.
So long as sustenance supports us, we do not
care afterwards who is the imām.

According to ʿAmr b. ʿAbd al-Malik al-ʿItrī: When Ṭāhir saw that they were not heeding the killing, destruction, and burning, he commanded that merchants be forbidden to take any flour or other commodities from his district into the City of Abū Jaʿfar, al-Sharqiyyah, and al-Karkh.[595] He commanded that boats coming from al-Baṣrah and Wāsiṭ be diverted at Ṭarnāyā onto the Euphrates, thence to al-Muḥawwal al-Kabīr, then into the Ṣarāt [Canal], and then into the trench by al-Anbār Gate.[596] Zuhayr b. al-Musayyab for a certain price would give protection up to Baghdad: from each ship containing cargo he took from 1,000 to 2,000 or even 3,000 dirhams, more or less. Ṭāhir's agents and forces in Baghdad did the same or worse on all the roads of the city. Prices rose. People were caught in the tightest kind of siege. Many of them despaired of relief and [891]
ease. Those who had left the city were glad; those who had remained regretted that they had done so.

In this year, Ibn ʿĀʾishah asked Ṭāhir for a guarantee of safety. He had fought on Muḥammad's side for a time in al-Yāsiriyyah.

The Battle of al-Kunāsah

In this year, Ṭāhir placed some of his commanders in [various] parts of Baghdad. He placed al-ʿAlāʾ b. al-Waḍḍāḥ al-Azdī with his companions and those he attached to him in al-

595. The translation follows the text of ed. Cairo, rather than ed. Leiden, which is corrupt at this point.

596. On the Trench of Ṭāhir and al-Anbār Gate, located about 1 mile due west of the Syrian Gate of the Round City, see Le Strange, *Baghdad*, 109–11.

Waḍḍāḥiyyah[597] over al-Muḥawwal al-Kabīr. He placed Nuʿaym b. al-Waḍḍāḥ, the brother of al-ʿAlāʾ, with the Turks and others who were with him next to the suburb of Abī Ayyūb on the shore of the al-Ṣarāt [Canal]. He fought continually[598] for months. Both sides held firm. During this time, they fought a battle in al-Kunāsah. Ṭāhir directed it in person. Many of Muḥammad's forces were killed in it. ʿAmr b. ʿAbd al-Malik [al-Warrāq] said:[599]

Sunday's battle
was something that will be spoken of forever.
How many bodies have I seen
thrown down, and how much blood!
For one onlooker
death was lying in wait:
A stray arrow came upon him
and tore through his liver.
Someone cries out, "O my father!"
and someone cries out, "O my son!"
Many a man is floating drowned,
who once was strong in endurance.
No one has missed him,
except the "ladies of the town."[600]
And how many a person has been lost who was valiant,
who was dear to the bereaved:
He was among the onlookers
in front, very silent.[601]
[892] If he had set eyes on what
[the bereaved] has set eyes on, he would not have returned.

---

597. Al-Waḍḍāhiyyah is the reading of ed. Cairo. The manuscript used for ed. Leiden has an undotted word that the editor conjecturally read as *bi-l-rābiṭah* ("at the post or garrison"). Al-Waḍḍāḥiyyah lay just outside the al-Baṣrah Gate of the Round City. See Le Strange, *Baghdad*, 58, 92.

598. Literally, "he went out early in the morning to fight and late in the afternoon."

599. Masʿūdī, VI, 467–68, quotes sixteen lines and attributes them the blind poet ʿAlī b. Abī Ṭālib.

600. On *banāt al-balad* as prostitutes, see ed. Leiden, *Glossarium*, CXLIII.

601. Ed. Leiden reads *shadīda l-kharadi* ("stong of bashfulness, virginity, or silence"). Ed. Cairo reads *shadīda l-ḥaradi* ("strong of anger").

There remains no mature man of them
who has escaped, nor any youth.
Ṭāhir's ravenousness
is like the ravenousness of a lion.
He has pitched his tent, not to depart,
on the battlefield, like a man who does not quit his abode.
His eyes emit at the time of
battle a blaze of fire.
One person says, "They have killed
a thousand, but not any more."
Another says, "Yea, more; indeed,
the slain cannot be counted."
One person flees toward them,
dreading the fear of the morrow.
In vain! You will see
of those who have passed away not a one!
Those who have passed away will never return to
those who remain, even to all eternity.
I said to one who had been pierced by a spear,
but whose spirit within him had not yet perished:[602]
"Who are you—alas for you,
poor man—in relation to Muḥammad?"
He replied, "Not through kinship am I
close [to him], nor am I from a town [of his].
"I have never seen him at all, and have never
received of him any gift."[603]
And he said, "Not because of error
did I fight, nor out of good sense;
"But only for something immediate
that comes from him into my hand."

According to ʿAmr b. ʿAbd al-Malik: Muḥammad commanded Zurayḥ, his slave (*ghulām*), to search for money and to [893]
demand it from people who held deposits in safekeeping and

602. The last word of the line is problematic. The translation follows ed. Cairo's *lam tabid(ī)*. Ed. Leiden reads *taʾadi*, with the note *sic in codice*. Perhaps this should be vocalized *lam taʾud(ī)* from the root *ʾ-w-d*, "to decline, return."

603. *Ṣafad* means both "bond" and "gift."

from others. He commanded al-Hirsh to obey Zurayḥ. He would force his way into people's houses, raid them by night, and make seizures on mere suspicion. In this way he collected a great deal of money and ruined many people. People escaped [from Baghdad] on the pretext of going on the pilgrimage. The rich fled. Al-Qarāṭīsī said concerning this:[604]

They have pretended to be making the pilgrimage, though not
intending to make it;
rather, they want to flee from al-Hirsh.
How many people were living a life of well-being,
when al-Hirsh was deputed to bring ruin upon them!
Anyone whose house Zurayḥ searches
experiences humiliation and is visited by plundering.

The Battle of Darb al-Ḥijārah

In this year, the Battle of Darb al-Ḥijārah[605] took place. A report of it follows.

It has been mentioned: This battle, which took place in the vicinity of Darb al-Ḥijārah, went in favor of Muḥammad's forces and against Ṭāhir's. Many people were killed in it. Concerning this, ʿAmr b. ʿAbd al-Malik al-ʿItrī said:

Saturday's battle, the day of Darb al-Ḥijārah,
cut off a company of onlookers.
That was after they wore themselves out, but
our rabble killed them with stones.
He came to the *shūrajī*s[606] with intent to kill;
he said, "I want the command for you."
[894] He was met by men each of whom was a suspicious thief

604. Ibn al-Athīr, VI, 190, quotes the first two verses; Masʿūdī, VI, 496, quotes the poem and attributes it to the blind poet ʿAlī b. Abī Ṭālib.

605. Darb al-Ḥijārah ("Street of Stones") was the location of a bridge that crossed the Karkhāyā Canal that paralleled the main road from the al-Kūfah Gate to Muḥawwal. Al-Kunāsah was located on the same road, about 1 mile to the west. See Le Strange, *Baghdad*, 150–51, 308.

606. The lacuna in the Leiden text of this hemistich is filled by ed. Cairo. A *shūrajī* (from Persian *shūra*, nitre) was either a slave employed in making salt-encrusted land fit for agriculture or the master of such land. See ed. Leiden, *Glossarium*, CCCXIX.

who had spent his term in prison for mischief,
One who had nothing on to conceal himself,
whose penis stood up like a minaret.
So they retreated from them, although in the past
they had fought well in every attack.
To us, these are the same as those:
they respect no man or woman with a right to protection.[607]
Everyone who was obscure has become a chief,
living a life of comfort and abundance:
Every day he carries in his right hand
a spear with a pennant on top.
The Mother of Evil has brought him forth from her house
to seek plunder—his vagrant mother.
He speaks abusively to people; he does not care
for nice words when he abuses, nor does he hint.
This is not a time of the noble and generous man;
this is the time of villains, people of evil nature.
Fighting once used to be fighting;
today, O Most High, it is a trade.

He also said: [895]

A reed mat coated with pitch on the back—
Muḥammad and Manṣūr are in it.
Strength and security are their watchwords,
and their saying is, "The wall has been taken."
What benefit will there be for you in their wall,
when you are slain or taken prisoner?
Your horsemen have been killed in conflict,
and many of your homes have been destroyed.
Bring for yourselves a single leader
who is well mannered, in whose face there is light.
You who ask about our condition,
Muḥammad is in the palace, besieged.

607. Ed. Cairo fills in the lacuna in the Leiden text of this hemistich.

The Battle of al-Shammāsiyyah Gate

In this year, a battle took place at al-Shammāsiyyah Gate.[608] Harthamah was taken prisoner in it. A report of the reasons for the battle, how it took place, and its results follows.

According to ʿAlī b. Yazīd, who said: Harthamah was encamped at the Bīn Canal (*Nahr Bīn*), protected by a wall and trench. He had prepared *manjanīq*s and *ʿarrādah*s, and had stationed ʿUbaydallāh b. al-Waḍḍāḥ at al-Shammāsiyyah. From time to time he would go forth, but he would halt at the Khurāsān Gate,[609] fearful of the men of the army, not desiring to fight. He would summon the people to his cause, but they would abuse him verbally and mock him. So he would stand
[896] for a time and then depart. Ḥātim b. al-Ṣaqr was one of Muḥammad's commanders. He had agreed with his forces—unclothed ones and vagrants (*ʿayyārūn*)—that they would give battle to ʿUbaydallāh b. al-Waḍḍāḥ by night. They descended upon ʿUbaydallāh suddenly, while he was unaware, and launched an attack on him, driving him from his position. He retreated in defeat, and they captured from him horses, weapons, and much equipment. Ḥātim b. al-Ṣaqr took control of al-Shammāsiyyah. When the news reached Harthamah, he brought his forces up to reinforce (ʿUbaydallāh) and to drive off the army from him back to its position. Muḥammad's forces came to [fight] him, and fighting broke out between them. One of "the unclothed" took Harthamah prisoner, not recognizing him. One of Harthamah's companions attacked the man, cut off his hand, and freed Harthamah. The latter came back in defeat. When news about him reached the men of his camp, it collapsed totally, and its men went fleeing in panic toward Ḥulwān. Night and their preoccupation with plundering and taking prisoners hindered Muḥammad's forces from pursuit. I have been told

608. Al-Shammāsiyyah Gate was located at the northern extremity of al-Shammāsiyyah quarter on the east bank of the Tigris, at the point where the main road north to al-Mawṣil left al-Shammāsiyyah. See Le Strange, *Baghdad*, 170, 199.

609. That is, the Khurāsān Gate of al-Mukharrim quarter on the East Bank, not to be confused with the similarly named gate of the Round City. See Gabrieli, "La successione di Hārūn ar-Rašīd," 385 (note 5).

that the men of Harthamah's army did not make their way back for two days. The "unclothed ones" became stronger because of what had come into their hands. Many poems were written about that battle. One of them is the following by ʿAmr al-Warrāq:

A naked one who owns no shirt
goes forth in the morning to look for a shirt.
He assaults someone who has a coat of mail
that blinds the eyes with its brightness.
In his hand is a banner
red that gleams like jewels.
He is eager to seek fighting,
more eager than a man who seeks pleasure.
He is easy to be led, as if
he were going forth to eat date candy.
He is a marauding lion, who has always been
an accomplished chief of robbers.
He is bolder and more resolute in advancing
in battle than a wounded lion.
He approaches on a contemptible mount,
and his stock is from the worst stock.
He escapes, if escape occurs, [897]
on something fleeter than a young camel.
A man in armor, if exposed to his murderous intent,
has no place of refuge.
How many a brave horseman
has he sold at a cheap price!
He calls out, "Oh who will buy
the head of an armored man for a handful of dates?"

One of Harthamah's companions said:

Time comes to an end, but their fighting never ends:
houses are pulled down, and wealth diminishes.
People are unable to do what they have sought to do:
they cannot fend off ruin, no matter how they try.
They bring us a report in which there is no light;
every day there are stories about the sons of harlotry.

When news of what the "unclothed ones" and Ḥātim b.

al-Ṣaqr had done to ʿUbaydallāh b. al-Waḍḍāḥ and Harthamah reached Ṭāhir, it grieved and distressed him. He commanded that a floating bridge be thrown across the Tigris above al-Shammāsiyyah. He dispatched his forces and set them in order; he himself went forth with them to the bridge. They crossed over toward the enemy and fought them in very fierce fighting. He reinforced them with his men periodically, until they turned back Muḥammad's forces and made them leave al-Shammāsiyyah. He sent ʿUbaydallāh b. al-Waḍḍāḥ and Harthamah back to the places that had been abandoned.[610]

After the victory of the "unclothed ones," Muḥammad had given out 2 million dirhams [in pay] by taking apart his palaces and audience rooms (*majālis*) at al-Khayzurāniyyah. Now, the forces of Ṭāhir burned them all—the roofs had been gilded—and killed many of the "unclothed ones" and looters. Concerning this, ʿAmr al-Warrāq says:[611]

Two heavy things[612] and Ṭāhir b. al-Ḥusayn
came upon us the morning of Monday.
[898] They assembled their host at night and proclaimed:
"Seek your vengeance today for al-Ḥusayn."[613]
They beat their drum, and to [fight] them rushed
men, each of them strong of spear and forearm.
You who were slain on the plain, who were cast down on the shore,

610. *Wa-radda al-mahājir / muhājir ʿUbaydallāh ibn al-Waḍḍāḥ wa-Harthamah.* This might mean, "He sent ʿUbaydallāh b. al-Waḍḍāḥ and Harthamah back to *al-Muhājir*," taking al-Muhājir as a place name. Such a place is attested (Le Strange, *Baghdad*, 59), but it was next to al-Kūfah Gate of the Round City, whereas the context implies that the two men reoccupied the positions in al-Shammāsiyyah, across the river from the Round City. I therefore take *mahājir* to be equivalent to *mahājīr*, "abandoned places."

611. Masʿūdī, VI, 471, quotes the lines with variants.

612. According to the lexicons, *thaqalāni* ("two heavy things") can mean two armies (because they are heavy in assault), or mankind and the *jinn* (because anything held in esteem can be called a *thaqal*). See Lane, *Lexicon*, I, 344. There is some uncertainty about the reading, which is Guyard's emendation of manuscript *baʿlāni* ("two lords"). Neither the original reading nor the emendation fits the meter, although the emendation is possible by poetic license.

613. That is, vengeance for al-Ḥusayn b. ʿAlī b. ʿĪsā b. Māhān. See pp. 108–14, above, for the circumstances surrounding his death.

the object of whose love was among Ṭayyi' of the Two Mountains:
What was in your hands? If
the people had made peace, would you have been in need?
Were you a vizier or a commander? Nay, you were as far
from both things as the stars of the Little Dipper.
How many a keen-sighted man went out early with two eyes
to see the situation [of the armies] and came back with one eye!
They do not miss what they intend:
their archers aim only at the eyes.
You who ask me about them, they are the worst people
I have ever seen among mankind; no others are like these two:
The worst of those still alive or those who have passed on—
of those who have passed on or those I have seen among the two heavy things (sc. mankind and *jinn*).

When what Ṭāhir had done was reported to Muḥammad, it caused him great distress and anxiety. A secretary to Kawthar [899] mentioned that Muḥammad composed the following verses, or that someone composed them and attributed them to him:

I have been sorely afflicted by the most brave-hearted among men and *jinn*,
who, when he excels, is like nothing else that excels.
With every man of power he has a spy
who watches him and knows what he says.
He is not inattentive to something because of stubbornness,
when an inattentive person would cause an affair to fail.

In this year, Muḥammad's situation weakened, and he became certain that he would perish. ʿAbdallāh b. Khāzim b. Khuzaymah fled from Baghdad to al-Madā'in.

According to al-Ḥusayn b. al-Ḍaḥḥāk: When he realized that Muḥammad entertained suspicions about him, and that low persons and rabble were biased against him, ʿAbdallāh b. Khāzim b. Khuzaymah became worried about himself and his property. He made his way to al-Madā'in at night in boats with his dependents and children and stayed there. He was not present at any of the fighting.

According to someone else: Ṭāhir sent a letter to him and warned him that his estates would be seized and that he would be liquidated. So he took warning, escaped from the strife, and remained safe. One of his relatives said concerning this:

Ibn Khāzim was not cowardly in the face of rowdies,
riffraff, and inferior persons:
But he feared the assault of a lion,
crushing in his strength, famous for his aggressiveness.

When his action became known among the people, the merchants of al-Karkh met among themselves and said, "We ought to disclose our position to Ṭāhir and show him that we are innocent of giving aid against him." They assembled and drafted a letter informing him that they were obedient and well disposed toward him because of what they had heard: namely, his commitment to obeying God, upholding the right, and repressing wrongdoers. They did not look on the war as legitimate, let alone fight [in it]. Anyone from their side who advocated
[900] it did not belong to them. "The common thoroughfares were choked with them. Indeed, the men . . . ,[614] nor do they own houses or real estate in al-Karkh. They are either cutpurses, makers and sellers of sweets,[615] or people from the prisons. Their only shelters are the baths and mosques. The merchants among them are mere street vendors who deal in trifles. A woman is forced to support herself by the mercy of a pimp for a while before she can escape.[616] An old man even falls on his face from weakness. A person carrying a purse in his waistband or in his hand has it cut away from him. We have no might or power against them, nor do we have anything for ourselves with them [here]. Indeed, some of us remove the stones from the road

614. There is a lacuna in the manuscript. The words with which ed. Cairo attempts to fill the lacuna turn out to be a dittography from the previous line.

615. *Sawwāṭ wa-naṭṭāf*: makers and sellers of *nāṭif*, a sweet paste that had to be kneaded a long time, drawn out, and pounded. See Fagnan, *Additions*, 83, s.v. *sawwāṭ*.

616. The translation follows the Leiden text as interpreted in *Glossarium*, CDXXXI. Ed. Cairo differs, but also seems to have suffered corruption: "A man meets a woman in the press of people, and the two tarry (*yaltaththāni*, an otherwise unattested form of the root *l.th.th*) before escaping."

because of the tradition (*ḥadīth*) concerning this that has been reported from the Prophet, may God bless him and grant him peace; how then [would we fail to act] if we had power to prevail against those it would benefit religion and life in this world to have kept off the street, put permanently into prison, and banished from the land, and [if we had power] to stop greed and riot and banish vice, purse-snatching, and stealing? God forbid that any of us should make war on you!"

It has been mentioned that they wrote a petition concerning this and that some men arranged[617] to slip through to him with it. But those who were wise and prudent among them said to them, "Do not think that Ṭāhir does not understand this or that he is unable to send spies among you and against you, so that it is as if he were present among you. The best plan is not to make yourselves conspicuous with this; for we cannot be sure but that if some base person sees you, it will lead to your destruction and the loss of your property. The danger of your being exposed to these base persons is too fearful for you to seek to clear yourself from disgrace in the eyes of Ṭāhir. Indeed, if you were sinners and wrongdoers, you would be more likely to receive his pardon, mercy, and forgiveness. So put your trust in God, who is blessed and exalted, and forbear." They deferred to them and forbore. Ibn Abī Ṭālib, the blind [poet], said:[618]

Never mind the people of the streets, for soon [901]
 the claws of the lion will get them.
The membrane around strong hearts will be torn asunder;
 soon they will go into the grave.
God will destroy all of them
 because of greed[619] and wickedness.

It has been mentioned: Al-Hirsh went out, and with him the rabble, "unclothed ones," and a multitude of all sorts of people,

---

617. The translation follows ed. Cairo's *itta'ada qawmun*, rather than ed. Leiden's *anfadhū qawman* ("they dispatched men"). The passage makes it clear that the petition was never sent. The two words are similar in Arabic script.

618. Quoted in Mas'ūdī, VI, 470.

619. Variant in Mas'ūdī: "rebellion."

and made his way to the Island of al-ʿAbbās.[620] A party of Ṭāhir's men came forth, and the two sides fought violently. It was a section in which no fighting had taken place, but after that day it became a battlefield. In the end, the victory went to (Ṭāhir); however, on the first day of the fighting, Muḥammad's forces gained the upper hand over Ṭāhir's forces, until they drove them back to the house of Abū Yazīd al-Sharawī.[621] The people of the suburbs in the areas next to the al-Anbār Gate Road became frightened.

It has been mentioned: When Ṭāhir saw this, he dispatched one of his commanders to them. He was occupied in many directions, fighting off Muḥammad's forces from them. He inflicted a heavy blow on them there: many men drowned in the Ṣarāt [Canal], and others were killed. Concerning the defeat of Ṭāhir on the first [day],[622] ʿAmr al-Warrāq said:

Ṭāhir's crier announced in our presence,
    "People, desist; remain at home.
"Tomorrow will come to you; so beware
    [a lion with a wide jaw in which there is . . .]"[623]
Then the rabble arose to confront him
    after midnight, before the prayer [of dawn].
On Saturday, they left his army
    confounded and silent in the darkness of night.

About the battle that went against Muḥammad's forces, he said:

How many a slain man have we seen!
    We did not ask him why!—

620. Jazīrat al-ʿAbbās, or more commonly, al-Jazīrah al-ʿAbbāsiyyah, was a large area, about one and one-half miles in length and half a mile in width, located west of the Round City, between two branches of the Ṣarāt Canal, which split below the plot and reunited above it. It had been granted as a fief to al-ʿAbbās, brother of the caliph al-Manṣūr, and was celebrated for its fertility. See Le Strange, *Baghdad*, 142.

621. That is, toward the Round City. The house of Abū Yazīd al-Sharawī was on the northwest side of the square outside al-Kūfah Gate. See Le Strange, *Baghdad*, 59.

622. The bracketed word is from ed. Cairo.

623. The second hemistich of the line is found only in ed. Cairo; the manuscript used by ed. Leiden has a lacuna. The last word of the line in ed. Cairo, *ʿuyūt*, is not recorded in any dictionary and almost certainly is corrupt.

One wearing mail, whom a "naked one"
met with violence and recklessness:
If the former met the latter with a spear, [902]
the latter met the former with boasting[624]—
An Ethiopian who kills people
over a piece of canvas,
Cloaked in [only] the sun, content
with every sustenance that is wished for.
He makes an attack and kills
none but the head of an army:
Such as ʿAlī Afrāhamard,[625]
or ʿAlāʾ, or Quraysh.
Beware of a shot, O Ṭāhir,
from the hand of the little Ethiopian!

ʿAmr al-Warrāq also said concerning this:

The beauty of Baghdad has departed—
and it indeed possessed beauty.
Every day there has broken it
one shock after another.
The earth has raised a cry unto God
from the abomination, crying aloud.
O you who have been slain,
you are not following the religion of the [true] way.
Would that I knew what you gained
when you journeyed by night.
Was it to Paradise that you were sent,
or are you being sent to the Fire?
Was it stones that killed you, or
were you killed perforce by spears?
If you fought in piety,
then a thousand pilgrimages be upon us![626]

According to ʿAlī b. Yazīd—a certain eunuch (*khādim*): Muḥammad ordered that whatever remained in the already

624. A pun is involved, since *faysh* means both "boasting" and "glans penis"—alluding to the "unclothed" state of the irregular troops.
625. He is referred to elsewhere by the variant name Farāhmard.
626. That is, to expiate the sin of murder.

despoiled storehouses should be sold. However, those in charge of them concealed[627] what was in them, to steal [it]. Muḥammad's situation became increasingly precarious: he had lost what he possessed, and the men were demanding pay (*arzāq*). One day, in vexation at what was befalling him, he said, "I wish that God Almighty would kill the two sides, both of them,[628] and give people rest from them. Not a one of them but is an enemy—both those who are on our side and those
[903] who are against us. The former want my money; the latter want my life." Some verses that he is said to have recited were mentioned to me:[629]

Disperse and leave me alone,
  you company of "helpers."
All of you are many-faced,[630]
  as is the nature of human beings,
And I see nothing but deceit
  and false hopes.
I possess nothing—
  ask my treasurers!
Alas for me, what has befallen me
  from the one who resides in the garden.[631]

[Continuing,] he said: Muḥammad's cause became weaker. His army dispersed and became frightened in its camp. He sensed that Ṭāhir was about to overcome him and defeat him.

In this year, al-ʿAbbās b. Mūsā b. ʿĪsā led the pilgrimage. Ṭāhir sent him to be in charge of the ceremonies at the command of al-Maʾmūn. Dāwūd b. ʿĪsā was in charge of Mecca in this year.

---

627. The translation follows the reading of ed. Cairo (*katama*). The original Leiden reading (*kamma*, "hid") is changed in the *Addenda* to *lamma*, "gathered up."

628. Ms. Ahmet III, 2929, the second manuscript used by ed. Cairo, ends at this point. The text of the remainder of this volume is based on the single manuscript available to the Leiden editor.

629. Masʿūdī, VI, 472, quotes the poem with variants.

630. The translation follows Gabrieli, "La successione di Hārūn ar-Rašīd," 387 n. 2, who takes *dhū wujūh* to mean "hypocrites."

631. That is, from Ṭāhir. Instead of *sākin*, the Masʿūdī version reads *nāzil*, "encamped," and glosses, "meaning Ṭāhir."

The Events of the Year 198

(September 1, 813–August 21, 814)

Ṭāhir Captures Baghdad

In this year, Khuzaymah b. Khāzim disobeyed Muḥammad b. Hārūn, separated himself from him, and sought a promise of safety from Ṭāhir b. al-Ḥusayn.[632] Harthamah entered the eastern part [of Baghdad]. A report concerning why Khuzaymah left Muḥammad, how this turned out, and how he became obedient to Ṭāhir follows.

It has been mentioned as the reason for this: Ṭāhir wrote to Khuzaymah, telling him that if he were to sever relations with
Muḥammad and offer him no effective aid, he (sc. Ṭāhir) would [904]
not be remiss in his regard.[633] When he received Ṭāhir's letter, Khuzaymah consulted his trusted friends and members of his family. They said to him, "By God, it seems to us that this man has our master by the nape of the neck; so make an arrangement for yourself and for us." He therefore wrote to Ṭāhir, announcing his obedience, and telling him that if he himself were the person encamped on the eastern side instead of Harthamah, he would

632. Parallels: Ibn al-Athīr, VI, 194–97; *Fragmenta*, 335.

633. The translation follows the emendation proposed in ed. Leiden, *Addenda*, DCCLXVII.

undertake every danger for him. He made known to (Ṭāhir) his lack of confidence in Harthamah and urged him not to lay any burden on the latter in the matter without guaranteeing to him (sc. Khuzayamah) that he would stand in his stead; Harthamah would then be brought into the affair. He (sc. Khuzaymah) would cut the bridges and as consequence bring about a situation that would elicit his approval and pleasure. If (Ṭāhir) did not guarantee him this, it would not be possible for him to expose himself to the mob, rabble, ruffians, and destruction. Ṭāhir accordingly wrote to Harthamah, rebuking him and accusing him of incompetence, saying, "You have gathered soldiers, wasted money, and given it in grants without the Commander of the Faithful or myself, when I am in such need of it to cover expenses and expenditures. You have failed to act against troops of little might and small significance, as if drawing back and afraid. This is surely an offense! Get ready to enter [the city], for I have decided to push back the army and cut the bridges. I hope that you will meet no significant opposition to this plan, God willing!" Harthamah wrote [back] to him, "I acknowledge your salutary opinion and excellent advice. Command as you wish; I will not oppose you." So Ṭāhir wrote to Khuzaymah to inform him of this.

It has been mentioned that when Ṭāhir wrote to Khuzaymah, he wrote a similar letter to Muḥammad b. ʿAlī b. ʿĪsā b. Māhān.

It has been said: On the eve of Wednesday, eight nights remaining in the month of Muḥarram of the year 198 (September 21, 813), Khuzaymah b. Khāzim and Muḥammad b. ʿAlī b. ʿĪsā seized the Tigris bridge and cut it.[634] They set up their banners on it, cast off their allegiance to Muḥammad,
[905] and proclaimed allegiance to ʿAbdallāh al-Maʾmūn. The people of ʿAskar al-Mahdī[635] remained quiet and stayed in their

634. Gabrieli, "La successione di Hārūn ar-Rašīd," 387 n. 4, identifies this as the main (middle) bridge, but notes that other bridges may have been cut as well, as implied by Ṭāhir's preceding message and the poem that follows.

635. ʿAskar al-Mahdī (al-Mahdī's Camp) was another name for the suburb of Ruṣāfah at the foot of the main bridge on the east bank of the Tigris. See Le Strange, *Baghdad*, 42, 187–89.

homes and markets that day. As soon as Harthamah entered, a few other commanders besides these two came to him and swore to him that he would see no misbehavior from them. He accepted this from them. Ḥusayn al-Khalīʿ composed the following about Khuzaymah's cutting of the bridge:[636]

We all owe Khuzaymah a debt of gratitude,
because God the Merciful has stilled the tumult of war.
He himself took charge of the affairs of the Muslims,
and defended and protected them most gloriously.
Had it not been for Abū al-ʿAbbās [Khuzaymah], fortune would not have ceased
being angry with us night and day.
Khuzaymah was not criticized for doing such a deed,
when the east of the country and the west were in turmoil.
He subjected the two Tigris bridges to cutting, while spears
were pointed and souls were in the palm of the sword.
He wounded the head of doom when it was threatening doom,
suffering distress because of one event, and laughing because of another event.
So it (sc. doom) was like a fire that a cloud has beguiled,
extinguishing by flame an encompassing flame.[637]
What is the killing of one soul among many souls,
if the world returns to peace and plenty? [906]
The heroic deed of Abū al-ʿAbbās requires no expiation,
when persistent trouble has recourse to trouble [to stop it].

According to Yaḥyā b. Salamah the Secretary (*al-Kātib*): Ṭāhir came early on Thursday against the city—al-Sharqiyyah[638] and its residential districts and al-Karkh and its markets. He demolished the two bridges over the Ṣarāt [Canal]—the old and the

636. The first five verses with variants are quoted by Ibn al-Athīr, VI, 194–95.

637. That is, as a cloud with flashing lighning puts out a fire by raining, so Khuzaymah by violence has extinguished violence. The translation of this and the preceding verse is uncertain.

638. Al-Sharqiyyah was a suburb of West Baghdad southeast of the Round City, between the main road leaving al-Baṣrah Gate and the shore of the Tigris. See Le Strange, *Baghdad*, 53, 90, 94. Ed. Leiden, *Addenda*, DCCLXVII, quotes from al-Khaṭīb al-Baghdādī, "It was named al-Sharqiyyah because it was to the east (*sharq*) of the Ṣarāt [Canal]."

new. There was heavy fighting at them. Ṭāhir tasked his forces severely and oversaw the fighting in person. Those who were with him fought at Dār al-Raqīq, and he[639] defeated the men until he drove them back to al-Karkh. Ṭāhir fought at al-Karkh Gate and al-Waḍḍāḥ Palace. He defeated Muḥammad's forces, and they were driven back in confusion. Ṭāhir passed through without turning aside for anything, until he had entered forcibly with the sword. He commanded his crier to proclaim security to anyone who remained in his house. At al-Waḍḍāḥ Palace, the market of al-Karkh, and the outskirts he placed commanders and soldiers in every location as required. He made his way to the City of Abū Jaʿfar and encircled it, along with the Palace of Zubaydah and al-Khuld Palace, from near the Bridge Gate,[640] to Khurāsān Gate, the Syrian Gate, al-Kūfah Gate, al-Baṣrah Gate, and the bank of the Ṣarāt [Canal] up to its outlet into the Tigris, with horses, equipment, and weapons. Ḥātim b. al-Ṣaqr, al-Hirsh, and the [North] African troops fought Ṭāhir steadfastly; so he set up *manjanīqs* behind the wall against the city and across from the Palace of Zubaydah and al-Khuld Palace and bombarded [them]. Muḥammad, with his mother and children, left for the City of Abū Jaʿfar. Most of his soldiers, eunuchs, and slave girls scattered from him into the streets and roads without turning aside for anything. The rabble and the low persons also scattered. ʿAmr al-Warrāq said about this:

[907] O Ṭāhir of strength,[641] whose
like has never been found!
O master (*sayyid*), son of a master,

---

639. The pronouns are ambiguous. I take the clause to mean that *Ṭāhir* (i.e., his forces) defeated *them* (i.e., the opposing forces of Muḥammad) and drove them back to al-Karkh. Ṭāhir then fought at the gate of al-Karkh, defeated Muḥammad's forces, and entered al-Karkh. The textual witness, however, is uncertain, probably because what we have is a condensation of a longer account. Ed. Cairo continues as follows: "Ṭāhir fought them at al-Karkh Gate and al-Waḍḍāḥ Palace: Muḥammad's forces defeated *them*, and they [i.e., Ṭāhir's forces] were driven back in confusion." This makes Ṭāhir's entry into al-Karkh and proclamation of security illogical.

640. *Fragmenta*, 335, reads: "from near the bridge to Khurāsān Gate."

641. *Yā ṭāhira l-ẓahri*: the Arabic plays on the similar sound of the two words and their visual similarity in Arabic script.

son of a master, son of master!
Back to their former occupations
have gone Muḥammad's "naked ones."
Makers and vendors
of sweets,[642] as well as impostors;
Bandits who were taking refuge with
vagrants and paupers;
Men in shackles who broke out of prisons
and became unshackled;
Men bold to plunder, who became masters,
though they were never entitled to be masters:
These have become obedient to your strength and have submitted,
after having been rebellious for a long time.

According to ʿAlī b. Yazīd, who said: One day I was at the home of ʿAmr al-Warrāq with a group of people, when a man came and told us about Ṭāhir's attack at al-Karkh Gate, and how the men had been driven back from it. ʿAmr said, "Hand me a cup," and he said concerning this:[643]

Take it, for wine has [many] names:
"medicine" is one, and "disease" is another.
Water improves it, when it is decanted—
sometimes—but water sometimes spoils it.
Someone said, "They had a battle
this very day," and [other] things.
I said to him, "You are an ignoramus.
You neglect the good things.
"Drink, and spare us reports about them.
People will make peace, if they want to."

Someone else then came among us and said, "So-and-so has fought with the 'naked ones'; so-and-so has come; so-and-so has plundered." Again, (al-Warrāq) said:

What a time we are in!
The great have died out.

642. For *naṭṭāf* and *sawwāṭ*, see note 615.
643. The text with minor variants is quoted in Ibn al-Athīr, VI, 195.

These low persons and rabble
 are commanders among us.
We have nothing,
 except what *He* wills.
[908] The earth has cried out,
 and the heavens, too, have cried out to God.
Religion has been taken away,
 and blood has become of little importance to God.
Abū Mūsā, take the good things:
 the time for the meeting has come.
Here is unmixed wine for you:
 the drinking companions have come to you.

ʿAmr al-Warrāq also said about this:

If you want to anger
 a soldier and get him to obey,
Say, "You soldiers,
 Ṭāhir has come to you!"

Muḥammad fortified himself in the city, along with those who were fighting on his side. Ṭāhir besieged him, taking the gates from him, and preventing flour, water, and other things from reaching him and the people of the city.

According to al-Ḥusayn b. Abī Saʿīd, who said that the eunuch (*khādim*) Ṭāriq, one of Muḥammad's courtiers (*khāṣṣah*) and one of al-Ma'mūn's after the arrival of the latter, told him that one day while under siege—or he may have said that it was on his last day—Muḥammad asked him to bring him something to eat: [Continuing, Ṭāriq] said: I entered the kitchen and found nothing. So I went to Jamrah the perfumer, who was al-Jawhar's slave girl, and said to her, "The Commander of the Faithful is hungry. Do you have anything, for I have found nothing in the kitchen?" She said to a girl of hers named Banān, "What do you have?" She brought a chicken and a loaf of bread. I brought them to him and he ate. He asked for water to drink, but there was none in the beverage closet.[644] By the evening he had decided

644. *Khizānat al-sharāb* may refer to a place where beverages were placed to be cooled. Cf. the description of the *meshrebeeyeh* (*mashrabiyyah*) in Lane, *Modern Egyptians*, 8–9.

to meet Harthamah, and he never again drank water until he perished.

According to Muḥammad b. Rāshid, who said that Ibrāhīm b. al-Mahdī[645] told him that he had been staying with Muḥammad the Deposed in the City of al-Manṣūr in his palace at the [909]
Golden Gate,[646] when Ṭāhir besieged him. [Continuing, Ibrāhīm] said: (Muḥammad) went out one night, wanting to relieve the dejection he was feeling. He went to al-Qarār Palace,[647] at Ṣarāt Point, below al-Khuld Palace, late at night. He sent for me, and I went to him. He said, "Ibrāhīm, don't you see the pleasantness of this night and the beauty of the moon in the sky, with its light in the water?" (We were on the bank of the Tigris at the time.) "Would you like to drink?" "As you will," I said, "may God make me your ransom!" So he called for a flagon (*raṭl*) of date wine (*nabīdh*). He drank it and then gave orders, and I was given a similar one to drink.

I began to sing to him without his asking me, for I knew in what bad humor he was. I sang something that I knew he liked. "How would you like someone to accompany you?" he said. "How I would like that!" I said. So he called for a favorite slave girl of his named Ḍaʿf. Given that we were in such a state of affairs, I found her name ominous.[648] When she came before him, he said, "Sing," so she sang from the poetry of al-Nābighah al-Jaʿdī:[649]

---

645. The ʿAbbāsid prince Ibrāhīm b. al-Mahdī was famous as a singer. See *EI*² s.v. (Sourdel). Another version of the incident is found in *Aghānī*, IV, 189 (ed. Cairo, V, 1794–96). Cf. Masʿūdī, VI, 426–30 (different *isnād* and details); *Fragmenta*, 335–36. Two shorter reports of apparently the same incident occur on pp. 231–33, below.

646. The Palace of the Golden Gate was at the center of the Round City. See Le Strange, *Baghdad*, 19, 30–33, 309–10.

647. On al-Qarār Palace, also known as the Palace of Zubaydah, see Le Strange, *Baghdad*, 102–3. Le Strange's explanation of the name is wrong. As Nabia Abbott noted, the meaning of *Qarār* was "permanency," alluding to the phrase *dār al-qarār* ("abode of permanency," i.e., heaven) in Qur'ān 40:39. See Abbott, *Two Queens of Baghdad*, 218 n.

648. *Ḍaʿf* means "weakness."

649. Al-Nābighah al-Jaʿdī (Ḥibbān b. Qays) was born before Islam, but lived most of his life as a Muslim and died in 65/684. The verse alludes to Kulayb b. Rabīʿah from the tribe of Taghlib. By killing a camel belonging to al-Basūs, a woman from the closely related tribe of Bakr (the camel had strayed onto his pasture and broken the eggs in a bird's nest), Kulayb precipitated the "War of

Kulayb, by my life, was a better defender
and less guilty than you, yet he became stained with [his own] blood.

What she sang distressed him and was ominous to him. He said to her, "Sing something else," so she sang:[650]

Their departure has made my eye tearful and sleepless:
verily, parting from loved ones provokes many tears.
The vicissitudes of their fortune continued to oppress them,
until they destroyed each other: verily the vicissitudes of fortune are oppressive!

He said to her, "May God curse you! Don't you know anything
[910] else to sing?" She replied, "Master, I only sang what I thought
you liked. I didn't mean to do anything you disliked. It was only
something that came to me." Then she started another song:[651]

By the Lord of repose and movement,
fate possesses many snares.
Night and day succeed each other,
and the stars revolve in the firmament,
Only to transfer prosperity from one king
occupied with the love of this world to another.
But the kingdom of the Possessor of the [Heavenly] Throne endures forever:
it neither passes away nor is shared with a partner.

"Get up," he said, "and may God be wrathful with you!" So she stood up. Now he had a beautifully made crystal cup—Muḥammad used to call it *Zubb Rubbāḥ*[652]—that had been

---

al-Basūs" between the two tribes. See Sezgin, *GAS*, II, 245–47; Nallino, *Le Poesie di an-Nābiġah al-Ǧaʿdī* (Rome, 1953), 105–8; *Shiʿr al-Nābighah al-Jaʿdī*, 143.

650. Quoted with minor variants in Ibn al-Athīr, VI, 196.

651. In *Aghānī*, III, 179, the poem is attributed to Abū al-ʿAtāhiyah. Seven verses of it are quoted in Ṭabarī, III, 450, where they are said to have been recited by a mysterious hidden voice (*hātif*) foreboding the death of al-Manṣūr in A.H. 158. Variants exist in Ibn al-Athīr, VI, 196.

652. The text and the meaning are uncertain. In the notes to his edition of *Fragmenta* (I, 125), de Goeje explains the name as derived from a kind of date from al-Baṣrah called *zubb rubbāḥ* or *zubb rubāḥ* (literally, "monkey penis"; cf. Lane, *Lexicon*, III, 1208). Ibn al-Athīr reads *rubb riyāḥ*, which is the name of a kind of mushroom.

placed before him. As the slave girl got up to leave, she tripped over the cup and broke it.

[Continuing,] Ibrāhīm said: The strange thing is that whenever we sat with this slave girl, we experienced something unpleasant in our assembly. (Muḥammad) said to me, "Alas, Ibrāhīm, don't you see what this slave girl has mentioned and what happened with the cup? By God, I think my time has come." "God," I said, "will lengthen your life, strengthen and preserve your kingdom for you, and subdue your enemy." Before I had finished my words, we heard a voice from the Tigris, saying: "Decided is the matter whereon you two enquire."[653] "Ibrāhīm," he said, "didn't you hear what I just heard?" "No, by God, I heard nothing," I said, although I had indeed heard. "You will hear a soft sound," he said. So I went down to the river bank, but I saw nothing. We resumed the conversation, and the voice returned: "Decided is the matter whereon you two enquire." He jumped up in distress from where he was sitting, mounted, and returned to his place in the city. It was only one or two nights later that the events of his death occurred—it was [911]
on Sunday, the 6th or 4th day of Ṣafar in the year 198.[654]

According to Abū al-Ḥasan al-Madā'inī,[655] who said: On the eve of Friday, seven days before the end of the Muḥarram in the year 198 (September 23, 813), Muḥammad b. Hārūn entered the City of Peace, fleeing from the palace called al-Khuld, because of the *manjanīq* stones that were landing on it. He commanded that his audience rooms (*majālis*) and carpets be burned, and they were. Then he went into the city. It had been fourteen months, less twelve days, since war had broken out with Ṭāhir.

---

653. Qur'ān 12:41.

654. The day of the week and the day of the month do not match. The 4th of Ṣafar (October 4, 813) fell on a Tuesday; the 6th of Ṣafar (October 6) fell on a Thursday. In the chronology of al-Madā'inī, which follows, the day and date do coincide.

655. The historian Abū al-Ḥasan ʿAlī b. Muḥammad b. ʿAbdallāh b. Abī Sayf al-Madā'inī (b. 135/752, d. ca. 228/843) was active at al-Baṣrah (his birthplace), al-Madā'in, and Baghdad, and was credited with over 200 works on history and literature, most of which survive only as quoted in the works of later authors. See *EI*[2] s.v. al-Madā'inī (U. Sezgin).

The Death of al-Amīn

In this year, Muḥammad b. Hārūn was killed.[656] The report of his death follows.

According to Muḥammad b. ʿĪsā al-Julūdī, who said: After Muḥammad had gone into the city and taken up residence there, his commanders realized that neither they nor he had equipment for the siege. Fearing that they would be defeated, Ḥātim b. al-Ṣaqr, Muḥammad b. Ibrāhīm b. al-Aghlab al-Ifrīqī, and his [other] commanders went before Muḥammad and said, "Your condition and ours has come to what you see. We have formed a plan which we submit to you. Consider it, and make up your mind to do it; for we hope that it will be right, and that God will make it prosper, if He will." "What is it?" he asked. They said, "The men have scattered from you, and your foe has encircled you on every side. Of your cavalry, 1,000 horses, the best and swiftest of them, remain with you. We think we should choose 700 of the *Abnā'*, men whom we know to love you. We will mount them on these horses and make a sortie by night from one of these gates; for the night belongs to its people,[657] and no
[912] one will stand firm against us, God willing. We will go out until we reach al-Jazīrah and Syria. You will raise troops and gather taxes, and will gain a large domain and a new kingdom. People will rally to you, and the soldiers will be cut off from pursuing you. It is for this that God, the Almighty and Exalted, has made new things happen in the succession of night and day." "How excellent your plan is!" he said to them, and he determined to do it. When word of this got out to Ṭāhir, he wrote to Sulaymān b. Abī Jaʿfar, Muḥammad b. ʿĪsā b. Nahīk, and al-Sindī b. Shāhak: "By God, if you do not make him stay and dissuade him from this plan, I will leave you not one estate unconfiscated, and my only objective will be your lives!" So they went before Muḥammad and said, "We have heard what you have decided to do. We beseech you for God's sake to take care for your life. These men are wretches. Now that the siege

656. Parallels: Yaʿqūbī, II, 536 (very brief); Dīnawarī, 395 (very brief); Masʿūdī, VI, 472–84; Ibn al-Athīr, VI, 197–202; *Fragmenta*, 337–41, 413–15.

657. Apparently a proverbial expression. See ed. Leiden, *Glossarium*, CXXII.

has resulted in what you see, they feel they have no place to go. They think there will be no security for their persons or property with your brother or with Ṭāhir and Harthamah because of the widespread knowledge of how they have applied themselves to the war and prosecuted it assiduously. We fear that if they make a sortie with you and you fall into their hands, they will take you prisoner and take your head. They will seek to gain favor by means of you and will make you the means to their own safety." And they cited examples of this to him.

[Continuing,] Muḥammad b. ʿĪsā al-Julūdī said: My father and his companions were sitting in the portico (*riwāq*) of the room (*bayt*) where Muḥammad and Sulaymān and his companions were. When they heard what they were saying and saw that he had accepted it for fear that matters would turn out as they had told him, they were on the verge of going in to them and killing Sulaymān and his companions. But then they changed their minds. They said, "War within, and war without!" and they ceased and desisted.

[Continuing,] Muḥammad b. ʿĪsā [al-Julūdī] said: When this made an impression on Muḥammad's heart and sank into his mind, he turned from his decision and returned to accepting the [913]
guarantee of safety (*amān*) and departure they had given him. He acceded to the request of Sulaymān, al-Sindī, and Muḥammad b. ʿĪsā [b. Nahīk]. They said, "Your only objective today is safety and diversion. Your brother will leave you [to go] where you like. He will set you apart in some place and give you everything that befits you and all you like and desire. No harm or evil will befall you from him." He trusted in this and agreed with them to go out to Harthamah.

[Continuing,] Muḥammad b. ʿĪsā [al-Julūdī] said: My father and his companions did not want to go out to Harthamah, because they had been his companions and knew his ways. They feared he would treat them roughly, would not favor them, and would give them no offices. So they went before Muḥammad and said to him, "Since you have refused to accept our advice to you—and it was the right advice—and have agreed with these flatterers, it would be better for you to go out to Ṭāhir than to Harthamah."

[Continuing,] Muḥammad b. ʿĪsā [al-Julūdī] said: He said to

them, "Alas, I do not like Ṭāhir! For I have dreamed: it was as if I were standing on a brick wall towering into the sky, broad-based and firm; never have I seen one like it in length, breadth, and firmness. I was wearing my black robes,[658] my belt, my sword, my hat (*qalansuwah*), and my boots. Ṭāhir was at the base of the wall, and he kept striking its base until the wall fell. I fell and my hat fell from my head. I have an ominous feeling about Ṭāhir. I am uneasy about him and therefore do not want to go out to him. But Harthamah is our *mawlā* and like a father. I am more comfortable with him and trust him more."

According to Muḥammad b. Ismāʿīl—Ḥafṣ b. Irmiyāʾīl: When Muḥammad wished to cross from the palace at al-Qarār to a house that was in the Garden of Mūsā[659]—he had a floating
[914] bridge in that place—he ordered that [carpets] should be spread in that audience room (*majlis*) and that it should be perfumed.

[Continuing,] he said: So my assistants and I spent the night getting perfume and aromatics, gathering apples, pomegranates, and citrons, and putting them in the rooms. My assistants and I stayed up all night. After I had prayed the morning prayer, I gave an old woman a piece of ambergris incense containing 100 *mithqāl*s,[660] like a melon, and said to her, "I've been up all night and am very tired. I have to get some sleep. If you see the Commander of the Faithful coming on the bridge, put this ambergris on the brazier"—and I gave her a small silver brazier with coals on it. I told her to blow until she burnt it all. I went onto a bark (*ḥarrāqah*)[661] and fell asleep. Before I knew what was happening, the old women came in a panic and woke me up. "Get up, Ḥafṣ," she said. "I've gotten into trouble." "What is

658. For the significance of black clothing as the official ʿAbbāsid color, see the references in note 245.

659. The exact location is unknown. The Mūsā Canal passed through al-Mukharrim quarter of East Baghdad. The reference may be to the Garden of Zāhir, which was located on the east bank of the Tigris, where the Mūsā Canal emptied into the river, a short distance below the main bridge. See Le Strange, *Baghdad*, 219–20.

660. I.e., 446.4 grams, or 15.75 ounces (see Hinz, *Islamische Masse und Gewichte*, 1–5).

661. On the kind of ship, see Mez, *The Renaissance of Islam*, tr. Khuda Bakhsh and Margoliouth; Kindermann, *"Schiff" im Arabischen*; and al-Nukhaylī, *Al-Sufun al-islāmiyyah*.

it?" I said. She said, "I saw a man coming on the bridge, alone, resembling the Commander of the Faithful in build. There was a group of people in front of him and one behind him, so I didn't doubt that it was he. So I burned the ambergris; and when he came, it was ʿAbdallāh b. Mūsā, and here is the Commander of the Faithful coming now!" I cursed her and upbraided her, and gave her another piece like the first to burn in his presence. She did so. This was when things began to take a turn for the worse.

According to ʿAlī b. Yazīd, who said: After the siege against Muḥammad had gone on for a long time, Sulaymān b. Abī Jaʿfar, Ibrāhīm b. al-Mahdī, and Muḥammad b. ʿĪsā b. Nahīk left him, and all of them made their way to ʿAskar al-Mahdī. Muḥammad remained besieged in the city Thursday, Friday, and Saturday. Muḥammad discussed with his companions and those who remained with him whether to ask for quarter (*amān*). He asked them about the way to escape from Ṭāhir. Al-Sindī said to him, "By God, master, if al-Ma'mūn were to get hold of us, it [915]
would be against our wishes and to our misfortune. I see no deliverance but Harthamah." "How by Harthamah," he asked him, "when death has surrounded me on every side?" Others advised him to go out to Ṭāhir. They said, "If you swore him oaths by which he became certain that you were committing your kingdom to him, perhaps he would trust you." But he said to them, "You have missed the mark in your advice, and I have erred in consulting you. If ʿAbdallāh my brother had toiled himself and taken charge of matters according to his own judgment, would he have accomplished one-tenth of what Ṭāhir has accomplished for him? I have tested Ṭāhir and inquired about his thinking. I have not found him inclined to break faith with ʿAbdallāh or to have any ambition except for him. If he agreed to obey me and turned to me, I would fear nothing, even if all the people of the earth opposed me. I wish he would agree to that: I would give him my treasuries; I would put my affairs into his hands and be pleased to live under his protection. But I have no hope that he will do so." Al-Sindī said to him, "You are right, Commander of the Faithful. Let us go quickly to Harthamah, for he thinks that there is no justification to act against you if you go out to him from the [capital of the] kingdom. He has already given me a guarantee that he will fight to defend you if

ʿAbdallāh moves to kill you. Go out at night, at an hour when people are asleep. I hope that what we do will escape the people's notice."

According to Abū al-Ḥasan al-Madāʾinī: When Muḥammad was about to go out to Harthamah and had agreed to his terms, Ṭāhir was troubled and refused to show leniency and allow him to depart. He said, "He is in my quarter, on the side [of the river] where I am. I have made him come out by siege and fighting,
[916] until he has come to ask for quarter (*amān*). I do not agree that he should go out to Harthamah, rather than me, so that the victory should be his."

When Harthamah and the commanders saw this, they met in the house of Khuzaymah b. Khāzim. Ṭāhir and his closest commanders went to them. Sulaymān b. al-Manṣūr, Muḥammad b. ʿĪsā b. Nahīk, and al-Sindī b. Shāhak came to them. They negotiated and arranged the matter. They informed Ṭāhir that al-Amīn would never come out to him: if what he requested were not granted, there was a risk that the result in his case would be like [what had happened] in the days of al-Ḥusayn b. ʿAlī b. ʿĪsā b. Māhān. They said to him, "He will come out in his person to Harthamah, for he feels safe with him and trusts his good intention, but is afraid of you. To you he will give the seal, the scepter, and the mantle—that being the caliphate.[662] Do not spoil this affair. Take advantage of it, since God has facilitated it." (Ṭāhir) granted this and agreed. But according to report, when al-Hirsh learned the news, he decided to gain favor with Ṭāhir; so he informed him that what had taken place between them and him was a trick, and that the seal, the mantle, and the scepter would be carried with Muḥammad to Harthamah. Ṭāhir accepted this and believed that it was as (al-Hirsh) had written. He became angry. He placed men in ambush around the Palace of Umm Jaʿfar and the Palaces of al-Khuld with weapons; they also had crowbars[663] and hoes. It was the

662. On these insignia of the caliphate, see note 41.

663. *ʿAtal* has a variety of meanings: an iron implement, perhaps like a machete, for cutting or lopping the side-shoots of palm trees; a kind of pickax used for digging; or an iron bar like a crowbar, used for demolishing walls. See Lane, *Lexicon*, V, 1949.

eve of Sunday, five days before the end of Muḥarram 198—the 25th of Aylūl (September), according to the Syriac month.

According to al-Ḥasan b. Abī Saʿīd—Ṭāriq the Eunuch (*khādim*), who said: When Muḥammad was about to go out to Harthamah, he became thirsty before leaving. So I looked for water in his beverage closet, but found none. In the evening, he hastened out, intending to go to Harthamah at the time that had been arranged between them. He put on the caliphal robes, a woolen tunic (*durrāʿah*), a shawl (*ṭaylasān*), and his tall hat (*qalansuwah*). Before him was a candle. When we reached the [917] guardhouse of al-Baṣrah Gate,[664] he said, "Get me a drink from the guards' wells." I handed him a cup of water, but it revolted him because of its foul odor, and he did not drink it. He went to Harthamah. Ṭāhir then assaulted him: he had hidden himself in ambush for him at al-Khuld; when Muḥammad went to the bark (*ḥarrāqah*), Ṭāhir and his companions came out and bombarded the bark with arrows and stones. [The passengers] leaned toward the water, and the bark overturned; Muḥammad, Harthamah, and those in it fell into the water. Muḥammad swam across and reached the Garden of Mūsā. But he suspected that his falling into the water had been a trick on the part of Harthamah, so he crossed the Tigris [again] and reached the vicinity of the Ṣarāt [Canal]. Those in charge of the garrison were Ibrāhīm b. Jaʿfar al-Balkhī and Muḥammad b. Ḥumayd. The latter was the son of the brother of Shaklah, the mother of Ibrāhīm b. al-Mahdī. Ṭāhir had put him in charge—whenever (Ṭāhir) gave one of his Khurāsānian companions a command, he joined men to him.[665] Muḥammad b. Ḥumayd, who was known as al-Ṭāhirī because Ṭāhir was promoting him in responsibilities, recognized (Muḥammad al-Amīn). (Al-Ṭāhirī) called out to his men, and they came down and took (Muḥammad). He himself quickly laid hold of Muḥammad. He grasped his legs and dragged him. He

664. Cf. another version on p. 189, below, where the cavalcade passes the Khurāsān Gate.

665. That is, he joined to Ibrāhīm b. Jaʿfar al-Balkhī (from Balkh in Khurāsān, as his name indicates) a man with Baghdad connections, in this case the nephew of the concubine Shaklah, the mother of Ibrāhīm b. al-Mahdī. On Shaklah, see Abbott, *Two Queens of Baghdad*, 33–34.

was placed on an ordinary horse,[666] a coarse soldier's waist-wrapper was thrown on him, and he was taken to the lodging of Ibrāhīm b. Jaʿfar al-Balkhī, who was staying at al-Kūfah Gate. (Al-Ṭāhirī) mounted a man behind him to hold him lcst he fall, as is done with prisoners.

According to al-Ḥasan b. Abī Saʿīd—Khaṭṭāb b. Ziyād: When Muḥammad and Harthamah fell into the water, Ṭāhir hastened to the Garden of Muʾnisah, opposite al-Anbār Gate, the site of his camp, lest he be accused of the drowning of Harthamah. [Khaṭṭāb continued,] saying: When Ṭāhir reached the Syrian Gate—we were with him in the cavalcade, along with al-Ḥasan b. ʿAlī al-Maʾmūnī and al-Rashīd's eunuch (*khādim*) al-Ḥasan al-Kabīr—Muḥammad b. Ḥumayd caught up with us and dismounted. He approached Ṭāhir and told him that he had taken
[918] Muḥammad prisoner and had sent him to al-Kūfah Gate, to the lodging of Ibrāhīm al-Balkhī. Ṭāhir turned to us and told us the news. "What do you say?" he asked. Al-Maʾmūnī said [in Persian], "*Ma-kun*"—that is, "Do not do as was done to Ḥusayn b. ʿAlī." Then Ṭāhir called a *mawlā* of his named Quraysh al-Dandānī and commanded him to kill Muḥammad. Ṭāhir followed him, heading for al-Kūfah Gate, toward the place.

According to al-Madāʾinī[667]—Muḥammad b. ʿĪsā al-Julūdī, who said: When (Muḥammad) had made ready to leave—it was after the final night prayer (*ʿishāʾ*), the eve of Sunday—he came out into the courtyard of the palace and sat down on a chair. He was wearing white robes and a black shawl (*ṭaylasān*). We came into his presence and stood before him with maces.

Kutlah the eunuch (*khādim*) came and said, "Master, Abū Ḥātim[668] sends you his greetings. He says, 'Master, I have come at the appointed time to transport you, but I think you should not come out tonight; for I saw by the Tigris, on the shore, something that made me suspicious. I fear that I may be overpowered, so that you may be taken from my hands or your life

---

666. A *birdhawn*, a hack or destrier, i.e., a non-Arabian, nonthoroughbred horse.

667. Ṭabarī highlights the contrasting nature of this account by introducing the *isnād* with the word *ammā*: "As for al-Madāʾinī, he mentioned . . ."

668. That is, Harthamah, whose *kunyah* (agnomen) was Abū Ḥātim. See Ṭabarī, III, 718.

be lost. Instead, stay where you are, until I go back and prepare myself. I will come tomorrow night and bring you out. If you are attacked, I will fight to defend you, and shall have my equipment with me.'" Muḥammad said to him, "Go back to him and say to him, 'Do not leave, for I am coming out to you now. It cannot be avoided. I will not stay until tomorrow.'"

(Muḥammad) was apprehensive. He said, "The people and the *mawālī* and guards in charge of my gate have scattered from me. I am afraid that if I wait for the morning and the report of their scattering reaches Ṭāhir, he will come in to me and take me." He called for a black horse of his—a bobtail with a blaze on its forehead and white on its legs; he called it "al-Zuhrī."[669] Then he called for his two sons. He embraced them, smelled them, and kissed them. He said, "I commend you to God." His eyes [919]
filled with tears, and he began to wipe them with his sleeve. Then he stood up and jumped onto the horse. We went out in front of him to the palace gate, until we had mounted our horses. Before him was a single candle. When we reached the arcades[670] next to Khurāsān Gate, my father said to me, "Muḥammad, stretch out your hand over him, for I fear that some man may strike him with a sword. If he is struck, the blow will hit you instead of him." So I threw the reins of my horse onto its mane and stretched out my hand over him, until we reached Khurāsān Gate. We ordered it to be opened and went out to the wharf. Harthamah's bark was there. (Muḥammad) went up to it. The horse began to hesitate and shy. He struck it with the whip and urged it onward, until he had ridden into the Tigris and boarded the bark. We took the horse, went back to the city, and entered it. We gave orders and the gate was locked. We heard the screaming, so we went up to the dome that was over the gate. There we stood, listening to the sound.

According to Aḥmad b. Sallām, the official in charge of peti-

669. The vowels are uncertain; al-Zahrī, al-Zuhrā, al-Zahrā, and al-Zuharī are other possibilities. Masʿūdī, VI, 476, reads al-Zuhayrī, al-Zuhayrā, or al-Zahīrī.

670. *Ṭāqāt*: The round city of Baghdad was surrounded by a triple wall (outer, main, and inner ramparts). The roadway into the city from each of the four main gates was bordered on either side between the main and inner wall by vaulted arcades. These originally contained shops, but later were occupied by the city police and horse guards. See Le Strange, *Baghdad*, 25–26.

tions and complaints,[671] who said: I was among the commanders who rode with Harthamah in the bark. When Muḥammad got into it, we stood up out of respect. Harthamah knelt on his knees and said, "Master, I cannot stand up because of my arthritis."[672] He embraced him, held him to his bosom, and then began kissing his hands, and feet, and eyes, saying, "My lord and master, the son of my lord and master!"

(Muḥammad) began to examine our faces. He looked at ʿUbaydallāh b. al-Waḍḍāḥ and said to him, "Which of them are you?" He replied, "I am ʿUbaydallāh b. al-Waḍḍāḥ." "Yes," he said. "May God reward you well. How thankful I am for what you did in the matter of the snow![673] If I meet my brother, may God preserve him, I will not fail to praise you before him and
[920] ask him to reward you on my behalf."

While we were about these things and Harthamah had given orders for the bark to push off, Ṭāhir's men attacked us in skiffs (*zawārīq*) and boats (*shadhawāt*). They raised a clamor and clung to the rudder. Some of them cut the rudder; others bored holes in the bark; others threw bricks and shot arrows. The bark was breached. Water entered it, and it sank. Harthamah fell into the water, and a sailor pulled him out. Each of us struck out as best he could. I saw how Muḥammad, having come to that state, was encumbered by his clothes, and how he threw himself into the water.

Then I came ashore. One of Ṭāhir's men caught hold of me and took me to a man who was sitting on an iron chair on the bank of the Tigris behind the Palace of Umm Jaʿfar with a fire lit before him. He said in Persian, "This is a man who came out of the water—one of the passengers in the bark who fell into the water." "Who are you?" he said to me. I said, "One of Harthamah's men. I am Aḥmad b. Sallām, the police chief (*ṣāḥib shurṭah*) of the *mawlā* of the Commander of the Faithful." "You're lying," he said. "Tell me the truth."

671. *Ṣāḥib al-maẓālim*: On the development of this insituation, see Amedroz, "The Maẓālim Jurisdiction in the Aḥkām Sulṭāniyya of Māwardī," *JRAS* (1911), 635–74; Levy, *The Social Structure of Islam*, 348–51.

672. *Niqris*: a swelling of the joints of the leg, either from arthritis or gout. See Lane, *Lexicon*, s.v.

673. *Sic.* I do not know to what this refers.

I said, "I have told you the truth." "Then what has happened to the Deposed One?" he said. I said, "I saw how he was encumbered by his clothes and how he threw himself into the water." He said, "Bring my horse." They brought his horse and he mounted. He gave orders that I should be led by his side.

A rope was put on my neck and I was led by his side. He turned onto al-Rushdiyyah Street. When he reached the Mosque of Asad b. al-Marzubān, I became out of breath from running and was unable to run. The person who was leading me said, "This man has stopped; he isn't running." "Dismount," he said, "and cut off his head." I said to him, "May I be made your ransom! Why will you kill me, when I am a man to whom God has shown favor? I wasn't able to run, but will ransom myself with 10,000 dirhams." When he had heard mention of the 10,000 dirhams, I said, "You shall detain me with you until the [921]
morning and give me a messenger for me to send to my agent in my home in ʿAskar al-Mahdī. If he doesn't bring you the ten thousand, cut off my head." "You've made a fair offer," he said, and he commanded that I should be mounted. So I was mounted behind one of his companions. He took me to the house of his master—it was the house of Abū Ṣāliḥ the secretary (*al-kātib*). He took me into the house and commanded his slaves to keep me. He gave them orders and instructions. He found out from me the news about Muḥammad and how he had fallen into the water; so he went to Ṭāhir to tell him the news about him. He turned out to be Ibrāhīm al-Balkhī.

His slaves took me into one of the rooms of the house. There were reed mats in it, two or three pillows—and, in one version, some rolled-up mats.[674] I sat down in the room. They brought a lamp into it, checked the door of the house, and sat down to talk.

---

674. The reading of ed. Leiden, *fī riwāyah*, implies that this is a parenthetical remark by al-Ṭabarī, alluding to a different version of Aḥmad b. Sallām's account. Cf. p. 194, below, which seems to be such a version. But the text is suspect. On p. 193, Aḥmad b. Sallām goes behind the mats rolled up "in the corner (*fī zāwiyah*) of the room." Since *riwāyah* and *zāwiyah* differ in Arabic script only in the order of two letters and the presence or absence of a dot over the first letter of the word, the original reading here may also have been: "and, in a corner, some rolled-up mats."

After an hour of the night had passed, we suddenly heard horses moving. People knocked on the door. It was opened for them, and they entered, saying, "*Pusar-i Zubaydah!*"[675] A man was brought in to me, unclothed, wearing drawers, a turban veiling his face, and a tattered piece of cloth on his shoulders. They put him with me, ordered those in the house to guard him, and left additional men behind with them.

After the man had settled down in the room, he removed the turban from his face. It was Muḥammad! I wept and said to myself, "Surely we belong to God, and to Him we return."[676] He began looking at me and said, "Which of them are you?" I said, "I am your *mawlā*, master." "Which of the *mawālī*?" he asked. I said, "Aḥmad b. Sallām, the official in charge of petitions and complaints." "I know you from somewhere else," he said. "You used to come to me in al-Raqqah." "Yes," I said. He said, "You used to come to me and often showed me kindness. You are not my *mawlā*; you are my brother and one of my own [family]." Then he said, "Aḥmad—." "At your service, master," I said. "Come close to me," he said, "and hold me. I feel very
[922] frightened." So I held him to myself. His heart was beating so hard that it was about to burst his chest and come out. I kept holding him to me and calming him. Then he said, "Aḥmad, what has happened to my brother?" I said, "He is alive." "May God bring evil upon their postmaster!" he said. "What a liar he is! He said that he had died." He seemed to be apologizing for waging war against him. I said, "Rather, may God bring evil on your ministers!" "Say nothing but good about my ministers," he said, "for they are not at fault. I am not the first person to have sought a thing and been unable to achieve it." Then he said, "Aḥmad, what do you think they will do to me? Do you think they will kill me, or will they keep their oaths to me?" I said, "No, they will keep them for you, master." He began to draw around himself the tattered rag that was on his shoulders, drawing it and holding it with his upper arm on the right and left. I took off a lined cloak that I was wearing and said, "Master, throw this over you." "Alas," he said, "let me be. This is from

675. Persian for "Zubaydah's son," i.e., Muḥammad al-Amīn.
676. See note 23.

God, who is magnified and exalted. In this place it is better for me."

While we were thus, there was a knocking on the door of the house, and it was opened. An armed man came in to us and looked closely at him to confirm that it was he. When he became certain that it was, he left and locked the door. This was Muḥammad b. Ḥumayd al-Ṭāhirī. Thus I realized that the man would be killed.

I had yet to perform the odd prostration of my prayer.[677] I feared that I would be killed with him without having completed the prayer. So I stood up to complete an odd number of prostrations. "Aḥmad," he said. "Do not go away from me. Pray next to me. I feel very afraid." So I drew near to him. At midnight or close to it, I heard the movement of the horses. There was a knocking at the door, and it was opened. Some Persians entered the house with drawn swords in their hands. When he saw them, he stood up and said, "'Surely we belong to God, and to Him we return!' By God, my life has perished for the sake of God! Is there no escape? Is there no one to help? Is there none of the *Abnā'*?" [923]

They came and stood at the door of the room where we were. They drew back from entering it. They started saying to each other, "Go on," and pushing each other. I stood up and went behind the mats rolled up in the corner of the room. Muḥammad got up and took a pillow in his hand and started saying, "Woe unto you! I am the cousin of the Messenger of God, may God bless him and grant him peace. I am the son of Hārūn. I am the brother of al-Ma'mūn. [Fear] God, [fear] God concerning my blood!" One of them came in to him—he was named Khumārawayh and was a slave (*ghulām*) of Quraysh al-Dandānī, Ṭāhir's *mawlā*. He struck him a blow with the sword. It landed on the front of his head. Muḥammad struck his face with the pillow that was in his hand and leaned on him to take the sword from his hand. Khumārawayh shouted in Persian, "He's killed

677. The reference is to a form of night prayer called *ṣalāt al-witr*, consisting of an odd number of prostrations (*rak'ahs*)—three or five. The narrator remembers that he has not yet completed the final one. See Lane, *Lexicon*, s.v. *watara*.

me! He's killed me!" A group of them came in. One of them pricked him in the hip with his sword. They got on top of him and slaughtered him, cutting the nape of his neck. They took his head and went with it to Ṭāhir. They left his body. A little before daybreak, they came for his body, wrapped it in a horse blanket, and carried it away.

In the morning, I was told, "Hand over the 10,000 dirhams, or we will cut off your head." So I sent to my agent. He came to me. I commanded him, he brought them, and I handed them over. Muḥammad's entry into the city had taken place on Thursday. He had gone out to the Tigris on Sunday.

Aḥmad b. Sallām is also reported to have said in this account: I said to Muḥammad, after he had come into the room with me and had become calm, "May God not reward your ministers well, for they brought you to this pass." He replied to me, "Brother, this is not the place for blame." Then he said, "Tell me about al-Ma'mūn, my brother: is he alive?" "Yes," I said, "this fighting—on whose behalf is it, if not his?" He said,
[924] "Yaḥyā, the brother of ʿĀmir b. Ismāʿīl b. ʿĀmir"—he was in charge of news in Harthamah's camp—"told me that al-Ma'mūn had died." I said to him, "He lied." Then I said to him, "This waist wrapper (*izār*) you are wearing is a coarse one. Put on mine and this shirt of mine, for it is soft." He said to me, "For someone in a state like mine, this is plenty." So I instructed him to turn his thoughts toward God[678] and pray for forgiveness, which he began to do.

While we were thus, suddenly there was a thud from which the floor almost shook, and behold, Ṭāhir's men had entered the house and headed toward the room. The door was narrow; so Muḥammad tried to hold them off with a pillow[679] that was

---

678. *Laqqantuhu dhikr Allāh*: The expression has a general sense here. In later times, the custom developed of whispering "instructions" into the ear of the dead man at the time of interment, so that he could answer the examining angels correctly. This instruction was called *talqīn* (from the same root as *laqqantuhu*). Cf. Lane, *Modern Egyptians*, 523–25; Dozy, *Supplément*, II, 553–54.

679. The text of the only manuscript reads *mijannah*, "shield." As ed. Leiden notes, the parallel in *Fragmenta*, 415a, reads *mikhaddah*, "pillow." The two words are easily confused in Arabic script. Because a pillow (referred to as a

with him in the room. As soon as they reached him, they threw him to the ground. Then they rushed at him and cut off his head. They went to meet Ṭāhir with it, and they carried his body to the Garden of Mu'nisah, to his camp. When ʿAbd al-Salām b. al-ʿAlā', the commander of Harthamah's guard, came, (Ṭāhir) gave him permission [to enter]. He had crossed over to him by the bridge that was in al-Shammāsiyyah. (ʿAbd al-Salām) said to him, "Your brother [Harthamah] sends greetings to you. What is your news?" (Ṭāhir) said, "Lad, bring the basin." They brought it. Muḥammad's head was in it. "This," he said, "is my news! Let him know." In the morning, he set Muḥammad's head on al-Anbār Gate.[680] Countless residents of Baghdad went out to look at it, and Ṭāhir came to say that it was "the head of Muḥammad the Deposed."

According to Muḥammad b. ʿĪsā: The Deposed One saw a louse on his garment. "What is this?" he said. They said, "Something that gets into the clothing of the people." He said, "May God protect me from the passing away of prosperity." He was killed that very day.

According to al-Ḥasan b. Abī Saʿīd: Both armies, that of Ṭāhir and that of the people of Baghdad, regretted the killing of Muḥammad because of the wealth they had been obtaining.

Also according to him: He mentioned that the repository (*khizānah*) holding the head of Muḥammad, the head of ʿĪsā b. [925]
Māhān, and the head of Abū al-Sarāyā[681] was entrusted to him. [Continuing,] he said: I looked at the head of Muḥammad. There was a blow on his face. The hair of his head and beard was intact: none of it had fallen[682] off, and its color was unchanged.

Ṭāhir sent the head of Muḥammad to al-Ma'mūn, along with

---

wisādah) already has been mentioned as in the room and it would be unlikely for the captors to have left al-Amīn in a room with military equipment with which to defend himself, *mikhaddah* is likely to have been the original reading.

680. Cf. *Fragmenta*, 415: "on the tower, the tower of the wall of the garden next to al-Anbār Gate. Al-Anbār Gate was opened and countless residents . . ."

681. I.e., al-Sarī b. Manṣūr, known by his *kunyah*, Abū al-Sarāyā, who in the following year (198/815) led an ʿAlid uprising in al-Kūfah in the name of Muḥammad b. Ibrāhīm (known as Ibn Ṭabāṭabā). The rebellion was put down, and Abū al-Sarāyā was executed on 10 Rabīʿ I 200 (October 19, 815). See Ṭabarī, III, 977–81, 984–87.

682. The reading of ed. Cairo (*yataḥātta*) is superior to that of ed. Leiden.

the mantle, the scepter, and the prayer rug—it was of palm leaves and lined—with Muḥammad b. al-Ḥasan b. Muṣʿab, his cousin.[683] Al-Ma'mūn ordered that he be given a million dirhams. I saw Dhū al-Ri'āsatayn bring the head of Muḥammad before al-Ma'mūn on a shield by his own hand. When the latter saw it, he prostrated himself.

According to al-Ḥasan [b. Abī Saʿīd]—Ibn Abī Ḥamzah—ʿAlī b. Ḥamzah al-ʿAlawī, who said: A number of members of the family of Abū Ṭālib[684] approached Ṭāhir while he was in the garden at the time of the death of Muḥammad the son of Zubaydah. We happened to be in the capital. He gave them and us gifts. He wrote to al-Ma'mūn granting us or some of us permission [for an audience]. So we set out for Marw, and then returned to Medina. People congratulated us on our good fortune. We met the residents and other people who were in Medina and described to them the death of Muḥammad and how Ṭāhir b. al-Ḥusayn had summoned a *mawlā* of his named Quraysh al-Dandānī and ordered him to kill him. A certain old man among them said to us, "How did you say [his name was]?" I told him. The old man said, "Praise God! That is what we used to relate—that Quraysh would kill him. We assumed this meant the tribe [of Quraysh], but the name has fit with the name."

According to Muḥammad b. Abī al-Wazīr—ʿAlī b. Muḥammad b. Khālid b. Barmak: When news of the death of Muḥammad reached Ibrāhīm b. al-Mahdī, he exclaimed "Surely we belong to God, and to Him we return!" He wept a long time and then said:[685]

Turn aside at a place of wind-swept ruins,
    at al-Khuld [Palace], with its stones and bricks;
[926] With its polished marble that was gilded,
    and the door that was a door of pure gold:
Turn aside at it, and learn there
    with certainty the power of the Almighty.

683. Literally, "the son of his father's brother."
684. That is, descendants of ʿAlī b. Abī Ṭālib.
685. The poem is quoted with variants in Ibn al-Athīr, VI, 201–2.

Take a message from me to the
master who is over the subordinate and the commander.
Tell him, "O son of him who was favored with [God's] guidance,[686]
cleanse God's lands of Ṭāhir."[687]
He was not satisfied with severing his jugular veins,
as sacrificial animals are slaughtered with butchers' knives,
But went so far as to come dragging his limbs
with a rope, destroying [his limbs] as far as one can go,[688]
Death having already settled upon him,
and his eye having lost its sight.

When news of this reached al-Ma'mūn, it was distressing to him.

According to al-Madā'inī: Ṭāhir wrote [the following letter] to al-Ma'mūn about the victory:

> To proceed: Praise be to God the Exalted, the Possessor of power and glory, kingdom and dominion; Who, when He wills a thing, says to it only "Be," and it is; save Whom there is no god; the Merciful, the Compassionate.[689]
>
> Among the things that God determined and confirmed, ordained and established, were how that the Deposed One should break his oath of allegiance, violate his covenant, and be overthrown[690] in his strife, and how that He would decree that he would be slain for the deeds his hands had earned; and God is never unjust to His servants.
>
> I have previously written to the Commander of the Faithful, may God lengthen his life, about how God's

686. The poet addresses al-Ma'mūn as a relative of the Prophet.
687. There is a pun on *ṭahhir* ("cleanse") and the name Ṭāhir.
688. The text of the second hemistich is uncertain. The translation follows the reading and interpretation suggested by ed. Leiden, *Addenda*, DCCLXVII.
689. Cf. Qur'ān 36:82.
690. The unusual word (*irtikās*) recalls Qur'ān 4:88, 91, where the same root is associated with God's overthrow of those who become hypocrites or cause civil strife (*fitnah*).

army surrounded the [Round] City and al-Khuld [Palace]; how they occupied its outlets, its roads, and its ways of access on the Tigris, up to the streets of the City of Peace; how garrisons were set up around it; how I brought down ships and boats with *ʿarrādah*s and fighters opposite al-Khuld and the Khurāsān Gate to keep watch over the Deposed One, lest he practice some guile
[927] or follow a course of action whereby he might find a way to stir up strife, arouse discord, or provoke combat, after God, who is exalted and glorified, had encircled him and abandoned him; how messengers went repeatedly, conveying what Harthamah b. Aʿyan, the *mawlā* of the Commander of the Faithful, was offering to him and asking of me: that the way should be cleared for him to go out to (Harthamah); how I met with Harthamah b. Aʿyan to discuss the matter; and how I disliked what (Harthamah) proceeded to do on his own initiative regarding him after God had exhausted him and cut off his hope concerning every stratagem or support, after requisites had been cut off, and after he had been prevented from reaching water, let alone other things, so that his own servants and followers among the people of the city and those who had taken refuge in it with him wanted to kill him and conspired to fall upon him to protect and save their own lives. And there were other things, such as I have explained to the Commander of the Faithful, may God lengthen his life, and such as I hope have reached him.

I now inform the Commander of the Faithful that I carefully considered what Harthamah b. Aʿyan, the *mawlā* of the Commander of the Faithful, had arranged regarding the Deposed One, what he had offered him, and what he had agreed to for him. I found that if he were to escape from his place, where God had made him dwell with humiliation and contempt, and where He had brought him into confinement and siege, civil strife would increase; the people lying in wait in the outlying areas would only grow more ambitious and unsettled. I informed Harthamah b. Aʿyan of this and of my dislike of what he had given (al-Amīn) hope of and had agreed to for him. Harthamah, for his part, said he did not think it right to go back on what he had granted him. Having despaired of his changing his mind, I made an agreement with him: the Deposed One would send ahead the Prophet's mantle, sword, and scepter before leaving; then I would give him free passage to go out to (Harthamah). I did not want there to be any disagreement between myself and (Harthamah), by which we might reach a situation that would give the enemies hope against us, or any falling out of hearts, instead of [928] our unity. The agreement was on this basis and that we would meet at our appointed time on the eve of Saturday. So, with my closest confidants, men I have relied on and whose self-possession, valor, and loyalty I trust, I went and made a full inspection of those whom I had put in charge of the city and al-Khuld on land and water, and commanded them to be vigilant and alert, on guard and cautious. Then I went back toward the Khurāsān Gate. I had prepared barks and ships in addition to the existing equipment, so that I might ride them myself at the time of my rendezvous with Harthamah. I boarded them, together with a group of my closest confidants and hired men (*shākiriyyah*). I stationed a group of them, horsemen and foot soldiers, between Khurāsān Gate and the wharf and on the shore. Harthamah b. Aʿyan approached until he came close to the Khurāsān Gate, equipped and ready. He had tried to outwit me by a message to the Deposed One: he was to go out to him when he reached the wharf, and he would transport him before I knew of it or before he had sent me the mantle, the sword, and the scepter according to the terms on which he had agreed with me. When the Deposed One's departure was reported to those whom I had stationed at Khurāsān Gate, they came hurrying as soon as he came into their sight to check the seal, for I had given them an order and warned them not to allow anyone to pass without my order. He, however, tried to reach the wharf before them. Harthamah brought the bark up to it, and

the promise breaker reached it before my men. Kawthar was in the rear; my *mawlā* Quraysh captured him and with him the mantle, the scepter, and the sword. He took him and the things he had. The companions of the Deposed One fled when they saw that my forces
[929] intended to prevent their Deposed One from leaving. Some of them rushed toward Harthamah's bark, which capsized with them, so that it filled with water and sank; others returned to the city. The Deposed One then threw himself out of the bark into the Tigris to reach safety on shore, regretting his having left, violating the promise, and proclaiming his rallying cry. A group of my aides, whom I had posted between the Khurāsān Gate wharf and al-Ṣarāt Point, hastened to him. They took him by force and compulsion, without pact or agreement. He proclaimed his rallying cry, persisted in his perfidy, and offered them 100 beads,[691] each of which, he said, had a value of 100,000 dirhams; but they insisted on being loyal to their caliph, may God preserve him, on upholding their religion, and on preferring their bounden duty. So they laid hold of him, God having delivered him up and left him solitary, each desiring him and wishing to obtain favor with me before his fellow, until disorder broke out among them.[692] They tried to subdue him with their swords, competing for him, and fearing lest he should elude them. Finally, there was appointed[693] for him one zealous for God, His religion, His Messenger, and His caliph, and he did away with him. Word of this reached me, and I commanded that his head should be carried to me. When it had been brought, I ordered those whom I had posted in the city, al-Khuld, and the surrounding area, and everyone else in the garrisons to remain in their places and secure

691. The word *ḥabbah* can mean either a bead, a small coin, or a unit of weight (0.0706 gram). See Dozy, *Supplément*, I, 241; Hinz, *Islamische Masse und Gewichte*, 1–5. Perhaps al-Amīn was carrying jewels.

692. Alternative translation: "they fought among themselves."

693. The verb used here, *utīḥa*, normally is used of things ordained or destined by God.

their immediate vicinity, until my order should come to them. Then I left. Thus God has granted great benefit and victory to the Commander of the Faithful—to him, and to Islam through him and in him.[694]

In the morning, the people became excited and disagreed about the Deposed One. Some believed he had been killed, whereas others denied it; some doubted, whereas others were certain. So I thought it wise to dispel their uncertainty about him. I brought out his head for them to look at, that it might be verified in their eyes. Thus the confusion in their minds would be ended, along with the evil of sedition by those who seek corruption and hasten to strife. I went toward the city early in the morning. Those in it surrendered, and its people rendered obedience. The areas adjoining the [930]
City of Peace on the east and the west—their quarters, suburbs, and districts—showed themselves loyal to the Commander of the Faithful. The war came to an end. (God) restored with peace and Islam the people of (peace and Islam). God has removed corruption from them. Through the blessing of the Commander of the Faithful, He has brought them into peace and tranquillity, into meekness, loyalty, and contentedness. Every benefit comes from God, the Almighty and Exalted, and every good thing; and to God be praise for this.

As I write this to the Commander of the Faithful, may God keep him, there is not in my presence any inciter to strife, or any instigator, or any mischief maker; there are only people who heed and obey, eager and ready. God has caused them to taste the sweetness of the Commander of the Faithful and the gentleness of his rule, so that they go about their affairs in its shadow, going early to their places of business, and returning late to their homes. God is the Bestower of this benefit, the Completer of it, and the One who will grant even more of it through His blessing.

I pray that God will gladden the Commander of the

694. The meaning of the end of the sentence is not clear.

Faithful with His favor; that He will continually increase it for him; that He will cause him to be thankful to Him for it; and that He will make His grace toward him continuous, lasting, and uninterrupted; until God unites for him the good of this world and of the world to come—for him, his friends, the upholders of his right, and for all the Muslims through his blessing, the blessing of his rule, and the good fortune of his caliphate. For He is their protector in this and faithful in it; and He is quick to hear and benevolent in what He desires.

Written on Sunday, four nights remaining in the month of Muḥarram 198.[695]

It has been mentioned concerning Muḥammad the Deposed that before his death, after he had gone into the city and had seen how events had turned against him and how his aides were slipping away and going out to Ṭāhir, he sat in the gallery[696] that he had made on [the Palace of] the Golden Gate.[697] (He had ordered it to be built some time earlier.) He commanded that all the commanders and soldiers who were with him in the city should be summoned; and so they were gathered in the courtyard (*raḥbah*). He looked down upon them and said:[698]

[931] Praise be to God who raises up and brings low, who gives and withholds, who straitens and enlarges; and to Him is the journeying. I praise Him even for time's misfortunes, the desertion of helpers, the scattering of men, the departure of wealth, the coming of misfortunes, and the arrival of disasters; praising Him with praise in return for which He will lay up for me the greatest reward and give me the best consolation. I bear witness

---

695. The day, Sunday, and the date (the 26th day of a thirty-day month) do not coincide. The last Sunday in Muḥarram, according to modern tables, was the 25th of the month (September 25, 813).

696. *Janāḥ* means "wing." Le Strange calls it a "belvedere" or "pinnacle," a covered gallery or balcony built high enough so that the caliph could look out at the courtyard of the palace and address a gathering. See Le Strange, *Baghdad*, 31–32.

697. On this palace, located at the center of the Round City, see Le Strange, *Baghdad*, 31–32.

698. Parallel: Masʿūdī, VI, 443–44.

that there is no god but God alone—no partner has He—as He has testified to Himself, and as His angels have testified to Him; and that Muḥammad is His faithful servant and His messenger to the Muslims (may God bless him and grant him peace). Amen, O Lord of the worlds!

To proceed: O company of the *Abnāʾ* and people who preceded [all others] in following right guidance! You know of my negligence in the days when al-Faḍl b. al-Rabīʿ was my vizier and adviser and how his days continued, causing me regret among courtiers (*khāṣṣah*) and commoners (*ʿāmmah*). Finally, you alerted me, and I took notice; you sought my aid in everything that displeased you in regard to myself and among you; and I gave you unsparingly what my kingdom contained and my power had obtained—what I had gathered and what I had inherited from my fathers. I named as commander someone who was not suitable and entrusted matters to someone who was not up to them. I strove—God knows—to gain your approval by every means I could; you strove—God knows—to displease me by every means you could. As part of this, I sent you ʿAlī b. ʿĪsā, an elder and senior man among you, and people who were merciful and affectionate toward you. It would take too long to mention what was done on your part. I forgave the offense and was generous. I acquiesced and told myself to be patient when I learned that victory had eluded him. I wanted you to remain as a garrison in Ḥulwān with the son of the elder statesman of your mission (*daʿwah*), the man under whose father you had glory and through whom your obedience became complete, ʿAbdallāh b. Ḥumayd b. Qaḥṭabah. You, however, reached a point in leaguing together against him that he could neither tolerate nor endure, led by a man of your [932]
own. Numbering 20,000, you aimed at me, revolting against your leader with Saʿīd al-Fard,[699] to whom you

699. Saʿīd "the Unique": The reference may be to Saʿīd b. Mālik b. Qādim. See p. 136, above.

listened and whom you obeyed. Then, under the leadership of al-Ḥusayn,[700] you revolted against me, deposed me, and reviled me. You seized me, imprisoned me, bound me, and you forbade me from mentioning some things. The hatred in your hearts and your disobedience became greater and greater. But I praise God, as one who has submitted to His command and accepted His decree. Peace!

It has been said: After Muḥammad had been killed and the tumult had ceased, and after a guarantee of safety (*amān*) had been given to all and sundry[701] and the people had become calm, Ṭāhir came into the city on Friday and led the people in worship, preaching to them an eloquent sermon in which he quoted the [verses called] *al-Qawāriʿ*[702] from the Qurʾān. Among what has been preserved of it is that he said: "Praise be to God, 'Master of kingship, who gives kingship to whom He will, and takes away kingship from whom He will; He exalts whom He will, and abases whom He will; in whose hand is the good; and He is powerful over everything.'"[703]—along with [other] verses of the Qurʾān, which he made to follow one after the other. He urged obedience and the maintenance of unity (*jamāʿah*) and exhorted the people to hold fast to the rope of obedience. Then he returned to his camp.

It is mentioned: When Ṭāhir ascended the pulpit on Friday, a large group of Hāshimites, commanders, and others were present before him. He said:

Praise be to God, "Master of kingship, who gives it to whom He will; who exalts whom He will, and abases

---

700. For the attempted coup against al-Amīn under the leadership of al-Ḥusayn b. ʿAlī b. ʿĪsā b. Māhān, see pp. 108 ff., above.

701. Literally, "had been granted to white and black."

702. The original meaning of *qawāriʿ* (plural of *qāriʿah*) is "calamities," or "disasters," and it is used as the title of Sūrah 101 of the Qurʾān. However, the word came to be used to designate "verses that one reads when one is afraid of the *jinn* or men, so that one feels secure, such as the Verse of the Throne [2:255], the verses at the end of the Sūrah of the Cow [2:284–86], and the Sūrah of Yāsīn [36]; for they avert fear from whoever reads them, as if they upbraided the devil." (*Lisān*, V, 3597c).

703. Cf. Qurʾān 3:26.

whom He will; in whose hand is the good; and He is powerful over everything." "He does not set right the work of those who do corruption,"[704] and "He does not guide the devising of the treacherous."[705] Truly, the emergence of our victory came not of our own hands, nor from our own devising; rather, God has chosen [what is best] for the caliphate.[706] For He has made it a stay for His religion and a support for His servants, the governance of the provinces and the barring of the borders, the readying of provisions and gathering of tribute (*fay'*), the execution of judgment, the propa- [933]
gation of justice, and the revival of the [Prophet's] tradition (*sunnah*) after vanities and reveling in destructive lusts had sapped it. He who inclines toward this world thinks well of the call of its beguilement: he draws out the milk of its prosperity, cleaves to the flower of its garden, and loves the splendor of its beauty. You have seen the fulfillment of God's promise—He is exalted and glorified—against the one who behaved insolently against Him: how He brought His strength and retribution upon him after he had turned from his promise, rebelled against Him, and disobeyed His commandment; and how His prohibition replaced him, and His admonition brought about his destruction.[707] So hold fast to the firm cords of obedience, and follow in the paths of unity (*jamā'ah*). Beware the fate of those who disobeyed and rebelled, who kindled the spark of civil strife and divided a people that had been at unity, so that God requited them with loss of this world and the next.

---

704. Qur'ān 10:81.

705. Qur'ān 12:52.

706. Either *ikhtāra Allāhu li-l-khilāfah* is to be rendered "has chosen [the best for] the caliphate"—a construction attested elsewhere (see Dozy, *Supplément*, I, 415)—or some words have fallen from the text. The version of the speech in *al-'Iqd al-Farīd* (II, 188 in ed. Bulaq; IV, 212 in the 1983 Beirut printing) reads: "God has chosen for the caliphate . . . him who will carry its burdens and assume its weight."

707. The text of the end of the sentence ("and how His prohibition . . .") is hopelessly corrupt. The phrase may originally have begun, "and altered His (i.e., God's) prohibition . . ." (*wa-ghayyara nahyahu*).

After Ṭāhir had conquered Baghdad, he wrote to Abū Isḥāq al-Muʿtaṣim[708]—one [authority] has mentioned that he in fact wrote this to Ibrāhīm b. al-Mahdī,[709] but [most] people have said that he wrote it to Abū Isḥāq al-Muʿtaṣim:

> To proceed: It is distressing to me to write to a man of the caliphal family without having been given authorization to do so. However, it has been reported to me that you lean in opinion and incline in affection toward the promise breaker who has been deposed. If that is so, what I have written to you of it is quite enough. If it is not so, then peace be upon you, prince, and the mercy of God and His blessing!

At the bottom of the letter he wrote the following verses:

Your embarking upon the matter while the proper time for it was not made manifest
was ignorance, and your heedless opinion was [indeed] heedlessness.
How ugly a world it is in which those who do wrong acquire
the portion of those who do right, and the vain man is deceived!

The Army Mutinies against Ṭāhir

In this year, the army mutinied against Ṭāhir after the killing of Muḥammad.[710] Ṭāhir fled from them and went into hiding for
[934] several days, until he set matters right with them. A report of why they mutinied against him and the consequences for him and them follows.

According to Saʿīd b. Ḥumayd, who mentioned that his father related [the following] to him: Ṭāhir's forces mutinied against him five days after the death of Muḥammad. Having no money at hand, he was hard pressed. He supposed that this had

---

708. He was the third son of al-Rashīd and ruled as caliph from 218/833 to 227/842.

709. Ibrāhīm b. al-Mahdī led a revolt against the rule of al-Maʾmūn in 202/817. See Ṭabarī, III, 1013–17, 1074–75, Cf. *Fragmenta*, 416.

710. Parallels: Ibn al-Athīr, VI, 207–8; *Fragmenta*, 416–17.

happened through the connivance of the people of the suburbs (*arbāḍ*) with them and that they were on the side of (the mutineers) against him. However, none of the people of the suburbs had made a move in the matter. The strength of his forces increased. Fearing for himself, he fled from the garden, and they plundered some of his property. He went to ʿAqarqūf,[711] having commanded the gates of the city and the gate of the palace to be guarded against Umm Jaʿfar and against Mūsā and ʿAbdallāh, the sons of Muḥammad. Afterward, he ordered that Zubaydah, along with Muḥammad's sons Mūsā and ʿAbdallāh, should be transferred from the Palace of Abū Jaʿfar to the Palace of al-Khuld. They were transferred on the eve of Friday, twelve nights before the end of Rabīʿ I (November 17, 813). They were taken the same night in a boat to Humayniyā on the west bank in the Upper Zāb district.[712] Afterward, he commanded that Mūsā and ʿAbdallāh should be taken to their uncle [al-Maʾmūn] in Khurāsān by way of al-Ahwāz and Fārs.

When the soldiers mutinied against Ṭāhir and demanded their pay (*arzāq*), they burned al-Anbār Gate, which was by the trench, and the Garden Gate (*Bāb al-Bustān*), and they brandished their swords. They continued thus that day and the next and shouted, "Mūsā, O Victorious One!"[713] People said that Ṭāhir had acted with good judgment in sending Mūsā and ʿAbdallāh away. Ṭāhir and the commanders who were on his side had withdrawn. Ṭāhir prepared to fight (the mutineers) and do battle with them, but when the commanders and notables learned of this, they went to him and apologized. They placed the blame on "foolish and immature persons" and asked him to pardon them, accept their apology, and be pleased with them. They guaranteed to him that they would never again do anything displeasing to [935]

---

711. ʿAqarqūf (vocalized ʿAqraqūf by Yāqūt) was a village four *farsakh*s (23.9 km, or 14.9 miles) from Baghdad on the Dujayl Canal, north of Baghdad and west of the Tigris. It was the site of a large mound, thought to be the grave of pre-Sasanian Persian kings. See Yāqūt, *Muʿjam*, s.v.; *EI*[2] s.v. ʿAḳarḳūf.

712. Humayniyā (or Humāniyah) was a village on the west bank of the Tigris about 60 miles downstream from Baghdad. See Le Strange, *Lands*, 37; Yāqūt, *Muʿjam*, s.v. Humāniyah.

713. *Yā Manṣūr*—indicating their acceptance of al-Amīn's young son as caliph.

him, as long as he remained with them. Ṭāhir said to them, "By God, I departed from you only in order to bring down my sword upon you. I swear by God that if you ever again do anything like this, I will go back to my intention concerning you and will go out to do something you won't like!" In this way he broke their spirit. He commanded that the men be given four months' pay (*rizq*). One of the *Abnā'* said concerning this:

The commander swore—his word and his deed
were true—in the assembly of the evildoers:
If any of them became unruly or rioted,
wherever in the area it might be,
He would not argue with people from their assembly;
he would not delay, like a just man or one who grants a respite,
Until he had brought upon them great tribulation
that would leave their homes vacant ruins.

According to al-Madā'inī: After the soldiers had rioted and Ṭāhir had withdrawn, Saʿīd b. Mālik b. Qādim, Muḥammad b. Abī Khālid, and Hubayrah b. Khāzim rode to him with elders of the people of the suburbs (*arbāḍ*). They swore solemn oaths that none of the people of the suburbs had made a move during those days: what had taken place had not accorded with their opinion, nor had they wanted it. They guaranteed him the good behavior of their areas of the suburbs and that each of them would undertake in his area everything incumbent upon him, so that nothing disagreeable to him would befall him from any direction. ʿAmīrah, the father of Shaykh b. ʿAmīrah al-Asadī, and ʿAlī b. Yazīd came to him with elders from the *Abnā'* and behaved toward him as Ibn Abī Khālid, Saʿīd b. Mālik, and Hubayrah had done. They told him that the *Abnā'* behind them were well disposed in their opinion and obedient to him. They had not been involved in anything his forces had done in the garden. Ṭāhir was pleased; however, he said to them, "The men are demanding their pay, and I have no money." So Saʿīd
[936] b. Mālik guaranteed them 20,000 dīnārs and conveyed them to him. Ṭāhir was pleased and went back to his camp in the garden. Ṭāhir said to Saʿīd, "I accept them from you as a debt to be owed by me." "No," he replied, "it is only a gift and a little

for your slave (*ghulām*) and for what God has made your due." So Ṭāhir accepted it from him and commanded that the soldiers be given four months' pay. They were satisfied and became quiet.

According to al-Madā'inī: There was a man named al-Samarqandī on Muḥammad's side. He used to shoot from *manjanīq*s that were on ships in the middle of the Tigris. Sometimes, the people of the suburbs (*arbāḍ*) would gain against Muḥammad's forces who were facing them in the trenches; so (Muḥammad) would send to (al-Samarqandī) and bring him to shoot at them. He was a marksman whose stones did not miss. (According to report, people had not yet been killed by stones at that time.) After Muḥammad was killed, the bridge was cut and the *manjanīq*s from which he had been shooting on the Tigris were burned. Al-Samarqandī feared for his life. Afraid that someone whom he had given cause to seek vengeance[714] would look for him, he went into hiding. The people looked for him. He hired a mule and left for Khurāsān, fleeing. While he was on the road, a man met him and recognized him. After he had passed on, the man said to the muleteer, "Alas for you! Where are you going with this man? By God, if you are taken with him, you will be killed. The least that will befall you is that you will be imprisoned." "Surely we belong to God, and to Him we return!" said the muleteer. "I recognized his name, by God, and had heard of him—God take his life!" So the muleteer hastened to his comrades—or he may have reached a garrison—and told them about him. The men [whom he told] were companions of Kundghūsh from Harthamah's forces. They took (al-Samarqandī) and sent him to Harthamah. Harthamah sent him to Khuzaymah b. Khāzim in the City of Peace, and Khuzaymah turned him over to someone whom al-Samarqandī had given cause to seek vengeance. He took al-Samarqandī out to the bank of the Tigris on the east side, and he was crucified alive.

People have mentioned: When they were about to fasten him
to his beam of wood, a crowd gathered. Before they had fastened [937]
him, he kept saying, "Yesterday you were saying, 'May God

714. That is, by killing one of the man's relatives.

not cause your hand to fail, O Samarqandī!' Today you have prepared your stones and arrows to shoot me." When the beam was raised, the people approached him, throwing stones, shooting arrows, and thrusting spears, until they killed him. Even after his death they kept shooting. The next morning they burned him: they brought fire to burn him and lit it, but it would not ignite. They threw cane and firewood on him and set fire to it. Part of him burned; part of him the dogs tore to pieces. This took place on Saturday, the 2nd of Ṣafar (October 1, 813).

A Description of Muḥammad b. Hārūn, His Agnomen, the Length of His Reign, and His Age[715]

According to Hishām b. Muḥammad[716] and others: Muḥammad b. Hārūn—Abū Mūsā—came to power on Thursday, eleven days before the end of Jumādā I 193.[717] He was killed the eve of Sunday, six days before the end of Ṣafar 198.[718] His mother was Zubaydah, the daughter of Jaʿfar al-Akbar b. Abī Jaʿfar. His caliphate lasted four years, eight months, and five days. His *kunyah* (agnomen) has also been given as "Abū ʿAbdallāh."

However, Muḥammad b. Mūsā al-Khwārizmī[719] is mentioned as having said: The caliphate passed to Muḥammad b. Hārūn on the middle day of Jumādā II 193 (March 6, 809). In the year

---

715. Parallels: Ibn al-Athīr, VI, 202–5; *Fragmenta*, 342–44, 418. Cf. the biography in al-Ṣafadī, *Kitāb al-Wāfī bi-al-wafayāt*, V, 135–39 (repeated in al-Kutubī, *Fawāt al-wafayāt*, IV, 46–48).

716. Hishām b. Muḥammad b. al-Sāʾib al-Kalbī (b. ca. 120/737, d. 204/819 or 206/821), often called "Ibn al-Kalbī" after his father (d. 146/763), who himself was a genealogist, historian, geographer, and Qurʾān commentator, was a Shīʿī native of al-Kūfah who wrote prolifically on many subjects. See *EI*² s.v. al-Kalbī (Atallah).

717. I.e., 19 Jumādā I (February 10, 809). Compare the dates given on p. 2, above; Yaʿqūbī, II, 536–37; Dīnawarī, 395–96; and *Fragmenta*, 342.

718. I.e., 23 Safar 198 (October 23, 813). Compare the date given on p. 181, above ("six days *from the beginning of* the month"). A confusion between the words *khalawna* ("having elapsed [since the beginning of the month]") and *baqīna* ("remaining [to the end of the month]") is possible. The 23rd of Ṣafar did indeed fall on a Sunday. Compare also the date given on p. 187 and implied below, placing al-Amīn's death on the 23rd of the previous month, Muḥarram.

719. Muḥammad b. Mūsā al-Khwārizmī was a great mathematician and chronologist. See *EI*² s.v. al-Khwārazmī (Vernet).

he came to power, Dāwūd b. ʿĪsā b. Mūsā, the governor of Mecca, led the pilgrimage. Abū al-Bakhtarī remained in charge of his governorship.[720] Ten months and five days after coming to power, Muḥammad dispatched ʿIṣmah b. Abī ʿIṣmah to Sāwah.[721] He appointed his son Mūsā heir apparent on the 3rd day of Rabīʿ I (December 15, 809). ʿAlī b. ʿĪsā b. Māhān was in charge of his police (*shurat*). In the year 194, the pilgrimage was led by ʿAlī b. al-Rashīd. Ismāʿīl b. al-ʿAbbās b. Muḥammad [938]
was in charge of Medina. Dāwūd b. ʿĪsā was in charge of Mecca. Between the appointment of his son [Mūsā as heir apparent] and the encounter of ʿAlī b. ʿĪsā b. Māhān with Ṭāhir b. al-Ḥusayn and the death of ʿAlī b. ʿĪsā b. Māhān in 195 there was one year, three months, and twenty-nine days. The Deposed One was killed the eve of Sunday, five nights before the end of Muḥarram (September 25, 813). His period in power accompanied by civil war was four years, seven months, and three days. After Muḥammad had been killed and the report of this reached al-Maʾmūn in a pouch from Ṭāhir on Tuesday, 12 Ṣafar 198 (October 11, 813), al-Maʾmūn made the report public. He gave permission to the commanders, and they came into his presence; al-Faḍl b. Sahl stood up and read the letter containing the report. He was congratulated on the victory, and they invoked God's blessing upon him. After the death of Muḥammad, Ṭāhir and Harthamah received a letter from al-Maʾmūn, saying that al-Qāsim b. Hārūn should be deposed [from the succession]. They made this public and sent out their letters to this effect. The letter deposing him was read on Friday, two nights before the end of the month of Rabīʿ I 198 (November 25, 813). According to what has reached me, Muḥammad's entire lifespan was twenty-eight years. He was tall, bald over the temples, fair, small eyed, hook nosed, handsome, big boned, and broad shouldered. His birthplace was al-Ruṣāfah.

It has been mentioned that Ṭāhir said after killing Muḥammad:

---

720. That is, the governorship of Medina. See Ṭabarī, III, 739, where Abū al-Bakhtarī Wahb b. Wahb is listed as Hārūn's last governor of Medina.

721. That is, ʿIṣmah b. Ḥammād b. Sālim. See p. 44, above. The *kunyah* of Ḥammād b. Sālim was "Abū ʿIṣmah." The date is mentioned here apparently as the first sign of military hostility on al-Amīn's part.

I killed the caliph in his residence,
and with the sword I caused his wealth to be plundered.

He also said:

I overcame people by force and strength,
and slew mighty heroes.
I dispatched the caliphate to Marw,
hastening its way to al-Ma'mūn.

Poems Composed about Muḥammad b. Hārūn and Elegies for Him

[939] Among the poems written in derision (*hijā'*) of him was the following:[722]

Why should we weep for you? Why?—because of [your] raptures,
Abū Mūsā [al-Amīn]? because of [your] promoting of amusement?
Because of [your] omission of the five [prayers] in their times,
in your eagerness for the juice of the grape?
For Shanīf[723] I do not weep;
as for Kawthar, the thought of his death gives me no grief.
You did not know what was the measure of [God's] pleasure,
nor did you know the measure of [His] wrath.
You were not fit to rule,
and the Arabs did not grant you obedience as ruler.
You who weep for him, may the eye
of whoever caused you to weep have wept only for wonder!
Why should we weep for you?—because you exposed us
to *manjanīq*s, and at times to being plundered,
And to people who made us their slaves—
because of them the tail seeks to gain power over the head—
In torment and wasting siege
that blocked the roads, so that there was no way to [obtain] one's needs?

---

722. Eleven verses of the poem with variants are quoted in Ibn al-Athīr, VI, 205.

723. Apparently, Shanīf, like Kawthar, was one of al-Amīn's eunuchs.

They have alleged that you are alive and recruiting [soldiers]:
anyone who has said this has lied.
Would that whoever has said it, in isolation
from all, were to go where he has gone!
God made it necessary for us to kill him:
when He necessitates something, it indeed becomes necessary.
By God, he was a trial for us:
God became angry with him and wrote [His decree].

ʿAmr b. ʿAbd al-Malik al-Warrāq composed the following, lamenting Baghdad, deriding Ṭāhir, and speaking evil of him:[724]

Who has smitten you, Baghdad, with the [evil] eye?
Were you not for a long time the delight of the eye?
Were there not in you people possessing nobility, [940]
who would meet me with good deeds and kindness?
Were there not in you people whose dwelling
and whose residence were a great adornment?
Time cried to them of departure; so they separated.
How the pain of departure grieved me!
I commend to God people whom I never remember
but that tears flow from my eye.
They once were; then a fate separated and dispersed them:
for fate it is that separates the two sides.
How many of them were helpers to me against my fate!
How many among them were generous to me with assistance!
How goodly was the time that united us!
Where is the time that has departed? Whence [has it departed]?
You who are devastating Baghdad that you may reside in it,
you have destroyed yourself between the two ways.
The hearts of all people were one—
ready money—and being ready money is not like [being] a debt [to be paid later]—

724. Five verses of this poem have been quoted on p. 137, above, with variant readings.

When you dispersed them. You divided them into parties,
and the people one and all were [divided] between two hearts.

According to ʿUmar b. Shabbah[725]—Muḥammad b. Aḥmad
[941] al-Hāshimī: Lubābah, the daughter of ʿAlī b. al-Mahdī, said:[726]

I weep for you not because of [lost] happiness and companionship,
but because of exalted deeds, the spear, and the shield.
I weep for a mortal[727] by whose death I have been grieved,
who made me a widow before the wedding night.

Some have said that this poem was composed by the daughter of ʿĪsā b. Jaʿfar, who was betrothed to Muḥammad.

Al-Ḥusayn b. al-Ḍaḥḥāk al-Ashqar,[728] a *mawlā* of [the tribe of] Bāhilah, composed [the following], lamenting Muḥammad. One of Muḥammad's boon companions, he did not believe Muḥammad had been killed and expected him to return.

Best of your family (though they alleged otherwise),
because of you I am sore wounded and grieving.
God knows that I have a liver
that is thirsty because of you, and an eye that weeps.
Though I lament the loss I have suffered,
I hold within me more than I express.
Why did you not remain to meet our need

725. Abū Zayd ʿUmar b. Shabbah (b. 173/789, d. 262/875), a traditionist and historian, was a pupil of al-Madāʾinī. According to Ṭabarī, II, 168, Ṭabarī personally studied ʿUmar b. Shabbah's *Kitāb Akhbār ahl al-Baṣrah* under the author. See Sezgin, *GAS*, I, 345.

726. The poem, with three additional verses, is quoted in Mubarrad, *al-Kāmil*, I, pt. 2, p. 773, with the following note in the margin: "Ibn Shādhān said that this poem about Muḥammad al-Amīn was by Lubābah, the daughter of Mūsā al-Hādī. She was al-Amīn's cousin and was betrothed to al-Amīn, but he was killed before the marriage was consummated." Ibn ʿAbd Rabbih, *al-ʿIqd al-farīd*, III, 225, gives the woman's name as Lubānah, the daughter of Rayṭah b. ʿAlī. "Her verses for the occasion became the type for the use of noble ladies who lost their husbands before the marriage was consummated" (Abbott, *Two Queens of Baghdad*, 222). Cf. also Masʿūdī, VI, 485.

727. Variant in Mubarrad and Masʿūdī: "a horseman" (*fāris*); Ibn ʿAbd Rabbih: "a master" (*sayyid*).

728. That is, the poet al-Ḥusayn al-Khalīʿ. Twenty verses are quoted in Ibn al-Athīr, VI, 202–3.

forever? Why did harm not come to someone else?
You succeeded caliphs who came before,
but after you the succession will surely be wanting.
May your kin not sleep after their offense:
after it I have come to hate your kin.
By rending open your inviolability, they rent open
the Prophet's sanctuary, before which [hang] curtains.
Your relatives who deserted [you] attacked:
all of them avow their disgrace.
When they came, they did not do at the shore
what a jealous, proud person would do.
They left their father's harem to be plundered,
while the chaste women were screaming and shouting.[729]
Beside themselves, they allowed their ankles to be seen—
the young girls among them—and the middle-aged lamented.
Their kerchiefs were snatched away: exposed was
she who wore a veil, and earrings were wrested away.
Among the plunder the women were like [942]
pearls that a shell has opened to reveal.
[He was] a king whose kingdom fate diminished,
so that he grew weak: time's shiftings are various.
How unlikely it is that after you
our[730] strength will endure and our honor last!

---

729. This line and the line below, "How unlikely it is that after you *their* strength will endure and *their* honor last," are quoted in *Aghānī*, VI, 204, with the following story: "According to al-Ṣūlī, from al-Ḥusayn b. Yaḥyā, who said that al-Ḥusayn b. al-Ḍaḥḥāk had told him: 'I was determined to write an elegy for al-Amīn, giving free rein to my tongue, and relieving my grief. However, Abū al-ʿAtāhiyah met me and said to me, "Ḥusayn, I sympathize with you and like you. I know how you feel about al-Amīn. He deserves to be elegized by you. But you have given your tongue free rein from grief and pain over him, saying things that verge on disparagement and defamation of someone else and incitement against him. Al-Maʾmūn is about to descend into Iraq to come against you. Save yourself! Alas, do you dare to say . . . ?"—and he quoted the two lines. "Curb your tongue's vehemence! Withdraw what has been published in your name, and remedy the excess you have committed." Realizing that he had given me good advice, I thanked him and stopped composing. Because of his advice I escaped—and just barely!'"

730. *Aghānī* reads "their strength," and "their honor," referring specifically to the members of the ʿAbbāsid family who sided with al-Maʾmūn. See note 729.

They did not respect solemn documents,
 under which there is the grave for betrayers.
After an oath to God will you kill him?
 Killing after a promise of safety is an outrage!
Tomorrow you shall know by an [evil] consequence
 the power of God; so consider and halt.
You whose sleep is diminished by sleeplessness,
 the lamentations have subsided, yet your heart is grieving.
To me you were a sufficient hope;
 then it passed away, and grief took its place.
The order of things became confused; things hateful to us became
 approved; and after your death, what was approved became hated.
Unity has been disrupted because of your loss:
 the world is left untended,[731] and the mind is grieved.[732]

He also said, lamenting him:

Whenever the trustworthy one remembers, he laments al-Amīn;[733]
 even if the carefree man sleeps, he makes his eyelids hot [with tears].
Dwellings between Buṣrā[734] and Kalwādhā
 have not ceased to arouse sadness for me.
The courtyards of kingship are empty;

---

731. The metaphor implicit in the Arabic *sudan* is that of an animal left to pasture by itself. There is an allusion to Qur'ān 75:36, "What, does man reckon he shall be left to roam at will?"

732. The reading of ed. Cairo *wa-l-bālu munkasifu* ("the mind is grieved," literally, "eclipsed, darkened") is preferable to ed. Leiden's *wa-l-bālu munkashifu* ("the mind is uncovered"), which the Leiden glossary (CDLIII) explains as meaning "the covering of the heart is uncovered from fear."

733. The Arabic text could also be translated, "When al-Amīn is mentioned, he (the poet) laments for al-Amīn; even if he goes to sleep free of [other] care, he causes his eyelids to become hot [with tears]." There is a pun on the name "al-Amīn" and the adjective *amīn*, "trustworthy, faithful."

734. The town of Buṣrā (not to be confused with a similarly named city in Syria) lay on the Tigris about 10 *farsakh*s (37.2 miles) upstream from Baghdad. See Le Strange, *Lands*, 50.

in them the winds blow to and fro, weaving them diversely.[735]
Time has diminished the might of their inhabitant—
[time], which made sport of the ancient generations.
After they had lived in unity, time scattered them:
I used to cling to the goodness of their friendship.
After their departure I have not seen goodness like them,
nor have the eyes of beholders seen them.
O my grief, though enemies rejoice [at his misfortune]!
Alas for the Commander of the Faithful!
After your death, those who seek bounty cannot find it,
and the mounts of petitioners are left to rest.[736]
To your court every day they used to [943]
come late and early with good fortune.
He was the mountain: the heights hurled themselves down
at the sound of his collapse, and the righteous were seized with fear.
After your death the world will mourn for [your] protection,
and after your death it will mourn for the religion that was defended [by you].
The brightness of everything has departed,
and religion has again become outcast and despised.
The might of one linked with Kisrā[737] and his nation
has become firmly established, and the Muslims have been humbled.

He also said, lamenting him:

O my grief over you! One closer [to you] in kinship than I has forgotten you,
while my griefs for you increase!

---

735. The image is borrowed from the descriptions of abandoned campsites in pre-Islamic poetry, where the sand blown into delicate ripples by the wind evokes the passage of time and the loss of dear ones.

736. That is, people no longer tire their camels in long journeys to seek al-Amīn's patronage. The theme of the journey across the desert to a patron of great generosity is common in pre-Islamic poetry.

737. The Arabs called any of the Persian kings who ruled Iraq and Iran before the Arab conquest "Kisrā" (from Persian *Khusraw*). The line alludes to al-Ma'mūn's "Persianness."

The following was composed by ʿAbd al-Raḥmān b. Abī al-Hudāhid, lamenting Muḥammad:

Flow, O tears: he has been cut off from his cord,
  and we have lost the copiousness of his rain.[738]
A disaster's hand snatched away your prosperity;
  you became a thing whose misfortunes we bear with patience.
Death has come to have a banner among us:
  death's tooth laughs from his banner.
What caused the blow of death to descend upon
  the most generous person who ever alighted on his family's soil—
God's viceroy (*khalīfah*)[739] in His creation?
  The hands of kings fell short of his virtues;
The radiance of a moon shone from his face;
  and from his light the darkness of its shadow was dispelled.
[944] The Earth was shaken in its quarters,
  when the sword was made to lap up his spilled blood.
Anyone whose soul is calm at his fall,
  whether he be an ordinary man or a member of his family,
May I see such a one in a situation like the one in which he saw [al-Amīn],
  so that they [all] taste something bitterer[740] than his illness.
How many a mighty one of a kingdom have we seen
  taken away from his family and his servants!
O king beyond whom there is no king
  among the nations of the Seal of the Prophets:
You who were generous and gave life to the place where you dwelt,
  and from whose rain an abundant dropping flowed:
If death desisted from a man worthy of trust,
  to the level of whose foot [and no higher] it (sc. death) was

738. The generosity of al-Amīn is compared to a continuous rain (*dīmah*, pl. *diyam*).

739. Both the title "caliph" and its literal meaning of "successor, viceregent" are intended.

740. The vocalization of ed. Cairo (*tadhūqa l-amarra*), followed here, yields a metrical line; ed. Leiden's vocalization *tadhawwaqa l-amra* is unmetrical.

made equal in strength;
Or [if death desisted from] a king whose power is not challenged,
save as the grim-faced [lion] is challenged in his lair:
Nobility would have made you immortal, as long as night passes away,
or the clouds of evening rise on high;
Sovereignty, when you clothed yourself in it,
would have caused the teeth of evildoers to gnash from regret;
He of the [Heavenly] Throne would have made a mark upon your enemies, [945]
as He made a mark upon His ʿĀd and His Iram.[741]
May God not deprive of effect a Sūrah[742] that has been recited
for the best caller [to Islam] He ever summoned into His sanctuary.
I was only like the dream of a dreamer
who was made to enter the door of happiness in his dream;
Until, when his sleep released him,
he again felt the absence [of happiness].

He also said, lamenting him:

I say, being about to flee,
"May you be watered with rain, O Palace of al-Qarār!"[743]
Time's hand shot you with an arrow to the eye,
and you became scorched by the smoke of fire.
Tell me of your assembly: Where have they alighted?
In what place may they be visited,[744] after [this] place of visiting?
Where are Muḥammad and his two sons? How is it
that I see as traces of their habitation blackened buildings?

---

741. ʿĀd (an ancient tribe) and Iram (a city) are cited as examples of God's destruction of evildoers. The two names are juxtaposed in Qurʾān 89:6–7.

742. Following ed. Cairo *Allāhu sūratan*; ed. Leiden's *Allāh ṣayyūratan* is metrically difficult. Both readings are conjectural emendations of a single manuscript reading.

743. Arabic elegies often express the hope that the grave may be rained on, as water is a sign of blessing.

744. Ed. Cairo's *mazāruhum* is metrically preferable to ed. Leiden's *zamruhum*, "their company."

It is as if they had never been made at ease in a tranquil kingdom,
that protected against kings by the best protector.
[He was] an imām who in times of trouble was a help
to us, and a cloud bestowing rain.
Time has left the sons of his father
overwhelmed by black seas.
They caused their sun to perish, so that misfortune came,
and they came to be in darkness without daylight.
They drove out from themselves a light-giving moon,
and the horses of evildoers trod them down.
Had they been a match for them and equal to them,
they would not have been crowned with crowns of shame.
Verily, the imām has departed, and his two heirs
have made our bowels burn with fire.
[946] They said, "Al-Khuld has been bought." I said, "In ignominiousness
that will bring its buyers to abasement."
Thus the kingdom will follow its former [rulers],
when stability is cut off from al-Qarār [Palace].[745]

Muqaddis b. Ṣayfī said, lamenting him:

My friend, what have events brought upon you,
that weeping has become your obedient servant?
From disaster's heights has descended
a disaster that hearts cannot resist.
In the cemetery of the garden is a grave:
dwelling beside his grave is an alien lion.
The disaster of his loss was grievous to anyone
who has a portion in deeds of nobility.
For men such as he tears are shed,
and in assemblies to mourn him garments are rent.
Zubaydah held back no tears from him
to be bestowed on kinswoman or kinsman.
Leave Mūsā his son to lament a calamity:
distress has befallen Mūsā his son.

---

745. The line puns on the meaning of *qarār*, "stability."

I have seen the assemblies of the caliphs
empty of him; in their court there is no one who answers.
May it gladden you that I, a mature man,
dissolve [in tears] for him, and my liver dissolves within me.
He who was far away was afflicted because of him and bowed down in grief;
he who caused disquiet saw his own day in him.[746]
I call from the bowels of the earth a person
whom the summons would stir, but he does not reply.
If wars[747] announce the death of any soul to him,
the wars [themselves] have been grieved by his fall.

Khuzaymah b. al-Ḥasan wrote [the following poem], lamenting him through the words of Umm Jaʿfar:[748]

To the best imām, risen from the best lineage;
to the most excellent person who ever ascended the boards of a pulpit;
To the inheritor of the ancients' knowledge and understanding;
to the king al-Ma'mūn,[749] from Umm Jaʿfar:
As I write to you, my tears fall heavily [947]
from my eyelids and eye, O my cousin.
Harm and the abjectness of grief have befallen me;
my thoughts have banished sleep from my eye, O my cousin.
I am distraught because of what I suffered after his affliction:
my state is grievous and most loathsome.
I will complain of what I suffered after the loss of him
to you, as one complains who is beside herself, overwhelmed.
I make request because of what has passed over me since I lost him,

746. The verse appears to be a veiled reference to al-Ma'mūn.

747. The text and meaning of the line are uncertain. The word "wars" (*ḥurūb*) is the editor's conjecture. The manuscript reads *ḥurūf*, "letters, sounds, words."

748. Ibn al-Athīr, VI, 203–4, quotes the text and adds: "After reading the poem, al-Ma'mūn wept and said, 'By God, I will seek vengeance for my brother—may God strike his murderers dead!'" Masʿūdī, VI, 486–87, quotes eight verses. Ibn ʿAbd Rabbih, *al-ʿIqd al-farīd*, III, 215, quotes six verses of the poem and attributes them to Abū al-ʿAtāhiyah.

749. Both the proper name and its meaning "the trustworthy one" are intended.

for you are the best person to rectify and remedy my sorrow.
Ṭāhir came—may God not account Ṭāhir pure![750]
In regard to what he did, Ṭāhir will never be purified!
He made me go out with my face uncovered and without a head cloth;
he plundered my wealth and burned my homes.
Hārūn would be grieved by what I have suffered
and what has befallen me from one who is deficient in nature, depraved.[751]
If what he perpetrated was because of a command you gave,
I will suffer patiently the command of a Powerful Ordainer.
Remember my kinship, O Commander of the Faithful:
I give my life as your ransom, worthy of reverence as you are, and given to remembering.

[948] He also said, lamenting him:

Glory be to your Lord, the Lord of might, the Everlasting!
How we were afflicted the morning of that Sunday!
How all Islam has been afflicted
with the decline and weakening of its two stays!
Whoever was not afflicted by [the death of] the Commander of the Faithful, and did not
come to be in peril, with anxiety increasing,
Yet I have been afflicted by him, until it has become evident in my mind and my religion, in my [enjoyment of] this world and my body.
O night, of whose passage Islam will complain—
and all mankind—until the end of eternity,
You betrayed the king who presaged good fortune,
the imām, the valiant lion.
Fate came to him: it disquieted him;
it accosted him with a multitude of villains,
With *shūrajīs*[752] and people of unclear language,[753] led by

---

750. The verse puns on the meaning of the name "Ṭāhir": "clean, pure, blameless."

751. *Aʿwar* ("one-eyed") seems to be used here in its extended sense of "bad, corrupt, abominable."

752. For the origin of this term, originally applied to slaves who worked reclaiming salt-encrusted land, see note 606.

Quraysh [al-Dandānī], with swords, in shirts of mail.
They encountered him when he was alone, having no one to help him
against them, without supporters to bring him aid.
They made him drink of death, when he was unable to defend himself:
alone—and what an unequalled submitter he was!
He met their faces[754] with a face not lacking dignity, [949]
more beautiful and unstained than new Qūhistān tunics.[755]
O my grief, when Quraysh closed in on him,
and the sword was quivering in a quivering hand!
He did not move; he remained erect,
with his head lowered; he did not say a word;[756]
Until, when the sword reached the middle of his head,
his hands brushed it away, as one does who is calm.
He arose; his hands held fast to the base of his neck,
like a fierce shaggy lion rushing into danger.
He dragged it;[757] it fell; he brought it
to the ground with the hand of a cornered, angry lion.
He almost had killed him, had they not outnumbered him;
he rose, freeing himself from him, but he hardly could.
This is the report about the Commander of the Faithful;
I have not omitted a word from it or added anything.
May I not cease to mourn him until death, even though
that destroyed him which destroyed Lubad.[758]

---

753. *Aghtām* are people who do not speak (Arabic) clearly or correctly. It is synonymous with *ʿajam*, Persians—just as the Greeks called all speakers of other languages "*barbaroi*," i.e., babblers. See Lane, *Lexicon*, VI, 2229.

754. The margin of the manuscript gives the alternate reading, "swords" [Leiden note].

755. Literally, than new *qūhī* garments; i.e., made of a white cloth imported from Qūhistān (Persian, Kūhistān) province. Cf. ed. Leiden, *Glossarium*, CDXLI.

756. Literally, "he did not [say] anything for the first time, nor anything for the second time." For the idiom, see Lane, *Lexicon*, I, 163.

757. Apparently the antecedent is the sword, but the pronouns are ambiguous and could refer to Quraysh (translate "him").

758. That is, even though time or fate destroyed him, as it destroyed Lubad, the last of the seven vultures of the legendary sage Luqmān, whose life was to end with the death of Lubad. See Lane, *Lexicon*, VII, 2646; *EI*[2] s.v. Luḳmān (Heller).

According to al-Mawṣilī, who said: When Ṭāhir sent the head of Muḥammad to al-Ma'mūn, Dhū al-Ri'āsatayn wept and said, "He has drawn down upon us people's swords and their
[950] tongues. We commanded him to send him as a prisoner, and he sent him slaughtered." Al-Ma'mūn said to him, "What is past is past. Use your ingenuity to find an excuse for it." So the men wrote and kept at the task. Aḥmad b. Yūsuf produced a small piece of paper containing the following:[759]

> To proceed: The Deposed One was indeed the partner of the Commander of the Faithful in lineage and kinship; however, God made a distinction between them in right of succession and honor; for the one forsook the bonds of religion and departed from the common interest[760] of Muslims. God, the Mighty and Exalted, relating to us the story of the son of Noah, says, "He is not of thy family; he is a deed not righteous."[761] Thus, there is no obedience to anyone in disobedience to God, and there is no rupture [of the obligations of kinship] if the rupture takes place for the sake of God. My letter to the Commander of the Faithful comes after God has slain the Deposed One and clothed him with the cloak of his perfidy. He has set the affairs of the Commander of the Faithful on a firm basis. He has accomplished His promise to him and what was expected from His sincere promise, when by him He restored union after it had been broken, joined together the community after it had

759. For Aḥmad b. Yūsuf, al-Ma'mūn's secretary, also known for his letters, aphorisms, and verses, see *EI*[2] s.v. (Sourdel). *Qirṭās* normally referred to papyrus at this period. Sourdel, *Vizirat ʿabbaside*, 206 n., summarizes the attributions given by other historians to the letter. Parallels: Yaʿqūbī, II, 536–37; *Fragmenta*, 418.

760. *Al-amr al-jāmiʿ*: the phrase means "the business that joins (the Muslims) together."

761. Qur'ān 11:46. Cf. the preceding verses: "And Noah called to his son, who was standing apart, 'Embark with us, my son, and be thou not with the unbelievers!' He said, 'I will take refuge in a mountain, that shall defend me from the water.' Said he, 'Today there is no defender from God's command but for him on whom He has mercy.' And the waves came between them, and he was among the drowned."

been fragmented, and restored the banners of Islam after they had become tattered.

Some Aspects of the Conduct and Mode of Life of the Deposed Muḥammad b. Hārūn[762]

According to Ḥumayd b. Saʿīd, who said: After he became ruler and after al-Maʾmūn wrote to him and gave him his allegiance, Muḥammad sought out eunuchs and purchased them, spending inordinately on them. He appointed them to [attend on] his private quarters by night and by day, his provisions of food and drink, and his decisions commanding or forbidding. Some he enrolled into a special unit (*farḍ*) that he named "al-Jarādiyyah," and others, Abyssinians, he enrolled into a special unit which he named "al-Ghurābiyyah."[763] He forsook both free women and [951] slave girls, so that they were sent away. Concerning this, a certain poet said:[764]

O you who stay long at your residence in Ṭūs,
 far from your family, who cannot be ransomed by [other] lives:
You have left behind a husband for the eunuchs—
 someone who has endured the bad luck of Basūs from them![765]
As for Nawfal, he is a person of importance.
 What a companion Badr is!

---

762. Parallel: Ibn al-Athīr, VI, 205–7.

763. Cf. the reference to the two groups in the poem quoted on p. 142, above, where the Jarādiyyah are identified as *Ṣaqālib*, or Slavs, and note 539, explaining the possible origin of the name. "Ghurābiyyah" is derived from the word for raven, *ghurāb*, with reference to their black skins. See Abbott, *Two Queens of Baghdad*, 210–11. On *farḍ*, troops not on the regular muster roll and paid contractually, see ed. Leiden, *Glossarium*, CDI; also Balādhurī, *Futūḥ*, glossarium, s.v.

764. Quoted with variants in Ibn al-Athīr, VI, 205–6.

765. The line echoes the proverb, "More unlucky than Basūs." The origin of the proverb was unclear even to the early Arabic lexicographers. One explanation is that Basūs was a pre-Islamic Arab woman whose camel caused a forty-year war between the tribes of Bakr and Taghlib. See *Lisan*, s.v. (ed. Cairo, I, 281). The translation follows the vocalization of ed. Leiden. I would prefer to vocalize *taḥammalu* (for *tataḥammalu*) and to translate, "a husband for the eunuchs, from whom you will endure the bad luck of Basūs."

Neither is Bashshār al-ʿUṣmī,
    when they are mentioned, the possessor of a lowly share with him;
Nor does young Ḥasan have a lowlier lot
    with him when the cups are passed round.
They have one half of his life;
    in the other half he applies himself to drinking old wine.
Young women have no share with him,
    except frowning with a gloomy face.
If the chief is so ill,
    how does it fare with us after the chief?
If the one staying in the residence of Ṭūs knew,
    it would distress the one staying in the residence of Ṭūs!

[Continuing,] Ḥumayd said: After Muḥammad became ruler, he sent to all the countries in search of entertainers. He attached them to his court and paid them salaries. He went all out in buying swift horses. He obtained wild animals, lions, birds, and such things.[766] He secluded himself from his brothers, family members, and military commanders and held them in contempt. He divided whatever was in the treasuries and the jewels that were in his residence among his eunuchs, table companions, and confidants. Whatever jewels, stores, and weapons were in al-Raqqah were also brought to him. He commanded the building of audience rooms (*majālis*) for his villas (*mutanazzahāt*) and his places of retreat, amusement, and sport at al-Khuld Palace, al-Khayzurāniyyah, the Garden of Mūsā, ʿAbdūyah[767] Palace, al-Muʿallā Palace, Raqqat Kalwādhā, al-Anbār Gate, Banāwarī,[768] and al-Hūb. He ordered five barks (*ḥarrāqāt*) to be built on the
[952] Tigris in the shape of a lion, an elephant, an eagle, a serpent, and a horse, spending a great deal of money on their construction. Abū Nuwās[769] said, praising him:

766. Cf. the anecdotes in Masʿūdī, VI, 431–33, about exotic fishes, lions, and so forth.

767. Also vocalized *ʿAbdawayh.*

768. Banāwarī (the reading is uncertain) was the name of the village (also called Bayāwarī) that had stood on the site of the Karkh suburb, south of the Kūfah Gate of Baghdad. See Le Strange, *Baghdad*, 67.

769. Abū Nuwās al-Ḥasan b. Hāniʾ al-Ḥakamī (b. 139/756, d. between 195 and 198) was known for his poems celebrating wine and young boys. See *EI*^{2} s.v. Abū

God has made subject to al-Amīn riding animals
that never were made subject to the master of the temple.[770]
Whereas the mounts of the latter traveled by land,
the former has traveled on the water riding a lion of the jungle:
A lion that stretches out its arms, advancing quickly,
wide of mouth, grim of teeth.
He does not master it with bridle or whip,
or with pressure of his foot in the stirrup.
People marveled when they saw you on the image
of a lion, moving as fast as the clouds.
"Praise God!" they shouted, when they saw you traveling on it:
What if they had seen you atop the eagle—
With its breast, its beak, and its wings,
cutting through wave after wave;
Outstripping the birds in the sky whenever one
urges it to speed in coming or going!
May God bless the commander and preserve him. [953]
May He preserve for him the garment of youth.
—A king for whom no praises are adequate,
a Hāshimite inspired to the right course!

According to al-Ḥusayn b. al-Ḍaḥḥāk, who said: The Commander [of the Faithful] built a great ship on which he spent 3 million dirhams. He also obtained one in the shape of a sea-creature called the dolphin. Abū Nuwās al-Ḥasan b. Hāni' said about this:[771]

The "moon of the night" has mounted the dolphin;
rushing into the water, he has sailed the deep.
The Tigris shone with his beauty;
the people[772] shone and rejoiced.

Nuwās (Wagner); Sezgin, *GAS*, II, 543–50. The poem, with variants, may be found in *Dīwān*, I, 265–66; Ibn al-Athīr, VI, 206, quotes six verses.

770. According to Qur'ān 34: 12–13, God subjected the wind and certain of the *jinn* to work for Solomon. The *jinn* assisted Solomon in his construction projects: "places of worship (*maḥārib*, pl. of *miḥrāb*, translated here as 'temple'), statues, porringers like water-troughs, and anchored cooking-pots."

771. The poem, with variants, can be found in *Dīwān*, I, 266.

772. Variant: "the banks (of the river)."

Never has my eye seen a boat like it,
better at going forward or veering round.
Urged on by its oars,
it speeds over the water or goes at a gentle pace.
God has bestowed it upon al-Amīn alone,
who has been crowned with the crown of kingship.

According to Aḥmad b. Isḥāq, who was the grandson of the Kūfan singer Barṣawmā,[773] and who said: Al-ʿAbbās b. ʿAbdallāh b. Jaʿfar b. Abī Jaʿfar was one of the important men
[954] of the Banū Hāshim in strength, intellect, and deeds. He used to keep eunuchs (*khadam*, pl. of *khādim*). One of his favorite eunuchs, who was named Manṣūr, became angry with him and fled to Muḥammad. He came to the latter while he was in the palace of Umm Jaʿfar known as al-Qarār. Muḥammad received him very warmly, and the eunuch enjoyed unusually good favor with him.

One day the eunuch rode out with a group of Muḥammad's eunuchs who were called *al-Sayyāfah* ("Swordsmen"). He passed by the gate of al-ʿAbbās b. ʿAbdallāh, wanting to show al-ʿAbbās's eunuchs his appearance and condition. Word of this was brought to al-ʿAbbās, who ran out in a shirt, without a turban, with a leather-covered staff in his hand. He overtook the eunuch in Suwayqat Abī al-Ward[774] and caught hold of the reins [of his horse]. The [other] eunuchs tried to put up a fight, but whenever he hit one, that one would lose courage, so that they finally scattered from him. Al-ʿAbbās led the eunuch back into his house. When a report of this reached Muḥammad, he sent a group of men to the house of al-ʿAbbās. The men stood in front of it, while al-ʿAbbās lined up his slaves (*ghilmān*, pl. of *ghulām*) and *mawālī* on the wall of his house with shields and arrows.

Aḥmad b. Isḥāq [continued his report,] saying: By God we

---

773. The musician Barṣawmā (actually a flute virtuoso, not a singer) was introduced to al-Rashīd's court by Ibrāhīm al-Mawṣilī. See *EI*², Supplement, s.v. Barṣawmā al-Zāmir (E. Neubauer).

774. A *suwayqah* (diminutive of *sūq*) is a small market. There was a well-known Sūq Abī al-Ward about half a mile south of al-Kūfah Gate in the Karkh suburb. Perhaps the two are to be identified. See Le Strange, *Baghdad*, 60.

were afraid that the fire might burn down our homes, for they wanted to burn down al-ʿAbbās's house. Rashīd al-Hārūnī came and asked to be admitted. He went before al-ʿAbbās and said, "What are you doing? Do you know what you are involved in and what has come upon you? If he allowed them, they would plunder your house at spearpoint! Aren't you under obedience?" "Yes," he said. "Then get up," he said, "and ride!" So al-ʿAbbās went out, wearing his black [court] robes. When he reached the gate of his house, he said, "Page, bring my horse!" "No way!" said Rashīd, "You shall go on foot." When al-ʿAbbās reached the street, he looked, and behold a crowd had gathered: al-Julūdī, al-Ifrīqī, Abū al-Baṭṭ, and al-Hirsh's forces had come for him. He looked at them. I saw him set off on foot, while Rashīd rode.

When a report of this reached Umm Jaʿfar, she went before Muḥammad and started to beg him. He said to her, "May I be [955] declared to be no relative of the Prophet, God bless him and grant him peace, if I don't kill him!" She began to implore him. "By God," he said to her, "I'll teach you a lesson!" She uncovered her hair and said, "And who will come into my presence when my head is uncovered?" While Muḥammad was in the midst of this—al-ʿAbbās had not yet arrived—the eunuch Ṣāʿid came before him, bringing news of the death of ʿAlī b. ʿĪsā b. Māhān. Muḥammad turned his attention to this. Al-ʿAbbās remained in the antechamber ten days. Muḥammad forgot about him. Then he remembered him and said, "Let him be imprisoned in one of the rooms of his house. Let three of his senior *mawālī* have access to him to serve him. Let him be given a three-course meal every day."

Al-ʿAbbās remained in this condition until Ḥusayn b. ʿAlī b. ʿĪsā b. Māhān revolted in the name of al-Maʾmūn and imprisoned Muḥammad. Isḥāq b. ʿĪsā b. ʿAlī and Muḥammad b. Muḥammad al-Maʿbadī then paid a visit to al-ʿAbbās b. ʿAbdallāh. He was in a belvedere (*manẓarah*). The two said to him, "Why are you sitting still? Go out to [join] this man!" They meant Ḥusayn b. ʿAlī. So he went out and came to Ḥusayn. Then he stood by the Bridge Gate and left no abuse of Umm Jaʿfar unspoken, while Isḥāq b. Mūsā was receiving oaths of allegiance to al-Maʾmūn.

Before long, al-Ḥusayn was killed. Al-ʿAbbās fled to the Bīn

Canal (Nahrabīn), to Harthamah. His son, al-Faḍl b. al-ʿAbbās, then went to Muḥammad and denounced to him what his father owned. Muḥammad sent men to al-ʿAbbās's house and took from it 4 million dirhams and 300,000 dīnārs, which were in bottles in a well. They overlooked two of the bottles. Al-Faḍl [later] said, "Nothing remained of my father's inheritance but these two bottles, with 70,000 dīnārs in them." After the civil war ended and Muḥammad was killed, he returned to his house and took the two bottles. He gave them . . .[775] He made the
[956] pilgrimage in that year—that is, 198.

According to Aḥmad b. Isḥāq: Afterward, al-ʿAbbās b. ʿAbdallāh used to say, "Sulaymān b. Jaʿfar said to me while we were in al-Maʾmūn's residence, 'Haven't you killed your son yet?' 'May I be made your ransom, uncle!' said I. 'Who would kill his own son?' 'Kill him,' he said to me, 'for he was the one who denounced you and your money and made you poor.'"

According to Aḥmad b. Isḥāq b. Barṣawmā, who said: After Muḥammad had been besieged and matters were pressing hard on him, he said, "Alas, there is no one to rely on!" "Yes, there is," he was told. "He is one of the Arabs, a Kūfan named Waḍḍāḥ b. Ḥabīb b. Budayl al-Tamīmī, one of the best of the Arabs, and a man of sound judgment." "Send for him," he replied.

So he came to us. When he had come to him, Muḥammad said to him, "I have been told of your conduct and judgment. Counsel us in our affair." He said to him, "Commander of the Faithful, today judgment has become unsound and has departed. However, use false rumors, for they are an instrument of war." So he appointed a man named Bakīr b. al-Muʿtamir, who used to go down to Dujayl.[776] Whenever Muḥammad suffered a reverse or defeat, he would say to Bakīr, "Come up with something, for we have suffered a reverse." Bakīr would then devise reports for him. But when the people spoke among themselves, they discovered that these were false.

---

775. There is a lacuna in the text.

776. A canal and a road in the Ḥarbiyyah suburb bore this name. See Le Strange, *Baghdad*, 127–31.

[Continuing,] Aḥmad b. Isḥāq said: I can still clearly picture Bakīr b. al-Muʿtamir—an old man with a large frame.

According to al-ʿAbbās b. Aḥmad b. Abān, the secretary (*kātib*)—Ibrāhīm b. al-Jarrāḥ—Kawthar, who said: One day, Muḥammad b. Zubaydah commanded that [cloths] should be spread for him on a raised bench (*dukkān*)[777] in al-Khuld [Palace]. A green carpet was spread for him on it, matching cushions and furnishings were placed on it, and a great many silver, gold, and jeweled vessels were made ready for him. He commanded the woman superintendent of his slave girls that [957] one hundred skilled slave girls should be readied for him. They were to be sent up to him in groups of ten, carrying lutes, and singing in unison. So she sent ten up to him. When they had settled themselves on the bench, they began to sing:

They killed him that they might take his place,
as once Kisrā was betrayed by his *marzubān*s.[778]

Muḥammad grumbled in displeasure at this, cursed her, and cursed the slave girls. He commanded, and they were taken down. He waited a while and then commanded her to send up [another] ten. When they had settled themselves on the bench, they began to sing:[779]

Whoever is glad at the death of Mālik,
let him come to our women at the beginning of the day:

777. *Dukkān* usually means a sitting room or alcove provided with raised stone or brick benches built against the wall. Pillows would be placed on these for sitting. See Lane, *Lexicon*, III, 900. The parallel in Masʿūdī, VI, 426, has al-Amīn sitting in a *ṭārimah*, a portable pavilion closed on three sides. The fact that he orders the structure to be torn down argues for some such interpretation. See Sourdel, "Questions de cérémonial ʿabbaside," 129, for a description of the *ṭārimah*.

778. The verse is by al-Walīd b. ʿUqbah, who was addressing the Banū Hāshim after the death of the caliph ʿUthmān. See Ibn al-Athīr, III, 28. *Kisrā* was the Arabic name for any king of the Sasanian dynasty of Iran; a *marzubān* was a noble charged with defending the borders of the Sasanian Empire.

779. The verses, by al-Rabīʿ b. Ziyād, are from an elegy for Mālik b. Zuhayr al-ʿAbsī, whose murder launched a forty-year-long war between the brother tribes of ʿAbs and Dhubyān in pre-Islamic times. The full text may be found in Abū Tammām, *Dīwān al-Ḥamāsah*, III, 34–41; German translation and commentary in Rückert, *Hamâsa*, No. 335–36.

He will find the women bareheaded, lamenting him,
beating their cheeks before the glow of dawn.

Muḥammad became angry and did what he had done with the first group. For a long time he bowed his head in silence. Then he said, "Send up [another] ten." She sent them up. When they had taken their place on the bench, they started to sing in unison:

Kulayb, by my life, was a better defender
and less guilty than you, yet he became stained with [his own] blood.[780]

Muḥammad rose from where he had been sitting and ordered the place to be torn down, so ominous did he find what had happened.

According to Muḥammad b. ʿAbd al-Raḥmān al-Kindī—Muḥammad b. Dīnār, who said: Muḥammad the Deposed was sitting one day. The siege had closed in on him, and he was very worried and depressed. He called for his boon companions and for drink to divert himself. It was brought. He had a slave
[958] girl whom he favored; he commanded her to sing, and he took a cup to drink. But God constrained her tongue, so that all she could sing was:

Kulayb, by my life, was a better defender
and less guilty than you, yet he became stained with [his own] blood.

He threw the cup he was holding at her. He gave orders concerning her, and she was thrown to the lions. He then took another cup and called for another girl. She sang:

They killed him that they might take his place,
as once Kisrā was betrayed by his *marzubān*s.

He threw the cup in her face. Then he took another cup from which to drink and said to another girl, "Sing!" So she sang:[781]

---

780. See note 649.

781. The poem by al-Ḥārith b. Waʿlah al-Dhuhlī may be found in Abū Tammām, *Dīwān al-Ḥamāsah,* I, 199–205; German translation and commentary in Rückert, *Hamâsa,* No. 43. The poem begins:

Arise, Umaymah, they have killed my brother . . .

He threw the cup in her face, kicked the tray with his foot, and returned to his dejection. He was killed a few days afterward.

According to Abū Saʿīd, who said:[782] Faṭīm, the mother of Mūsā, the son of the deposed one, Muḥammad b. Hārūn, died, and he showed himself to be greatly grieved. Word of this reached Umm Jaʿfar, and she said, "Carry me to the Commander of the Faithful." So she was carried to him, and he received her. He said, "My lady, Faṭīm has died!" She said:

May my soul be your ransom! Let grief not destroy you;
for in your life there is a succession to those who have passed away.
With Mūsā as your compensation, every affliction has become insignificant;
after [the birth of] Mūsā there is no sadness for a woman lost.

And she said, "May God make great your reward! May He make your patience abundant, and make consolation for her your treasure!"[783]

According to Ibrāhīm b. Ismāʿīl b. Hāniʾ (the nephew of Abū Nuwās)—his father [Ismāʿīl b. Hāniʾ], who said [to Ibrāhīm]: Your uncle, Abū Nuwās, satirized Muḍar in his poem in which he said:[784] [959]

Arise, Umaymah, they have killed my brother;
and if I shoot, my arrow will hit me.
If I forgive, I forgive something enormous;
and if I assault, I weaken my own bone.

The poet's brother had been killed by his own tribesmen. The poet faced the dilemma of taking revenge against his own kin and thereby weakening his own tribe or allowing his brother's death to go unavenged.

782. Parallel in Masʿūdī, VI, 430, where the name is given as Naẓm, with Faṭm as a variant.

783. That is, may God consider your bearing her death with patience as a meritorious deed to be kept as a deposit for your benefit on the day of judgment. See Lane, *Lexicon*, III, 956, s.v. *dhakhara*.

784. The poem praises the South Arabian tribes, to which Abū Nuwās himself belonged, and satirizes the North Arabian tribes. Muḍar was originally a powerful confederation of North Arabian tribes. Quraysh, the Prophet's tribe (and the tribe of the caliph) belonged to the Muḍar group. See *EI*[1], Supplement,

As for Quraysh, it has no reason to boast,
 except its profits from its trade.[785]
If you mention a claim to glory,
 Quraysh comes slandering the one who overcomes her.[786]
When Quraysh gives her genealogy,
 (trade)[787] has half of her affiliations.

He meant [in the second line] that its noblest part is contested. This was reported to al-Rashīd during his lifetime, and he imprisoned Abū Nuwās, who remained imprisoned until Muḥammad came to power. Abū Nuwās, who had been Muḥammad's companion during the time he was prince, then said, praising Muḥammad:[788]

Remember, O trustworthy one of God[789]—and acquaintance should be remembered—
 how I stood and recited to you, while the people were present;
How I scattered pearls on you, O pearl of Hāshim—
 Oh, who has ever seen pearls being scattered on pearls!
Your father [Hārūn] was one whose like never ruled the earth;
 your paternal uncle was Mūsā [al-Hādī], his equal, the chosen;
Your grandfather was al-Mahdī, rightly guided, whose closest brother,
 Abū al-Faḍl Jaʿfar, was the father of your mother.[790]
There are none like your two Manṣūrs—the Manṣūr of Hāshim,
 and the Manṣūr of Qaḥṭān, when claims to glory are counted.

---

s.v. Rabīʿa and Muḍar. For the full text of the poem, with variants, see Abū Nuwās, *Dīwān*, II, 1–11.

785. The more martial Bedouin tribes looked down on tribes that supported themselves, as did Quraysh, from the caravan trade.

786. In the *Dīwān*, the second half of the line reads, "her merchants bring her most of it." The meaning of the text in Ṭabarī is unclear.

787. *Dīwān*: "We have," i.e., the Yemeni tribes of whom Abū Nuwās considered himself the spokesman. The scholium on the poem says that this alludes to the Yemeni and Azdi grandmothers of the Prophet's grandfather, ʿAbd al-Muṭṭalib.

788. Text, with variants, in Abu Nuwās, *Dīwān*, I, 241.

789. Punning on the name *al-Amīn*, which means "the trustworthy one."

790. Muḥammad's mother, Zubaydah, was the daughter of Abū al-Faḍl Jaʿfar, the son of Abū Jaʿfar al-Manṣūr.

Who is there who can shoot at the heights with your two arrows,
when ʿAbd Manāf[791] and Ḥimyar[792] are your two progenitors?

A slave girl sang these verses before Muḥammad. He said to her, "By whom are the verses?" He was told that they were by Abū Nuwās. "How is he?" he asked. He was told that he was in prison. "He has nothing to fear," he said. He sent to him Isḥāq b. Farāshah and Saʿīd b. Jābir (the latter had been Muḥammad's nursing brother). The two of them said, "The Commander of the Faithful mentioned you yesterday and said, 'He has nothing to fear.'" Abū Nuwās then composed some verses and sent them to him. They are these verses:[793] [960]

I was wakeful, and slumber flew from my eye;
the evening companions fell asleep, but they did not share [their sleep with me].
O trustworthy one (*amīn*) of God, you have been made ruler of a kingdom
in which the fear of God is your garment.
Your face sheds dew, whereby
people in every place live.
It is as if mankind were in the likeness of a spirit
having one body, with you as its head.
O *Amīn* of God, prison is a fearsome thing;
and you have sent, saying, "You have nothing to fear."

When it was recited to Muḥammad, he said, "He has spoken the truth. Fetch him to me." So he was brought at night. His fetters were broken, and he was taken out [of prison] and brought into Muḥammad's presence. He recited:[794]

Welcome! Welcome to the best imām
ever shaped from the mettle of the caliphate in character.[795]

791. ʿAbd Manāf was the father of Hāshim, the common ancestor of the ʿAbbāsid family and the Prophet.

792. Ḥimyar was a Yemeni tribe. Through his grandmother Khayzurān, the wife of al-Mahdī, al-Amīn could claim Yemeni ancestry.

793. See Abū Nuwās, *Dīwān*, I, 242.

794. Text, with variants, in Abū Nuwās, *Dīwān*, I, 261.

795. For "in character" (*naḥtan*), the *Dīwān* reads, "purely" (*baḥtan*), which is probably the original reading.

O *Amīn* of God, God watches over you,
  when you are at rest and when you travel, wherever you go.
The entire earth is a habitation for you;
  for God is your friend, wherever you are.

[961] Muḥammad gave him a robe of honor, freed him, and made him one of his companions.

According to ʿAbdallāh b. ʿAmr al-Tamīmī—Aḥmad b. Ibrāhīm al-Fārisī, who said: Once Abū Nuwās drank wine, and this was reported to Muḥammad during his days [as caliph]. He therefore ordered him to be imprisoned, and al-Faḍl b. al-Rabīʿ put him in prison for three months. Muḥammad then thought of him and ordered him to be brought. The Banū Hāshim and others were with Muḥammad, and he called for the sword and leather mat,[796] to threaten Abū Nuwās with death. Abū Nuwās then recited the following verses to him:

Remember, O trustworthy one of God—and acquaintance
  should be remembered . . .

He continued with the poem we have quoted above, and added to it:[797]

This world has become beautiful with the beauty of a caliph
  who is the full moon, except that he always shines;
An imām who will rule the people for seventy years:
  for that has he put on the garment and girdle [of rule].
Generosity points to him from his cheeks,
  and looks from his sides when he looks.
O best object of hope, I am one
  who is held in custody, incarcerated in your prisons, destitute.
Three months have past since I was imprisoned,
  as if I had committed an unpardonable crime.
If I have committed no crime, why is fault being found with
  me?[798]

---

796. The *naṭʿ* or *niṭʿ* was a leather mat used to receive an executed man's head.

797. Text, with variants, in Abū Nuwās, *Dīwān*, I, 241–42.

798. The reading of the *Dīwān* is more likely to be original: "why am I being treated with rigor," reading *taʿannutī* for ed. Leiden's *taʿaqqubī*.

But if I have committed a crime, your pardon is greater. [962]

Muḥammad then said to him, "If you drink it—." "My blood," he said, "shall be yours to shed, Commander of the Faithful." He released him. Abū Nuwās therefore used to smell wine, but not drink it—as he said:

I will not taste aged wine, except as a fragrance.

According to Masʿūd b. ʿĪsā al-ʿAbdī—Yaḥyā b. al-Musāfir al-Qarqisāʾī, who said: Duḥaym, the slave (*ghulām*) of Abū Nuwās told me that Muḥammad reproved Abū Nuwās for drinking wine and imprisoned him. Al-Faḍl b. al-Rabīʿ had a maternal uncle who used to examine the inmates of the prisons, visit them, and investigate them. He entered the place where the *Zindīqs*[799] were being held and, seeing Abū Nuwās, whom he did not know, said to him, "Young man, are you with the *Zindīqs*?" "God forbid!" he replied. "Perhaps," he said, "you are one of those who worship the ram?" "No," he replied, "I eat rams, wool and all!" "Perhaps," he said, "you are one of those who worship the sun?" "In fact," he replied, "I find the sun so loathsome that I avoid sitting in it." "Then for what misdeed were you imprisoned?" he asked. Abū Nuwās replied, "I was imprisoned on a charge of which I am innocent." "Is it nothing but that?" he asked. "By God," he replied, "I have told you the truth."

So the uncle came to al-Faḍl and said to him, "Sir, you are not being good caretakers of God's blessings. Are people to be imprisoned [merely] on suspicion?" "What is it?" he asked. So the uncle told him what Abū Nuwās claimed about his misdeed. Al-Faḍl smiled and went before Muḥammad and told him about it. Muḥammad summoned Abū Nuwās and ordered him to avoid

799. The *Zindīqs* (Arabic *zindīq*, pl. *zanādiqah*) comprised mainly Manichaean dualists, and probably also Mazdakites and other remnants of once-flourishing Mesopotamian sects. They were subject to persecution. See G. Vajda, "Les zindîqs en pays d'Islam au début de la période abbaside," *RSO*, XVII (1938), 173–229; Gabrieli, "La ≪zandaqa≫ au Ier siècle abbasside," in *L'élaboration de l'Islam*, 23–38; Omar, "Some Observations on the Reign of the ʿAbbāsid Caliph al-Mahdī 775–778 A.D.," in *ʿAbbāsiyyāt*, 89–93; Lieu, *Manichaeism in the Later Roman Empire and Medieval China*, 83–84; and *EI*[1] s.v. Zindīḳ.

wine and drunkenness. "Yes," he said. He was told, "By an oath by God?" "Yes," he said.

So Abū Nuwās was allowed to leave. Some young fellows from Quraysh then sent for him. He said to them, "I will not drink." They said, "Even if you do not drink, entertain us with your conversation." So he accepted. As the cup was being passed among them, they said, "Didn't you once like it?" He answered,
[963] "By God, there is no way for me to drink it!" And he recited:[800]

You two who go speaking reproof, reprove on!
    I will not taste aged wine, except as a fragrance.
I was reproved on account of it by an imām
    whom I do not think it right to disobey.
So pass it to someone else,
    for I am a boon companion only for conversation.
My share in the wine, when it is passed round,
    is to see it and smell the scent.
As for my approving of it,
    I am like a *Qaʿadī* extolling *Khārijism*:[801]
Unable to carry a weapon into battle,
    he advises anyone who can [carry one] not to stay home.

According to Abū al-Ward al-Subʿī, who said: We were at the home of al-Faḍl b. Sahl in Khurāsān, when al-Amīn was mentioned. He said, "How can it not be considered justified to fight against Muḥammad, when his poet says in his assembly:[802]

'Yea, give me wine to drink, and say to me that it *is* wine;
    do not give it to me to drink secretly, if it is possible to declare it openly'?"

When the story reached Muḥammad, he commanded al-Faḍl b. al-Rabīʿ, and the latter took Abū Nuwās and imprisoned him.

800. Text, with variants, in Abū Nuwās, *Dīwān*, III, 273–74.

801. A *Qaʿadī*, as explained in the margin of the *Dīwān*, was any of the Khārijites who held the opinion that "Judgment belongs to God alone" (the formula known as *taḥkīm*, used to challenge the legitimacy of the ruling caliph), but who did not actually rebel against the ruling caliph. The word is derived from *qaʿada*, "to sit, stay behind (from a battle)." See Lane, *Lexicon*, II, 618 (for *taḥkīm*), and *Dīwān*, ad. loc.

802. For the full text of the poem, see Abū Nuwās, *Dīwān*, III, 126–29.

According to Kāmil b. Jāmiʿ, on the authority of one of the companions of Abū Nuwās and transmitters of his poetry, who [964] said: Abū Nuwās composed some verses that were reported to al-Amīn. At the end of them was the following:[803]

What makes me behave even more proudly toward people
 is that I see myself as the wealthiest of them, even when I am in poverty.
Even if I had obtained[804] no [other] glory,
 my tongue's having protected me from all men would be glory enough for me.
Let no one hope to overcome me in this—
 not even the owner of the crown secluded in the palace.

So al-Amīn—Sulaymān b. Abī Jaʿfar[805] was with him—sent for him. When he came before him, al-Amīn said, "You biter of your whore mother's clitoris! Son of a stinking uncircumcised woman!"[806] (And he cursed him with the foulest curses.) "With your poetry you earn filth from the hands of the wicked, and then you say, 'Not even the owner of the crown secluded in the palace!' My God, you had better not slander *me* ever in any way!" Sulaymān b. Abī Jaʿfar said to him, "By God, Commander of the Faithful, he is one of the biggest dualist heretics." Muḥammad said, "Can anyone witness to it against him?" Sulaymān brought a group of witnesses. One of them said that Abū Nuwās had been drinking on a rainy day and had set his cup under the open sky, so that raindrops fell into it, and had said, "They say that with each drop an angel descends. How many angels do you think I'm drinking now?"—and he drank what was in the cup. Muḥammad therefore ordered him to be imprisoned. Concerning this, Abū Nuwās said:[807]

803. For the full text, with variants, see Abū Nuwās, *Dīwān*, I, 339–40.

804. The reading of the *Dīwān* (*arith*) is superior—"Even if I had *inherited* no glory": Abū Nuwās often boasted of his descent from Yemeni tribes that carried on the traditions of the South Arabian kingdoms.

805. He was al-Amīn's great uncle on both the paternal and maternal sides.

806. The adjective *lakhnāʾ*, meaning "stinking, malodorous," is applied particularly to women whose genitals are malodorous or who are uncircumcised (i.e., have not had their clitoris removed at puberty). See *Lisan*, s.v.

807. See Abū Nuwās, *Dīwān*, I, 340.

Lord, men have wronged me;
without my having committed dereliction[808] they have imprisoned me.
[965] To [the charge of] unbelief (*juḥūd*), though you know that the opposite
is true of me—to this [charge] have they linked me by their cunning.[809]
Running in their racecourse
in every race and the fear [of God] have been my only religion.
My excuse is not accepted, so that their witness against me
fears, nor are they satisfied with the oath of my right hand.
Truly Kawthar was more deserving of imprisonment
in a house of reproach and home of shame.
As for al-Amīn, I have no hope that he will defend me:
Who will today be my helper with al-Ma'mūn?

When these verses by him reached al-Ma'mūn, the latter said, "By God, if I reach him, I will enrich him with wealth he had not hoped for!" However, Abū Nuwās died before al-Ma'mūn entered the City of Peace.

After Abū Nuwās had been imprisoned for a long time, he composed the following about his imprisonment—it was related on the authority of Diʿāmah:

Praise God all together,
all you Muslims.
Then say, and do not flag,
"Lord, grant life to al-Amīn!"
He has promoted eunuchs, until
he has made impotence a religion.
And people one and all have emulated
the Commander of the Faithful.

---

808. Instead of *taʿaṭṭul* ("dereliction"), the *Dīwān* reads *khaṭī'ah* ("offense, sin").

809. The text is difficult, but seems to represent real variant, not merely a miscopying of the text in the *Dīwān*, which is syntactically simpler:

To repudiation of that to which my heart is resolved,
by falsehood and slander they have linked me.

These verses also reached al-Ma'mūn when he was in Khurāsān. He said, "I will take care of him, if he flees to me."

According to Ya'qūb b. Isḥāq, on the authority of someone who reported this from Kawthar, the eunuch (*khādim*) of the Deposed One: Muḥammad was unable to sleep one night while he was engaged in his war with Ṭāhir. He wanted someone [966] to spend the night conversing with him, but no one from his entourage was at hand. So he summoned his chamberlain (*ḥājib*) and said, "Alas, my mind is full of thoughts. Bring me a witty poet with whom I can spend the rest of this night." The chamberlain went to the closest person in his presence. He found Abū Nuwās and said to him, "Comply with the request of the Commander of the Faithful." Abū Nuwās replied, "Perhaps you were seeking someone else?" The chamberlain said, "I was seeking no one but you." So he brought Abū Nuwās to him. Muḥammad said, "Who are you?" "Your servant," he replied, "al-Ḥasan b. Hāni', whom you released yesterday." "Don't be afraid," said Muḥammad. "Certain proverbs came into my mind, and I wanted you to set them into poetry. If you do it, I will reward you with whatever you ask." Abū Nuwās asked, "What are they, Commander of the Faithful?" Muḥammad said, "They are these sayings of the Arabs: 'God has effaced what has past.'—'How badly, by God, my horse has run!'[810]—'Break a stick on your nose!'[811]—and, 'Refuse, and he will desire you even more.'"[812] Abū Nuwās said, "My wish is four shapely maidservants. Muḥammad ordered them to be brought, and Abū Nuwās recited:

Your long making of excuses has been for nought;
I see no wisdom in delaying with you.

---

810. See Freytag, *Proverbia*, I, 208. The proverb is said to be used referring to anyone who has done less than he should have done or to whom too little has been presented.

811. Ibid., II, 404. The proverb (addressed to a woman) is said to be used referring to anyone whom people want to compel by force or deceive by trickery.

812. Ibid., I, 218. The proverb is said to come from what a man once said to a woman: "Make a show of refusing when I court you, and it will arouse even more desire." It can be used to refer to a person who pretends not to want to sell something in order to sell the thing for a higher price, since desire increases for a thing withheld.

You wanted to avoid me,
  but I wanted dalliance with you.
What did you want by this?—
  "Refuse, and he will desire you even more."

He took a maidservant by the hand and set her aside. Then he recited:

The oaths of your swearing were firm,
  and I cried out till I died from your staying away.
By God, my lady, violate your oath just once;
  then "break a stick on your nose!"

He set the second one aside, and then he recited:

May I be your ransom! Why this disdain?
  Why do you revile people of honor?
Grant a rendezvous to a wearied lover
  for whose misdeed there has been repentance.
[967] Do not remember bygones:
  "God has effaced what has past."

He set the third one aside, and he recited:

Certain women sent to me in the darkness of night,
  saying, "Come to us, but beware of the watchmen."
And so, when the enemies had been lulled to sleep,
  and I feared no observer or fire's glow,
I mounted my colt and went joyfully toward
  creatures dark-eyed, fair, soft, and dark-lipped.
But I came when morning had already risen:
  "How badly, by God, my horse had run!"

Said Muḥammad, "Take them [all]—may God not prosper you with them!"

According to al-Mawṣilī—Ḥusayn, al-Rashīd's eunuch (*khādim*), who said: When the caliphate came to Muḥammad, one of his lodgings on the bank [of the Tigris] was readied for him by spreading the best and most splendid of the carpets of the caliphate. He[813] said, "Master, your father never had any

813. The subject is unclear—presumably, someone in charge of furnishing the residence, perhaps Ḥusayn the eunuch.

better carpet than this to impress kings and visitors who came to him; so I wanted to spread it for you." He replied, "I wanted to have what was inherited[814] spread out for me at the beginning of my caliphate." And he said, "They have cut it up!" By God, I saw that the servants and grooms had caused it to be cut up and had divided it.

According to Muḥammad b. al-Ḥasan, who said: Aḥmad b. Muḥammad al-Barmakī told me that Ibrāhīm b. al-Mahdī once sang to Muḥammad b. Zubaydah:[815]

I shunned you, until they said, "He knows not passion";
and I visited you, until they said, "He has no patience."

Muḥammad was delighted and said, "Fill his boat with gold."

According to ʿAlī b. Muḥammad b. Ismāʿīl—Mukhāriq,[816]
who said: I was with Muḥammad b. Zubaydah on a rainy [968]
day. He was drinking a morning drink, and I was sitting near him, singing. There was no one with him. He was wearing an embroidered coat.[817] Never, by God, had I seen a better one. So I began to look at it. He said, "You seem to like it, Mukhāriq." I said, "Yes, master, on you, because your face is beautiful in it. I am looking at it, and praying for your protection." "Slave (*ghulām*)," he said; and the eunuch (*khādim*) responded to him. He called for another coat, put it on, and gave me the one he had been wearing. After a little while, I looked at him again. He repeated something similar, and I gave the same reply. So he called for another coat; and this went on until he had done this with three coats, which I put on, one over the other. However, when he saw me wearing them, he regretted what he had done, and his expression changed. "Lad," he said, "go to the cooks.

814. The word used (*al-m.r.d.raj*) apparently corresponds to Persian *murdarīg*, "inheritance, patrimony." The reading may be corrupt. See ed. Leiden, *Glossarium*, CDLXXXIII.

815. The rest of the poem by Abū Ṣakhr al-Hudhalī can be found in al-Qālī, *Kitāb al-Amālī*, I, 148–50. Muḥammad b. Zubaydah is al-Amīn.

816. Mukhāriq was a virtuoso singer at the court of al-Rashīd. He continued at court until his death in the reign of al-Wāthiq in 230/844–45. See *EI*[1], Supplement, s.v. Mukhārik (Farmer).

817. The *jubbah* was an outer garment with broad sleeves. See Dozy, *Dictionnaire détaillé des noms des vêtements chez les Arabes*, 107–17.

Tell them to cook us a roast and prepare it quickly.[818] Bring it to us right away." No sooner had the lad gone than the table was brought. It was pretty and small, and in the middle of it was a huge bowl and two loaves of bread. It was set before him. He broke off a morsel, dipped it into the dish, and said, "Eat, Mukhāriq!" I said, "Sir, excuse me from eating." "I won't excuse you. Eat!" he said. So I broke off a morsel and took something. When I put it into my mouth, he said, "God curse you! What a glutton you are! You've ruined it for me. You've spoiled it and stuck your hand into it." Then he lifted the bowl with his hand, and suddenly it was in my lap. "Get up!" he said, "and God curse you!" So I got up, with the fat and the gravy dripping from the coats. I took them off and sent them home. I called for the fullers and embroiderers. I tried my best to restore them to their original condition, but they were not restored.

According to al-Buḥturī Abū ʿUbādah[819]—ʿUbaydallāh b. Abī Ghassān, who said: I was with Muḥammad on a very cold
[969] winter day. He was in one of his audience rooms (*majlis*) that was set apart and spread with a carpet such that I have rarely seen one more precious or more beautiful. On that day I had for three days and nights consumed nothing but date wine (*nabīdh*) and could hardly speak or think. Muḥammad went to relieve himself. I said to one of the personal eunuchs (*khādim*), "Alas, by God, I am dying. Is there any way to get something to put into my stomach to soothe what I am feeling?" "Give me a chance," he said, "and I will use cunning on your behalf. Pay attention to what I say and say that my words are true." When Muḥammad returned and sat down, the servant looked at me and smiled. Muḥammad, seeing him do so, asked, "Why did you smile?" He said, "It was nothing, sir." Muḥammad became angry. [Continuing,] al-Buḥturī said: (The servant) then said, "There is something about ʿUbaydallāh b. Abī Ghassān: he cannot smell the odor of watermelons or eat them. He becomes very upset because of them." (Muḥammad) said, "ʿUbaydallāh,

818. Ed. Cairo reads, "prepare it well."

819. The poet al-Walīd b. ʿUbayd(allāh) b. Yaḥyā Abū ʿUbādah was born in 206/821 and died in 284/897. See *EI*² s.v. al-Buḥturī (Pellat); Sezgin, *GAS*, II, 560–64.

is this true about you?" I said, "Yes, sir, it is something from which I suffer." "Too bad for you," he said, "seeing how good watermelons are and how good they smell!" "But that's how I am," I said. He expressed amazement and said, "Bring me some watermelon." Several were brought. When I saw them, I made a show of shuddering and of recoiling from them. "Take it," he said [to the servants], "and set the watermelon before him." I began to show him how upset and agitated I was about this, while he kept laughing. Then he said, "Eat one!" "Sir," I said, "you will kill me. You will ruin my stomach and make me sick. God help me!" "Eat a watermelon," he said, "and you shall have the carpet of this room! I swear to God." I said, "What shall I do with the room's carpet, when I die if I eat it?" I kept refusing, but he insisted. The servant[820] came with knives; they cut up a watermelon and began stuffing it into my mouth, while I screamed and struggled. Withal, I swallowed, making it appear to him that I was doing it against my will. I struck my head and [970]
cried out, while he kept laughing. When I finished, he moved into another room. He called the carpet spreaders, and they carried the carpet of that room to my house. Then he bandied words with me about the carpet of the [second] room for another watermelon. He did as he had done the first time, and gave me the carpet of the room, until he had given me three carpets and had made me eat three watermelons. My condition, by God, became good, and I felt strong.

Now Manṣūr b. al-Mahdī used to make a show of giving (Muḥammad) sincere advice. He came when Muḥammad had gotten up to wash himself. I realized that Muḥammad would seek to do me some evil out of regret for what he had given away. Having heard the news, Manṣūr approached me while Muḥammad was out of the chamber and said, "Son of a whore! Will you cheat the Commander of the Faithful and take his property? By God, I was on the verge of doing something, and will." "Sir," I said, "it did happen, but the reason was such

820. *Al-Khādim*: Ed. Leiden, *Glossarium*, CCXV, argues that the word has a collective sense and should be translated "servants." This is unnecessary. One servant (or eunuch) brought in the knives, and those present began to cut up the watermelon and feed it to ʿUbaydallāh.

and such"—and I explained. "If you would like to kill me and commit a sin, that's up to you! But if you act with graciousness, that would be worthier of you. I will not do it again." He replied, "I will be gracious to you."

Muḥammad then came and said, "Spread carpets for us by that pool.[821] They spread them for him by it. He sat down, and we sat down also. The pool was full of water. Muḥammad said, "Uncle,[822] I have longed to do something—throw ʿUbaydallāh into the pool, so that you can laugh at him." Al-Manṣūr replied, "Sir, if you do it, he will die, because the water is very cold and it is a very cold day today. But I will tell you about something very nice I have tried." "What is it?" he asked. He replied, "Command that he be tied to a board and placed at the door of the lavatory. Everyone who comes to the door of the lavatory will urinate on his head." "By God, that's good!" he said. A board was brought, and I was tied to it. Then he gave orders, and I was carried off and set at the door of the lavatory. The servants came. They loosened the cord from me and approached, letting him see that they were urinating on me, while I screamed. This
[971] went on God knows how long, while he kept laughing. Then he gave orders and I was untied. I let him see that I had cleaned myself and changed my clothes, and then I got away from him.

According to ʿAbdallāh b. al-ʿAbbās b. al-Faḍl b. al-Rabīʿ—his father, the Deposed One's chamberlain (*ḥājib*), who said: I was standing beside him. The morning meal was brought. He ate alone, and had a wonderful meal. Sometimes it used to be prepared for the caliphs before him in the manner in which it used to be prepared for each one of them; he would eat of each food, and then he would be brought his food.[823] He ate until he had finished; then he raised his head toward Abū al-ʿAnbar, who was one of his mother's eunuchs (*khādim*), and said, "Go to the kitchen and tell them to prepare *bizmāward*[824] for me. Let

---

821. *Birkah* can refer either to a natural lake or to a man-made pool or tank.

822. That is, Manṣūr b. al-Mahdī, who was al-Amīn's uncle.

823. The text is almost certainly corrupt, and the original meaning of the sentence cannot be determined.

824. *Bizmāward* (other forms of the same, originally Persian word are *bazmāward, buzmāward,* and *zumāward*) are described as meatballs wrapped in dough. See ed. Leiden, *Glossarium*, CXXXIII; and Lane, *Lexicon*, III, 1250.

them leave them very long, and not cut them up. The filling should be fat pieces of chicken, clarified butter, herbs, eggs, cheese, olives, and nuts. Let them make a lot of them, and hurry." It was only a short time before they brought them on a square table. The long *bizmāward* had been placed on it in the shape of the Dome of ʿAbd al-Ṣamad,[825] so that the top [of the pile] was a single *bizmāward*. It was placed before him. He took one and ate it, and he kept eating until he had left nothing on the table.

According to ʿAlī b. Muḥammad—Jābir b. Muṣʿab—Mukhāriq, who said:[826] I once passed a night the like of which I had never passed before. I was at home after nightfall, when a messenger came from Muḥammad, who was then caliph. He galloped off with me, and brought me to Muḥammad's residence. I was taken inside. There was Ibrāhīm b. al-Mahdī, who had been sent for, as I had been. We went forward and reached a gate that led to a courtyard. Behold, the courtyard was filled with some of Muḥammad's large candles; it was as if the courtyard were in daylight. Muḥammad was on a hobby horse,[827] and the residence was full of maidservants and menservants (*khadam*). [972]
The players were playing, and Muḥammad in the midst of them was on the hobby horse, dancing about with it. A messenger came to us and said, "He has said, 'Stand in this spot, by this door next to the courtyard, and raise your voices, singing loudly or softly after the oboe,[828] following it in its melody.'" Now the oboe, the maidservants, and the players were [singing and playing] one thing:

Lo, Danānīr forgets me, but I remember her[829]—

825. ʿAbd al-Ṣamad b. ʿAlī, the uncle of al-Manṣūr, had died in 185 (801–2) during the reign of al-Rashīd (see Ṭabarī, III, 650).

826. Parallel: *Aghānī*, XVI, 138–39.

827. The word used (*kurraj*) is an Arabicized version of Persian *kurrah*, "colt." The word was applied to wooden horses used as toys by children. From the context, this must have been something like the representations of horses that Spanish dancers sometimes wear suspended from their shoulders in dances representing the movements of a battle. See Dozy, *Supplément*, II, 461; also Gaudefroy-Demombynes, "Sur le cheval-jupon et al-kurraj," 155–59.

828. On the *sūrnāy*, see Dozy, *Supplément*, I, 831.

829. Danānīr was the celebrated singer Danānīr al-Barmakiyyah, the freed slave girl of Yaḥyā b. Khālid al-Barmaki. She was a favorite of al-Rashīd, and

and were following the piper. Ibrāhīm and I remained standing, reciting it, and splitting our throats with it, until daybreak. Muḥammad was on the hobby horse; he neither wearied nor grew bored until morning. Sometimes he would come near us and we would see him; sometimes the maidservants and menservants came between him and us.

According to al-Ḥusayn b. Firās, a *mawlā* of the Banū Hāshim, who said: In the time of Muḥammad, men went on military expedition on condition that he return to them the fifth.[830] It was returned to them. A man would obtain six dīnārs, which was a lot of money.

According to Ibn al-Aʿrābī, who said: I was present with al-Faḍl b. al-Rabīʿ. Al-Ḥasan b. Hāniʾ[831] was brought. Al-Faḍl said, "The charge has been raised before the Commander of the Faithful that you are a *Zindīq.*" Al-Ḥasan began to declare his innocence and to swear. Al-Faḍl kept repeating what he had said about him and asked him to speak to the caliph about him. He promised, and [al-Faḍl] released him. As al-Ḥasan left, he said:[832]

My family, I have come to you from the grave,
    while [other] people wait in vain for resurrection.
Were it not for Abū al-ʿAbbās [al-Faḍl b. al-Rabīʿ],
    my eye would not be looking at children or at abundance.
Through him, God has clothed me with benefits
    the recounting of which has occupied the hands of my gratitude.
I was made to receive[833] them from a counselor of quick intelligence,
    and I counted[834] them with ten fingertips.

---

some of Abū Nuwās's love poems are addressed to her, e.g., *Dīwān*, IV, 11–12. See *Aghānī*, XVI, 136ff.; also Abbott, *Two Queens of Baghdad*, 138–40.

830. That is, that he return to them the one-fifth share (*khums*) of any booty that was normally reserved for the ruler under Islamic law. See Dozy, *Supplément*, I, 404.

831. That is, Abū Nuwās.

832. See Abū Nuwās, *Dīwān*, I, 249–50.

833. The translation follows the vocalization of the *Dīwān*, rather than that of ed. Leiden, which is metrically impossible.

834. The reading (*ʿaqadtuhā*) of the *Dīwān* is preferable. Ed. Leiden has *madadtuhā*, "I drew them (up, as from a well)."

According to al-Riyāshī—Abū Ḥabīb al-Mūshī, who said: I was with Mu'nis b. ʿImrān. We were on our way to al-Faḍl b. [973]
al-Rabīʿ in Baghdad. Mu'nis said to me, "Why don't we go to visit Abū Nuwās?" So we went into the prison to see him. He said to Mu'nis, "Abū ʿImrān, where are you heading?" He replied, "I was on my way to see Abū al-ʿAbbās al-Faḍl b. al-Rabīʿ." Abū Nuwās said, "Will you deliver to him a note that I give you?" "Yes," he replied. So Abū Nuwās gave him a note containing the following:[835]

Not a single hand is there among men
but that Abū al-ʿAbbās is its master.[836]
Trusted friends slept on their beds,
but *he* came to my soul by night and revived it.
I feared you, but then there made me feel safe
from fearing you your fear of God.
You pardoned me, as one pardons who is powerful
and entitled to exact punishments, but remitted them.

These verses were the cause of his release from detention.

According to Muḥammad b. Khallād al-Sharawī—his father [Khallād], who said: Muḥammad heard Abū Nuwās's poem that says:[837]

Yea, give me wine to drink, and say to me that it *is* wine—

also, his poem that says:[838]

Give me it to drink, Dhufāfah,
tart in taste and unsullied.
Inglorious in my eyes is he who hates it
out of hope or out of fearing;[839]
Just as after the death of Hārūn
the caliphate became inglorious and neglected.

---

835. See Abū Nuwās, *Dīwān*, I, 248

836. The reading of the *Dīwān* may be preferable: "Not a single hand is there among men *like* the hand of which Abū al-ʿAbbās is the master."

837. See note 802.

838. For additional lines and variants, see Abū Nuwās, *Dīwān*, III, 210–11. Dhufāfah al-ʿAbsī was in charge of al-Rashīd's horses.

839. That is, hope for heaven or fear of hell.

Then the following was recited to him:[840]

[974] He brought it olive-golden,
and we could not restrain ourselves from worshiping it.

Muḥammad imprisoned him for this, saying: "Enough! You are an unbeliever! You are a *Zindīq*!" Abū Nuwās wrote to al-Faḍl b. al-Rabīʿ concerning this:[841]

You, Ibn al-Rabīʿ, taught me goodness[842]
and accustomed me to it, and goodness became a habit.
My life of vanity stopped, my mindless behavior ceased,
and I manifested fear of God and abstemiousness.
If you saw me, you would compare to me al-Ḥasan al-Baṣrī
in his asceticism, or Qatādah,[843]
Because of bowings that I adorn with prostrations,
and a paleness like that of the locust.
Summon me then—may you not fail to evaluate someone like me—
and note with your eye the prostration mark [on my forehead].[844]
If a hypocrite ever saw it,
he would buy it to use as evidence [of his piety].

---

840. Ibid., 131.

841. Ibid., I, 246–47. Discussion and German translation in Wagner, *Abū Nuwās*, 82–83; discussion and English translation in Nicholson, *Literary History of the Arabs*, 293–94.

842. For *khayr*, "goodness," the *Dīwān* reads *nusk*, "piety, asceticism."

843. Al-Ḥasan al-Baṣrī was a famous ascetic. Qatādah, a scholar also from al-Baṣrah (Abū Nuwās was himself a native of the city), was a contemporary of al-Ḥasan. He died in 735.

844. That is, the mark (*sajjādah*) left by repeatedly touching the forehead to the ground in prayer.

Bibliography of Cited Works

I. Primary Sources: Texts and Translations

Abū Nuwās, al-Ḥasan b. Hāni' al-Ḥakamī. *Der Dīwān des Abū Nuwās.* Bibliotheca Islamica 20a–d. Vol. 1, edited by Ewald Wagner; Wiesbaden and Cairo, 1958. Vol. 2, edited by Ewald Wagner; Wiesbaden, 1972. Vol. 3, edited by Ewald Wagner; Wiesbaden, 1988. Vol. 4, edited by Gregor Schoeler; Wiesbaden, 1982.

Abū Tammām, Ḥabīb b. Aws al-Ṭā'ī. *Dīwān al-Ḥamāsah.* With commentary by al-Tabrīzī, edited by Muḥammad Muḥyī al-Dīn ʿAbd al-Ḥamīd. 4 vols. Cairo, 1938. German translation by Friedrich Rückert as *Hamâsa, oder die ältesten arabischen Volkslieder.* 2 vols. Stuttgart, 1846.

Aghānī. See al-Iṣbahānī.

al-Balādhurī, Abū al-Ḥasan Aḥmad b. Yaḥyā. *Futūḥ al-buldān.* Edited by M. J. De Goeje. Leiden, 1866.

al-Dīnawarī, Abū Ḥanīfah Aḥmad b. Dāwūd. *Kitāb al-Akhbār al-ṭiwāl.* Edited by Vladimir Guirgass. Leiden, 1888.

Fragmenta Historicorum Arabicorum. Edited by M. J. De Goeje. Vol. 1 contains the anonymous *Kitāb al-ʿUyūn wa-al-ḥadā'iq fī akhbār al-ḥaqā'iq*; Leiden 1869. Vol. 2 contains years A.H. 196–251 of Miskawayh's *Kitāb Tajārib al-umam wa-taʿāqib al-himam*; Leiden, 1871.

Ibn ʿAbd Rabbih, Aḥmad b. Muḥammad al-Andalusī. *Al-ʿIqd al-farīd.* Edited by Muḥammad Saʿīd al-ʿAryān. 8 vols. Cairo, 1940.

Ibn al-Athīr, ʿIzz al-Dīn. *Kitāb al-Kāmil fī al-ta'rīkh.* Edited by C. J. Tornberg. 12 vols. Leiden, 1870–71.

Ibn Khaldūn, Walī al-Dīn Abū Zayd ʿAbd al-Raḥmān b. Muḥammad. *Al-Muqaddimah.* Translated by F. Rosenthal as *The Muqaddimah, an Introduction to History.* 3 vols. New York, 1958.

Ibn Khallikān, Abū al-ʿAbbās Aḥmad b. Muḥammad. *Kitāb Wafayāt al-aʿyān*. Translated by Baron Mac Guckin de Slane as *Ibn Khallikān's Biographical Dictionary*. 4 vols. 1843–71. Reprinted, New York and London, 1961.

Ibn Manẓūr, Jamāl al-Dīn Abū al-Faḍl Muḥammad b. Mukarram al-Anṣārī. *Lisān al-ʿarab*. 6 vols. Cairo, 1981.

al-Iṣbahānī, Abū al-Faraj ʿAlī b. al-Ḥusayn. *Kitāb al-aghānī*. Edited by Ibrāhīm al-Abyārī. 31 vols. Cairo, 1969.

al-Khafājī, Shihāb al-Dīn Aḥmad. *Shifā' al-ghalīl fīmā fī kalām al-ʿarab min al-dakhīl*. Edited by Muḥammad ʿAbd al-Munʿim Khafājī. Cairo, 1952.

al-Khuraymī, Abū Yaʿqūb Isḥāq b. Ḥassān b. Qūhī. *Dīwān al-Khuraymī*. Edited by ʿAlī Jawād al-Ṭāhir and Muḥammad Jabbār al-Muʿaybid. Beirut, 1971.

al-Kutubī, Muḥammad b. Shākir. *Fawāt al-wafayāt*. Edited by Iḥsān ʿAbbās. 5 vols. Beirut, 1973.

Lisān. See Ibn Manẓūr.

al-Masʿūdī, Abū al-Ḥasan ʿAlī b. al-Ḥusayn. *Murūj al-Dhahab wa-maʿādin al-jawhar*. Edited and translated by C. Barbier de Meynard and Pavet de Courteille as *Les Prairies d'or*; 9 vols., Paris, 1861–77. Also edited and partially translated by C. Pellat as *Les Prairies d'or*; 7 vols., including 2 of indices, Paris and Beirut, 1962–79.

al-Maydānī, Abū al-Faḍl Aḥmad b. Muḥammad. *Majmaʿ amthāl al-ʿarab*. Cairo, 1959. Translated by G. W. Freytag as *Arabum Proverbia*. 2 vols. Bonn, 1838–43.

Michel le Syrien. *Chronique*. Edited and translated by J.-B. Chabot as *Chronique de Michel le Syrien, Patriarche jacobite d'Antioche (1166–1199)*. Paris, 1905.

al-Mubarrad, Abū al-ʿAbbās Muḥammad b. Yazīd. *Al-Kitāb al-kāmil*. Edited by W. Wright. 2 vols. in 3. Leipzig, 1864–92.

al-Nābighah al-Jaʿdī, Ḥibbān b. Qays. *Le Poesie di an-Nābiġah al-Ǧaʿdī*. Edited and translated by Maria Nallino. Rome, 1953.

———. *Shiʿr al-Nābighah al-Jaʿdī*. Edited by ʿAbd al-ʿAzīz Rabbāḥ. Damascus, 1384/1964.

al-Qālī, Abū ʿAlī Ismāʿīl b. al-Qāsim. *Kitāb al-Amālī*. 2 vols. Beirut, 1965.

al-Ṣafadī, Ṣalāḥ al-Dīn Khalīl b. Aybak. *Kitāb al-Wāfī bi-al-wafayāt*. Bibliotheca Islamica 6a–. Vol. 5, edited by Sven Dederling; Wiesbaden, 1970. Vol. 17, edited by Dorothea Krawulsky; Wiesbaden, 1982.

al-Ṭabarī, Abū Jaʿfar Muḥammad b. Jarīr. *Jāmiʿ al-bayān fī tafsīr al-qur'ān*. 30 vols. Būlāq, 1323/1905. Reprinted Beirut, 1398/1978.

———. *Ta'rīkh al-rusul wa-al-mulūk*. Edited by M. J. De Goeje et al. as

Annales quos scripsit Abu Djafar . . . at-Tabari. 13 vols. and 2 vols. *Indices* and *Introductio, glossarium, addenda et emendanda*. Leiden, 1879–1901. Also edited by Muḥammad Abū al-Faḍl Ibrāhīm. 10 vols. Cairo, 1960–69.

al-Yaʿqūbī, Abū al-ʿAbbās Aḥmad b. Isḥāq, called Ibn Wāḍiḥ. *Taʾrīkh*. Edited by M. T. Houtsma as *Historiae*. 2 vols. Leiden, 1883.

Yāqūt, Abū ʿAbdallāh Yāqūt b. ʿAbdallāh al-Ḥamawī al-Rūmī. *Muʿjam al-buldān*. Edited by Muḥammad Amīn al-Khānijī and Aḥmad b. al-Amīn al-Shanqīṭī. 8 vols. Cairo, 1323/1906.

al-Zamakhsharī, Jār Allāh Abū al-Qāsim Maḥmūd b. ʿUmar. *Asās al-balāghah*. Beirut, 1399/1979.

II. Secondary Sources and Reference Works

Abbott, Nabia. *Two Queens of Baghdad: Mother and Wife of Hārūn al-Rashīd*. Chicago, 1946. Reprinted London, 1986.

Amedroz, H. R. "The Maẓālim Jurisdiction in the Aḥkām Sulṭāniyya of Māwardī." *JRAS* (1911): 635–74.

Ayalon, D. "The Military Reforms of Caliph al-Muʿtaṣim: Their Background and Consequences." Unpublished communication to the International Congress of Orientalists, New Delhi, 1964. Printed in offset, Jerusalem, 1963.

Barthold, W. *Turkestan Down to the Mongol Invasion*. 4th edition. Gibb Memorial Series. London, 1977.

Bell, Richard. *Bell's Introduction to the Qurʾān*. Revised and enlarged by W. Montgomery Watt. Edinburgh, 1970.

Bosworth, C. E. *The ʿAbbāsid Caliphate in Equilibrium*. Vol. 30 of *The History of al-Ṭabarī*. Albany, 1989.

Bravmann, M. M. *The Spiritual Background of Early Islam: Studies in Ancient Arab Concepts*. Leiden, 1972.

Brockelmann, C. *Geschichte der arabischen Litteratur*. 5 vols. Leiden, 1937–49.

Combe, E., J. Sauvaget, and G. Wiet, eds. *Répertoire chronologique d'épigraphie arabe*. Vol. 1. Cairo, 1931.

Crone, Patricia. *Slaves on Horses: The Evolution of the Islamic Polity*. Cambridge, 1980.

Day, Florence E. "Dated Ṭirāz in the Collection of the University of Michigan." *Ars Islamica* 4 (1937): 421–46.

De Goeje, M. J. *Bibliotheca Geographorum Arabicorum*. Vol. 4, *Indices, Glossarium et Addenda et Emendanda*. Leiden, 1879. Reprinted, 1967.

Dozy, R. P. A. *Dictionnaire détaillé des noms de vêtements chez les arabes.* Amsterdam, 1845. Reprinted Beirut, n.d.

———. *Supplément aux dictionnaires arabes.* 2 vols. Leiden, 1881. Reprinted Beirut, 1968.

El-Hibri, Tayeb. "Harun al-Rashid and the Mecca Protocol of 802: A Plan for Division or Succession?" *IJMES* 24 (1992), 461–80.

Encyclopaedia of Islam. 1st edition. 4 vols. and Supplement. Leiden, 1913–42.

Encyclopaedia of Islam. 2nd edition. 6 vols. and Supplement. Leiden, 1960–.

Fagnan, E. *Additions aux dictionnaires arabes.* 1923. Reprinted Beirut, [1974].

Freytag, G. W. *Arabum Proverbia.* See al-Maydānī in Section I.

Gabrieli, Francesco. "Documenti relativi al califfato di al-Amīn in aṭ-Ṭabarī." *RCAL,* 6th series, vol. 3 (1927): 191–220.

———. "La successione di Hārūn ar-Rašīd e la guerra fra al-Amīn e al-Ma'mūn." *RSO* 11 (1926–28): 341–97.

———. "La «zandaqa» au Ier siècle abbasside." In *L'Élaboration de l'Islam.* Paris, 1961.

Gaudefroy-Demombynes, M. "Sur le cheval-jupon et al-karraj." In *Mélanges offerts à William Marçais.* Paris, 1950.

von Grunebaum, Gustav E. *Muhammadan Festivals.* Chicago, 1951. Reprinted London, 1976.

Hinz, Walther. *Islamische Masse und Gewichte.* Handbuch der Orientalistik, Ergänzungband 1, Heft 1. Leiden, 1955.

Kaabi, M. "Les Origines ṭāhirides dans la *da'wa* 'abbāside." *Arabica* 19 (1972): 145–64.

Kennedy, Hugh. *The Early Abbasid Caliphate: A Political History.* London and Totowa, 1981.

Kimber, R. A. "Hārūn al-Rashīd's Meccan Settlement of A.H. 186/A.D. 802." *University of St. Andrews, School of Abbasid Studies, Occasional Papers* 1 (1986): 55–79.

Kindermann, H. *"Schiff" im Arabischen: Untersuchung über Vorkommen und Bedeutung der Termini.* Zwickau-im-Sa., 1934.

Lane, Edward William. *An Account of the Manners and Customs of the Modern Egyptians.* London, 1836. Reprinted New York, 1973.

———. *An Arabic-English Lexicon.* London, 1863–93. Reprinted Beirut, 1968.

Lassner, Jacob. *The Shaping of 'Abbāsid Rule.* Princeton, 1980.

———. *The Topography of Baghdad in the Early Middle Ages: Text and Studies.* Detroit, 1970.

Le Strange, G. *Baghdad during the Abbasid Caliphate.* Oxford, 1900. Reprinted Westport, Conn., 1983.

———. *The Lands of the Eastern Caliphate.* Cambridge, 1905.

Levy, R. *The Social Structure of Islam.* Cambridge, 1957.

Lieu, Samuel N. C. *Manichaeism in the Later Roman Empire and Medieval China: A Historical Survey.* Manchester, 1985.

Mez, Adam. *The Renaissance of Islam.* Translated by Salahuddin Khuda Bakhsh and D. S. Margoliouth. Patna, 1937.

Morony, Michael G. *Iraq after the Muslim Conquest.* Princeton, 1984.

Nicholson, Reynold A. *A Literary History of the Arabs.* Cambridge, 1907. Reprinted Cambridge, 1969.

al-Nukhaylī, Darwīsh. *Al-Sufun al-islāmiyyah ʿalā ḥurūf al-muʿjam.* [Alexandria], 1974.

Omar, F. *ʿAbbāsiyyāt: Studies in the History of the Early ʿAbbāsids.* Baghdad, 1976.

Ostrogorsky, Georg. *Geschichte des byzantinischen Staates.* 2d ed. Munich, 1952.

Rückert, Friedrich. *Hamâsa.* See Abū Tammām in Section I.

Serjeant, R. B. *Islamic Textiles: Material for a History up to the Mongol Conquest.* Beirut, 1972.

Sezgin, Fuat. *Geschichte des arabischen Schrifttums.* Vol. 1, *Qur'ānwissenschaften, Ḥadīt, Geschichte, Fiqh, Dogmatik, Mystik bis ca. 430 H.*; Leiden, 1967. Vol. 2, *Poesie bis ca. 430 H.*; Leiden, 1975.

Shaban, M. A. *Islamic History: A New Interpretation.* Vol. 1, *A.D. 600–750*; Cambridge, 1971. Vol. 2, *A.D. 750–1055*; Cambridge, 1976.

Sourdel, D. "Questions de cérémonial ʿabbaside." *REI* 28 (1960): 121–48.

———. *Le Vizirat ʿabbāside de 749 à 936 (132 à 324 de l'Hégire).* 2 vols. Damascus, 1959–60.

Vajda, G. "Les Zindîqs au pays d'Islam au début de la période abbaside." *RSO* 17 (1938): 173–229.

Vasiliev, A. A. *History of the Byzantine Empire 324–1453.* Madison and Milwaukee, 1952.

Wagner, Ewald. *Abū Nuwās: Eine Studie zur arabischen Literatur der frühen ʿAbbāsidenzeit.* Wiesbaden, 1965.

Wüstenfeld, F., and E. Mahler. *Vergleichungs-Tabellen der mohammedanischen und christlichen Zeitrechnung.* Leipzig, 1926. Arabic translation by A. M. Magued; Cairo, 1980.

Yule, H. "Notes on Hwen Thsang's Account of the Principalities of Tokháristán, in which some Previous Geographical Identifications are Reconsidered." *Journal of the Royal Asiatic Society* (New Series) 6 (1873): 92–120.

Index

The index contains all proper names of persons, places, and tribal and other groups, as well as topographical data, occurring in the introduction and the text (but not normally in the footnotes), together with technical terms.

The definite article al-, *the abbreviations* b. *(*ibn, *"son of") and* bt. *(*bint, *"daughter of"), and everything in parentheses are disregarded for the purposes of alphabetization. Where a name occurs in both the text and the footnotes on the same page, only the page number is given.*

B

L

M

Z